Handbook of
ORGANIZATIONAL
CREATIVITY

Handbook of
ORGANIZATIONAL
CREATIVITY

Edited by

JING ZHOU • CHRISTINA E. SHALLEY

Lawrence Erlbaum Associates
Taylor & Francis Group

New York   London

Lawrence Erlbaum Associates
Taylor & Francis Group
270 Madison Avenue
New York, NY 10016

Lawrence Erlbaum Associates
Taylor & Francis Group
2 Park Square
Milton Park, Abingdon
Oxon OX14 4RN

© 2008 by Taylor & Francis Group, LLC
Lawrence Erlbaum Associates is an imprint of Taylor & Francis Group, an Informa business

Printed in the United States of America on acid-free paper
10 9 8 7 6 5 4 3 2 1

International Standard Book Number-13: 978-0-8058-4072-8 (Hardcover)

Visit the Taylor & Francis Web site at
http://www.taylorandfrancis.com

and the LEA and Routledge Web site at
http://www.routledge.com

This book is dedicated to Xiaohui and Dave
For their unfailing support.
To our children: Russell, Quinn, Cal, and Reilly.
They are wonderful inspirations for learning and creativity.

CONTENTS

PREFACE

Ten years ago, publishing an edited volume of the magnitude of the present volume on organizational creativity research would have been unthinkable. At that time, the foundation for research on creativity in the workplace had just been laid and seeds planted. Theoretical frameworks had been borrowed mainly from personality and social psychology, and empirical research had been pursued by a tiny number of researchers. Few people could envision that in such a short period of time, the field of organizational creativity could grow into a full-fledged research field.

Today, ten years later, the solid foundation built and seeds planted earlier have turned into a beautiful garden. Central constructs have been defined. Theoretical frameworks have been proposed, tested, and refined. Techniques for assessing creativity in the behavioral laboratory have been adapted from social psychology, and some of them have gained wide acceptance among organizational creativity researchers. Scales for measuring employee creativity in field settings have been developed and widely used. Systematic research streams have been formed involving several key contextual factors. All in all, the field of organizational creativity research has accomplished a great deal and accumulated a wealth of knowledge that has substantial theoretical and practical significance. More importantly, even more exciting possibilities for research await researchers to pursue, discover, and create. It is within this background and at this critical junction of creativity research that we worked with a group of leading researchers to put together this *Handbook of Organizational Creativity*.

The contributors to this volume represent many of the leading researchers in the field of organizational creativity to date. We cover cutting-edge theorizing and research on creativity in the workplace, discuss emerging areas, and highlight promising future research trends. Our general organizing principle is to go from general to specific research topics, from micro to meso to macro topics, and from presenting theory and research to discussing practical implications of organizational creativity research.

Chapters in this volume are divided into four sections. The first section, entitled "Organizational Creativity in Historical Context," provides a general overview of the origin and current state of the field of organizational creativity, addresses important theoretical and methodological issues, and links organizational creativity research to classic texts of administrative science.

More specifically, in the first chapter of the first section, Shalley and Zhou provide a historical overview of the organizational creativity research field. They start by discussing relevant research within the fields of social and personality psychology. Then they lay out the main theoretical frameworks and conceptual models that have been presented within the area of organizational creativity. Following this, they discuss common methods used in organizational creativity and highlight some measurement issues. Finally, they present a brief summary of the empirical findings to date.

In the second chapter, Amabile and Mueller present the componential theory of creativity, which identifies major elements for creative performance. These elements include domain-relevant skills, creativity-relevant processes, intrinsic motivation, the work environment, the creative process, and creative outcomes. Next, Amabile and Mueller describe various ways of measuring and assessing each of these elements, with a focus on assessing creative products or outcomes. They then review different research methodologies for studying creativity (i.e., lab experiment, single-time correlational study, case study, and a variation of the experience sampling technique–work diaries study) and use previous studies to illustrate each of these methodologies.

In the third chapter, Ford and Kuenzi analyze classic management texts such as Thompson's (1967) "Organizations in Action," March and Simon's (1958) "Organizations," and Katz and Kahn's (1966) "The Social Psychology of Organizations" to cull insights for current and future organizational creativity research. They take an evolutionary perspective (e.g., Campbell, 1960) focusing on variation, selection, and retention (VSR), and use Weick's "Social Psychology of Organizing" text as an organizing frame for the analysis. Ford and Kuenzi review some recent organizational creativity research to highlight potential ties to

VSR theory. Finally, they offer future research ideas that are suggested by their review and analysis of these classics.

In the second section titled "Distinctive Contributions from Organizational Creativity Research," more detailed coverage of specific researched topics is presented in each of the chapters. The chapters included in this section represent several distinct and systematic research streams on organizational creativity. They are organized from more micro topics, to meso, and finally to macro topics.

More specifically, in the first chapter in this section, Tierney develops a creativity leadership model that serves to integrate and categorize previous research on effects of leadership on employee creativity, and to highlight possibilities for future research. According to the model, three issues warrant special research attention: leadership levels (individual, dyadic, group, and organizational), leader facets (traits, behaviors, relations), and spheres of leadership influence (cognition, motivation, and capacity). Using this model as a guiding framework, she then reviews previous studies and suggests many paths that future researchers can follow to advance our understanding of effects of leadership on creativity in the workplace.

In the second chapter, Zhou develops a conceptual framework that addresses issues related to the nature and components of feedback (i.e., feedback valence and feedback style, developmental orientation, and person-focused vs. task-focused feedback), characteristics of the feedback recipient (i.e., achievement orientation, power motivation, and emotional intelligence), characteristics of the feedback giver (i.e., knowledge and expertise, and seniority and status). In addition, she theorizes that these categories of variables independently or jointly affect creativity via several psychological mechanisms (i.e., intrinsic motivation, understanding of creativity standards, and acquisition of creativity skills and strategies). Although parts of this theoretical framework have been examined in previous research, much awaits testing and further refinement. More importantly, Zhou suggests that this framework needs to be tested as a whole. Finally, Zhou provides guidelines for practicing managers on how to promote creativity through feedback.

In the third chapter, Shalley argues that role expectations for creative performance should increase individuals' frequency of engaging in creative activities, which ultimately will result in higher levels of creative performance. That is, if managers want employees to be more creative they need to encourage them to undertake creative activities. On the basis of previous research, Shalley elaborates that role expectations can be created by providing either goals for creativity or establishing creative job requirements, both of which should lead to higher creative performance. In addition to role expectations, Shalley points out that an employee's work context needs to support these goals or job requirements in order to facilitate creativity.

The next set of chapters moves from a micro or individual level of analysis to a meso level of analysis. Specifically, Paulus discusses research that has examined ways to encourage creativity in groups and teams. His specific focus is on ideational creativity, which involves creativity in the idea-generation stages of brainstorming. Paulus reviews the literature on group brainstorming and highlights research findings that can aid in facilitating or constraining group brainstorming. Finally, he discusses important issues to consider that may lead to the generation of higher levels of creative ideas.

Following Paulus's chapter on creativity in groups and teams, Perry-Smith brings a social network perspective to organizational creativity research. She examines how social relationships, both formal and more importantly, informal can affect individuals' and teams' creativity at work. Specifically, Perry-Smith discusses the importance of weak rather than strong ties for creativity. She also emphasizes the role of the structure of the network, and how it is important for creativity to either be central in the social network with few ties outside the network or be on the periphery of the network with many outside ties. Finally, she stresses the importance of informal interactions for exposing individuals to diverse viewpoints that may at some point be transmitted into helpful information.

In the last of this set of meso-level chapters, West and Richter discuss the role of climate and culture for creativity and innovation in organizations. They primarily review literature relevant to group- and organizational-level influences on creativity and innovation. West and Richter propose that culture and climate factors may vary in their influence on both creativity and innovation. Finally, they present results of relevant research to substantiate their arguments.

At this point, the chapters move to a macro-level of analysis. The Dougherty and Tolboom chapter focuses on how to creatively organize firms in order to have sustained product innovation. Dougherty and Tolboom discuss how product innovation involves integrating market and technology knowledge, collaboration, and the controlling of the innovation. They highlight three deep structures that should enable sustained product innovation. First, work needs to be collectively understood as professional practice of value creation, rather than as a set of clearly defined, discrete jobs. Second, work needs to be differentiated into autonomous communities of practice, each in charge of discrete problems in innovation management. Third, the communities of practice are integrated by creating actionable standards. Finally, they discuss how these deep structures can successfully enable sustained product innovations.

Next, Drazin, Kazanjian, and Glynn focus on the role of professionals in creativity and innovation. They suggest that researchers should approach the study of creativity by using the lens of sensemaking, rather than the more traditional structural functionalist perspective used in organizational sciences in general, and in creativity research. Drazin, Kazanjian, and Glynn discuss the conflicts that can arise between different frames of references held by professional groups and how these conflicts are played out in organizations. Finally, they argue that creativity and innovation come about not from the contributions of single professional groups but from political actions of multiple professional groups asserting and defending their points of view.

In the last chapter of the second section of this volume, Woodman discusses the interrelationships of creativity, innovation, and organizational change. Specifically, he proposes a domain model in which he views each of these as nested within each other, with creativity nested within innovation, which is nested within organizational change. Woodman conceptualizes about how research on organizational creativity can inform research on organizational change. He also discusses how research on organizational change can inform creativity research. Finally, he discusses how creativity theory and research may help to inform the practice of change management.

The third section of this volume is entitled "Normative Implications of Organizational Creativity Research." In the first chapter of this section, Gilson focuses on whether being creative has real value beyond the actual act of creating. That is, she explores when employees are creative, whether this leads to other positive and valued outcomes such as higher levels of performance, job satisfaction, or work efficiency. Gilson takes a multilevel approach to examining the questions she poses at the individual, group, and organizational levels. Her review of the literature highlights some interesting preliminary research findings. Finally, her overall discussion points to the need for much more research in this area at all levels of analysis.

In the second chapter, Hargadon discusses a set of activities that are necessary for creativity to occur. He suggests that these activities are critical but are often underestimated or even overlooked because conventional wisdom tends to regard creativity as the sole act of inventing a new product or having an inspirational idea. These activities include, for example, connecting with others in similar and different areas of knowledge and experience, learning about what already exists, remembering what you already know, and thinking in other boxes. According to Hargadon, this set of activities can set the stage, work backstage, and help to find a niche for an idea to sell to others. Finally, he presents many examples showing how organizational creativity contributed to business successes.

The fourth section is entitled "Suggestions for Future Organizational Creativity Research." In the sole chapter included in this section, Zhou and Shalley identify and integrate common threads of the chapters included in this volume, and suggest future research directions aimed at broadening the scope and deepening the impact of organizational creativity research. First, Zhou and Shalley introduce a typology that would enable researchers to expand research on antecedents of creativity to multilevel analysis. Second, they call for broadening the scope of creativity research especially concerning affect, reward, time, and bridging with other research fields. Third, they introduce three different approaches that can be used to expand creativity research to international or cross-cultural context. Finally, Zhou and Shalley argue that future research is needed to investigate positive and negative consequences of creativity.

The targeted readers for this edited volume include researchers in the field of organizational creativity, researchers in other fields of management research (e.g., organizational behavior, organizational theory, entrepreneurship, strategic management, human resource management, and change management), and psychology (e.g., industrial and organizational psychology, social psychology, and educational psychology) who are interested in building bridges with the field of organizational creativity, and new and aspiring researchers and PhD students. Researchers and PhD students in marketing, sociology, and education may also find this book very useful and relevant. Thoughtful managers and executives, professional and knowledge workers who are not directly involved in creativity research, and thoughtful and aspiring managers and MBA students would also find this book beneficial in sharpening their thinking, and in helping them to identify the right tools for managing creativity.

We wish to thank a number of distinguished researchers who over time have made tremendous contributions to research on creativity in the workplace, and whose work in this field has influenced our thinking. Although not all of them were able to participate in this project, their contributions to the field and to our thinking are evident in this volume.

We thank Cameron Ford for having a great vision and starting this project. Last, but not least, we tremendously appreciate Jeremy Schoen's help in reading and commenting on various versions of the manuscripts.

Jing Zhou and Christina E. Shalley

CONTRIBUTORS

Teresa M. Amabile is the Edsel Bryant Ford Professor of Business Administration at the Harvard Business School. Her research over the past three decades has focused primarily on the ways in which work environments and other social environments influence creativity, with an emphasis on motivational mechanisms. Her current research examines how particular events and patterns of events over time, within organizations, influence daily subjective experience at work—emotions, perceptions, and motivations—as well as how subjective experience influences work performance. She received her PhD in psychology from Stanford University, and taught in the Psychology Department at Brandeis University before joining the Harvard Business School in 1995.

Deborah Dougherty. After working for ten years in large public bureaucracies, Deborah Dougherty received her PhD in management from MIT. She has held academic positions at the Wharton School and McGill University, and is now professor at Rutgers University. Her scholarship concerns organizing for sustained innovation in complex organizations, new product development, innovation in services, and knowledge management. She teaches managing technology and innovation, principles of management, managing strategic transformation, and PhD seminars in qualitative methods and organization theory. She was elected chair of the Technology and Innovation Management Division of the Academy of Management, is a senior editor for *Organization Science*, and has served or is now serving on the editorial boards for six other journals.

Robert Drazin is a professor of organization and management, and faculty director for the Center for Entrepreneurship and Corporate Growth at Goizueta Business School, Emory University. Prior to joining the Goizueta Business School faculty, Robert taught at the Graduate School of Business at Columbia University. His research interests include organization design, organization theory, and the management of innovation and growth in large corporations.

Cameron Ford earned his PhD in Business Administration from Penn State University in 1990 and served on the faculty of Rutgers University's Graduate School of Management before joining the University of Central Florida. He recently established and serves as the director of the UCF Center for Entrepreneurship and Innovation, one of the fastest growing entrepreneurship centers in the country. Cameron's scholarly interests focus on evolutionary processes whereby novel proposals generate economic value. He is especially interested in how sensemaking processes related to creative visions serve to organize knowledge, people, and resources during new venture emergence processes. Cameron's research has appeared in journals such as the *Academy of Management Review, Journal of Management, Journal of Organizational Behavior, Journal of Applied Behavioral Science,* and *IEEE Transactions on Engineering Management.* He has also published numerous book chapters related to creativity and entrepreneurship, and edited the book *Creative Action in Organizations.* He is an associate editor for *Creativity and Innovation Management* and serves on the editorial board of *Journal of Creative Behavior.*

Lucy L. Gilson is an associate professor and Ackerman Scholar at the University of Connecticut's School of Business. She received her PhD form the Georgia Institute of Technology. Her research interests focus on work groups and what makes them effective and creative. For the most part, her work has examined group processes, empowerment, mentoring, trust, and, in particular, creativity. Her research has been published in such outlets as the *Academy of Management Journal, Journal of Applied Psychology, Journal of Management, Journal of Organizational Behavior,* and *Journal of Vocational Behavior.* Professor Gilson is on the editorial board of the *Journal of Management.*

MaryAnn Glynn is a fellow of the Winston Center for Leadership and Ethics and professor of organizational studies at the Carroll School of

Management, Boston College. Prior to joining Boston College, MaryAnn served on the faculties at Goizueta Business School, Emory University, and the Yale School of Management. Her research interests are at the intersection of micro-level cognitive processes (such as learning, creativity, and intelligence) and cultural influences (social norms, institutional arrangements) on identity, symbolism, and organizational leadership.

Andrew Hargadon is associate professor of technology management and director of Center for Entrepreneurship at the Graduate School of Management at University of California, Davis. He received his PhD from the Management Science and Engineering Department in Stanford University's School of Engineering, where he was Boeing fellow and Sloan Foundation Future Professor of Manufacturing. He received his B.S. and M.S. in Stanford University's Product Design Program in the Mechanical Engineering Department. He is author of *How Breakthroughs Happen* (HBS Press, 2003).

Robert K. Kazanjian is a professor of organization and management at the Goizueta Business School, Emory University. Previously, he was a faculty member at the Ross School of Business, University of Michigan. He received his PhD in organization and strategy from the Wharton School of the University of Pennsylvania. His research interests center on the management of innovation and growth in both small, young firms as well as large, diversified firms. Particular interests relate to issues of capability creation, attaining synergies, innovation processes, and broad-scale organization design and change.

Maribeth Kuenzi is currently a doctoral student at the University of Central Florida. Her research interests focus on ethics, organizational justice, and innovation processes, and her dissertation addresses dimensions of organizational work climates. Her research has been published in *Organizational Dynamics,* and been presented at the National Academy of Management and Society for Industrial Organizational Psychology meetings.

Jennifer S. Mueller is an assistant professor of management at the Wharton School, University of Pennsylvania. Her research primarily focuses on how social relationships aid or hinder team performance at work. Specifically, she is interested in how relational losses contribute to individual performance in larger teams, and how close relationships contribute to and shape the process of innovation at work. She received her PhD in social psychology from Brandeis University and has taught at New York University in the Stern School of Business as well as the Yale School of Management. Jennifer has published her work on creativity in several leading journals including *Administrative Science Quarterly* and the *Academy of Management Journal*.

Paul B. Paulus is dean of the College of Science and professor of psychology at the University of Texas at Arlington. He received his PhD from the University of Iowa. His areas of interest are group dynamics, group decision making, and group creativity. His most recent book is *Group Creativity: Innovation through Collaboration* by Oxford University Press.

Jill Perry-Smith is an assistant professor of organization and management at the Goizueta Business School, Emory University. She received her PhD in organizational behavior from Georgia Institute of Technology. Her research focuses on understanding how organizational contexts, particularly the informal social structure, enable individual creativity. Her ongoing work explores the role of social networks in facilitating different types of creativity at various levels of analysis. In addition, her work explores work-family initiatives as an instance of a creative response to a particular problem domain. Her research has appeared in *Academy of Management Journal, Academy of Management Review,* and *Organizational Behavior and Human Decision Processes*.

Andreas W. Richter is an assistant professor of organizational behavior at Instituto de Empresa Business School, Madrid, Spain. He earned his PhD from Aston Business School in 2005 (intergroup conflict and teamworking effectiveness). His work has been published in journals such as the *Academy of Management Journal*, the *European Journal of Work and Organizational Psychology*, and the *Journal of Applied Psychology*. His current research interests include intergroup relations and intergroup conflict, organizational creativity, and research methodology.

Christina E. Shalley is GT Advance Professor in the College of Management at the Georgia Institute of Technology. She received her PhD in business administration from the University of Illinois at Urbana–Champaign. Her research interests concern how to structure jobs and the work environment to support creative work. Her work focuses on investigating the effects of various social and contextual factors in enhancing and stifling employee creativity. Her research has been published in such outlets as the *Academy of Management Journal, Academy of Management Review, Creativity Research Journal, Journal of Applied Psychology, Journal of Management, Organizational Behavior and Human Decision Processes,* and *Research in Personnel/Human Resources Management,* among others. She is on the editorial board of the *Journal of Management,* and she was co-editor of a special issue on managing exploration versus exploitation appearing in the *Academy of Management Journal.*

Pamela Tierney is the Ames Professor of Innovation and Technology Management in the School of Business Administration at Portland State University. She earned her PhD in organizational behavior from the University of Cincinnati. Her research interests include employee creativity, leadership, and self-efficacy. Her research on these topics has appeared in journals such as the *Academy of Management Journal, Personnel Psychology,* and the *Journal of Management.*

J. Neill Tolboom is a PhD candidate at Rutgers University, majoring in organizational management. He received his BCom in commerce from the University of Manitoba. He earned a MDiv in divinity from New Brunswick Seminary, New Jersey, and a DMin in ministry from Drew University, New Jersey. He is a United Methodist minister and his interests include structuring religious organizations for sustained innovation.

Michael A. West is a professor of organizational psychology and head of research at Aston Business School, Birmingham, UK. He graduated from the University of Wales in 1973 and received his PhD in 1977 ("The Psychology of Meditation"). He then spent a year working in the coalmines of South Wales. He has authored 17 books and over 150 scientific and practitioner articles and book chapters. He is a fellow of the British Psychological Society, the American Psychological Association (APA), the Chartered Institute of Personnel and Development, the International Association of Applied Psychology, and the Royal Society for the Encouragement of Arts, Manufactures, and Commerce. His current research interests include team innovation and effectiveness, team-based organizations, and people management and performance in health-care systems.

Richard W. Woodman (PhD, Purdue University) is the Fouraker Professor of Business and Professor of Management at Texas A & M University where he teaches organizational behavior, organizational change, organizational creativity and innovation, and research methodology. He is editor of the *Journal of Applied Behavioral Science* and co-editor of the annual series *Research in Organizational Change and Development* published by Elsevier. He has been division chair and program chair of the Organization Development and Change division of the Academy of Management. His research interests focus on organizational change and organizational creativity. In a previous life, Dr. Woodman was a military intelligence officer in the U.S. Army, worked in both the petroleum and banking industries, and served for several years as vice-president of a financial institution.

Jing Zhou is Professor of Management in the Jesse H. Jones Graduate School of Management at Rice University. She received her PhD from the University of Illinois at Urbana–Champaign. Her current research interests include contextual factors that promote or inhibit employee creativity and innovation. Prior to joining the Jones School at Rice University, she was associate professor and Mays fellow in the Management Department at the Mays Business School at Texas A&M University. Her work has been published or is forthcoming in such journals as *Academy of Management Journal, Creativity Research Journal, Journal of Applied Psychology, Journal of Creative Behavior, Journal of Management, Journal of Organizational Behavior,* and *Personnel Psychology,* as well as *Research in Personnel/Human Resources Management.* Currently, she serves on several editorial boards including the boards of *Academy of Management Journal, Academy of Management Review, Journal of Applied Psychology,* and *Journal of Management.* She is an incoming Associate Editor of *Journal of Applied Psychology.*

SECTION I

Organizational Creativity
in Historical Context

CHAPTER 1

Organizational Creativity Research
A Historical Overview

Christina E. Shalley
Georgia Institute of Technology

Jing Zhou
Rice University

INTRODUCTION

Organizational creativity represents a relatively new and emerging research area within the field of organizational behavior. As a research area, it owes its intellectual roots to a great deal of research on creativity in general, which has been conducted primarily within psychology. This work has provided a rich foundation from which to draw upon for a conceptual and empirical stream of work focused exclusively on factors that can enhance or constrain creativity within organizations or within the context of work. Creativity in the context of work is possible in any job or by any employee (Shalley, Gilson, & Blum, 2000), given the appropriate conditions, which will be discussed in this chapter.

In the field of psychology, some of the conceptual and empirical work has been focused on individuals' creativity at work, but the majority of the research examines creativity in general. For example, there is work on creativity in the arts, creativity in solving short-term problems (e.g., a problem-solving task in the behavioral laboratory that lasts a few minutes), creativity of scientists, creativity of eminent scholars, the study of children's creativity in educational environments, and work on how individuals can improve their ability to think creatively (e.g., Runco, 1986; Runco & Chand, 1995; Runco & Okuda, 1988; Taylor, 1964, 1988; Taylor & Barron, 1963; Torrance, 1974). Thus, what distinguishes the study of creativity in these two fields is organizational creativity's exclusive focus on variables that have direct implications for the workplace, and creativity in a work or organizational context.

This chapter starts with defining what we mean by creativity in general and organizational creativity. Then, a brief overview of the major research conducted on creativity in the field of psychology is presented. It is by no means a comprehensive review, but provided as both an acknowledgement of the excellent work conducted in psychology on creativity, and because organizational creativity researchers have benefited and will continue to benefit from this work (see Sternberg, 1999, for an overview of this area). Next, we move on to a discussion of organizational creativity and present the prominent conceptual pieces in this area, followed by our discussion of the major methodologies used and highlighting of some methodological issues to consider. Finally, we briefly summarize the major research findings to date in the field of organizational creativity.

DEFINITION OF CREATIVITY

Creativity can be described as both an outcome and a process. Specifically, in order to produce creative outcomes, individuals need to first engage in certain processes that can help them to potentially be more creative. For example, they may examine unknown areas to find better or unique approaches to a problem, or seek out novel ways of performing a task, and link ideas from multiple sources. As a process, creativity can involve continuously finding and solving problems and implementing new solutions (Basadur, 2004; Basadur, Graen, & Green, 1982). Also, it is an iterative process, involving reflection and action, seeking feedback, experimenting, and discussing new ways to do things in contrast to just relying on habit or automatic behavior.

Koestler (1964) said that creativity involves a bisociative process, which is the deliberate connecting of two previously unrelated thoughts, ideas, or things to produce a new insight or invention. Essentially, he stressed the importance of seeing things differently from the way most people see them. Also, he placed value on the ability to recognize new information and to use it to help problem solving.

Wallas's (1926) classic model of the creative thought process identifies four stages of creativity thinking. These stages are preparation (e.g., examination of the problem and goals for addressing it), incubation (e.g., no longer consciously working on the problem but unconscious work may be ongoing), illumination (e.g., solution presents itself — the "aha experience"), and verification (use of logic and knowledge to make the idea into an appropriate solution). Amabile (1983) proposed a related model of the creative process which included five stages of creative thought. These five stages are task presentation (e.g., problem presented through external or internal stimulus), preparation (e.g., gather relevant information to solve the problem), idea generation (e.g., production of possible responses), idea validation (e.g., check each idea generated for appropriateness), and finally, outcome assessment (e.g., choose a solution). Stein (1967) described the creative process as having three stages: hypothesis formulation, hypothesis testing, and communication. Parnes, Noller, & Biondi (1977) had a five-stage model of the creative problem-solving process: fact finding, problem finding and defining, idea finding, solution finding, and acceptance finding. Finally, Hogarth (1980) proposed that four stages comprise the creative process. These stages are preparation, production, evaluation, and implementation. As can be seen by all these process models, they involve some similar stages, along with some minor differences in terms of what is included. Nonetheless, they all include the identification of a problem or opportunity, gathering information, generating ideas, and evaluation of these ideas. Although engagement in creative processes does not always lead to creative outcomes, at times it does result in the production, conceptualization, or development of creative ideas, products, or processes.

In general, creativity as an outcome has been defined as something that is viewed as novel. Beyond the point of novelty, there are some differences in some of the ways to define creative outcomes between the psychological and organizational literatures. In the psychological literature, some researchers define creative outcomes usually generated in a brainstorming session in terms of fluency, flexibility, and originality, with these three concepts being highly correlated. Fluency is the number of ideas generated. Flexibility is the number of categories of ideas referenced. For example, if a person is brainstorming uses for a box, and she says to use it as a flowerpot, to hold my shoes, and to pack groceries, researchers would consider that she produced three ideas for fluency, but only one category (i.e., a container) for flexibility. However, if the same box can hold her shoes, be cut up to make paper dolls, and flatten out to cover her head for protection from the rain, again she would have three ideas for fluency but also three categories for flexibility. Finally, originality is the production of ideas that are unique from all other ideas generated for a group of individuals. So in evaluating the originality of the uses generated for a box, you would check to see how many people generated a particular use, such as holding paper dolls, and that idea would be given a score on how common or rare the idea appears to be. Therefore, originality deals with statistical uniqueness but does not examine usefulness or appropriateness of the idea generated.

Other definitions in both psychology and organizational behavior consider creativity to be novel and useful or involve appropriate ideas, processes, or procedures (Amabile, 1988; Mumford & Gustafson, 1988; Shalley, 1991). For example, Rogers (1954) defined creativity as the emergence of a novel relational product coming out of the uniqueness of an individual and the context (i.e., circumstances, events, people) of their existence at that time. Using Barron's (1955) definition, Amabile (1983) stated that creativity is the production of novel and appropriate ideas by either an individual or small working group. Novel ideas are those that are unique compared to other ideas currently available. Useful or appropriate ideas are those that have the potential to add value in either the short or long term. Therefore, creative outcomes can range from suggestions for incremental changes in procedures to major, radical breakthroughs (Mumford & Gustafson, 1988).

Also, in the organizational literature, creativity has been commonly referred to as the ideation component of innovation, while innovation includes both ideation and the application of new ideas (i.e., implementation). Another issue for creativity is that there has been some differentiation between whether problems are externally presented versus discovered. For example, Getzels and colleagues (e.g., Getzels, 1975; Getzels & Csikszentmihalyi, 1976) suggested that discovered problems are more likely to be solved creatively than presented problems, and other theorists have proposed that problem discovery itself is an important part of creative activities (e.g., Campbell, 1960). Ward, Smith, and Finke (1999) noted that there are different kinds of creative contributions, and that this may explain disagreements among creativity scholars about what "truly" underlies creativity. For example, there can be differences between goal-oriented or focused creativity versus exploratory creativity. Also, Ward and his colleagues (1999) talked about differences between domain-specific and universal creativity skills. Finally, Unsworth (2001) recently developed a matrix of four creativity types that varied on two dimensions: the driver for the engagement (external or internal) and the problem type (closed or open). Open ideas are those discovered by an individual, while closed ideas are presented to him. Unsworth argued that there may be differences in processes and predictors for each of the four types of creativity.

CREATIVITY IN THE FIELD OF PSYCHOLOGY

The field of psychology has a long history of studying creativity. Empirically there are two main approaches for research in this area: the study of individual differences and cognitive processes. There are also a number of conceptual models and frameworks that we will briefly discuss.

Individual Differences

Much of the historical work on creativity has examined individual differences. First, there is a body of work looking at the lifetime and characteristics of individuals who have exhibited creativity in their work, such as in art or scientific discoveries. For example, researchers have studied biographies and autobiographies of famous creative individuals in order to determine whether a particular personality factor or type of intellect makes a difference (Cox, 1926; Galton, 1870). A related approach primarily taken by MacKinnon and Barron (MacKinnon, 1962; Barron, 1968) was to intensively study one or more creative individuals, in what could be described as a living laboratory. Also, Simonton's (e.g., 1975, 1976a, 1976b, 1977) research focused on the creative productivity of musicians, artists, writers, scientists, and philosophers over long periods of time and throughout history. He used archival research to detect causal patterns between social variables and the creativity and productivity of these individuals. Some of his work has followed particular individuals, while other pieces have looked at groups of these individuals by generation and examined aggregate trends. In general, these studies have produced some intriguing results for a special population of creators. That is, the work described in this paragraph has focused on those who are involved in creative works that are of a relatively high level of creativity (i.e., eminent scientists, artists, philosophers). Zuckerman and Cole (1994) examined the work methods used by eminent, innovative scientists versus their more "run of the mill" counterparts with regard to procedural knowledge. They found that the work methods of these two groups differed, with eminent scientists focusing more on strategic research methods and strategic sites.

The majority of the work on individual differences in creativity has focused on ordinary individuals. Typically, a battery of intelligence, personality, and creativity tests are given to try to identify what characteristics are more likely to be associated with someone exhibiting creativity. For example, Guilford (1959) has tried to identify and measure a "creativity" trait. Also, a number of researchers have tried to identify personality traits related to creative production (e.g., Barron & Harrington, 1981; Gough, 1979; MacKinnon, 1962; Torrance & Khatena, 1970). Some of the major research findings with regard to individual differences that have been identified by researchers such as Cattell and Butcher (1968), Gough (1979), and MacKinnon (1975) are that creative individuals tend to be higher on self-confidence, aggressiveness, flexibility, self-acceptance, unconcern with social constraints or others' opinions, sensitivity, introversion, and intuitiveness. Therefore, all of this research has contributed to our knowledge about the individual differences that are associated with being creative, and we now turn to cognitive processes.

Cognitive Processes

A second major research area concerns the cognitive processes involved in attempting to be creative. For example, Newell, Shaw, and Simon (1962) have considered the cognitive skills needed in order to be creative. Using an information-processing approach, they viewed the creative process as the application of particular set-breaking heuristics. Kirton's (1976, 1994) Adaption–Innovation theory posits that individuals have a preferred style of problem solving. Kirton proposed a bipolar continuum of cognitive styles with adaptors and innovators located at opposite ends. Adaptors tend to operate within known procedures and paradigms, whereas innovators tend to take risks and violate traditional ways of doing things in order to develop problem solutions that are unique.

A number of researchers have focused on examining various cognitive processes or skills involved in creative problem solving (see Reiter-Palmon & Illies, 2004 for a recent review). For example, Mumford and his colleagues have examined the cognitive skills of problem finding, problem construction, generation of alternatives, and idea evaluation, among others (e.g., Mumford, Baughman, Maher, Costanza, & Supinski, 1997; Reiter-Palmon, Mumford, Boes, & Runco, 1997; Vincent, Decker, & Mumford, 2002).

There are also tests that have been developed to try to tap the creative process, such as Guilford's (1963, 1967) Alternative Uses Task that seeks to tap the divergent thinking component of his structure-of-intellect theory (1956). Building on Guilford's work, Torrance developed the Torrance Tests of Creative Thinking (Torrance, 1962, 1974). These tests have been widely used, as has Duncker's (1945) Functional Fixedness Problem.

Additionally, there are well-established training programs to facilitate cognitive processing for creativity. For example, Osborn's (1953) work on brainstorming involves a set of four rules: (a) no evaluation of any kind, (b) encouragement of wild ideas, (c) encouragement of many ideas, and (d) build upon or modify the ideas of others, which should be followed in order to get the highest frequency of ideas generated as well as the most original ideas. Gordon (1961) developed a creativity stimulation program called Synectics that, among other things, was guided by two principles: (a) make the familiar strange (i.e., take something ordinary and find new ways of viewing it through the use of analogy), and (b) make the strange familiar (i.e., take a new problem and through the use of metaphors and analogy transform it into something familiar). DeBono (1985) developed his "thinking hats" in which individuals wear different hats, such as a red hat for intuitive thinking, a green hat for generative thinking, and a black hat for critical thinking, as a way to metaphorically encourage people to see things from a number of different viewpoints. Finally, Parnes (1967) developed a creative problem solving training program that consisted of a variety of both individual and group techniques.

In summary, there are a number of tests that can be used to measure individual levels of creative ability, and training programs that can try to help develop individuals' creative thinking. Also, a body of research exists that examines the cognitive processes involved in being creative. We will now turn to a brief discussion of various conceptual models that have been developed.

CONCEPTUAL MODELS OF CREATIVITY WITHIN PSYCHOLOGY

In general, researchers (e.g., Amabile, 1983; Rokeach, 1965; Simon, 1985; Steiner, 1965) have theorized that ability, intrinsic motivation, and engagement in certain cognitive stages are necessary for creative performance. For example, in order to be creative, individuals have to be inherently interested in the issue or problem and motivated to find a solution (e.g., Amabile, 1983; Barron, 1965; Crutchfield, 1962; Runco & Chand, 1995; Steiner, 1965). Csikszentmihalyi's work on problem discovery (Csikszentmihalyi & Robinson, 1986; Getzels & Csikszentmihalyi, 1976) led him to suggest that the identification of problems that hold the potential for creative solutions is partly driven by intense interest in and curiosity about a subject and by perseverance. He proposed that a highly motivated state is achieved when people are engaged in an activity where the challenge matches their skill level (Csikszentmihalyi & Csikszentmihalyi, 1988). When this is the case, individuals are totally involved in the task they are working on, resulting in a state he called flow (Csikszentmihalyi, 1990). Furthermore, some researchers have developed specific models of the creative process that will be briefly described here in the order of their appearance in the literature.

Campbell's (1960) evolutionary model of creativity argued that creativity is not a mysterious process performed by only brilliant individuals. Campbell proposed that creativity requires extensive trial and error and hard work. Campbell believed that people had to generate multiple solutions to difficult problems, and in order to do this they needed to use a wide variety of approaches. Thus, his model strongly focused on variation, in terms of ideas, and also selective retention of promising ideas and the culling of less desirable ideas. Selective retention requires individuals to use their background, knowledge, and skills to decide which alternatives generated should be retained and which should be discarded.

Amabile (1983) introduced a componential model of the social psychology of creativity with three necessary components: domain-relevant skills, creativity-relevant skills, and task motivation. Although all three components are conceptually relevant to her model, she primarily focused on motivation and proposed an "intrinsic motivation hypothesis of creativity." Essentially, she argued that individuals need to be intrinsically motivated by the task in order to be creative, and that extrinsic motivators are detrimental for creativity. Her empirical work primarily with preschool and elementary-aged children on verbal and artistic tasks has supported this argument. However, her more recent work in organizations has found that some extrinsic motivators can be conducive to creativity, suggesting that there may be synergy between intrinsic and extrinsic motivation in promoting creativity.

Csikszentmihalyi (1988, 1996) took a "systems" approach and highlighted the interaction of the individual and his or her environment. The individual's environment has two salient aspects: the domain, which is cultural or symbolic, and the field, which is social. According to this system's perspective, an individual uses information from a domain and transforms or extends it through his or her personality, cognitive processes, and motivation. The field evaluates and selects from the new ideas presented. The domain, a culturally defined symbolic system, preserves and transmits creative products to other individuals and future generations.

Sternberg and Lubart (1991, 1995) proposed an investment theory of creativity, which argues that creative thinkers are similar to good investors. They argued that six resources are available for creativity: intellectual processes, knowledge, intellectual style, personality, motivation, and environmental context, with creativity resulting from a combination of these elements. Creative thinkers generate ideas that initially are rejected, possibly because they defy the crowd or threaten existing interests. These ideas are like undervalued stocks, in that the creative thinker has to convince others that his or her idea has value. Once others view the idea as valuable, which increases the perceived value of the investment, the creative thinker sells high by leaving the idea to others and moves to a new idea.

Simonton's (1999) evolutionary theory of creative thinking built on both Darwin's theory of organic evolution and Campbell's (1960) evolutionary model of the creative process. Simonton proposed a process of variation and selective retention. Variation primarily contributes to idea novelty, while the process of selection primarily contributes to idea usefulness. Since novelty is usually viewed as what distinguishes creative work over and above work that is useful, Simonton focused his theory on variation. He argued that variation does not need to be blind or random, rather it can be guided by the existence of knowledge elements that can be combined into new variations. The initial selection of ideas occurs in the creators' minds, as they test ideas against relevant criteria for usefulness or appropriateness, as well as using novelty criteria. At a certain point, ideas are shared with others, and additional variation and selection of ideas can then occur.

Sternberg (1999) proposed a propulsion model of types of creative contributions. His model characterized seven types of creative contributions that can occur in any domain. He argued that creative contributions differ both in the amount of creativity they exhibit and in the type of creativity they display. Four of the contribution types accept current paradigms and attempt to extend them. These contribution types are replication, redefinition, forward incrementation, and advance forward incrementation. Three of the contribution types reject current paradigms and attempt to replace them. They are redirection, reconstruction or redirection, and reinitiation.

Now that we have summarized the work appearing primarily in the psychology literature on creativity in general, the rest of this chapter focuses on conceptual and empirical work in the area of organizational creativity.

ORGANIZATIONAL CREATIVITY

Research on organizational creativity, as a subarea in the field of organizational behavior, is relatively new. Researchers began to actively work in this area during the late 1980s. For example, Amabile (1988) built on her work on the social psychology of creativity, described earlier, to propose a theory-based componential framework to understand what factors can facilitate or inhibit employee creativity. In the early 1990s, Woodman, Sawyer, and Griffin (1993) proposed that creativity was affected by the interaction of personal and organizational factors, and reviewed many individual, group, and organizational factors that could interact to influence employee creativity. At the same time, empirical research started to be conducted examining various personal and contextual factors that may affect individual creative performance (e.g., Amabile, 1996; Eisenberger & Selbst, 1994; Farmer, Tierney, & Kung-McIntyre, 2003; George & Zhou, 2001, 2002; Gilson & Shalley, 2004; Madjar, Oldham, & Pratt, 2002; Oldham & Cummings, 1996; Perry-Smith, 2006; Shalley, 1991, 1995; Shalley & Oldham, 1997; Shalley & Perry-Smith, 2001; Tierney & Farmer, 2002; Zhou, 1998, 2003; Zhou & George, 2001), with the number of studies greatly increasing each year.

CONCEPTUAL FRAMEWORKS

There are two main theoretical models that have guided the area of organizational creativity, that of Amabile (1988, 1996) and Woodman and colleagues (1993). What is common about both of these conceptual frameworks is the importance that is given to social and contextual influences for employee creativity. Also, there are a few other more recent conceptual pieces that have helped to inform us in this area (e.g., Ford, 1996; Unsworth, 2001). The two main theoretical models, along with the relevant other conceptual frameworks, will be briefly presented here in the order they appeared in the literature.

Amabile's (1988, 1996) componential model of creativity proposes that there are three key components of creativity: domain-relevant skills, creativity-relevant processes, and task motivation. Domain relevant skills include factual knowledge and expertise in a given domain. These skills can be affected by formal and informal education and training, as well as an individual's perceptual, cognitive, and motor abilities. The second component, which was originally called creativity-relevant skills but has been changed recently to creativity-relevant processes, includes explicit or tacit knowledge concerning strategies for producing creative ideas, appropriate cognitive styles, and work styles for creative-idea production.

Amabile posited that training in creative skills and strategies, experiences in creative activities, and possessing certain personality characteristics are likely to positively influence creativity-relevant processes. Task motivation is the third component and it includes individuals' attitudes toward a task and their perceptions of their own motivation for working on the task. Motivation can be either intrinsic (i.e., arising from individual's interest, involvement, curiosity, or satisfaction) or extrinsic (i.e., arising from sources outside of the task itself) in nature. Amabile argued that intrinsic motivation rather than extrinsic motivation was critical for creativity, and the componential model of creativity is often considered an intrinsic motivation perspective of creativity. Recently, the intrinsic motivation principle has been modified, such that it is now recognized that certain extrinsic motivators may not undermine intrinsic motivation or creativity. In the case when an extrinsic motivation actually serves to enhance intrinsic motivation, Amabile (1993) calls this motivational synergy.

Woodman and colleagues' (1993) interactionist perspective of organizational creativity is premised on the idea that creativity is an individual level phenomenon that is affected by both situational and dispositional factors. They stress that it is the interaction of an individual's disposition and contextual factors in the work environment that fully predicts creative performance. Furthermore, their model stresses influences across levels of analysis, and they argue that cross-level influences are critical in identifying and understanding group and organizational factors that can facilitate or stifle creative behavior in a complex social system. Specifically, Woodman and colleagues (1993) describe creative performance in organizations as a function of a number of individual, group, and organizational characteristics that interact in affecting whether creativity occurs. For individual characteristics they discuss how cognitive abilities or style, personality, intrinsic motivation, and knowledge are important. For group characteristics, they focus on norms, cohesiveness, size, roles, diversity, task- and problem-solving approaches. The organizational characteristics that they discuss are culture, resources, rewards, strategy, structure, and technology. In their model, creative persons, groups, and the organization are inputs that are transformed by the creative process and situation, with the potential outcome of this transformation leading to a creative product.

Ford's (1996) model of individual creative action argued that creativity action by an individual is a result of a combination of sensemaking, motivation, and knowledge and ability. He argued that creative and habitual actions are competing behavioral options for an individual. Normally, as long as habitual actions are attractive, even when the context may be conducive to creative activity, individuals will continue their habitual actions. Therefore, although creative action is very important, he predicted that creative actions would occur rarely in organizations. His theory covered multiple social domains such as group, organizational, institutional, and market.

Drazin, Glynn, and Kazanjian (1999) proposed a multilevel model of organizational creativity. They defined creativity as a process rather than an outcome. Specifically, creativity was an individual's psychological engagement in creative activity regardless of whether the outcomes are creative or not. Thus, they focused on an individual's attempt to undertake creative activities. They posited that individuals form frames of references that mediate their engagement in creative activities. Their model targeted longer term, large-scale organizational projects.

Mumford (2000) hypothesized about the type of human resource management strategies that might enhance creativity. He argued that organizations should consider multiple interventions at multiple levels in the organization, taking into account the individual, the group, the organization, and the strategic environment when selecting interventions intended to enhance creativity. For example, at the individual level, he argued that organizations should provide incentives for ongoing knowledge development. At the group level, Mumford proposed that the organization should provide diversity in project assignment, as well as providing multiple career tracks for advancement. For the organizational level, it would be beneficial to develop rotational assignment programs, and conduct innovation audits. Finally, at the environmental level, one thing he proposed was to assess the implications of strategic changes for expertise requirements.

Mainemelis (2001) proposed a model describing how individuals experience timelessness by being totally engaged in their work activities. This model looks at the effect of timelessness on the creativity of employees and how contextual conditions can help to facilitate or impair this engrossment process. He suggests that four experiences comprise timelessness: a feeling of immersion, recognition of time distortion, a sense of mastery, and a sense of transcendence. His model is focused on the experience of working on a specific task and the resultant affective processes that could occur to increase the likelihood of creative performance.

As mentioned earlier, Unsworth (2001) developed a matrix of four types of creativity that vary on two dimensions (i.e, the driver of the engagement and the problem type). Essentially, she argued that creativity is not a unitary construct so the commonly used definition of creativity (e.g., novel ideas appropriate for the situation) does not examine the type of idea generated, why it was generated, or how the process began. She proposed that there should be a more fine-grained analysis of the processes that occurred leading up to idea generation. As such, the four creativity types she identified were responsive (closed, external), expected (open, external), contributory (closed, internal), and proactive (open, internal).

Perry-Smith and Shalley (2003) focused on the social side of creativity by highlighting the importance of others for individuals generating creative ideas. Taking a more macro perspective, they used concepts from social network theory to explore the association between the context of social relationships and individual creativity. They argued that weaker ties are more beneficial, in general, than stronger ties for creativity. They also posited that one's position in the network can make a difference for creativity. Specifically, a peripheral position with many connections outside the network was argued to be more likely to be associated with more creative insights. However, they suggested that once a high level of creativity has been achieved, peripheral individuals would start to become more central to the network, with exposure to diverse people and information sparking new ideas and creative insights. The journey from a peripheral position to the center of the network continues with increasing creativity only up to a point, when the individual becomes too entrenched in the status quo this constrains creativity unless he or she maintains connections outside of the social field.

Elsbach and Hargadon (2006) proposed a framework for designing professionals' jobs to include "mindless" work in order to enhance their creativity. Specifically, they focused on designing entire workdays rather than specific tasks, as is commonly done within the job design literature. They argue that today's professionals are chronically overworked, and this workload pressure causes them to be less creative. They introduce the concept of "mindless" work, which is work low in both cognitive difficulty and performance pressures. They suggest that the creativity of professionals could be enhanced by designing the workday to include hours of cognitively challenging, high-pressure work interspersed with planned hours of mindless work.

Hargadon and Bechky (2006) introduced a model of collective creativity, which focuses on how the locus of creative problem solving can shift from individuals to interactions of a collective. Their model was grounded in observations, interviews, informal conversations, and archival data gathered in field studies of employees in professional service firms. They built a model of collective creativity that identifies the roles of four different types of social interactions: help seeking, help giving, reflective reframing, and reinforcing.

COMMON METHODOLOGIES

The majority of empirical studies on organizational creativity have been conducted either in the behavioral laboratory or in organizations primarily using field surveys. There also have been a few case studies and some longitudinal work that will be discussed briefly. There have been no field experiments or archival-based studies that we are aware of. Below we discuss common practices and procedures for the laboratory studies and field studies, and give a few examples of some other types of methodologies that have been used.

Laboratory Studies

For laboratory studies on organizational creativity (e.g., Amabile, 1996; Madjar & Oldham, 2002; Shalley, 1991, 1995; Shalley & Oldham, 1997), two critical issues are (1) how applicable are the treatment conditions for enhancing our knowledge of creativity in a work context and (2) the type of task the participants work on. First, the field has recognized the value of conducting controlled experiments in the laboratory with adults (e.g., typically undergraduate students). For example, there is no question that certain phenomena can be examined better in the laboratory, such as isolating and controlling different factors and directly examining the effect of different manipulations to establish causality. For example, Shalley and Perry-Smith (2001) were able to address an ongoing question in the creativity literature: Can expected evaluation sometimes have a beneficial rather than negative effect on individual creativity? They hypothesized that when the informational component of an expected evaluation is made salient it can have a positive effect on creative performance, as opposed to when the controlling component is salient. By actually manipulating the informational and controlling components of an expected evaluation, they were able to indeed show that their hypothesis was correct. Also, some organizational creativity research has begun in the laboratory and then continued in the field. For example, Zhou and colleagues (e.g., Zhou, 1998; Zhou & Oldham, 2001) examined the effects of different types of feedback (e.g., informational versus controlling) on creative performance. In her first study in the laboratory (Zhou, 1998), she was able to directly manipulate the effects of different types of feedback on participants' subsequent creativity. Much was learned from this study that could then be brought to the field and examined by surveying employees as to the type of feedback they perceived they had received from their supervisors or coworkers. In addition, Zhou and colleagues (Zhou, 2003; Zhou & George, 2001) investigated the main and interactive effects of various types of feedback and other personal and contextual variables on supervisors' ratings of the employees' actual creativity.

The second factor to consider in laboratory studies is the type of tasks participants are asked to work on. Specifically, it has been argued (Amabile, 1983; McGraw, 1978) that in order to be creative, individuals need to work on complex, open-ended tasks where a heuristic rather than algorithmic solution or outcome is possible. Complex heuristic tasks are open ended and ill structured, with no known straightforward path to a solution. Prior laboratory studies have used a few different types of tasks. For example, Amabile and her colleagues have used a number of tasks. Amabile (1996) categorized these tasks as falling into three categories: artistic (e.g. paintings), problem-solving (e.g., ideas for high-tech products), and verbal (e.g., stories) tasks. Also, Madjar and Oldham (2002) have used an idea generation task. Finally, Shalley (1991) developed an in-basket type of memo task in which participants are asked to read through a number of human resource and management problems that are stated in brief paragraphs. They are given information about their role as the human resource director in a large steel-manufacturing company. Participants are then encouraged to respond to each memo presented as the human resource director in the company, in a complete and thoughtful manner, without worrying about how many memos they responded to. The original task consisted of 22 problems, and various studies conducted since have used subsets of this original number (e.g., Shalley, 1995; Zhou, 1998).

In terms of measurement, laboratory studies have typically used Amabile's (1983) consensual assessment technique to measure creative performance. Using this technique, a product is judged as creative if appropriate, independent judges reliably agree that it is creative. It is important to gain agreement from multiple judges who are experts or have some advanced knowledge within the domain studied (e.g., relevant educational background or years of work experience). These judges' assessments need to reach an acceptable level of agreement concerning the extent to which an idea or product is considered creative (i.e., novel and appropriate).

Currently, the common method used in studies to check interrater agreement is by calculating R_{wg} (James, Demaree, & Wolf, 1984).

Earlier work in this area had used Spearman Brown or Cronbach's alpha calculations to assess interrater agreement. In most studies conducted to date, the overall creativity of a solution or product is rated on a 7-point scale that ranges from not at all creative to extremely creative (e.g., Shalley, 1991, 1995; Shalley & Perry-Smith, 2001; Zhou, 1998). Assuming an acceptable interrater reliability for the judges, a creativity score is then computed as an average of the creativity ratings for each individual across their generated solutions. Therefore, most of the studies conducted have used an overall creativity rating approach where the judges rate each of the products as to level of novelty and appropriateness and these ratings are then combined to form one composite rating. One study took a different approach. Here Zhou and Oldham (2001) had two judges separately evaluate both the originality and usefulness of the solutions. Once they had acceptable agreement between the judges' originality and usefulness ratings, they took averages of each, respectively. Next, a creativity index was formed for each participant by multiplying the originality and usefulness scores for a component measure. Although both of these approaches to measuring creativity are consistent with the definition of creativity common in the literature, future research needs to examine the relative effectiveness of these two different approaches.

Finally, one factor that is critical for laboratory research on organizational creativity is to establish the validity of testing particular phenomena in the laboratory, and discussing how these findings would generalize to an organizational setting. Given this, many of the prior laboratory studies have selected contextual factors to examine that are important for employees in organizations and have tried to structure the laboratory setting so that it is as close as feasible to a typical work environment. That said, while laboratory studies have inherent methodological strengths, like all methodologies, they have their weaknesses as well. For example, laboratory studies lack external validity. No matter what steps laboratory researchers take (and we would encourage future research to continue to try to increase realism in the laboratory), we recognize that participants are not real employees and the laboratory is not a work setting. Therefore, the use of multiple methods in the area of organizational creativity is strongly encouraged.

Field Studies

Most of the field studies on organizational creativity have used survey data to assess employees' perceptions of their work context and to collect personality and demographic data. In field studies the most common way to measure creativity is to have supervisors rate the creativity of their employees (e.g., George & Zhou, 2001, 2002; Oldham & Cummings, 1996; Scott & Bruce, 1994; Shin & Zhou, 2003; Tierney & Farmer, 2002; Tierney, Farmer, & Graen, 1999; Zhou, 2003; Zhou & George, 2001). There are a number of rating scales that have been used in this research. For example, there is George and Zhou's (2001, 2002) 13-item scale; Oldham & Cummings' (1996) 3-item scale; Scott and Bruce's (1994) 6-item scale, which also taps implementation of ideas as well as their generation; and Tierney and colleagues' (Tierney et al., 1999) 9-item scale, which has been used with only 6 items as well (Tierney & Farmer, 2002). These scales all share similarities but differ in their emphasis on certain types of jobs (e.g., R&D employees versus employees with jobs that naturally require lower levels of creativity), and their balance between asking questions only about idea or product generation as opposed to also questioning about implementation. Future research can tease out the extent to which these four scales, and other potential ones, converge and under what conditions certain scales are more suitable for certain types of jobs, employees, or different stages of the creative process. Moreover, it could be helpful if future studies attempted to include multiple evaluations of employees' creativity, by, for example, co-workers, self, and other supervisors, in order to see whether there is good interrater reliability or if particular evaluators are more appropriate under certain circumstances. Of course, similar to what has been found for ratings of general performance, it is possible that ratings of creativity from multiple sources may not yield more useful information (see LeBreton, Burgess, Kaiser, Atchley, & James, 2003).

Some field studies also have used objective measures of creativity, such as number of patents, patent disclosures, technical reports and research papers, and ideas submitted to organizational suggestion systems (e.g., Oldham & Cummings, 1996; Pelz & Andrews, 1966; Perry-Smith, 2006; Scott & Bruce, 1994; Tierney et al., 1999). Obviously, some of these objective measures are only appropriate for certain types of jobs or industries, where, for example, patents or technical reports are possible outcomes of the work. Similarly, if an organization does not have a suggestion program, this would be a meaningless metric to use. More importantly, while many studies have found similar results between objective measures and supervisory ratings of employee creativity, some studies have found different results, and some have found varying results between the different objective measures. For example, Tierney and colleagues (1999) found that supervisor ratings were significantly correlated with invention disclosures and research reports, with the pattern of results for these three measures being the same. Also, Scott and Bruce (1994) found that supervisor ratings were significantly correlated with number of invention disclosures. In addition, Oldham and Cummings (1996) found similar results for patent disclosures and supervisory ratings of creativity. However, in this same study they found different results for patent disclosures written and contributions to the employee suggestion program. Therefore, more research is needed to examine the value of using a more subjective measure of creativity, such as a supervisor rating, versus more objective measures, such as patents. It also should be noted that supervisor ratings of creativity could suffer from some of the same reliability issues that have been found with their ratings of general performance (see Rothstein, 1990; Viswesvaran, Ones, & Schmidt, 1996). Finally, research also needs to examine the utility among different objective measures of creativity.

Field studies are strong on external validity, but because they are usually cross-sectional in design, results cannot inform us about causality. That is, since the independent and dependent variables are measured at the same time or within a short time frame of each other, one cannot conclude that one factor caused another factor, just that they may be associated with each other. In addition, all extraneous factors and noise cannot be definitively controlled in field studies. On the other hand, the strength of field studies is that employees in their work organizations are being studied, so there is the potential for higher generalizability of results and greater external validity than compared to laboratory studies.

Other Research Designs

Currently, besides laboratory and field studies, there have only been a few other research designs used to study organizational creativity. These will be briefly discussed. First, Hargadon and Sutton (1997) in an ethnographic study over 2½ years, conducted observations, interviews, informal discussions, and gathered archival data of a product design firm. Their results led them to develop a technology-brokering model of product innovation. This model described how organizations acted as technology brokers, using the network position of a product design–consulting firm working with a number of clients across industries to broker, transfer, and adapt existing knowledge from one industry to another or combining preexisting ideas and products into new products. Second, Amabile and Conti (1999), in a longitudinal study, examined creativity-enhancing or -inhibiting work environments before, during, and after a major downsizing. They found that creativity and most of the creativity-supporting aspects of the work environment declined significantly but did moderately increase later. For creativity-undermining aspects, they found the opposite pattern of results. What was interesting in the methodology was that instead of following all employees in all waves of the data, they randomly sampled a different group of employees for each wave of data collection. Finally, Amabile, Barsade, Mueller, and Staw (2005), using a hybrid methodology, compiled qualitative and quantitative longitudinal data to explore how affect related to creativity. Specifically, they analyzed daily diary entries of employees from seven companies. They found that positive affect related positively to creativity. Positive affect also was found to be an antecedent to creative thought, as well as a consequence of creative-thought events.

MAIN EMPIRICAL RESEARCH FINDINGS
ON ORGANIZATIONAL CREATIVITY

In this section, we will provide a brief summary of the main research findings on organizational creativity. There have been a number of relatively recent comprehensive reviews of the literature that a reader wanting more detail can peruse (e.g., Mumford, 2000; Mumford, Scott, Gaddis, & Strange, 2002; Shalley & Gilson, 2004; Shalley, Zhou, & Oldham, 2004; Zhou & Shalley, 2003). Additionally, although Anderson, De Dreu, and Nijstad's (2004) review was concerned with innovation, they included some creativity studies in their review, which readers may find interesting and thought provoking.

In general, most of the major research findings have focused on creativity as an outcome. There has been relatively little research on the creative process within organizational creativity, with the exception of a few studies. Some recent empirical research has examined employees' overall engagement in creative processes at work (e.g., Gilson, Mathieu, Shalley, & Ruddy, 2005; Gilson & Shalley, 2004; Kazanjian, Drazin, & Glynn, 2000). Also, most of the organizational creativity research has examined the creative performance of individual employees rather than groups or teams of employees, but there is related work on team innovation and group brainstorming (e.g., Paulus, 2000; Sosik, Avolio, & Kahai, 1998; Sutton & Hargadon, 1996; West & Farr, 1990). The studies that have been conducted to date on the creativity of teams represent an initial start in this area (e.g., Ford & Sullivan, 2004; Gilson, Mathieu, Shalley, & Ruddy, 2005; Gilson & Shalley, 2004; Leenders, van Engelen, & Kratzer, 2003; Nemiro, 2002; Pirolo-Merlo & Mann, 2004; Taggar, 2001, 2002).

In general, the key finding in the literature is the value of a supportive and stimulating work environment. Consistently, research studies have found in the laboratory and the field that a supportive and stimulating work environment (cf. Oldham, 2003) is positively associated with creativity, and that a nonsupportive or controlling work environment is negatively associated with creativity (e.g., Amabile & Conti, 1999; Madjar et al., 2002; Oldham & Cummings, 1996; Stahl & Koser, 1978; Zhou, 2003). Support and stimulation can come from a variety of sources such as in the form of supportive and stimulating leadership (e.g., Amabile et al., 1996, 2004; Frese, Teng, & Wijnen, 1999; Shin & Zhou, 2003; Tierney & Farmer, 2002, 2004; Zhou, 2003; Zhou & George, 2003), supportive and stimulating coworkers (e.g., Amabile et al., 1996; Zhou, 2003; Zhou & George, 2001), or expected evaluation and feedback communicated in a supportive, informational manner rather than in a more controlling, punitive manner (e.g., Amabile, 1979; Amabile, Goldfarb, & Brackfield, 1990; Shalley, 1995; Shalley & Perry-Smith, 2001; Zhou, 1998, 2003; Zhou & Oldham, 2001). For further details concerning the research conducted to date on creative performance and the impact of leadership or expected evaluation and feedback, see chapters by Tierney and Zhou in this handbook.

A second consistent finding is that goals can be set to facilitate the occurrence of creative performance (e.g., Carson & Carson, 1993; Shalley, 1991, 1995). For more detail about the effects of creativity goals on creative performance, see the chapter by Shalley in this handbook.

Also, research has indicated that complex jobs (e.g., jobs with high levels of autonomy, feedback, significance, identity, and variety) (Hackman & Oldham, 1980) are associated with higher levels of creative performance as compared to simpler jobs (e.g., Amabile & Gryskiewicz, 1989; Farmer et al., 2003; Hatcher, Ross, & Collins, 1989; Oldham & Cummings, 1996; Tierney & Farmer, 2002, 2004). For example, Tierney and Farmer in two studies (2002, 2004) found positive, significant associations between supervisor's ratings of creativity and objective measures (i.e., using the *Dictionary of Occupational Titles*) of the employees' job complexity.

Finally, a number of studies have begun to explore the interactional effects of personality factors or cognitive style with contextual factors for creative performance. For the interaction of personality with a variety of contextual characteristics (e.g., supportive supervision, feedback, coworker support), most of the studies have used either Gough's (1979) Creative Personality Scale (CPS) or one or more dimensions of the Five Factor Model of Personality (FFM; Costa & McCrae, 1992), with openness to experience being examined the most (e.g., George & Zhou, 2001; Madjar et al., 2002; Oldham & Cummings, 1996; Zhou, 2003; Zhou & Oldham, 2001). In general, a mixed pattern of interactions has been found between personality factors and contextual factors (see Shalley et al., 2004 for a discussion). Therefore, much more research is needed to examine possible interactive effects.

Of the studies that have looked at the interaction of cognitive style and contextual factors (e.g., Baer, Oldham, & Cummings, 2003; Tierney et al., 1999), they have primarily used Kirton's Adoption-Innovation (KAI) inventory to examine the interactive effect of having an adaptive versus innovative style with some contextual factor (e.g., supportive supervision, rewards, job complexity). In general, cognitive style has been found to have a moderating effect in the two studies conducted in this area (Baer et al., 2003; Tierney et al., 1999). More research examining the interactive effect of cognitive style and different contextual factors on creative performance is warranted.

CONCLUSION

This chapter presents a historical overview of the field of organizational creativity. First, we provide a definition of creativity as both an outcome and a process. Then we describe the foundational work on creativity in general that has been conducted primarily in the field of psychology. In doing this, we discuss how creativity as an outcome has been defined in two different ways in the psychology literature (i.e., novel and appropriate versus statistical uniqueness as an originality measure), while in the organizational creativity literature it has consistently been defined as novel and useful or appropriate ideas, processes, or procedures. Then we discuss what differentiates the area of organizational creativity from creativity in general, by having this area focus exclusively on creativity at work or in organizations, as opposed to, for example, in elementary school settings or the arts. Next, we introduce the emerging, but rapidly growing, area of organizational creativity and discuss the major conceptual work, key measures, and design issues, and give a brief overview of the major findings to date in the area of organizational creativity. We hope that this chapter, as well as the rest of this handbook, will help guide future researchers to further develop this important research area.

REFERENCES

Amabile, T. M. (1979). Effects of external evaluation on artistic creativity. *Journal of Personality and Social Psychology, 37,* 221–282.

Amabile, T. M. (1983). *The social psychology of creativity.* New York: Springer-Verlag.

Amabile, T. M. (1988). A model of creativity and innovation in organizations. In B. M. Staw & L. L. Cummings (Eds.), *Research in behavior* (pp. 123–167). Greenwich, CT: JAI.

Amabile, T. M. (1993). Motivational synergy: Toward new conceptualizations of intrinsic and extrinsic motivation in the workplace. *Human Resource Management Review, 3,* 185–201.

Amabile, T. M. (1996). *Creativity in context.* Boulder, CO: Westview.

Amabile, T. M., Barsade, S. G., Mueller, J. S., & Staw, B. M. (2005). Affect and creativity at work. *Administrative Science Quarterly, 50,* 367–403.

Amabile, T. M., & Conti, H. (1999). Changes in the work environment for creativity during downsizing. *Academy of Management Journal, 42,* 630–640.

Amabile, T. M., Conti, R., Coon, H., Lazenby, J., & Herron, M. (1996). Assessing the work environment for creativity. *Academy of Management Journal, 39,* 1154–1184.

Amabile, T. M., Goldfarb, P., & Brackfield, S. C. (1990). Social influences on creativity: Evaluation, coaction, and surveillance. *Creativity Research Journal, 3,* 6–21.

Amabile, T. M., & Gryskiewicz, N. D. (1989). The creative environment scales: Work environment inventory. *Creativity Research Journal, 2,* 231–252.

Amabile, T. M., Schatzel, E. A., Moneta, G. B., & Kramer, S. J. (2004). Leader behaviors and the work environment for creativity: Perceived leader support. *Leadership Quarterly, 15,* 5–32.

Anderson, N., De Dreu, C. K. W., & Nijstad, B. A. (2004). The routinization of innovation research: A constructively critical review of the state-of-the-science. *Journal of Organizational Behavior, 25,* 147–173.

Baer, M., Oldham, G. R., & Cummings, A. (2003). Rewarding creativity: When does it really matter? *Leadership Quarterly, 14,* 569–586.

Barron, R. (1955). The disposition toward originality. *Journal of Abnormal and Social Psychology, 51,* 478–485.

Barron, F. (1965). The psychology of creativity. In T. Newcomb (Ed.), *New directions in psychology* (Vol. 2). New York: Holt, Rinehart, & Winston.

Barron, F. (1968). *Creativity and personal freedom.* New York: Van Nostrand.

Barron, F., & Harrington, D. M. (1981). Creativity, intelligence, and personality. *Annual Review of Psychology, 32,* 439–476.

Basadur, M. S. (2004). Leading others to think innovatively together: Creative leadership. *Leadership Quarterly, 15,* 103–121.

Basadur, M. S., Graen, G. B., & Green, S. G. (1982). Training in creative problem solving: Effects on ideation and problem solving in an applied research organization. *Organizational Behavior and Human Decision Processes, 30,* 41–70.

Campbell, D. T. (1960). Blind variation and selective retention in creative thought as to other knowledge processes. *Psychological Review, 67,* 380–400.

Carson, P. P., & Carson, K. D. (1993). Managing creativity enhancement through goal setting and feedback. *Journal of Creative Behavior, 27,* 36–45.

Cattell, R. B., & Butcher, H. J. (1968). The prediction of achievement and creativity. Oxford, England: Bobbs-Merrill.

Costa, P. T., & McCrae, R. R. (1992). *Revised NEO Personality Inventory (NEO PI-R) and NEO Five-Factor Inventory (NEO-FFI) professional manual.* Odessa, FL: Psychological Assessment Resources.

Cox, C. M. (1926). Genetic studies of genius: Vol. 2. In *The early mental traits of three hundred geniuses.* Stanford, CA: Stanford University Press.

Crutchfield, R. (1962). Conformity and creative thinking. In H. Gruber, G. Terrelly, & M. Wertheimer (Eds.), *Contemporary approaches to creative thinking* (pp. 120–140). New York: Atherton.

Csikszentmihalyi, M. (1988). Society, culture, and person: A systems view of creativity. In R. J. Sternberg (Ed.), *The nature of creativity* (pp. 325–330). Cambridge: Cambridge University Press.

Csikszentmihalyi, M. (1990). The domain of creativity. In M. A. Runco & R. S. Albert (Eds.), *Theories of creativity* (pp. 190–212). Newbury Park, CA: Sage.

Csikszentmihalyi, M. (1996). *Creativity.* New York: HarperCollins.

Csikszentmihalyi, M., & Csikszentmihalyi, I. S. (Eds.). (1988). *Optimal experience: Psychological studies of flow in consciousness.* Cambridge: Cambridge University Press.

Csikszentmihalyi, M., & Robinson, R. (1986). Culture, time and the development of talent. In R. Sternberg & J. Davidson (Eds.), *Conceptions of giftedness* (pp. 264–284). Cambridge: Cambridge University Press.

DeBono, E. (1985). *Six thinking hats.* Boston: Little, Brown.

Drazin, R., Glynn, M., & Kazanjian, R. (1999). Multilevel theorizing about creativity in organizations: A sensemaking perspective. *Academy of Management Review, 24,* 286–307.

Duncker, K. (1945). On problem solving. *Psychological Monographs, 68*(5, whole no. 270).

Eisenberger, R., & Selbst, M. (1994). Does reward increase or decrease creativity? *Journal of Personality and Social Psychology, 66,* 1116–1127.

Elsbach, K. D., & Hargadon, A. B. (2006). Enhancing creativity through "mindless" work: A framework of workday design. *Organization Science, 17,* 470–483.

Farmer, S. M., Tierney, P., & Kung-McIntyre, K. (2003). Employee creativity in Taiwan: An application of role identity theory. *Academy of Management Journal, 46,* 618–630.

Ford, C. M. (1996). A theory of individual creative action in multiple social domains. *Academy of Management Review, 21,* 1112–1142.

Ford, C. M., & Sullivan, D. M. (2004). A time for everything: How the timing of novel contributions influences project team outcomes. *Journal of Organizational Behavior, 25,* 279–292.

Frese, M., Teng, E., & Wijnen, C. J. (1999). Helping to improve suggestion systems: Predictors of making suggestions in companies. *Journal of Organizational Behavior, 20,* 1139–1155.

Galton, F. (1870). *Hereditary genius.* London: MacMillan, London, & Applegate.

George, J. M., & Zhou, J. (2001). When openness to experience and conscientiousness are related to creative behavior: An interactional approach. *Journal of Applied Psychology, 86,* 513–524.

George, J. M., & Zhou, J. (2002). Understanding when bad moods foster creativity and good ones don't: The role of context and clarity of feelings. *Journal of Applied Psychology, 87,* 687–697.

Getzels, J. W. (1975). Problem finding and the inventiveness of solutions. *Journal of Creative Behavior, 9,* 12–18.

Getzels, J. W., & Csikszentmihalyi, M. (1976). *The creative vision: A longitudinal study of problem finding in art.* New York: Wiley.

Gilson, L. L., Mathieu, J. E., Shalley, C. E., & Ruddy, T. M. (2005).Creativity and standardization: Complementary or conflicting drivers of team effectiveness? *Academy of Management Journal, 48,* 521–531.

Gilson, L. L., & Shalley, C.E. (2004). A little creativity goes a long way: An examination of teams' engagement in creative processes. *Journal of Management, 30,* 453–470.

Gordon, W. J. J. (1961). *Synectics: The development of creative capacity.* Oxford, England: Harper.

Gough, H. G. (1979). A creativity scale for the Adjective Check List. *Journal of Personality and Social Psychology, 37,* 1398–1405.

Guilford, J. P. (1959). Traits of creativity. In H. H. Anderson (Ed.), *Creativity and its cultivation* (pp. 142–161). New York: Harper.

Guilford, J. P. (1963). Intellectual resources and their values as seen by scientists. In C. W. Taylor & F. Barron (Eds.), *Scientific creativity: Its recognition and development.* New York: Wiley.

Guilford, J. P. (1967). *The nature of human intelligence.* New York: McGraw-Hill.

Hackman, J. R., & Oldham, G. R. (1980). *Work redesign.* Reading, MA: Addison-Wesley.

Hargadon, A., & Sutton, R. I. (1997). Technology brokering and innovation in a product development firm. *Administrative Science Quarterly, 42,* 716–749.

Hargadon, A. B., & Bechky, B. A. (2006). When collections of creatives become creative collectives: A field study of problem solving at work. *Organization Science, 17,* 484–500.

Hatcher, L., Ross, T. L., & Collins, D. (1989). Prosocial behavior, job complexity, and suggestion contribution under gainsharing plans. *Journal of Applied Behavioral Science, 25,* 231–248.

Hogarth, R. (1980). *Judgement and choice.* Chichester, England: Wiley.

James, L. R., Demaree, R. G., & Wolf, G. (1993). R_{wg}: An assessment of within-group interrater agreement. *Journal of Applied Psychology, 78,* 306–309.

Kazanjian, R. K., Drazin, R., & Glynn, M. A. (2000). Creativity and technological learning: The roles of organization architecture and crisis in large-scale projects. *Journal of Engineering and Technology Management, 17,* 273–298.

Kirton, M. J. (1976). Adaptors and innovators: A description and measure. *Journal of Applied Psychology, 61,* 622–629.

Kirton, M. J. (1994). *Adaptors and innovators: Styles of creativity and problem solving* (2nd ed.). New York: Routledge.

Koestler, A. (1964). *The act of creation.* New York: Macmillan.

LeBreton, J. M., Burgess, J. R. D., Kaiser, R. B., Atchley, E. K., & James, L. R. (2003). The restriction of variance hypothesis and interrater reliability and agreement: Are ratings from multiple sources really dissimilar? *Organizational Research Methods, 6,* 80–128.

Leenders, R. Th. A. J., van Engelen, J. M. L., & Kratzer, J. (2003). Virtuality, communication, and new product team creativity: A social network perspective. *Journal of Engineering and Technology Management, 20,* 69–92.

MacKinnon, D. W. (1962). The personality correlates of creativity: A study of American architects. *Proceedings of the Fourteenth Congress on Applied Psychology: Vol. 2* (pp. 11–39). Copenhagen: Munksgaard.

MacKinnon, D. W. (1975). IPAR's contribution to the conceptualization and study of creativity. In I. A. Taylor & J. W. Getzels (Eds.), *Perspectives in creativity* (pp. 60–89). Chicago: Aldine.

Madjar, N., & Oldham, G. R. (2002). Preliminary tasks and creative performance on a subsequent task: Effects of time on preliminary tasks and amount of information about the subsequent task. *Creativity Research Journal, 14,* 239–251.

Madjar, N., Oldham, G. R., & Pratt, M. G. (2002). There's no place like home? The contributions of work and non-work creativity supports to employees' creative performance. *Academy of Management Journal, 45,* 757–767.

Mainemelis, C. (2001). When the muse takes it all: A model for the experience of timelessness in organizations. *Academy of Management Review, 26,* 548–565.

McGraw, K. (1978). The detrimental effects of reward on performance: A literature review and a prediction model. In M. Lepper & D. Greene (Eds.), *The hidden costs of reward.* Hillsdale, NJ: Lawrence Erlbaum Associates.

Mumford, M. D. (2000). Managing creative people: Strategies and tactics for innovation. *Human Resources Management Review, 10,* 313–351.

Mumford, M. D., Baughman, W. A., Maher, M. A., Costanza, D. P., & Supinski, E. P. (1997). Process based measures of creative problem solving skills: 4. Category combination. *Creativity Research Journal, 10,* 59–71.

Mumford, M. D., & Gustafson, S. B. (1988). Creativity syndrome: Integration, application, and innovation. *Psychological Bulletin, 103,* 27–43.

Mumford, M. D., Scott, G. M., Gaddis, B., & Strange, J. M. (2002). Leading creative people: Orchestrating expertise and relationships. *Leadership Quarterly, 13,* 705–750.

Nemiro, J. E. (2002). The creative process in virtual teams. *Creativity Research Journal, 14,* 69–104.

Newell, A., Shaw, J. C., & Simon, H. A. (1962). The process of creative thinking. In H. Gruber, G. Terrell, & M. Wertheimer (Eds.), *Contemporary approaches to creative thinking* (pp. 43–62). New York: Atherton.

Oldham, G. R. 2003. Stimulating and supporting creativity in organizations. In S. E. Jackson, M. A. Hitt, & A. S. DeNisi (Eds.), *Managing knowledge for sustained competitive advantage* (pp. 243–273). San Francisco, CA: Jossey-Bass.

Oldham, G. R., & Cummings, A. (1996). Employee creativity: Personal and contextual factors at work. Academy of Management Journal, 39, 607–634.

Osborn, A. F. (1953). *Applied imagination.* New York: Scribner's.

Parnes, S. (1967). *Creative behavior guidebook.* New York: Scribner's.

Parnes, S. J., Noller, R. B., & Biondi, A. M. 1977. *Guide to creative action.* New York: Charles Scribner's Sons.

Paulus, P. B. (2000). Groups, teams, and creativity: The creative potential of idea-generating groups. *Applied Psychology—An International Review, 49,* 237–262.

Pelz, D. C., & Andrews, F. M. (1966). *Scientists in organizations: Productive climates for research and development.* Oxford, England: John Wiley.

Perry-Smith, J. E. (2006). Social yet creative: The role of social relationships in facilitating individual creativity. *Academy of Management Journal, 49,* 85–101.

Perry-Smith, J. E., & Shalley, C. E. (2003). The social side of creativity: A static and dynamic social network perspective. *Academy of Management Review, 28,* 89–106.

Pirolo-Merlo, A., & Mann, L. (2004). The relationship between individual creativity and team creativity: Aggregating across people and time. *Journal of Organizational Behavior, 25,* 235–257.

Reiter-Palmon, R., & Illies, J. J. (2004). Leadership and creativity: Understanding leadership from a creative problem-solving perspective. *Leadership Quarterly, 15,* 55–77.

Reiter-Palmon, R., Mumford, M. D., Boes, J. O., & Runco, M. A. (1997). Problem construction and creativity: The role of ability, cue consistency, and active processing. *Creative Research Journal, 10,* 9–23.

Rogers, C. (1954). Toward a theory of creativity. *A Review of General Semantics, 11,* 249–262.

Rokeach, M. (1965). In pursuit of the creative process. In G. A. Steiner (Ed.), *The creative organization.* Chicago: University of Chicago Press.

Rothstein, H. R. (1990). Interrater reliability of job performance ratings: Growth to asymptote level with increasing opportunity to observe. *Journal of Applied Psychology, 75,* 322–327.

Runco, M. A. (1986). Maximal performance on divergent thinking tests by gifted, talented, and nongifted children. *Psychology in the Schools, 23,* 308–315.

Runco, M. A., & Chand, I. (1995). Cognition and creativity. *Educational Psychology Review, 7,* 243–267.

Runco, M. A., & Okuda, S. M. (1988). Problem discovery, divergent thinking, and the creative process. *Journal of Youth and Adolescence, 17,* 211–220.

Scott, S. G., & Bruce, R. A. (1994). Determinants of innovative behavior: A path model of individual innovation in the workplace. *Academy of Management Journal, 37,* 580–607.

Shalley, C. E. (1991). Effects of productivity goals, creativity goals, and personal discretion on individual creativity. *Journal of Applied Psychology, 76,* 179–185.

Shalley, C. E. (1995). Effects of coaction, expected evaluation, and goal setting on creativity and productivity. *Academy of Management Journal, 38,* 483–503.

Shalley, C. E., & Gilson, L. L. (2004). What leaders need to know: A review of social and contextual factors that can foster or hinder creativity. *Leadership Quarterly, 15,* 33–53.

Shalley, C. E., Gilson, L. L., & Blum, T. C. (2000). Matching creative requirements and the work environment: Effects of satisfaction and intentions to leave. *Academy of Management Journal, 43,* 215–223.

Shalley, C. E., & Oldham, G. R. (1997). Competition and creative performance: Effects of competitor presence and visibility. *Creativity Research Journal, 10,* 337–345.

Shalley, C. E., & Perry-Smith, J. E. (2001). Effects of social-psychological factors on creative performance: The role of informational and controlling expected evaluation and modeling experience. *Organizational Behavior and Human Decision Processes, 84,* 1–22.

Shalley, C. E., Zhou, J., & Oldham, G. R. (2004). The effects of personal and contextual characteristics on creativity: Where should we go from here? *Journal of Management, 30,* 933–958.

Shin, S., & Zhou, J. (2003). Transformational leadership, conservation, and creativity: Evidence from Korea. *Academy of Management Journal, 46,* 703–714.

Simon, H. A. (1985). *Psychology of scientific discovery.* Keynote presentation at the 93rd annual meeting of the American Psychological Association, Los Angeles, CA.

Simonton, D. K. (1975). Sociocultural context of individual creativity: A transhistorical time-series analysis. *Journal of Personality and Social Psychology, 32,* 1119–1133.

Simonton, D. K. (1976a). Biographical determinants of achieved eminence: A multivariate approach to the Cox data. *Journal of Personality and Social Psychology, 33,* 218–226.

Simonton, D. K. (1976b). Philosophical eminence, beliefs, and Zeitgeist: An individual-generational analysis. *Journal of Personality and Social Psychology, 34,* 630–640.

Simonton, D. K. (1977). Creative productivity, age, and stress: A biographical time-series analysis of 10 classical composers. *Journal of Personality and Social Psychology, 35,* 791–804.

Simonton, D. K. (1999). Creativity as blind variation and selective retention: Is the creative process Darwinian? *Psychological Inquiry, 10,* 309–328.

Sosik, J. J., Avolio, B. J., & Kahai, S. S. (1998). Inspiring group creativity: Comparing anonymous and identified electronic brainstorming. *Small Group Research, 29,* 3–31.

Stahl, M. J., & Koser, M. C. (1978). Weighted productivity in R&D: Some associated individual and organizational variables. *IEEE Transactions on Engineering Management, EM-25,* 20–24.

Stein, M. I. (1967). Creativity and culture. In R. Mooney & T. Razik (Eds.), *Explorations in creativity* (pp. 109–119). New York: Harper.

Steiner, G. A. (1965). Introduction. In G. A. Steiner (Ed.), *The creative organization.* Chicago: University of Chicago Press.

Sternberg, R. J. (Ed.) (1999). *Handbook of creativity.* Cambridge: Cambridge University Press.

Sternberg, R. J., & Lubart, T. I. (1991). An investment theory of creativity and its development. *Human Development, 34,* 1–32.

Sternberg, R. J., & Lubart, T. I. (1995). *Defying the crowd: Cultivating creativity in a culture of conformity.* New York: Free Press.

Sutton, R. I., & Hargadon, A. (1996). Brainstorming groups in context: Effectiveness in a product design firm. *Administrative Science Quarterly, 41,* 685–734.

Taggar, S. (2001). Group composition, creative synergy, and group performance. *Journal of Creative Behavior, 35,* 261–286.

Taggar, S. (2002). Individual creativity and group ability to utilize individual creative resources: A multilevel model. *Academy of Management Journal, 45,* 315–330.

Taylor, C. W. (1964). *Widening horizons in creativity.* New York: Wiley.

Taylor, C. W. (1988). Various approaches to and definitions of creativity. In R. J. Sternberg (Ed.), The nature of creativity: *Contemporary psychological perspectives* (pp. 99–121). Cambridge: Cambridge University Press.

Taylor, C. W., & Barron, F. (Eds.). (1963). *Scientific creativity: Its recognition and development.* New York: Wiley.

Tierney, P., & Farmer, S. M. (2002). Creative self-efficacy: Potential antecedents and relationship to creative performance. *Academy of Management Journal, 45,* 1137–1148.

Tierney, P., & Farmer, S. M. (2004). The Pygmalion process and employee creativity. *Journal of Management, 30,* 413–432.

Tierney, P., Farmer, S. M., & Graen, G. B. (1999). An examination of leadership and employee creativity: The relevance of traits and relationships. *Personnel Psychology, 52,* 591–620.

Torrance, E. P. (1962). *Guiding creative talent.* Englewood Cliffs, NJ: Prentice-Hall.

Torrance, E. P. (1974). *The Torrance tests of creative thinking.* Bensonville, IL: Scholastic Testing Services.

Torrance, E. P., & Khatena, J. (1970). What kind of person are you? *Gifted Child Quarterly, 14,* 71–75.

Unsworth, K. (2001). Unpacking creativity. *Academy of Management Review, 26,* 289–297.

Vincent, A. S., Decker, B. P., & Mumford, M. D. (2002). Divergent thinking, intelligence, and expertise: A test of alternative models. *Creativity Research Journal, 14,* 163–178.

Visweswaran, C., Ones, D. S., & Schmidt, F. L. (1996). Comparative analysis of the reliability of job performance ratings. *Journal of Applied Psychology, 81,* 557–574.

Wallas, G. (1926). *The art of thought.* London: Cape.

Ward, T. B., Smith, S. M., & Finke, R. A. (1999). Creative cognition. In J. Sternberg (Ed.), *Handbook of creativity* (pp. 189–212). New York: Cambridge University Press.

West, M. A., & Farr, J. L. (1990). Innovation at work. In M. West & J. Farr (Eds.), *Innovation and creativity at work: Psychological and organizational strategies* (pp. 3–13). Chichester, England: Wiley.

Woodman, R. W., Sawyer, J. E., & Griffin, R. W. (1993). Toward a theory of organizational creativity. *Academy of Management Review, 18,* 293–321.

Zhou, J. (1998). Feedback valence, feedback style, task autonomy, and achievement orientation: Interactive effects on creative performance. *Journal of Applied Psychology, 83,* 261–276.

Zhou, J. (2003). When the presence of creative coworkers is related to creativity: Role of supervisor close monitoring, developmental feedback, and creative personality. *Journal of Applied Psychology, 88,* 413–422.

Zhou, J., & George, J. M. (2001). When job dissatisfaction leads to creativity: Encouraging the expression of voice. *Academy of Management Journal, 44,* 682–696.

Zhou, J., & George, J. M. (2003). Awakening employee creativity: The role of leader emotional intelligence. *Leadership Quarterly, 14*, 545–568.

Zhou, J., & Oldham, G. R. (2001). Enhancing creative performance: Effects of expected developmental assessment strategies and creative personality. *Journal of Creative Behavior, 35*, 151–167.

Zhou, J., & Shalley, C. E. (2003). Research on employee creativity: A critical review and directions for future research. In J. Martocchio (Ed.), *Research in personnel and human resource management* (pp. 165–217). Oxford, England: Elsevier.

Zuckerman, H., & Cole, J. R. (1994). Research strategies in science: A preliminary inquiry. *Creativity Research Journal, 7*, 391–406.

CHAPTER 2

Studying Creativity, Its Processes, and Its Antecedents
An Exploration of the Componential Theory of Creativity

Teresa M. Amabile
Harvard University

Jennifer S. Mueller
University of Pennsylvania

INTRODUCTION

We know what we know about creativity through research. To the extent that we understand the skills, personality styles, motivations, and conditions that are conducive or detrimental to creativity, or the processes through which it emerges, we have creativity researchers to thank. Yet this field of inquiry has not traditionally enjoyed the most stellar reputation. In the preface to his 1968 classic, *Creativity and Personal Freedom*, the psychologist, Frank Barron described the vilification of creativity research by the poet and social critic, Kenneth Rexroth. Rexroth, who had been a subject in one of Barron's early studies of creative writers, wrote an article called "The Vivisection of a Poet" for *The Nation*. According to Barron, Rexroth portrayed psychological research on creativity as not only useless but actually dangerous, because it had the power to potentially destroy the delicate phenomenon by excessive study and wrong-headed conclusions.

Creativity research has enjoyed only a slightly better reputation among the broader group of psychology scholars, management scholars, and business leaders. Many who are unfamiliar with recent advances in the field assume that it has little broad relevance because it focuses only on the arts (and perhaps the sciences), has little validity because creativity is too ill defined, ephemeral, and "soft" to study rigorously, and provides little practical applicability because creativity cannot be influenced. But they are wrong.

In recent years, a number of first-rate scholars in psychology and in management have devised ingenious methods for studying creativity in a broad range of domains, including organizational behavior. Moreover, they have clearly demonstrated systematic influences on creativity—some of which are amenable to change within organizations. Certainly, the study of creativity presents enormous challenges. It is difficult to assess and, given its complexity, its causes are difficult to discover except in extremely well-controlled psychology experiments where only one variable is manipulated and where all subjects complete the same task in a single laboratory session. In organizational settings, where well-controlled experiments are either infeasible or highly artificial, the challenges are much greater. Not only can creativity be influenced by a broad array of contextual factors at multiple levels (from individual skills to team dynamics to organizational climate), but participants are working over long periods of time on very different projects whose outcomes vary on a number of dimensions. Given the complexity of creativity, very little research has examined this phenomenon in the context of real organizations. Along with other scholars, we are currently trying to fill that void by building on the assessment tools and research methodologies of previous experimental and nonexperimental research. This undertaking, in itself, requires considerable creativity.

In this chapter, we will describe the componential theory of creativity (Amabile, 1983, 1988, 1996), which is a comprehensive theory that includes a description of the creative process as well as a specification of influences on creativity within and outside the individual. We will then illustrate various approaches to meeting the challenges of organizational creativity research by describing methods that address each aspect of the theory. To facilitate the adoption of potentially powerful new methods by organizational researchers, we will describe methods from both the organizational and the psychological literatures. We will discuss the assessment of creativity, its antecedents, and its processes, as well as the major research designs for studying creativity. We hope that this chapter will be useful for scholars planning research on organizational creativity and for anyone trying to evaluate such research and its conclusions.

THE COMPONENTIAL THEORY OF CREATIVITY

In keeping with most scholars who study the phenomenon, we define creativity as a process resulting in a product; it is the production of a novel and appropriate response, product, or solution to an open-ended task. The response must be new, but it must also be appropriate to the task to be completed or the problem to be solved. In addition, the task must be open ended, rather than having a single, obvious solution. The componential theory of creativity (Amabile, 1983, 1988, 1996), a theory designed to be comprehensively useful for both psychological and organizational creativity research, describes the creative process and the various influences on the process and its outcomes. Its basic elements, and the creative process it describes, are similar in the aggregate to other theories of creativity in both psychology (Simonton, 1999; Sternberg & Lubart, 1990; Wallas, 1926) and organizational studies (Ford, 1996; Woodman, Sawyer, & Griffin, 1993), although with different emphases and somewhat different proposed mechanisms.

In the componential theory, the influences on creativity include three components within the individual problem-solver—domain-relevant skills, creativity-relevant processes, and intrinsic task motivation—and one component outside the individual—the work environment. Figure 2.1 presents a simplified depiction of the updated theory (Amabile, 1996). Domain-relevant skills include knowledge, expertise, technical skills, intelligence, and talent in the particular domain where the problem-solver is working—such as microbiology or marketing. Creativity-relevant processes (originally called creativity-relevant skills) include a cognitive style and personality characteristics that are conducive to independence, risk-taking, and taking new perspectives on problems, as well as a disciplined work style and skills in generating ideas. Intrinsic task motivation is the motivation to undertake a task or solve a problem because it is interesting, involving, personally challenging, or satisfying—rather than undertaking it out of the extrinsic motivation arising from contracted-for rewards, surveillance, competition, evaluation, or requirements to do something in a certain way. Research evidence supports the inclusion of each of these components in the model (see Amabile, 1996).

The outside component is the work environment or, more generally, the social environment. This includes all of the extrinsic motivators (such as expected external evaluation) that have been shown to undermine intrinsic motivation, as well as a number of other factors in the environment that can serve as obstacles or as stimulants to intrinsic motivation

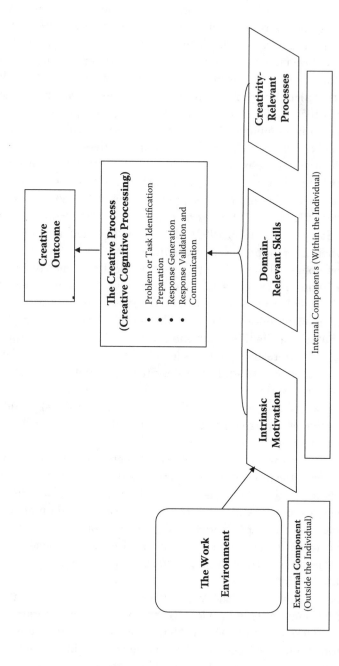

Figure 2.1 Simplified depiction of componential theory of creativity. Only major influences are depicted in the model. *Note:* Adapted from *Creativity in Context* (p. 113), by Amabile, 1996, Boulder, CO: Westview Press.

and creativity. Research in organizational settings has revealed a number of work environment factors that can block creativity, such as an emphasis on the status quo, a conservative, low-risk attitude among top management, norms of harshly criticizing new ideas, political problems within the organization, and excessive time pressure (e.g., Amabile, Conti, Coon, Lazenby, & Herron, 1996; Kanter, 1988). Other factors can stimulate creativity, such as freedom in carrying out the work; a sense of positive challenge in the work; work teams that are collaborative, diversely skilled, and idea focused; supervisors who encourage the development of new ideas; top management that supports innovation through a clearly articulated creativity-encouraging vision and through appropriate recognition for creative work; mechanisms for developing new ideas; and norms of actively sharing ideas across the organization (e.g., Amabile et al., 1996; Kanter, 1988; West & Anderson, 1996).

The theory specifies that all components are necessary for creativity and that, generally, the higher the level of each of the components, the higher the ultimate level of creativity. In other words, creativity requires a confluence of all components; creativity should be highest when an intrinsically motivated person with high domain expertise and high skill in creative thinking works in an environment high in supports for creativity. As depicted in Figure 2.1, all four of these components should facilitate the creative process. The creative process is, essentially, creative cognitive processing of problems and tasks—that is, all of the cognitive processes that contribute to the production of creative works. Creative cognitive processing consists of several subprocesses: analyzing and articulating the exact nature of the problem to be solved, preparing to solve the problem by gathering information and improving any required skills, generating ideas for solving the problem, testing or validating the chosen solution, and communicating that solution to others. Although these processes may often follow this sequence, they can occur in any sequence and will often recur iteratively until a creative outcome has been attained.

For example, an employee might start by considering a particular customer need (problem identification) and immediately come up with an idea (response generation) followed by reading and talking with colleagues about existing work in the area (preparation). She might then present the idea to top management (communication). If top management accepts the new idea as something potentially novel and useful, the employee might then be asked to test the idea (validation). The testing process could involve a series of tests, followed each time by refinement of the original idea and, perhaps, additional preparation through information gathering or even reformulation of the original problem identification. Once a final validated idea is accepted as novel and appropriate, then a creative outcome has been generated. However, if the idea is rejected, the employee must continue the process of refining the problem definition, preparing, generating, testing, and communicating ideas—or terminate the process. Ultimately, higher levels of each of the four components should lead to more effective creative cognitive processing, which, in turn, should lead to more creative outcomes. Those outcomes can be any observable product, performance, response, or idea, such as a poem, a new software program, a dance, a market research project, a new drug, a training course, a scientific experiment, or a completed consulting engagement.

The theory applies to any realm of human activity, with the basic components and processes and their mechanisms of influence remaining the same. The necessary intraindividual components should be the same in organizational contexts as in other contexts; in organizations, as elsewhere, people need domain expertise, creativity-oriented skills and processes, and intrinsic motivation for their work. Furthermore, creative activity can be affected by the work environment in any context—whether it is the environment of a school, a home, a studio, or a corporation. However, certain elements of the model are likely to be particularly distinctive in organizations. The work environment component in organizations contains features, such as team dynamics and top management behaviors, that are unlikely to be as important, or even present, in nonorganizational settings. In addition, outcomes are distinctive to each realm of human activity, as illustrated by our previous list that includes both poems and consulting engagements (which may, admittedly, be sheer poetry when they go well!). Even within organizations, the wide variety of activities makes for very different types of outcomes. In addition, it is possible that the creative process differs to some extent across realms of activity. In organizations, for example, the ways in which people identify problems or validate possible solutions are likely to be quite different from the ways in which those activities are carried out in the arts or in basic science laboratories. It is important to keep these distinctive features in mind when considering and evaluating methods for studying the components, the processes, and the outcomes in different domains.

As depicted in Figure 2.1, of the three intraindividual components, intrinsic motivation should be the most directly influenced by the work environment. This influence is captured in the componential theory's intrinsic motivation principle of creativity: People will be most creative when they feel motivated primarily by the interest, enjoyment, satisfaction, and challenge of the work itself—and not by extrinsic motivators. However, it is also important to note that the work environment undoubtedly has effects on domain-relevant skills (e.g., West & Anderson, 1996) and creativity-relevant processes, in addition to its effects on intrinsic motivation.

Recent research has suggested a modification of the intrinsic motivation principle. Although many extrinsic motivators in the work environment do appear to undermine intrinsic motivation and creativity, some may not. If rewards or other motivators are presented in a controlling fashion, leading people to feel that they are being bribed or dictated to—as is so often the case in organizations—the undermining effects are likely to occur. However, if rewards confirm people's competence (for example, by recognizing the value of their work), or enable them to become more deeply involved in work they are excited about doing (for example, by giving them more resources to do the work effectively), intrinsic motivation and creativity might not be undermined; in fact, they may be enhanced. This process is termed "motivational synergy" (Amabile, 1993). Thus, the theory suggests that, in addition to hiring people with domain-relevant expertise, creativity-relevant skills, and high intrinsic motivation for the work, managers should set up work environments that avoid control-oriented extrinsic motivators and instead focus on synergistic ones. Anything that supports the development of expertise, creativity-relevant skill, and intrinsic motivation should facilitate creativity.

METHODS FOR ASSESSING THE ELEMENTS OF THE THEORY

In order to fully understand the phenomenon of creativity, it is important to adequately assess each creativity component, the creative process, and creative outcomes. Table 2.1 provides examples of methods that have been used to assess these various elements. It is not meant to be comprehensive, but rather illustrative of the major approaches that have been taken. (For a comprehensive review of creativity assessment methods, see Puccio & Murdock, 1999.) As indicated in the table, some of these methods have been used primarily in psychological studies of creativity, and others have been used primarily in organizational studies. Some were developed specifically for creativity research, and some were developed for more general research purposes. We have tried to sample

Table 2.1 Some Methods for Assessing the Elements of Creativity As Presented in the Componential Theory of Creativity

ELEMENT OF CREATIVITY	BASIC METHODS USED	EXAMPLES*
Domain-relevant skills	a) Intelligence tests b) Skill/achievement tests c) Education level reports/experience level reports	a) IQ tests; Scholastic Aptitude Tests (G, P) b) Academic examinations (G, P/O) c) The Biographical Inventory: Creativity (Schaefer, 1969) (G, C) d) Reports of tenure within a field or an organization (G, P/O)
Creativity-relevant processes	a) Creative-thinking ability tests (fluency, flexibility, originality, and/or elaboration) b) Cognitive style assessments c) Personality inventories d) Creative thinking strategies	a) Torrance Tests of Creative Thinking (Torrance, 1966) (C, P) a) Remote Associates Test (Mednick & Mednick, 1966) (C, P/O) a) Unusual Uses Test (Guilford, 1967) (C, P/O) b) Kirton Adaption-Innovation Inventory (KAI) (Kirton, 1976) (C, P/O) b) Jabri, 1991 (G, P) c) Creative Personality Scale (Gough, 1979) of the Adjective Check List (Gough & Heilbrun, 1983) (C, P) c) Barron-Welsh Art Scale (Welsh & Barron, 1963) (C, P) c) Myers-Briggs Type Indicator (Myers, 1962) (G, O) c) NEO Personality Inventory (Costa & McCrae, 1985) (G, P) d) Creativity Styles Questionnaire (Kumar, Kemmler, & Holman, 1997) (C, P) d) Creative self-efficacy (Tierney & Farmer, 2002) (P, O)
Intrinsic versus extrinsic motivation	a) Trait motivation (stable individual differences) b) State motivation (motivation toward a particular task at a particular point in time)	a) Work Preference Inventory (Amabile et al., 1994) (G, P/O) b) Amabile, 1979 (G, P)

	Examples	Basic Methods Used
Work environment/social environment	a) Work environment questionnaires b) Biographical questionnaires and interviews	a) KEYS: Assessing the Climate for Creativity (Amabile, 1995) (C, O) b) The Biographical Inventory: Creativity (Schaefer, 1969) (C, P)
The creative process (creative cognitive processing)	a) Protocol analysis (analysis of problem-solving statements or behaviors) b) Specific reports of thinking or idea generation	a) Ericsson & Simon, 1993; Getzels & Csikszentmihalyi, 1976; Ruscio, Whitney, & Amabile, 1998 (G, P) b) Amabile et al., 2005 (C, O)
Creative outcome	a) Judge ratings (by experts, supervisors, or peers) of specific products or a person's body of work b) Counts of products meeting a creativity standard (such as patents) c) Mentions in compendia of creative individuals d) Originality of the product, defined as statistical infrequency e) Awards and honors for creativity f) Specific creative achievements	a) Consensual Assessment Technique (Amabile, 1982; Shalley, 1991, 1995; Zhou, 1998) (C, P/O) a) Getzels & Csikszentmihalyi, 1976; MacKinnon, 1962; Sobel & Rothenberg, 1980 (C, P) a) Gilson & Shalley, 2004; Madjar, Oldham, & Pratt, 2002; Oldham & Cummings, 1996; Zhou & George, 2001 (C, O) a) McDermid, 1965 (C, P/O) a) O'Quin & Besemer, 1989 (C, P) b) Simonton, 1997 (C, P) b) Andrews, 1979 (G, O) c) Galton, 1870; Simonton, 1975 (C, P) d) Simonton, 1980 (C, P) e) Feist, 1993; Simonton, 1992 (C, P) f) The Lifetime Creativity Scales (Richards, Kinney, Lunde, Benet, & Merzel, 1988) f) The Creative Achievement Scale (Ludwig, 1992) (C, P)

* The letter before each item in the "Examples" column matches the example to the specific approach with the same letter in the "Basic Methods Used" column of the same row. "G" or "C" signifies whether the method is used in general research or is specific to creativity research. "P" or "O" signifies whether the method is used primarily in psychological (P) or in organizational (O) research; "P/O" signifies that it is used in both.

from each of these types, including a few illustrative studies as examples of each method.

Of all the approaches to studying creativity that are listed in Table 2.1, the most commonly used approach in contemporary research on organizational creativity is the assessment of creative *outcomes* by *judge ratings*. Other contemporary studies rely on one or more of several methodologies listed in Table 2.1, including frequency counts of ideas generated (a modification of methods developed by Guilford [1967] and Torrance [1966] to assess creativity-relevant processes rather than outcomes), patent data, and qualitative accounts of creativity. Most creativity studies done in organizational settings assess creativity at the group or individual level, although some have examined the company or industry level (e.g., Taylor & Greve, 2006).

Judge ratings of creativity generally take one of two forms in contemporary organizational research: supervisor ratings, or ratings by multiple experts using the consensual assessment technique (CAT) (Amabile, 1982). Reliance on supervisor ratings draws on a decades-long tradition in the organizational literature of using such assessments to obtain quantitative measures of an employee's performance. More recently, researchers have applied this approach to assessments of creativity (e.g., Oldham & Cummings, 1996). Often, ratings are made by a single rater—the employee's direct supervisor.

The CAT, originally developed for psychological studies of creativity, is now widely used in organizational studies as well. The CAT is similar to the supervisor-based approach in its reliance on expert subjective assessment, but differs in its use of a consensus among multiple experts. The basic philosophy behind the consensual assessment technique is that, although creativity is difficult for people to define and very difficult to measure objectively in most domains, people who are familiar with a domain can recognize creativity when they see it, and their independent judgments generally agree as to the level of creativity in a given set of products. In essence, this sort of subjective assessment is what people rely on in the real world—although usually in a less rigorous manner.

The CAT is based on four key assumptions: First, that creativity exists on a continuum from the lowest "garden variety" levels to the highest genius levels; second, that people who are familiar with a domain (i.e., experts) can make reasonable judgments about the relative creativity of different works in that domain; third, that consensual assessment by multiple experts familiar with the domain is preferable to assessment by single individuals, to correct for the possible idiosyncrasies of any one rater; and, fourth, that having judges make comparative ratings of a number of works or individuals is preferable to having them rate only single works or individuals to achieve calibration along the creativity continuum. The CAT involves having judges who are familiar with the domain in which the work was done (generally, experts, supervisors, or peers) make scale-rated creativity assessments of several products or bodies of work done by different individuals in that domain. Generally, the judges are asked to use their own subjective definitions of what is creative in the domain, and to rate the products relative to one another (rather than relative to some absolute standard).

Ideally, in order to establish the reliability of the CAT measure, assessments are obtained from several judges working independently (all of whom have access to the same information about the products or bodies of work). If the judges' ratings agree at an acceptable level, then consensual assessment has been established; the mean of their ratings is taken as the measure of creativity for each product. Although single-expert ratings, in the form of supervisor ratings, have been shown to correlate significantly with some objective measures such as invention disclosures (Scott & Bruce, 1994; Tierney, Farmer, & Graen, 1999), we believe that it is preferable to use multiple expert raters (if available) to improve the reliability of the assessments.

Despite its widespread use in organizational and psychological research on creativity, the CAT has its own limitations. Many of these limitations are shared by other techniques relying on subjective assessments, such as single-supervisor ratings of individuals. First, like creativity judgment in the real world, the value of any subjective assessment technique is questionable at the highest levels of creativity in any domain. The history of art, science, and the humanities is replete with stories of path-breaking work that was soundly rejected by contemporary members of the field, only to later be celebrated as genius-level creativity. We argue that no method, including the CAT, can provide accurate measures of creativity at these levels. The reason is that, although this kind of creativity may lie along a continuum from lower levels, there are undoubtedly huge gaps in the distribution between more ordinary creativity and these flashes of genius, rendering comparison difficult. Occasionally, highly creative work creates a new domain, by combining two or more previously unconnected lines of thought. Thus, there exist no true experts at the time that the work is first produced. Accurate assessments of the true novelty and value of the work often require a long passage of time and considerable evolution of the relevant fields until enough people gain the necessary expertise to make accurate judgments. Moreover, because they are socially based, consensual judgments even at lower levels of creativity are subject to social bias—the political and personal forces that can lead observers to shade their judgments positively or negatively. Thus, subjective-assessment techniques are most useful at the more common levels of creativity most often seen in organizations and elsewhere. Moreover, when assessments are made by judges who know the people who produced the work, the potential for bias always exists. Therefore, these assessments must be interpreted cautiously. Nonetheless, because the true novelty and value of work ultimately depend on social judgment, we believe that observer assessments of creativity are an indispensable part of the researcher's repertoire.

It is interesting to note that, although subjective ratings by external judges are used extensively in both psychological and organizational creativity research, self-ratings are virtually absent from the empirical literature. The common wisdom among creativity researchers is that self-ratings are suspect because they are likely subject to several forms of bias. Moreover, appropriate consensual assessment requires judges to rate the products or bodies of work of several people relative to one another. Self-ratings may lack this comparison base. In addition, the ratings of several external judges are generally used in creativity studies in order to obtain more stable estimates. Obviously, each self-rated product would be rated by just a single judge. Despite these causes of concern, however, it would be useful for future research to investigate the utility of self-ratings, because individuals do have access to information about certain aspects of their own work that no one else has. For example, researchers could attempt to obtain comparative self-ratings in order to examine possible sources of bias in these ratings and to determine the correspondence between self-ratings and ratings by external judges. [A meta-analysis in the organizational literature has revealed an overall correlation of about 0.30 between self-ratings and ratings by others on a variety of dimensions not focused on creativity (Harris & Schaubroeck, 1988).]

Some theorists have proposed that creativity assessment is not just a way of identifying when creativity has happened, but rather is a crucial element of the overall process by which creativity happens. For example, Csikszentmihalyi (1999) argues that the assessment of a person's products or body of work is a part of a "creativity system." The system includes the individual who produces novel responses, the domain (or organized body of knowledge) that transmits information to the individual trying to work in that arena, and the field (the experts or gatekeepers in the domain) who judge whether the individual's work is worthy of inclusion in the domain. In this systems perspective, creativity does not exist without this acceptance by the field. This view gives prominence to the validation stage of the creative process (see Figure 2.1), highlighting the importance of cycling back through communication to and validation by *external* sources following individual validation of one's own ideas.

Clearly, whether they see it as an integral part of the creative process or not, contemporary organizational researchers view the assessment of outcomes—work products and bodies of work—by external judges as essential to the empirical study of organizational creativity. We agree wholeheartedly.

METHODS FOR STUDYING CREATIVITY

In the previous section, we surveyed ways in which researchers can assess each of the elements of creativity—the necessary components within and outside the individual, creative cognitive processing, and the outcomes that result from that processing. There is a variety of methodologies for studying just how these components and processes result in creative outcomes. In other words, there are a variety of ways in which these basic assessment tools can be combined for investigating what causes creativity, what relates to it, and the mechanisms by which it occurs. In this section, we will give a brief overview of some of the major methodologies in creativity research, with illustrations from our own and others' research. [For good overviews of some methods for studying creativity, also see the chapters in the "Methods for Studying Creativity" section of the *Handbook of Creativity* (Sternberg, 1999).]

RESEARCH METHODS AND CRITERIA FOR SELECTING THEM

Table 2.2 outlines some of the major methods in psychological and organizational studies of creativity along with examples from the literature and notes on some of the prominent strengths and drawbacks of each method. The methods at the beginning of the table afford researchers greater levels of control over observations, while those toward the end of the table afford greater ecological validity—that is, closeness to the actual phenomenon as it unfolds in an individual's life or in an organization. We have tried to make it clear, from the examples that we have chosen, that each of the major categories of methods has been used in both psychological and organizational studies.

In characterizing the methods in Table 2.2, we focused on the major methodological questions that any organizational researcher should

Table 2.2 Some Methods for Investigating Influences on, Correlates of, and Processes of Creativity

METHODS & DESCRIPTION	EXAMPLES*	MOST USEFUL FOR	LEAST USEFUL FOR
Experiments: One or more independent variables are manipulated under controlled conditions, and effects on creativity are assessed using inferential statistics. Other measures, usually assessed by questionnaires, may be analyzed as moderators or mediators.	• Amabile, 1979 (P) • Amabile, 1985 (P) • Choi & Thompson, 2005 (P/O) • Hennessey, 1989 (P) • Paulus & Yang, 2000 (P/O) • Shalley & Perry-Smith, 2001 (P/O) • Zhou, 1998 (P/O) • Goncalo & Staw, 2006 (P/O)	• Determining causal influences on creativity (hypothesis testing)	• Adequately capturing the complexities of organizational creativity • Discovering new influences on creativity and new relationships between creativity and other variables (hypothesis generation) • Studying the creative process • Suggesting how the creative process might unfold over time
Single-time correlational studies: Two or more variables are assessed quantitatively, often through questionnaires (but sometimes through observations or archives), and statistical relationships are tested.	• Amabile, Conti, Coon, Lazenby, & Herron, 1996 (O) • Ford & Gioia, 2000 (O) • Oldham & Cummings, 1996 (O) • Perry-Smith, 2006 (O) • Ruscio, Whitney, & Amabile, 1998 (P) • Scott & Bruce, 1994 (O) • Shin & Zhou, 2003 (O) • Zhou, 2003 (P/O)	• Determining the relationships between creativity and other factors (hypothesis testing) • Hinting at possible causal influences on creativity	• Discovering new influences on creativity and new relationships between creativity and other variables (hypothesis generation) • Studying the creative process • Suggesting how the creative process might unfold over time • Determining causal influences
Longitudinal correlational studies: Two or more variables are assessed quantitatively, often through questionnaires or historical records, at different points in time. Statistical analyses examine the extent to which variables at one point in time predict variables at a later point in time, and/or the extent to which variables change over time.	• Amabile & Conti, 1999 (O) • Simonton, 1977 (P) • West & Anderson, 1996 (P/O)	• Determining the relationships between creativity and other factors (hypothesis testing) • More directly suggesting possible causal influences on creativity • Suggesting how the creative process might unfold over time	• Discovering new influences on creativity and new relationships between creativity and other variables (hypothesis generation)

Small-sample longitudinal case studies: Using case study interviews, ethnographic observations over time, or historical records, information is obtained on one or a few individuals, groups, or organizations. Records are examined for patterns that point toward possible influences on, correlates of, and/or processes of creativity.	• Gruber, 1981 (P) • Hargadon & Bechky, 2006 (O) • Sutton & Hargadon, 1996 (O) • Wallace & Gruber, 1989 (P)	• Discovering new influences on creativity and new relationships between creativity and other variables (hypothesis generation) • Studying the creative process over time • Capturing the complexities of organizational creativity • Suggesting possible causal influences on creativity	• Determining causal relationships between creativity and other factors (hypothesis testing) • Generalizing to other individuals, groups, or organizations (due to the small number of data sources).
Large-sample hybrid method: Real-time longitudinal data collected on large, representative samples of individuals and/or groups. Data include longitudinal experience-sampling reports of specific events, questionnaires, creativity assessments over time, interviews, and observations. Multiple levels of analysis used to analyze quantitative and qualitative data.	• Amabile, 2003 (P/O) • Amabile, Barsade, Mueller, & Staw, 2005 (P/O) • Amabile, Hadley, & Kramer, 2002 (O) • Amabile, Schatzel, Moneta, & Kramer, 2004 (P/O) • Kurtzberg, 2005 (P/O) • Kurtzberg & Mueller, in press (P/O) • Mueller, 2002 (P)	• Discovering new influences on creativity and new relationships between creativity and other variables (hypothesis generation) • Studying the creative process over time • Capturing the complexities of organizational creativity • Determining likely causal influences on creativity • Generalizing to other individuals, groups, or organizations • Illuminating the role of specific types of events, within particular organizational contexts	• Testing causal relationships

* "P" or "O" signifies whether the study was published in or aimed at the psychological (P) or the organizational (O) literature or both (P/O).

consider: Will the method make it possible to determine causal influences on creativity? Can hypotheses about relationships between creativity and other constructs be tested? Might interesting new hypotheses about causes and relationships be generated? Will the method be likely to provide insight into how the creative process operates? Will it allow a glimpse into the complexities of organizational creativity; that is, will it have good ecological validity? Will it allow the researcher to generalize results to other individuals, groups, or organizations?

But there are many other issues to be considered in choosing a methodology to study creativity. One important issue concerns the researcher's ability to understand the perceptions and thoughts of individuals involved in creative work. Here, no simple ordering of the methods in Table 2.2 is possible. Interestingly, experiments can often be quite useful as a means for assessing people's thoughts and perceptions in real time as they are doing (or have just finished) a creativity task. Case studies may also be quite effective in getting at psychological states, but only if they include interviews along with observations and/or archival data collection. Another important issue concerns the possibility for bias in the data. Researcher bias, the tendency for the results to be influenced by the researcher's expectations or mere presence, is likely to be low in well-controlled experiments, in well-constructed surveys, and in archival data sources (which can be used for single-time correlational studies, longitudinal correlational studies, or case studies). Respondent (or subject) bias, the tendency for the results to be influenced by what respondents think is expected or by how they wish to appear to the researcher, is likely to be low in well-controlled experiments and archival data sources; however, it may be a problem in surveys. Both forms of bias can be a serious problem in observational and interview methods, which are most common in case studies.

Clearly, each methodology has its strengths and its drawbacks, forcing researchers to make tradeoffs. Generally, these tradeoffs can be made by considering the nature of the research question(s), the methods that others have used to address those questions (suggesting gaps that might be filled), the methodological strengths of the researcher (and the desire to expand those strengths), the availability of research participants and data of various kinds, and the desired publication outlet or audience for the research. Ultimately, our understanding of creativity will be best served by a number of careful researchers addressing important questions using a variety of methods—and by good theory building and theory testing that attempts to integrate and make sense of the findings.

We will illustrate the major types of methods for studying creativity by describing studies relevant to a seemingly simple question: What effect, if any, does evaluation have on creativity? Most of the studies that we will describe come from our own program of research (carried out with many collaborators over the past 30 years). Because we have not used case studies as a research tool, that example comes from another pair of researchers. Note that only the first example, the experiment, was designed solely to examine evaluation and creativity.

Example 1: An Experiment

The laboratory experiment examining the effects of expected evaluation on creativity (Amabile, 1979) used college students as subjects. In individual sessions, each subject was given an identical set of art materials and asked to use those materials to make a paper collage. Some of the subjects were randomly assigned to evaluation expectation conditions, where they were told that expert artists would be making a detailed evaluation of their collages, "noting the good points and criticizing the weaknesses." They were also told, "And since we know that our subjects are interested in how they are evaluated, we will send you a copy of each judge's evaluation of your design in about two weeks." Other subjects were assigned to nonevaluation conditions, where they were told that the focus of the study was not the collage itself but the effect of the collage-making activity on their subsequent mood; this was done to negate any assumptions they might have made about their collages being evaluated. After the study was completed, the consensual assessment technique was used to provide outcome data. Expert judges independently rated the creativity of the collages, without knowing the experimental condition or identity of the subjects who made the collages. The results clearly showed a negative effect of expected evaluation on creativity, with generally parallel effects on subjects' intrinsic motivation. (The only exception was a special evaluation condition where subjects were told exactly what to do in their collages to get a good evaluation from the judges. However, because these subjects were essentially given an algorithm for making a "creative collage," their task was no longer truly open-ended—one of the requirements of the basic definition of true creativity.) Although the essential finding of a negative effect of expected evaluation on creativity has been replicated by other researchers (e.g., Hennessey, 1989), some studies have found that certain types of evaluation can, under certain conditions, support creativity (e.g., Shalley, 1995; Shalley & Perry-Smith, 2001).

Example 2: A Single-Time Correlational Study

Although the results of the evaluation experiment were clear, they cannot be used to predict the extent to which expected evaluation might affect creativity in organizations. Is there, in fact, a measurable relationship between expected evaluation and creativity in organizations? If so, is it indeed a negative relationship? Or, might any connection between the experimental results and organizational work be negated by the obvious differences between real organizational behavior and a laboratory experiment on college students doing an essentially meaningless task for an unknown experimenter? To examine the effects of expected evaluation, as well as many other aspects of the work environment, we conducted a single-time correlational study in a large high-technology organization (Amabile et al., 1996). The primary data collection instrument was the KEYS questionnaire (Amabile, 1995), which assesses employee perceptions of several different aspects of the work environment as well as overall creativity in the work. We asked middle-level R&D managers in the company to nominate the most creative and least creative projects with which they had been associated over the previous three years. We then asked them to complete KEYS twice, once describing the work environment of the most creative project and once describing the work environment of the least creative project. The creativity nominations were later validated by higher-level managers in the company, who were unaware of which projects had previously been nominated as high or low in creativity for our study. The work environment descriptions on KEYS were also validated by asking other people on the most creative and least creative projects to fill out KEYS just once to describe the work environment surrounding their projects. These project team members did not know that their projects had been identified as particularly high or low on creativity.

We found that the high-creativity projects scored significantly higher than the low-creativity projects on several KEYS scales. Of particular interest here is the Organizational Encouragement scale, which includes several items concerning evaluation: "Performance evaluation in this organization is fair;" "Ideas are judged fairly in this organization;" "Failure is acceptable in this organization, if the effort on the project was good;" and "People in this organization can express unusual ideas without the fear of being called stupid." In addition, the low-creativity projects scored significantly higher than the high-creativity projects on the Organizational Impediments KEYS scale. That scale also included items on evaluation: "People are quite concerned about negative criticism of their work in this organization;" "People are too critical of new ideas in this organization;" and "Destructive criticism is a problem in this organization." Although, obviously, the form and meaning of evaluation in this correlational study were quite different from the form and meaning of the evaluation manipulation in the experiment, the overall result seems to be the same: Expecting critical evaluation from external sources is associated with lower creativity.

Example 3: A Longitudinal Correlational Study

Once we knew that evaluation did indeed seem to play a role in creativity in a real organization, we set out to discover something about the mechanisms by which the evaluative environment in an organization might change over time and whether there would be commensurate changes in creativity. A dramatic change in a high-technology organization we had studied earlier allowed us to begin this discovery process with a longitudinal correlational study (Amabile & Conti, 1999). As part of that earlier study, we had done a broad KEYS assessment of the current work environment across the firm. Several months after we had completed that data collection, the organization announced a major downsizing of the workforce. It seemed likely that such a major organizational event might lead to shifts in the work environment—including the evaluative environment—and, as a consequence, shifts in creativity itself.

We reentered the organization and administered KEYS at three additional points in time; we also conducted interviews with a subset of the people who completed the KEYS questionnaire. We discovered that, like several other aspects of the work environment, Organizational Encouragement declined significantly during the downsizing (relative to the predownsizing baseline). Although it recovered somewhat when the downsizing ended, it was still marginally lower than baseline even five months after the end of the downsizing. Moreover, Organizational Impediments increased significantly during the downsizing; by the time the downsizing ended, however, they had returned to baseline. Our statistical analyses revealed that the impact of downsizing on declines in perceived creativity was completely mediated by the changes in the work environment, including the evaluative environment as assessed by items on the KEYS instrument. Thus, although this study's design did not allow for definitive conclusions about causality, it allowed us to move one step beyond the single-time correlational study. Here, the longitudinal design allowed us to glimpse possible causes of changes in organizational creativity over time, including changes in the evaluative environment.

Example 4: A Case Study

We, ourselves, have not done case study research designed to examine evaluation processes in organizations and their possible relationship to creativity. The closest case study that we have found was published by Sutton and Hargadon (1996). These researchers did an ethnographic study of brainstorming sessions in a major and highly successful industrial design firm (IDEO), closely observing a large number of such sessions over a fairly long period of time. This study is relevant to questions about evaluation in a broad sense, because one of the chief characteristics of brainstorming is the guideline to suspend judgment during idea generation, avoiding all evaluation of ideas until later (Osborn, 1957). The study is relevant to questions about creativity in a broad sense as well; the motivating research question was, "How does IDEO innovate routinely?" The study, which did not examine a specific connection between evaluation and creativity, did reveal that brainstorming served a number of useful organizational functions. We believe that, in general, case studies can be a useful starting point for research programs on little-studied, little-understood phenomena—including particular questions about creativity in organizations.

Before turning to the fifth methodology and its example, we consider some of the challenges facing research on creativity in organizations.

CHALLENGES OF ORGANIZATIONAL CREATIVITY RESEARCH AND SOME WAYS TO MEET THEM

On the basis of our own research experience, and our reading of the literature, we have come to favor hybrid methodologies for studying creativity. These are methods that use a variety of approaches to examine people's thoughts, feelings, reactions, and performance, in the context of a given work environment and a given set of individual skills and styles. We believe that such methodologies are the best way to begin to understand the complex phenomenon of organizational creativity. We also believe that it is time to pay more attention to the specific ways in which work environments support or impede creativity, something that only a few researchers (e.g., Scott & Bruce, 1994) have attempted to do. In essence, it is time to illuminate the particular events and patterns of events that might lead to differential levels of creativity in organizations. Clearly, this is an immensely complex task. Although psychological and organizational theories can help us identify possible influences, careful and creative exploration will be required to discover previously unsuspected forces impacting organizational creativity. To truly understand the complexities of creativity in organizations, it will be necessary to combine the advantages of rigorous quantitative methods (such as measures from survey instruments) with the power of the rich and detailed (if messy) information that can be gained from carefully collected and analyzed qualitative data.

In addition, we believe that it is time for organizational creativity researchers to take on two particular challenges: the multilevel nature of organizational phenomena, and temporal issues. Compared to creativity in the visual and literary arts, which often takes the form of a single individual working on one particular product at a time, creativity in organizations is generally a multiperson, multitask affair. Within organizations, several levels of analysis must be considered: events involve individuals, individuals generally work in teams or groups, teams are embedded within companies, and companies are embedded within industries; creative outcomes can be assessed at any of these levels. Factors at each of these levels—from particular events on particular days, to industry dynamics—can affect the creativity of outcomes. Thus, multilevel designs and analyses are required. Such analyses require large samples.

Moreover, creative ideas and products often evolve over long periods of time in organizations, and influences on creativity might only reveal themselves through a temporal lens. Studying creative processes and influences over time is the only way, ultimately, to examine the dynamic evolution of creativity, as well as possible reciprocal influences among the elements outlined in the componential theory. All of this, of course, complicates the researcher's task immensely. Perhaps for this reason, few studies of organizational creativity attempt to examine multiple levels simultaneously, and very few look at creative work and its potential influences over time.

Example 5: The Large-Sample Hybrid Method of the Work Diaries Study

We took on these methodological challenges by creating a large-sample hybrid method for our Work Diaries Research Program (also called the T.E.A.M. Study, for Team Events And Motivation Study). In this research program, we examined creativity in situ, as it unfolded in different organizational contexts over long periods of time. We attempted to "trap creativity in the wild," observing it on the days that it happened, and then explaining its appearance by looking at the events, patterns of events, and work environment influences that surrounded and preceded it. The central data from this research program consisted of daily reports from 238 individual participants working in 26 project teams in

7 companies within 3 industries. Top management within each of the companies had identified each of these projects as requiring creativity for successful completion. Using a modification of the Experience Sampling Methodology (Csikszentmihalyi & Larson, 1987), we studied each of these teams daily over the entire course of their projects (or a discrete project phase). On average, teams were in the study for 19 weeks. Every work day, each individual member of each participating team received and privately completed an e-mailed Daily Questionnaire that included a number of quantitative items such as the number of hours they had spent on the project that day, the number of team members they had worked with, and Likert Scale ratings of their work environment perceptions, work motivation, work creativity and progress, affect, and assessments of the team's work that day. With a response rate of 75%, we collected nearly 12,000 Daily Questionnaires. Our data collection covered several calendar years.

Information on the events unfolding in the work of these individuals, teams, and organizations came through a narrative Event Description section at the end of each Daily Questionnaire. There, participants were asked to "Briefly describe one event that occurred today," with instructions to write a concise, specific account of any event that stood out in their mind from the day. They were encouraged to report any events that were in any way relevant to the project, their own work or feelings about the project, or their team's work or feelings about the project. They were told that these events could be drawn from private cognitive events, interpersonal events, task or project events, events occurring within the organization, or even events involving individuals or institutions outside the organization. Our aim was to obtain broad, representative samples of everything that might influence or give evidence of creativity in the work of our participants. The purpose was to enable both hypothesis testing and exploratory hypothesis generation about a broad range of antecedents, consequences, and processes of creativity—including evaluation.

The Work Diaries Study included assessments of each element of the componential theory of creativity (see Table 2.1). For this reason, in addition to the Daily Questionnaires, we also used longer questionnaire instruments to obtain single-time or periodic measures of the work environment, creativity and other aspects of performance, characteristics and skills of the individual participants, and characteristics of the team and the project. Domain-relevant skills were assessed by simple items on a biographical questionnaire concerning participants' education and experience levels. Two aspects of creativity-relevant processes were measured: cognitive style by the Kirton Adaption-Innovation Inventory (KAI) (Kirton, 1976), and personality by the NEO (Costa & McCrae, 1985). We assessed intrinsic and extrinsic motivation both as a stable trait, using the Work Preference Inventory (WPI) (Amabile, Hill, Hennessey, & Tighe, 1994) and as a daily state, using Likert Scale items on the Daily Questionnaire. Work-environment perceptions were assessed daily with Likert Scale items on the Daily Questionnaire, but more detailed assessments were obtained from the validated KEYS instrument (Amabile, 1995) administered three times during the study. Other aspects of the work environment, stemming from characteristics of the team and the project, were assessed with periodic questionnaires completed by the team leaders and team members.

As a measure of creative cognitive processing, we used coder-identified segments from the daily Event Descriptions. Our coding scheme defined creative thought as any of the following: (a) a discovery, insight, or idea; (b) the act of searching for a discovery, insight, or idea; (c) solving a problem in a nonrote way; or (d) the act of searching for a problem solution in a nonrote way. Trained coders, who were not familiar with the research participants or companies, were able to reliably identify instances of creative thought in the Event Descriptions. (See Amabile et al., 2005 and Amabile, Mueller, & Archambault, 2003a, 2003b for details on the coding methodologies used in the Work Diaries Research Program.) Thus, for each daily Event Description from each individual, we had a frequency count of the individual's creative thought instances reported that day—a quasi-behavioral measure of creative thinking.

We obtained measures of creative outcomes primarily through the standard consensual assessment technique: monthly peer ratings of each individual's creativity, and monthly expert ratings of each project's creativity. Importantly, the peer ratings correlated significantly with the quasi-behavioral frequency counts of creative thought instances identified in the individuals' diary narratives. In addition, at the end of their projects, the team members gave a final, overall assessment of the creativity of the project. Finally, we obtained daily and monthly self-ratings of creativity.

Despite all of these quantitative measures, some of the richest and most illuminating data come from qualitative sources. Shortly after completing data collection on each of the 26 teams, we wrote a detailed research case study recording basic background information on and our own impressions of the company, the team, the project, the individual team members, the team dynamics, and the major events that seemed to impact the team during the project. Information for these cases came from many sources, including the four in-person meetings we had with each team, meetings we had with company executives, the private meetings we had with team leaders and some team members, and the frequent telephone calls and e-mails between us and the participants. Perhaps most importantly, we have read and re-read the narrative Event Descriptions to identify events, influences, and dynamics that might be particularly important for understanding creative work in organizations. Our ultimate aim is to present a picture of creativity (and other aspects of organizational life) painted with both our statistical analyses and the human stories told in our participants' own words.

We have already conducted a number of studies on the Work Diaries data. Here, we will briefly describe two. Because, in reading the Event Description narratives, we were struck by the frequency and intensity of emotion expressed, we decided to try identifying the events that made the difference between the best days—those of the highest positive affect, and the worst days—those of the highest negative affect. This study revealed that evaluation and feedback were among the most prominent differentiators (Amabile, 2003). Receiving positive recognition or feedback frequently induced joy, and receiving criticism or negative feedback frequently induced anger, fear, or sadness.

It was clear that work evaluation—including seemingly minor, informal comments—evokes affect in organizations. The question remained, however, as to whether and how affect might relate to creativity in organizations. We investigated this question in a subsequent study, using multilevel statistical models to analyze three measures of affect (daily self-ratings on Daily Questionnaire scales, coder-rated mood in the diary narratives, and coder-rated discrete emotions in the diary narratives), the measure of coder-identified creative thought, and the peer ratings of creativity (Amabile et al., 2005). Overall positive mood on a given day (as well as the specific emotion of joy) was positively related to creative thought that day; anger, fear, and sadness were negatively related. The relationship was a simple linear one. Moreover, positive affect on a given day predicted creativity the next day and (to some extent) the day after that, even controlling for affect on the subsequent days. Also, self-rated daily positive mood over a given month was positively related to peer-rated creativity that month. Thus, the study provided strongly suggestive evidence that positive affect, which can be influenced by evaluation, is an antecedent of creativity in organizations. It also suggests that the creativity-relevant cognitive processes set in motion by positive affect can incubate over time to yield a creative response. Finally, detailed qualitative analysis of the diary narratives reporting creative thought events revealed that affect is also a consequence of creativity. By far, the emotion most frequently evoked by solving a problem or coming up with an idea was joy.

Figure 2.2 summarizes these findings as an elaboration of part of the componential theory of creativity. The elaboration goes beyond earlier presentations of the theory in three ways. First, it includes affect and the events in the daily work environment that can induce affect. Second, it proposes a new indirect link in the theory: how the work environment can influence creativity-relevant processes, which, in turn, influence creative responses. Third, it proposes a feedback loop from creativity back to affect.

Not surprisingly, the data collection and analysis effort in our hybrid-method research program was enormously labor intensive, expensive, and time consuming, requiring the collaboration of several academic researchers and industry practitioners. (See Amabile, Patterson, Mueller, Wojcik, Odomirok, Marsh, & Kramer, 2001 for a description and analysis of the early stage of this collaboration.) Nonetheless, we believe that the effort resulted in a rich, unique database that has yielded important insights into organizational creativity (and other organizational processes), and still has more to yield over the next several years. Also, we believe that future studies by other researchers, using other hybrid methods, could do much to provide the additional elaborations and corrections to existing theory that will be necessary to truly advance our field.

CONCLUSION

In describing our Work Diaries Study, we are not suggesting that all organizational creativity researchers must take a similarly comprehensive approach. On the contrary, we would warn that such undertakings require enormous commitments of resources, time, and energy. We are suggesting, though, that researchers expand their thinking about the methods they might use in their research by considering methods that might traditionally be considered the province of another discipline or subspecialty. For example, although experiments and psychometric instruments (such as personality or cognitive style questionnaires) have been favorite tools of psychological researchers for decades, a few organizational scholars have begun making good use of them to understand causal influences on creativity (through experiments) or the role of individual-difference factors (through psychometric tools). In addition, we are recommending

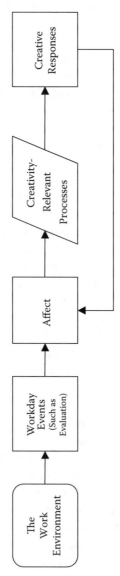

Figure 2.2 Affect: A recent elaboration of part of the componential theory of creativity. Note. Based on "Affect and Creativity at Work," by Amabile et al., 2005, *Administrative Science Quarterly, 50*, p. 392.

that organizational scholars begin to adopt multilevel methods to enable them to truly understand creativity in context, and longitudinal methods to enable them to discover how organizational influences on creativity play out over time. To the extent possible, it will also be important to expand our methods to allow simultaneous exploration of the various elements of creativity specified in the componential theory, and how they might interact dynamically to form a creativity system.

Ultimately, it is important to combine a variety of methodological approaches—not necessarily in the same study, as we have done with the Work Diaries Research Program, but at least sequentially. The principle of triangulation is no less applicable to organizational studies than it is to the natural sciences. It is only by taking different methodological viewing angles on a particular research question that we can overcome the blind spots of any one method and capitalize on the focal lens of each. As results from different methods converge, we will become more confident in painting a comprehensive, detailed picture of creativity in organizations—how it happens, what influences it, what its consequences are, and how we might get more of it. These insights will be useful not only to scholars interested in creativity, but to scholars and practitioners concerned with the broader issues of individual, group, and organizational performance. We cannot pretend to understand excellence in organizations or the people who work within them unless we understand how they invent, explore, and create things that have never existed before.

ACKNOWLEDGMENTS

We would like to express our appreciation to the editors and to four additional colleagues who provided valuable help on this chapter: Gerard Puccio, Giovanni Moneta, Dean Simonton, and Cameron Ford.

REFERENCES

Amabile, T. M. (1979). Effects of external evaluation on artistic creativity. *Journal of Personality and Social Psychology, 37,* 221–233.

Amabile, T. M. (1982). Social psychology of creativity: A consensual assessment technique. *Journal of Personality and Social Psychology, 43,* 997–1013.

Amabile, T. M. (1983). Social psychology of creativity: A componential conceptualization. *Journal of Personality and Social Psychology, 45,* 357–376.

Amabile, T. M. (1988). A model of creativity and innovation in organizations. In B. M. Staw & L. L. Cummings (Eds.), *Research in organizational behavior, Vol. 10,* 123–167. Greenwich, CT: JAI Press.

Amabile, T. M. (1993). Motivational synergy: Toward new conceptualizations of intrinsic and extrinsic motivation in the workplace. *Human Resource Management Review, 3,* 185–201.

Amabile, T. M. (1995). *KEYS: Assessing the climate for creativity*. Greensboro, NC: Center for Creative Leadership.

Amabile, T. M. (1996). *Creativity in context*. Boulder, CO: Westview Press.

Amabile, T. M. (2003). *Positive psychology in the workplace: The best (and worst) days at work*. Presented at the annual meeting of the American Psychology Association, Toronto, Canada.

Amabile, T. M., Barsade, S. G., Mueller, J. S., & Staw, B. M. (2005). Affect and creativity at work. *Administrative Science Quarterly, 50,* 367–403.

Amabile, T. M., & Conti, R. (1999). Changes in the work environment for creativity during downsizing. *Academy of Management Journal, 42,* 630–640.

Amabile, T. M., Conti, R., Coon, H., Lazenby, J., & Herron, M. (1996). Assessing the work environment for creativity. *Academy of Management Journal, 39,* 1154–1184.

Amabile, T. M., Hadley, C. N., & Kramer, S. J. (2002). Creativity under the gun. *Harvard Business Review, August 2002,* 52–61.

Amabile, T. M., Hill, K. G., Hennessey, B. A., & Tighe, E. M. (1994). The Work Preference Inventory: Assessing intrinsic and extrinsic motivational orientations. *Journal of Personality and Social Psychology, 66,* 950–967.

Amabile, T. M., Mueller, J. S., & Archambault, S. (2003a). *Coding manual for the DENA Coding Scheme (Detailed Event Narrative Analysis)* (Harvard Business School Working Paper #03-079). Boston, MA.

Amabile, T. M., Mueller, J. S., & Archambault, S. (2003b). *DENA Coding Scheme (Detailed Event Narrative Analysis)* (Harvard Business School Working Paper #03-080). Boston, MA.

Amabile, T. M., Patterson, C., Mueller, J. S., Wojcik, T., Odomirok, P. W., Marsh, M., & Kramer, S. J. (2001). Academic-practitioner collaboration in management research: A case of cross-profession collaboration. *Academy of Management Journal, 44,* 418–431.

Amabile, T. M., Schatzel, E. A., Moneta, G. B., & Kramer, S. J. (2004). Leader behaviors and the work environment for creativity: Perceived leader support. *The Leadership Quarterly, 15,* 5–32.

Andrews, F. M. (Ed.). (1979). *Scientific productivity: The effectiveness of research groups in six countries*. Cambridge: Cambridge University Press.

Barron, F. (1968). *Creativity and personal freedom*. Princeton, NJ: Van Nostrand.

Choi, H.-S., & Thompson, L. (2005). Old wine in a new bottle: Impact of membership change on group creativity. *Organizational Behavior and Human Decision Processes, 98,* 121–132.

Costa, P. T., & McCrae, R. R. (1985). *The NEO Personality Inventory Manual*. Odessa, FL: Psychological Assessment Resources.

Csikszentmihalyi, M. (1999). Implications of a systems perspective for the study of creativity. In R.J. Sternberg (Ed.), *Handbook of creativity,* 313–335. New York: Cambridge University Press.

Csikszentmihalyi, M., & Larson, R. W. (1987). Validity and reliability of the Experience Sampling Method. *Journal of Nervous and Mental Disease, 175,* 526–536.

Ericsson, K. A., & Simon, H. A. (1993). *Protocol analysis*. Cambridge, MA: The MIT Press.

Feist, G. J. (1993). A structural model of scientific eminence. *Psychological Science, 4,* 366–371.

Ford, C. M. (1996). A theory of individual creative action in multiple social domains. *Academy of Management Review, 21,* 1112–1142.

Ford, C. M., & Gioia, D. A. (2000). Factors influencing creativity in the domain of managerial decision making. *Journal of Management, 26,* 705–732.

Galton, F. (1870). *Hereditary genius.* London: MacMillan, London & Appleton.

Getzels, J., & Csikszentmihalyi, M. (1976). *The creative vision: A longitudinal study of problem-finding in art.* New York: Wiley-Interscience.

Gilson, L. L., & Shalley, C. E. (2004). A little creativity goes a long way: An examination of teams' engagement in creative processes. *Journal of Management, 30,* 453–470.

Goncalo, J. A., & Staw, B. M. (2006). Individualism-collectivism and group creativity. *Organizational Behavior and Human Decision Processes, 100,* 96–109.

Gough, H. G. (1979). A creative personality scale for the adjective check list. *Journal of Personality and Social Psychology, 37,* 1398–1405.

Gough, H. G., & Heilbrun, A. B. (1983). *The Adjective Check List manual.* Palo Alto, CA: Consulting Psychologists Press.

Gruber, H. E. (1981). *Darwin on man: A psychological study of scientific creativity* (rev. ed.). Chicago: University of Chicago Press.

Guilford, J. P. (1967). *The nature of human intelligence.* New York: McGraw-Hill.

Hargadon, A. B., & Bechky, A. (2006). When collections of creatives become creative collectives: A field study of problem solving at work. *Organization Science, 17,* 484–500.

Harris, M. M., & Schaubroeck, J. (1988). A meta-analysis of self-supervisor, self-peer, and peer-supervisor ratings. *Personnel Psychology, 41,* 43–62.

Hennessey, B. A. (1989). The effects of extrinsic constraints on children's creativity while using a computer. *Creativity Research Journal, 2,* 151–168.

Jabri, M. (1991). The development of conceptually independent subscales in the measurement of modes of problem solving. *Educational and Psychological Measurement, 51,* 975–983.

Kanter, R. M. (1988). When a thousand flowers bloom: Structural, collective, and social conditions for innovation in organizations. In B. M. Staw & L. L. Cummings (Eds.), *Research in organizational behavior* (Vol. 10). Greenwich, CT: JAI Press.

Kirton, M. (1976). Adaptors and innovators: A description and measure. *Journal of Applied Psychology, 61,* 622–629.

Kumar, V. K., Kemmler, D., & Holman, E. R. (1997). The creativity styles questionnaire-revised. *Creativity Research Journal, 10,* 51–58.

Kurtzberg, T. R. (2005). Feeling creative, being creative: An empirical study of diversity and creativity in teams. *Creativity Research Journal, 17*(1), 51–65.

Kurtzberg, T. R., & Mueller, J. S. 2005.) The influence of daily conflict on perceptions of creativity: a longitudinal study. *International Journal of Conflict Management, 16,* 335–353.

Ludwig, A. M. (1992). The Creative Achievement Scale. *Creativity Research Journal, 5*, 109–124.

MacKinnon, D. W. (1962). The nature and nurture of creative talent. *American Psychologist, 17*, 484–495.

Madjar, N., Oldham, G. R., & Pratt, M. G. (2002). There's no place like home? The contributions of work and nonwork creativity support to employees' creative performance. *Academy of Management Journal, 45*, 757–767.

Mednick, S. A., & Mednick, M. T. (1967). *Remote Associates Test examiner's manual.* Boston: Houghton Mifflin.

Mueller, J. S. (2002). The effects of expressive writing on performance and well-being in the workplace. *Dissertation Abstracts International: Section B: The Sciences and Engineering, 63(3-B)*, 1599.

Myers, I. B. (1962). *The Myers-Briggs Type Indicator.* Palo Alto, CA: Consulting Psychologists Press.

Oldham, G. R., & Cummings, A. (1996). Employee creativity: Personal and contextual factors at work. *Academy of Management Journal, 39*, 607–634.

O'Quin, K., & Besemer, S. P. (1989). The development, reliability, and validity of the revised Creative Product Semantic Scale. *Creativity Research Journal, 2*, 267–278.

Osborn, A. F. (1957). *Applied imagination.* New York: Scribner.

Paulus, P. B., & Yang, H. (2000). Idea generation in groups: A basis for creativity in organizations. *Organizational Behavior and Human Decision Processes, 82*, 76–87.

Perry-Smith, J. E. (2006). Social yet creative: The role of social relationships in facilitating individual creativity. *Academy of Management Journal, 49*, 85–101.

Puccio, G. H., & Murdock, M. C. (Eds.). (1999). *Creativity assessment: Readings and resources.* Buffalo, NY: Creative Education Foundation.

Richards, R., Kinney, D. K., Lunde, I., Benet, M., & Merzel, A. P. C. (1988). Assessing everyday creativity: Characteristics of the Lifetime Creativity Scales and validation with three large samples. *Journal of Personality and Social Psychology, 54*, 476–485.

Ruscio, J., Whitney, D. M., & Amabile, T. M. (1998). Looking inside the fishbowl of creativity: Verbal and behavioral predictors of creative performance. *Creativity Research Journal, 11*, 243–263.

Schaefer, C. E. (1969). The prediction of creative achievement from a biographical inventory. *Educational and Psychological Measurement, 29*, 431–437.

Scott, S. G., & Bruce, R. A. (1994). Determinants of innovative behavior: A path model of individual innovation in the workplace. *Academy of Management Journal, 37*, 580–607.

Shalley, C. E. (1991). Effects of productivity goals, creativity goals, and personal discretion on individual creativity. *Journal of Applied Psychology, 76*, 179–185.

Shalley, C. E. (1995). Effects of coaction, expected evaluation, and goal setting on creativity and productivity. *Academy of Management Journal, 38*, 483–503.

Shalley, C. E., & Perry-Smith, J. E. (2001). Effects of social-psychological factors in creative performance: The role of informational and controlling expected evaluation and modeling experience. *Organizational Behavior and Human Decision Processes, 84,* 1–22.

Simonton, D. K. (1975). Sociocultural context of individual creativity: A transhistorical time-series analysis. *Journal of Personality and Social Psychology, 32,* 1119–1133.

Simonton, D. K. (1977). Creative productivity, age and stress: A biographical time-series analysis of 10 classical composers. *Journal of Personality and Social Psychology, 35,* 791–804.

Simonton, D. K. (1980). Thematic fame, melodic originality, and musical Zeitgeist: A biographical and transhistorical content analysis. *Journal of Personality, 38,* 972–983.

Simonton, D. K. (1997). Creative productivity: A predictive and explanatory model of career trajectories and landmarks. *Psychological Review, 104,* 66–89.

Simonton, D. K. (1999). *Origins of genius: Darwinian perspectives on creativity.* New York: Oxford University Press.

Sobel, R. S., & Rothenberg, A. (1980). Artistic creation as simulated by superimposed versus separated visual images. *Journal of Personality and Social Psychology, 39,* 953–961.

Sternberg, R. J. (Ed). (1999). *Handbook of creativity.* New York: Cambridge University Press.

Sternberg, R. J., & Lubart, T. I. (1991). An investment theory of creativity and its development. *Human Development, 34,* 1–31.

Sutton, R. I., & Hargadon, A. (1996). Brainstorming groups in context: Effectiveness in a product design firm. *Administrative Science Quarterly, 41,* 685–718.

Taylor, A., & Greve, H. R. (2006). Superman or the fantastic four? Knowledge combination and experience in innovative teams. *Academy of Management Journal, 49,* 723–740.

Tierney, P., & Farmer, S. M. (2002). Creative self-efficacy: Its potential antecedents and relationship to creative performance. *Academy of Management Journal, 45,* 1137–1148.

Tierney, P., Farmer, S. M., & Graen, G. B. 1999. An examination of leadership and employee creativity: The relevance of traits and relationships. *Personnel Psychology, 52,* 591–620.

Torrance, E. P. (1966). *The Torrance test of creative thinking: Norms-technical manual.* Lexington, MA: Personnel Press.

Wallace, D. B., & Gruber, H. E. (Eds.). (1989). *Creative people at work: Twelve cognitive case studies.* New York: Oxford University Press.

Wallas, G. (1926). *The art of thought.* New York: Harcourt, Brace.

Welsh, G. S., & Barron, F. (1963). *Barron-Welsh Art Scale.* Palo Alto, CA: Consulting Psychologists Press.

West, M. A., & Anderson, N. R. (1996). Innovation in top management teams. *Journal of Applied Psychology, 81,* 680–693.

Woodman, R. W., Sawyer, J. E., & Griffin, R. W. (1993). Toward a theory of organizational creativity. *Academy of Management Review, 18,* 293–321.

Zhou, J. (1998). Feedback valence, feedback style, task autonomy, and achievement orientation: Interactive effects on creative performance. *Journal of Applied Psychology, 83*, 261–276.

Zhou, J. (2003). When the presence of creative coworkers is related to creativity: Role of supervisor close monitoring, developmental feedback, and creative personality. *Journal of Applied Psychology, 88*, 413–422.

Zhou, J., & George, J. M. (2001). When job dissatisfaction leads to creativity: Encouraging the expression of voice. *Academy of Management Journal, 44*, 682–696.

CHAPTER 3

"Organizing" Creativity Research Through Historical Analysis of Foundational Administrative Science Texts

Cameron Ford and Maribeth Kuenzi

University of Central Florida

INTRODUCTION

Evolutionary models have a prominent history in theorizing related to creativity and social change. Donald Campbell (1960, 1965) is generally credited as the first to apply Darwinian concepts related to variation, selection, and retention (VSR) processes to better understand complex dynamic interactions among established knowledge, social convention, and new ideas. Many prominent psychologists such as Simonton (2000), Csikszentmihalyi (1988), and Gardner (1993) have advocated this approach to understanding creativity, and Campbellian reasoning has had a substantial impact on theories of stability and change in the administrative sciences (Baum & McKelvey, 1999). Weick (1969, 1979) elaborated Campbell's ideas to create a general model of organizing that relies on describing interlocking enactment (variation), selection, and retention processes. Others have applied Campbell's and Weick's ideas more specifically to creativity in organizations (e.g., Ford, 1996; Staw, 1990).

One of the most important features of VSR models is the assertion that variations emerge from elements of previously retained solutions. Analogous to the process of combining elements of existing strands of previously selected DNA to create new offspring, the development of new ideas has been described as a consequence of associating elements of existing ideas. Hargadon and Sutton (1997) described a process they labeled "knowledge brokering" to describe how "old" solutions create new value when applied to novel settings. It is in this spirit that we cull through passages from some of the most prominent books in the history of the management field to produce recombinant knowledge (cf. Hargadon, 2003) capable of generating new research proposals. Our effort is motivated by three premises: (a) there are many timeless challenges related to organizing; (b) balancing competing creating and organizing processes, what Thompson (1967) refers to as "the paradox of administration," is one of these timeless challenges; and (c) classic texts that offer broad descriptions of organizing processes are a unique source of ideas relative to more narrowly framed descriptions characteristic of contemporary contributions to the field. We hope to identify valuable old ideas, and provide examples of how reconsidering these ideas in a novel context can motivate new avenues of inquiry.

In the past 20 years or so, there has been a surge of research that has focused on creativity in organizations and on the conditions that facilitate and hinder creative work performance. Most of the seminal contributors to this emerging research literature are represented in this volume. We will employ a definition of creativity that has been used in slightly different versions by most of these contributors, and was originally argued by Teresa Amabile as a necessary precursor to understanding creativity in social contexts. We favor the wording we have used previously (Ford, 1996) to define creativity as a "domain-specific, subjective judgment of the novelty and value of an outcome of a particular action" (1996, p. 1115). This definition works well in the context of VSR theorizing because it emphasizes characteristics of domains (retention), judgments and criteria (selection), and observable outcomes (variations). The dimensions of novelty and value are also usefully distinguished, thus allowing for exploration of inherent tensions between variation (novelty) and selective-retention (value) processes (Campbell, 1960; Weick, 1979).

Although creativity has not been a central topic of inquiry in the management field until recently, we believe that strands of useful theoretical reasoning have been articulated in classic works that attempted the ambitious challenge of describing how organizations work. Such ambitious process theorizing is seldom attempted in the more fragmented theories and studies that dominate current discourse among management scholars. We wonder if something has been lost over the years as domains of inquiry have become narrower and less connected. We hope that by examining classic texts that offer broad, powerful principles for organizing that we can derive useful insights for interpreting prior creativity research and motivating future creativity research.

SELECTING CLASSIC TEXTS

To assist scholars with looking into the past, Bedeian and Wren (2001) polled the members of the Fellows Group of the Academy of Management and asked them to vote on "the 25 most influential books of the 20th century." The purpose of this endeavor was to establish a list of books that have had a major impact in the field of management due to their progressive thinking. Bedeian and Wren describe the motivation for this effort by quoting Sir Isaac Newton, "If we have seen a little farther it is by standing on the shoulders of the giants who have gone before us."

In this paper we examine three of the field's most comprehensive and influential efforts to provide thorough descriptions of organizational functioning that were on this list developed by Bedeian and Wren— Katz and Kahn's "The Social Psychology of Organizations" (1966), March and Simon's "Organizations" (1958) (embellished with related contributions from Cyert and March, 1963), and Thompson's "Organizations in Action" (1967)—as a pool of ideas from which we hope to gain additional insights into processes related to organizational creativity. Although creativity received little explicit attention in these seminal works, we believe that many concepts they offer can be framed within the theoretical language of Campbellian VSR theory to help reveal connections to recent creativity research. Our admiration of Campbell and Weick's depictions of creating and organizing processes led us to adopt Weick's description of Campbellian VSR theory from his influential book "The Social Psychology of Organizing" (1979) as a framework for organizing our historical analyses of these important texts. Although Weick's book did not make Bedeian and Wren's top 25 list, it was noted as one of the "Best of the Rest" for the significant number of votes it received.

Next we offer a brief description of Weick's version of VSR theorizing, and then analyze ways in which classic texts enrich our understanding of this general approach to describing creativity and change. We will then conclude by describing connections between our findings and current efforts to investigate organizational creativity, and offer a few suggestions for future research motivated by our analyses.

OUR "ORGANIZING" FRAMEWORK: WEICK'S VARIATION/ ENACTMENT–SELECTION–RETENTION MODEL

As we just mentioned, Weick (1979) developed a model to describe the process of organizing based on an evolutionary model of social creativity proposed by Campbell (1960). We selected Weick's VSR model to help us organize contributions from different texts because VSR logic has been widely employed in the administrative sciences at multiple levels of analysis to address a wide range of theoretical issues (Baum & McKelvey, 1999). We believe it offers a versatile and robust meta-theoretical foundation for understanding creativity (cf. Simonton, 2000) and organizing that can reveal common features as well as potential omissions in theorizing and empirical research. Consequently, we will provide a brief overview of Weick's model and then use it to organize our comparison of the three classics texts we have selected. There are four elements to the model and three feedback loops (see Figure 3.1). The four elements are ecological change, variation/enactment, selection, and retention.

Environmental Change

Environmental change affects individuals' perceptions of uncertainty or ambiguity in their environment. These perceptions provide the raw material for subsequent sensemaking processes. Individuals in organizations receive enormous amounts of information from the environment that affect their decisions and behaviors. The meaning of these signals is typically equivocal and requires individuals to impose meaning on events. Sensemaking processes that construct meaning are guided by previously retained schemas that provide prototypical depictions of frequently experienced environments. Weick makes the important point that individuals create their own environments to some extent by selectively noticing, interpreting, and acting on ambiguous environments in ways that are influenced by an individual's prior experiences and resulting schema. This leads Weick to describe much of organizing in terms of self-fulfilling prophecies, wherein individuals make sense of ambiguous circumstances, use those interpretations to take action, and create outcomes that mirror their prior sensemaking. Put in somewhat more romantic terms that might resonate with creators or entrepreneurs, sensemaking processes triggered by environmental change and resulting ambiguity are the basis for turning ideas into realities. Unfortunately, environmental changes often go unnoticed when individuals' sensemaking processes do not attend to or recognize the significance of heightened ambiguity. In this case, previously retained routines and habits may

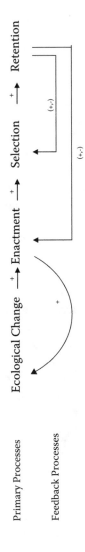

Figure 3.1 Weick's (1979) variation/enactment–selection–retention model of organizing.

overwhelm active sensemaking of environmental change and result in sustained patterns of routine behavior (Ford, 1996).

Variation/Enactment

Enactment is the term used by Weick to describe Darwinian variation processes as previously described by Campbell (1960). Enactment is the process through which individuals interact with their environment. Enactment is typically based on utilizing previously retained routines to produce relatively predictable outcomes from one's environment. However, novel forms of enactment may provoke change in one's environment that results in new task and social structures (see Ford, 1996, for a description of structuration processes related to creative action). In organizational settings, novel enactment typically results from knowledge transfer whereby analogical reasoning reveals how solutions retained in one domain can be applied in another, or through associationistic reasoning whereby previously retained knowledge is recombined to fashion novel solutions (Hargadon, 2003). Individuals who frequently engage in these types of thought processes and introduce novel solutions to others are likely to be considered "creative."

Selection

Selection is the point in the process where meanings and interpretations are preserved for future use. Choices are made regarding the relative usefulness of alternative interpretations and enacted environments. Selection processes result in an individual developing an interpretation, or schema, of an environment that then serves to act as tentative rules, screens, or constraints that guide subsequent decision making and action. Individual's schemas depict important attributes or variables and causal relationships among variables in specific settings. New situations are interpreted in light of an individual's repertoire of schema, thus reducing ambiguity and guiding actions in a manner that often reinforces existing schema (cf. self-fulfilling prophecies; Weick, 1979). Thus, selection processes are characterized by substantial inertia that tends to favor routine actions because their consequences are relatively certain. Novel solutions may receive favorable reviews on occasion, but this is likely only in cases where routine options can no longer be enacted or when environmental change reveals undeniable and consequential shortcomings in familiar solutions (Ford, 1996). It is also important to consider that the selection and retention of a novel solution implies a failure of previously retained solutions. Thus, it is not surprising that selection processes suppress "mutations" in order to preserve some degree of continuity and organization across generations (Campbell, 1960).

Retention

Retention processes are the repositories of previously created and enacted solutions that have survived the selection process. This knowledge may be related to routines, strategies, norms, cultures, technology, and disciplinary know-how. The more eclectic and broad one's pool of retained knowledge, the more potential one has to develop novel associations or remote analogies that foster creativity. Narrow, limited experience limits the amount of raw materials available to promote novel ideas. Retention processes also serve to organize and categorize incoming information, usually in ways that are consistent with previously retained interpretations.

Feedback Loops

Weick's (1979) model also has three feedback loops that can have either a positive or negative effect on enactment. Ecological change and enactment (variations) are linked by a feedback loop. This feedback loop describes how an individual's behavior instigates environmental change. One consequence of considering this relationship is the realization that individuals and environments cannot be meaningfully considered in isolation from one another (cf. Woodman, Sawyer, & Griffin, 1993). It also requires that one consider dynamic processes through which creative action and environmental change provoke each other over time (cf. Ford, 1996).

Enactment is linked to selection. The quantity and rigor of selection processes are affected by the frequency and novelty of an individual's choices and actions. Moreover, selection has an effect on retention in that selected interpretations may enrich the pool of previously retained knowledge. However, retention is connected to selection and enactment via two additional feedback loops. These two relationships reflect the ways in which learning affects selection and enactment. Specifically, the character of selection processes can be affected through retained experiences. Selection criteria may be added, removed, or prioritized differently as a result of learning more about causal relationships in a particular environment. Retention also affects future enactment because it presents a modified array of knowledge from which an individual may draw upon to formulate new solutions to environmental changes. These feedback loops describe three specific dynamic processes that can be used to propose relationships among action, learning, and environmental change.

Summary

Creating and organizing are best considered as dynamic processes that can be effectively described by Darwinian VSR reasoning (Simonton, 2000). Individuals make sense of environmental changes and formulate actions based on prior knowledge and existing preferences. The results of specific actions may induce further environmental change, as well as changes in knowledge and preferences. The evolutionary cycle linking environments and action has been usefully employed to understand creativity, innovation, entrepreneurship, strategy, organizational inertia, and changes in populations of firms (Baum & McKelvey, 1999; Ford, 1996; Simonton, 2000). Thus, these concepts have advanced theory at the individual, organization, and industry levels of analysis. Our faith in the robustness of these proposals leads us to analyze historical texts by describing how they address these process descriptions. Once these analyses are complete, we will turn our attention to recent organizational creativity research to reveal potential ties to VSR theorizing, and offer future research ideas suggested by our review of classic contributions. A summary of the analyses and comparisons of our three selected classic texts that follow is presented in Table 3.1.

KATZ AND KAHN'S ROLE EPISODE MODEL

Katz and Kahn's "The Social Psychology of Organizations" (1966) applies social psychology principles to the study of organizations as open systems to understand collective action in organizations. According to Katz and Kahn, social structures are manufactured by individuals by inventing and enacting patterns of behaviors. They emphasize that "These social systems are anchored in the attitudes, perceptions, beliefs, motivations, habits, and expectations of human beings" (1966, p. 37). Consequently, the main problem that social systems are concerned with "... is that of reducing the variability and instability of human actions to uniform and dependable patterns" (1966, p. 41).

Because they define organizations as open systems of roles, Katz and Kahn (1966) underscore the fact that organizations are contrived in nature and the structure is primarily characterized by retained patterns of interlocking expectations and actions. All individuals in an organization are part of a role set that helps define the organization. Thus, the key property of organizations is the recurrence of expected behavior patterns in relation to organizational roles. Katz and Kahn (1966) proposed a model of role episodes, similar in many respects to Weick's

(1979) enactment model, to explain individual action in organizational settings. They propose that a role episode consists of four elements: sent role, role behavior, received role, and role expectations (see Figure 3.2). Role episodes are described as cyclical and ongoing and are characterized by dynamic, reciprocal relationships between environments and actions, consistent with the tenets of VSR theorizing. The following sections attempt to describe Katz and Kahn's proposals within the context of VSR reasoning and theoretical language to facilitate comparisons across texts.

Environmental Change

Environmental change in the Katz and Kahn model is depicted primarily through their description of the sent role. The sent role consists of communications of role expectations or evaluative standards that are sent by individuals to influence the focal person's role set. Role sending is a cyclical process by which individuals become socialized in a role, receive feedback on the acceptability of their behavior in relation to the role, and then correct their behaviors as necessary.

Variation/Enactment

Role behavior is the response of the focal person to influences in his or her environment. It is a recurring action of an individual related to the actions of other individuals in that there is a predictable outcome. These repetitive behaviors make up a social system of collective behaviors where individuals each play their specific part. Received role expectations are the evaluative standards applied to (role) behavior of an individual in a specific position or organizational office (1966, p. 195). Interestingly, Katz and Kahn's descriptions were primarily oriented toward facilitating routine rather than creative performance.

Selection

The received role is the focal person's perception of role-sending information. How close the received role is to the sent role will depend on things such as the characteristics of the sender and focal person, expectations, and the communication process. It is through the sent role that the organization informs individuals about the expectations of their roles. The received role will also be affected by individual's perceptions of the organization. Role expectations are the evaluative standards that an individual applied to select among various behavioral options. They

Table 3.1 Analysis and Comparison of Historical Texts

	PRIMARY PROCESSES				FEEDBACK PROCESSES		
	ECOLOGICAL CHANGE (TASK ENVIRONMENT)	VARIATION/ ENACTMENT	SELECTION	RETENTION (ENACTED ENVIRONMENT)	VARIATION → ECOLOGICAL CHANGE	RETENTION → VARIATION	RETENTION → SELECTION
Katz & Kahn (1966)	Sent role: Influence attempts by members of a focal person's role set that communicate role expectations (evaluative standards)	Role behavior: Responses of a focal person to received and reflexive role expectations	Received role: Received role expectations— "evaluative standards applied to [role] behavior" (p. 195)	Received role: Reflexive role expectations— "the focal person 'sends' to himself or herself"	Extent to which focal person's role behavior influences role sender's role expectations and influences attempts (moderated by attributes of the person and interpersonal factors, see Figure 3.2)	Extent to which reflexive role expectations facilitate and constrain deviant (positive or negative) role behavior	Extent to which reflexive role expectations affect received role expectations

	Environmental stimuli / Domain	Programs/Innovations / Discretionary	Satisficing / Norms of rationality	Organizational learning produces / Domain consensus	Extent to which performance programs... / discretionary action	Extent to which organizational learning outcomes / domain consensus	Extent to which organizational learning / domain consensus affects
March & Simon (1958) / Cyert & March (1963)	Environmental stimuli within the "negotiated environment" ranging from routine to relatively novel (pp. 139–140) reveal disparity between aspiration levels and achievement (p. 120)	Programs/ Innovations: • Routine stimuli evoke appropriate performance programs. • Novel stimuli evoke problemistic search, problem solving and innovation.	Satisficing: Alternative is selected when it meets or exceeds set of acceptable-level decision rules; alternatives are evaluated sequentially	Organizational learning produces: • aspiration levels • attention rules • search rule • performance programs	Extent to which performance programs or innovations affect achievement and character of the negotiated environment	Extent to which organizational learning outcomes facilitate and constrain the adoption of performance programs or innovations	Extent to which organizational learning affects acceptable-level decision rules and sequencing of alternatives
Thompson (1967)	Domain: • technology included • population served • services rendered (Chap. 3)	Discretionary (Chap. 9) behavior regarding: • technology included • population served • services rendered resulting from problemistic search • opportunistic surveillance (Chap. 11)	Norms of rationality— Suggest ordering of standards of desirability: 1. Efficiency tests (technical core) 2. Instrumental tests (managerial level) 3. Social tests (institutional level) (Chap. 7)	Domain consensus (chap. 3)—Shared expectations about what the organization will and will not do regarding: • technology included (Chap. 5) • population served (Chap. 6) • services rendered	Extent to which discretionary action affects the domain	Extent to which domain consensus (shared expectations and knowledge) facilitate and constrain discretionary action	Extent to which domain consensus (shared expectations and knowledge) affects the character of efficiency tests, instrumental tests, and social tests

form the basis for subjective judgments regarding the respective value or appropriateness of different solutions, strategies, or routines. Role expectations inform individual choice, and to the extent that they correspond with sent roles will also affect social and organizational evaluations as well.

Retention

We believe that retention in Katz and Kahn's model is best reflected by their description of a focal person's reflexive role expectations. These are the expectations that the focal person sends to himself or herself. Again, it is through the sent role that the organization informs individuals about the expectations of their roles. However, the extent to which these expectations are received (retained) will determine motivation and readiness for effective role performance.

Variation to Environmental Change Feedback Loop

A focal person's role behavior influences role sender's role expectations and influences attempts. Katz and Kahn add that this relationship may be moderated by attributes of the person and interpersonal factors (see Figure 3.2). Katz and Kahn propose that personality is the product of these types of interaction cycles and it is continually being modified through an individual's life. Not surprisingly, individuals will tend to be attracted to roles that have expectations for which they are well suited. Although their description emphasizes the ways in which individuals align themselves with others' role expectations, their theory provides a means for understanding how role behavior can shape how others view a role. In this way, individuals can influence role expectations to better match their interests and styles.

Retention to Variation Feedback Loop

This relationship defines the extent to which reflexive role expectations facilitate and constrain deviant (positive or negative) role behavior. The information that the individual "sends" to himself or herself will affect how he or she responds in certain situations. How they perceive their role in the organization will affect how they behave. Individuals will have an understanding of behaviors that will meet the expectations of their office, the organization, and their own personal interests. This feedback loop also takes into consideration an individual's internal motivation to perform a specific role and his perceptions about his own abilities and values in relation to his role.

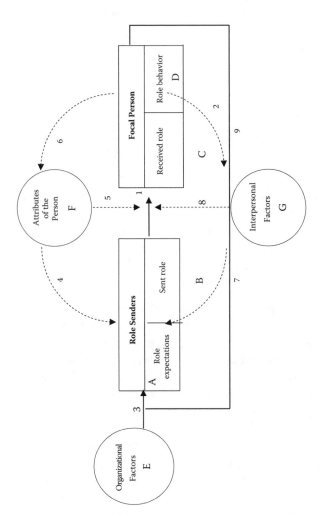

Figure 3.2 Katz and Kahn's (1966) model of organizational roles.

Retention to Selection Feedback Loop

This is the extent to which reflexive role expectations affect received role expectations. Again, individuals "send" information to themselves and this will in turn affect the evaluative standards applied to how they respond in certain situations. An individual's received role expectations is, therefore, a result of the interaction between sent role expectations and reflexive role expectations. The resultant mix will influence the manner in which individuals prioritize and choose among different behavioral options.

Summary

Katz and Kahn's description of role episodes offers a dynamic, evolving description of how individuals enact and alter role expectations in organizations. Their description emphasizes the evolutionary character of these processes by noting that:

> "... the response of the focal person feeds back to each sender in ways that alter or reinforce that sender's expectations and subsequent role-sending. The current role-sendings of each member of the set depend on that member's evaluations of the response to his or her last sendings, and thus a new episode begins" (1966, p. 195).

With respect to creativity, Katz and Kahn's theory would lead one to be pessimistic regarding creative contributions from those whose roles emphasize routines (Ford, 1996), are not associated with creativity goals (Shalley, 1991), or lack leader support for innovation (Amabile, Schatzel, Moneta, & Kramer, 2004). Put simply, when creativity is not given priority over routine behaviors, then individuals will have a tendency to follow convention. Alternatively, sent and received role expectations could significantly increase creative performance, as can be seen in organizations such as IDEO that compete on the basis of creative design (Hargadon & Sutton, 1997). Overall, we believe that Katz and Kahn's description offers strong direction for describing interactions between contextual features such as climate perceptions and individual differences, and offers language and rationales for investigating dynamic relationships between creative action and social structures.

MARCH AND SIMON'S ADMINISTRATIVE PROCESS MODEL

March and Simon published "Organizations" in 1958 and offered an amazing propositional inventory meant to serve as a guide for developing a theory of formal organizations to rival those offered in economics.

Cyert and March's "A Behavioral Theory of the Firm" (1963) further advanced the ideas offered by March and Simon. According to these authors, decision making and action are affected by four primary organizing processes: quasi-resolution of conflict, uncertainty avoidance, problemistic search, and organizational learning.

March and Simon devote considerable attention to innovation in organizations. They introduced the idea that cognitive limits on rationality affect organizational change and program development. In particular, they emphasized that aspiration–performance gaps motivate the search for satisfactory (not optimal) solutions that address sources of uncertainty. These processes were proposed to promote the creation of organizational routines for addressing frequently faced problems or sources of uncertainty. Over time, they proposed that problemistic search and organizational learning result in the creation of robust routines for avoiding uncertainty. However, these same processes were also used to describe occasions when organizations innovate. Specifically, when current routines do not offer satisfactory solutions to sources of uncertainty, or when individual aspirations exceed current performance, problemistic search will seek new solutions. This process is especially likely to occur when facing environmental change because "the rate of innovation is likely to increase when changes in the environment make the existing organizational procedures unsatisfactory" (1958, p. 183).

Environmental Change
Environmental stimuli and related uncertainty motivate search for solutions to problems. Alternatively, if individuals view the environment as stable they will adhere to current routines. The extent to which individuals will be motivated to enact novel solutions will be based on their aspiration levels and their satisfaction regarding their current circumstances. Their description suggests that some measure of dissatisfaction is necessary to motivate innovation and the creation of new organizational routines. When changes in the environment are too subtle to create dissatisfaction with current routines, then the status quo will prevail.

Variation/Enactment
March and Simon propose that organizations address sources of environmental uncertainty by employing organizational routines. In the case where existing routines are ill suited for a specific problem, organizations will engage in problemistic search. Problemistic search is not always rigorous, however, and is typically simpleminded and biased. Search

processes begin with simple solutions first and then progress to increasingly complex solutions only when simple solutions are unsatisfactory. Simple solutions are found in the neighborhood of the problem, or in the neighborhood of the current routine. If these simple search strategies fail to offer satisfactory solutions, then more comprehensive search ensues. Additionally, search is biased by previously retained understandings of the environment and causal relationships that affect solutions. Overall, these search processes lead to adopting new solutions that are closely related to current solutions. Highly novel alternatives are rarely proposed or adopted.

Selection

Alternative actions are selected based on their correspondence to specific problems, and the extent to which they are expected to produce satisfactory results. Alternatives are evaluated sequentially with obvious routines in the front of the line, followed by locally familiar options, and then by increasingly novel alternatives. The first option that minimally satisfies the joint preferences or criteria of different subunits in an organization (e.g., finance, marketing, operations, etc.) will be selected. In this manner, organizational goals serve as constraints that must be satisfied by enacted solutions.

Retention

The process of addressing organizational uncertainty with local and biased problemistic search results in organizational learning. This learning takes the form of organizational routines or programs. Short-term adaptations engage existing routines to address current problems. However, long-term adaptation is possible through innovation of novel routines created to address new sources of uncertainty brought on by environmental change. Associations between specific environmental cues and currently available performance routines allow organizations to address recurring problems effectively and efficiently.

Variation to Ecological Change Feedback Loop

March and Simon primarily argue that organizational action can address sources of organizational uncertainty. However, they also argue that organizations have the ability to negotiate with their environments as a means of avoiding uncertainty. Thus, some organizational routines serve to create repetitive, predictable transactions with stakeholders who might otherwise create uncertainty for decision makers.

Retention to Variation Feedback Loop

This reflects the extent to which organizational learning outcomes facilitate and constrain the adoption of performance programs or innovations. As is the case in all evolutionary theorizing, March and Simon depict a tension between routine and innovative action. The more elaborate an organization's set of performance routines, the more likely it is for subsequent actions to be based on those routines. Attempts to enact innovations run counter to efforts to avoid uncertainty and capitalize on prior organizational learning. In order for retained knowledge to be employed for developing novel solutions, performance must dip below aspiration levels sufficiently to motivate search and innovation.

Retention to Selection Feedback Loop

This is the extent to which organizational learning affects acceptable decision rules and sequencing of alternatives. As organizational learning occurs, the acceptable decision rules will reflect the new information learned about the environment. More importantly, aspiration levels will tend to conform to prior experiences in a manner that makes it less likely for substantial aspiration–performance gaps to arise. Narrowing this gap limits incentives to search and innovate. Consequently, organizations can become gradually insensitive to poor performance and continue to employ routines that have become ineffective at addressing critical sources of uncertainty.

Summary

March and Simon's attempt to develop a comprehensive theory of organizational action describes dynamic evolutionary processes whereby organizational actions become routines through processes of search and learning, and organizational environments are negotiated to limit uncertainty facing decision makers. Their emphasis on the motivations and cognitive limitations of individual actors, as well as structural dynamics that create and cope with conflict, transformed the administrative sciences. Finally, their descriptions of organizational routines and innovations fit well with VSR theorizing in that they depict the tension between variation and selective retention processes (Campbell, 1960). March subsequently elaborated the description of this tension in his influential work describing tradeoffs between exploitation (routine) and exploration (creative) actions in organizations (March, 1991).

THOMPSON'S MODEL OF ORGANIZING
UNDER NORMS OF RATIONALITY

Thompson's classic work "Organizations in Action" (1967) views organizations as open systems. It explores the influence of technology and uncertainty on organizational structure. Thompson's description of organizations as open systems emphasizes that organizations are designed to address environmental change and uncertainty. However, he also proposes that organizations are subject to norms of rationality that are based on the assumption of complete certainty in decision making. This poses a dilemma: How can one simultaneously organize in a manner that enables an organization to address environmental change while creating levels of certainty necessary to address norms of rationality? Thompson's solution was to suggest that organizations create buffers that insulate their technical cores from environmental disruptions. This suggests a rather proactive approach to enacting the organization's environment. He proposes that organizations create their own domain. The domain of an organization will determine the points where the organization is dependent on the environment. Organizations can then use a variety of tactics like buffering, forecasting, and negotiating to reduce dependency and gain greater control over the environment. In this manner, organizations can insulate their technological core from uncertainty and make decisions under norms of rationality. As is the case with Katz and Kahn (1966) and March and Simon (1958), Thompson's work is notable for its description of dynamic evolutionary processes that describe how contextual features and organizational actions affect each other over time.

Environmental Change

Thompson defines the domain in an organization as identifying the points where the organization is dependent on inputs from the environment. The domain takes into consideration, and is defined by, three elements: technology included, population served, and services rendered. When accounting for these elements, no two organizations will be identical. Thompson's descriptions resonate with Weick's proposals in the sense that organizations are assumed to have considerable control over how they define and enact their organizational environment.

Variation/Enactment

Organizations have to deal with uncertainty in their domain, and this is done through the exercise of discretion by employees. Individuals have to make decisions regarding the technology included, the population served, and the services rendered. According to Thompson, "Individuals exercise discretion whenever they believe it is to their advantage to do so and seek to evade discretion on other occasions" (1967, p. 118). Thompson describes acts of discretion as resulting from two different administrative processes, problemistic search and opportunistic surveillance. Problemistic search as described by March and Simon (1958) is motivated by when a problem arises and the search is focused on finding a solution to the problem. Problemistic search would be seen most in the technical core where uncertainty is relatively low. Alternatively, opportunistic search does not require an instigating problem, and does not necessarily stop when a satisfactory solution is found. Instead, it is an active monitoring of the environment in search of opportunities. Thompson describes it as something akin to curiosity in individuals. Opportunistic surveillance would be mostly associated with the institutional level, the parts of the organization between the technical core and the environment that absorb uncertainty and initiate innovation.

Selection

Thompson describes three primary types of tests used to assess the value of different solutions or choices. The first are efficiency tests, which refer to the degree to which choices are optimized. These types of tests are typical in the technical core where optimal allocations of personnel, materials, and technology are calculated to utilize resources most efficiently. The second type consists of instrumental tests. They test the degree to which choices produce desirable results and are most typically employed by those who manage the technical core. Unlike efficiency tests, which are based on mathematical methodologies, instrumental tests are based on less rigorous criteria that can be subjected to dispute. Social tests are the third type used when standards are ambiguous or decision makers face incomplete information. These kinds of tests are likely to be relevant to creative solutions that do not meet or even address the requirements of efficiency or instrumental tests. By utilizing all of these kinds of tests, organizations are able to adapt to their environments while simultaneously optimizing their utilization of resources. The division of labor between those insulated from uncertainty in an organization's technical core, and those proactively negotiating with the environment in an organization's institutional level, is a key feature of Thompson's proposals.

Retention

Thompson emphasizes the development of domain consensus as a primary retention outcome allowing organizations to function under norms of rationality. To function under norms of rationality, an organization's employees must develop a prior consensus regarding the domain. Thompson argues that "Domain consensus defines a set of expectations both for members of an organization and for others with whom they interact, about what the organization will and will not do" (1967, p. 29). This shared understanding provides a way for individuals to understand an organization's goals and stakeholders, and can serve as a guide to decision making. Thompson also follows the descriptions of March and Simon (1958) by acknowledging the importance of established routines, especially in the technical core.

Variation to Ecological Change Feedback Loop

This relationship is effectively described by Thompson's proposals regarding the exercise of discretion. He argues that individuals in discretionary positions are the ones who affect domain definitions and resulting sources of uncertainty facing an organization. Decisions regarding technology, populations served, and services rendered suggest that organizations have substantial degrees of agency with respect to enacting their environment.

Retention to Variation Feedback Loop

This is the extent to which domain consensus facilitates and constrains discretionary action. Once commitments have been made (retained) regarding technology to be utilized, populations to be served, and services to be rendered, future discretionary actions will be constrained by the resources, processes, and relationships established by prior choices. Although organizations have a measure of discretion when engaging their environment, significant changes in these commitments become increasingly difficult as a firm matures.

Retention to Selection Feedback Loop

This is the extent to which domain consensus affects the character of efficiency tests, instrumental tests, and social tests. The shared expectations about what the organization will and will not do will affect the standards of desirability for the organization. This in turn will influence the character of the tests used to evaluate the organization. The choice of tests will depend on the direction the organization has taken and the areas of the organization (technology, population served, or services rendered) to be evaluated. Specifically, commitments that emphasize low-cost leadership are likely to require emphasizing efficiency tests, and commitments to innovation leadership suggest a greater emphasis on social tests.

Summary

Thompson proposes that technological and environmental uncertainty is a primary challenge to be addressed by organizing processes. Consequently, dependence on environmental resources represents the primary threat to an organization's long-term viability. This leads organizations to seek control over environmental dependencies through strategies such as buffering and negotiating. Individuals in discretionary roles make decisions that affect the commitments an organization has with its environment, and utilize efficiency, instrumental, and social tests to balance the need to adapt with norms of rationality. Decisions based on norms of rationality motivate problemistic search in the technical core. However, organizations must also search for new opportunities and promote adaptation at the institutional level.

As a final note, Thompson offers a description of what he calls "the variable human." He proposes that individuals come to a job with aspirations and knowledge, and the roles individuals take present opportunities and constraints. Thompson assumes that an individual "will try to exploit his opportunities (as he sees them) in the direction of his aspirations and that, within the limits of the constraints he believes to be operating, he will be guided in this endeavor by his beliefs about causation and by the standards or norms he believes are appropriate" (1967, p. 102). We believe this description resonates with many of the proposals offered by Katz and Kahn (1966) and March and Simon (1958), and supports our assertion that ideas from this influential work are consistent with a general Campbellian VSR approach to understanding creativity and social change.

CONNECTIONS TO RECENT ORGANIZATIONAL CREATIVITY RESEARCH

At this point we have argued that Campbellian VSR theorizing is a useful way to integrate proposals related to creativity and change, that Weick's (1979) enactment theory offers a useful generalization of VSR reasoning to describe organizing processes, and that several classic texts offer useful embellishments on the themes presented by Weick. At this point, we turn our attention to recent research on organizational creativity; first, by showing how one might think of its relationship to VSR reasoning and the classic organizational texts we have described, and second, by proposing useful directions for future research motivated by our analyses.

Environmental Change

Several recent contributions to the organizational creativity literature speak to the issues of environmental change, ambiguity, and sensemaking. Drazin, Glynn, and Kazanjian (1999) describe sensemaking processes that fuel creativity in organizational settings. Central to their arguments are environmental changes or crises that shift attention from one creative challenge to another, and implicate different sources of retained knowledge (e.g., engineering, administration) likely to serve as the ingredients for creative advances. Fong (2006) offers experimental evidence that shows that when individuals experience emotional ambivalence, it serves as a cue to engage in active sensemaking to resolve environmental ambiguity, and results in heightened awareness of novel and potentially valuable associations with the potential to allay ambiguity and resolve ambivalence. Creative goal setting has also been shown to affect creative performance (Shalley, 1991). In part, this may result by sending role expectations that focus attention on specific environmental changes and require individuals to reduce specific sources of ambiguity by developing creative proposals. Another fascinating set of findings that may benefit from associated ideas related to environmental change and ambiguity was presented in Elsbach and Kramer's (2003) study of Hollywood pitch meetings. Their study shows that assessments of creativity are highly subjective (ambiguous) and are significantly affected by social psychological processes related to the appearance and mannerisms of those pitching novel proposals. This research setting provides an excellent example of Thompson's proposals regarding discretionary decisions at the institutional level where organizations enact their environment. Once these commitments are made, technical professionals (e.g., lighting, set design, sound, post-production, etc.) are assembled and asked to execute their craft reliably and efficiently. Research on problem finding (Csikszentmihalyi, 1988) suggests that there may be individual differences in the extent to which people are "looking for trouble," or actively searching for environmental changes that suggest creative conundrums.

Variation

Recent research on processes leading to novel ideas suggests that developing novel associations drawn from existing solutions is the key to useful innovations (Hargadon, 2003). This reasoning is consistent with March and Simon's emphasis on organizational routines and their proposals regarding local and distant search as sources of novel solutions. Recent research in the innovation literature (e.g., Christensen, 1997) also emphasizes the importance of embedding novel solutions within a "value network" of robust, well-understood solutions in order to yield value from novelty. Novel solutions that do not interface effectively with existing technologies, organizational routines, or user habits are unlikely to be selected and retained. All of the classic texts reviewed here agree in the assertion that novelty destroys previously retained routines, violates established role expectations, and violates norms of rationality. This conclusion supports the assertion offered by Ford (1996) that managing creativity requires reducing the seductiveness of existing routines in addition to supporting the generation of novel solutions.

Selection

Most of the recent organizational creativity research examining selection processes has focused on role expectations in the form of supervisor expectations and feedback. For example, Shalley and Perry-Smith (2001) showed that expectations of controlling feedback were negatively associated with creative performance, and expectations of informational feedback was positively associated with creative performance (see also Shalley, 1995). Interestingly, individuals who were shown a creative example also had higher creative performance. Mumford (2002) reviewed several studies that examined output requirements and feedback on creativity and concluded that technical feedback, clear expectations, and an absence of punishment promote creativity in organizational settings. Innovation research has examined the role that aspiration–performance gaps play in motivating creative solutions (Greve, 2003), and behavioral-decision research has demonstrated that aspiration–performance gaps substantially influence risk taking (Shapira, 1995). It would be interesting to explore the possibility that aspiration–performance gaps are related to intrinsic motivation measures that have been previously linked to creative performance (Amabile, 1996).

Retention

Domain-specific knowledge was proposed by Amabile (1988) as one of the central influences on individual creativity in organizational settings. This is consistent with findings that professional eminence seems to require up to a decade of prior learning and experience before significant professional achievements are attained (Simonton, 2000). The importance of knowledge as a facilitator of creativity has also been examined in collective activity. Perry-Smith and Shalley (2003) presented a depiction about how social networks form as a means of bringing together diverse knowledge that can lead to creative solutions, but cautioned that retained knowledge residing within the network may eventually lead to lower levels of creative performance because little novel information is present.

Feedback Processes

Few empirical research efforts examining organizational creativity have used longitudinal research designs. One notable exception was offered by Amabile and Conti (1999) when they examined the effect that downsizing had on climate dimensions related to organizational creativity. Not surprisingly, aspects of climate that suggested prioritizing creativity and favorably assessing creative efforts declined significantly. Clearly, employee variation and selection processes were affected by the uncertain and threatening character of the environment. Also, the aforementioned studies that examined supervisor feedback suggest that it is likely that selection processes can be influenced through interactions with those who offer role expectations. Another interesting longitudinal study was presented by Hargadon and Bechky (2006) who examined how collectives of creators become creative collectives. They showed that individuals who conceived of a novel variation were able to instigate collective creativity by seeking help from others. Help giving was a form of feedback that led to heightened aspirations and more favorable assessments. Insights were often reframed as a way of exploring new analogies and suggesting new associations (variations). Longitudinal studies such as these offer valuable insights into learning and momentum-building processes related to creative proposals in organizational settings.

SUGGESTIONS FOR FUTURE RESEARCH

Our review of classic texts, organized within VSR theoretic categories, reveals several potentially fruitful avenues for future organizational creativity research. Although it is beyond the scope of this chapter to attempt a comprehensive description of these possibilities, we would like to conclude by offering a few illustrative examples that demonstrate the usefulness of this exercise.

We believe that future organizational creativity research needs to examine dynamic processes between environments and variations. Each of the texts examined here offers specific, relatively similar proposals for how creative action affects organizational processes and structures. Although most organizational creativity studies (including ours) offer a perfunctory description of the benefits of creative performance, evidence that individual creativity promotes organizational innovation, internal venturing, or strategic differentiation is scant. We suspect that the relationship between creativity and other positive organizational outcomes is likely to be curvilinear, with too much or too little being harmful rather than helpful. March and Simon (1958), for example, might describe how solutions that venture too far from existing routines destroy competence and waste resources (March, 1991). Current research is oriented primarily to examine the effects of environments of creativity. We think it would be interesting to emphasize how creativity affects organizational environments (e.g., climate, structure, etc.).

The explicit recognition that current routines and creative paths to adaptation are fundamentally at odds with one another represents another strong theme across each text. We believe that organizational creativity research should pursue more nuanced arguments regarding the ways in which novel solutions create and destroy value. Ford and Gioia (2000) provide empirical evidence that factors that influenced the novelty of managerial choices were completely different from the factors that affected their value to the organization. This unexpected finding suggests that novelty and value might be better considered as loosely coupled dimensions affected differentially by variation and selective retention processes. Some environments, such as Thompson's (1967) institutional level, might find novel solutions to be inherently valuable. Alternatively, novel solutions introduced to an organization's technical core would likely be disruptive and negatively or intermittently associated with value. We believe that contextual differences in the value of novel solutions are likely in organizational environments, and that future research should adopt assessment procedures that permit these relationships to be explored.

Other more-focused research questions are suggested by our analyses. For example, it would be interesting to see whether sequential presentation of information affects individual creative performance. In a similar vein, our analyses suggest that multiple, complex decision criteria must be jointly considered to develop satisfactory solutions to environmental changes. We believe organizational creativity research could benefit from considering more organizationally relevant selection criteria similar to those used to evaluate business plans in the context of entrepreneurship. The extent to which social or technical considerations dominate creativity assessments would be interesting to explore, as would the sequence with which criteria should be addressed in order to improve the odds that a novel solution would be selected and retained (e.g., does one need to prove that an invention works before financial considerations are brought to decision makers?). In general, we believe that infusing explanations for creative performance with organizational features and processes such as goals, roles, routines, structure, technology, and strategy will enable creativity research to impose a bigger intellectual footprint on the management discipline.

We hope that our exercise of examining historically important and influential texts reveals that broad theorizing that emphasizes dynamic relationships between action and structure is well established and available for motivating new investigations of organizational creativity. We also suggest that connecting new proposals to robust ideas from prior decades may broaden the scope of organizational creativity theorizing to address issues related to innovation, entrepreneurship, and organizational adaptation. Overall, we believe that our analyses demonstrate that many classic works offer powerful ideas capable of inspiring new areas of empirical inquiry.

REFERENCES

Amabile, T. M. (1988). A model of creativity and innovation in organizations. In B. M. Staw & L. L. Cummings (Eds.), *Research in Organizational Behavior, 10* (pp. 123–167). Greenwich, CT: JAI Press.

Amabile, T. M. (1996). *Creativity in context: Update to the social psychology of creativity.* Boulder, CO: West View Press.

Amabile, T. M., & Conti, R. (1999). Changes in the work environment for creativity during downsizing. *Academy of Management Journal, 42,* 630–640.

Amabile, T. M., Schatzel, E. A., Moneta, G. B., & Kramer, S. J. (2004). Leader behaviors and the work environment for creativity: Perceived leader support. *Leadership Quarterly, 15,* 28–32.

Baum, J. A., & McKelvey, B. (Eds.). (1999). *Variations in organizational science: In honor of Donald T. Campbell.* Newbury Park, CA: Sage.

Bedeian, A., & Wren, D. (2001). Most influential management books of the 20th century. *Organizational Dynamics, 29,* 221–225.

Campbell, D. T. (1960). Blind variation and selective retention in creative thought as in other knowledge processes. *Psychological Review, 95,* 380–400.

Campbell, D. T. (1965). Variation and selective retention in socio-cultural evolution. In H. R. Barringer, G. I. Blanksten, & R. W. Mack (Eds.), *Social change in developing areas: A reinterpretation of evolutionary theory* (pp. 19–48). Cambridge, MA: Schenkman.

Christensen, C. M. (1997). *The innovator's dilemma.* Cambridge, MA: Harvard Business School Press.

Csikszentmihalyi, M. (1988). Society, culture, and person: A systems view of creativity. In R. J. Sternberg (Ed.), *The nature of creativity: Contemporary psychological perspective* (pp. 325–339). New York: Cambridge University Press.

Cyert, R., & March, J. (1963). A summary of concepts in the behavioral theory of the firm. In *A behavioral theory of the firm*. Englewood Cliffs, NJ: Prentice-Hall.

Drazin, R., Glynn, M. A., & Kazanjian, R. K. (1999). Multilevel theorizing about creativity in organizations: A sensemaking perspective. *Academy of Management Review, 24*(2), 286–307.

Elsbach, K. D., & Kramer, R. M. (2003). Assessing creativity in Hollywood pitch meetings: Evidence for a dual-process model of creativity judgments. *Academy of Management Journal, 46*(3), 283.

Fong, C. (2006). The effects of emotional ambivalence on creativity. *Academy of Management Journal, 49,* 1016–1030.

Ford, C. (1996). A theory of individual creative action in multiple social domains. *Academy of Management Review, 21,* 1112–1142.

Ford, C. M., & Gioia, D. A. (2000). Factors influencing creativity in the domain of managerial decision making. *Journal of Management, 26*(4), 705–732.

Gardner, H. (1993). *Creating minds.* New York: Basic Books.

Greve, H. R. (2003). A behavioral theory of R&D expenditures and innovations: Evidence from shipbuilding. *Academy of Management Journal, 46,* 685–702.

Hargadon, A. (2003). *How breakthroughs happen: The surprising truth about how companies innovate.* Boston: Harvard Business School Press.

Hargadon, A. B., & Bechky, B. A. (2006). When collection of creatives become creative collectives: A field study of problem solving at work. *Organization Science, 17*(4), 484–500.

Hargadon, A. B., & Sutton, R. I. (1997). Technology brokering and innovation in a product development firm. *Administrative Science Quarterly, 42,* 716–749.

Katz, D., & Kahn, R. (1966). *The social psychology of organizations.* New York: John Wiley.

March, J. G. (1991). Exploration and exploitation in organizational learning. *Organization Science, 2*(1), 71–87.

March, J., & Simon, H. (1958). Organizations. New York: John Wiley & Sons.

Mumford, M. D. (2002). Social innovation: Ten cases from Benjamin Franklin. *Creativity Research, 14,* 253–266.

Perry-Smith, J. E., & Shalley, C. E. (2003). The social side of creativity: A static and dynamic social network perspective. *Academy of Management Review, 28*(1), 89–106.

Shalley, C. E. (1991). Effects of productivity goals, creativity goals, and personal discretion on individual creativity. *Journal of Applied Psychology, 76,* 179–185.

Shalley, C. E. (1995). Effects of coaction, expected evaluation, and goal setting on creativity and productivity. *Academy of Management Journal, 38,* 483–503.

Shalley, C. E., & Perry-Smith, J. E. (2001). Effects of social-psychological factors on creative performance: The role of informational and controlling expected evaluation and modeling experience. *Organizational Behavior and Human Decision Processes, 84,* 1–22.

Shapira, Z. (1995). *Risk taking: A managerial perspective.* New York: Russell Sage Foundation.

Simonton, D. K. (1999). Creativity as blind variation and selective retention: Is the creative process Darwinian? *Psychological Inquiry, 10*(4), 309–328.

Simonton, D. K. (2000). Creativity: Cognitive, personal, development, and social aspects. *American Psychologist, 55,* 151–158.

Staw, B. M. (1990). An evolutionary approach to creativity and innovation. In M. A. West & J. L. Farr (Eds.), *Innovation and creativity at work* (pp. 287–308). Chichester, England: Wiley.

Thompson, J. (1967). *Organizations in action.* New York: McGraw-Hill.

Weick, K. (1969). *The social psychology of organizing.* Reading, MA: Addison-Wesley.

Weick, K. (1979). *The social psychology of organizing* (2nd ed.). Reading, MA: Addison-Wesley.

Woodman, R. W., Sawyer, J. E., & Griffin, R. W. (1993). Toward a theory of organizational creativity. *Academy of Management Review, 18,* 293–321.

Zhou, J., & George, J. M. (2001). When job dissatisfaction leads to creativity: Encouraging the expression of voice. *Academy of Management Journal, 44*(4), 682–697.

SECTION II

Distinctive Contributions from Organizational Creativity Research

CHAPTER 4

Leadership and Employee Creativity

Pamela Tierney
Portland State University

INTRODUCTION

Given the dynamic environment facing today's organizations, a hallmark of contemporary leadership is the capacity to foster employee creativity. As such, the topic of leading for creativity has received increasing attention in the literature by those attempting to conceptually and empirically formulate what it means to lead in a creativity context. Such work includes overviews of various aspects relevant to leading for creativity (see Mumford, Scott, Gaddis, & Strange, 2002; Shalley & Gilson, 2004; Shalley, Zhou, & Oldham, 2004) as well as special journal issues devoted explicitly to the topic (see *Leadership Quarterly, 14,* 2003, and *15,* 2004). Although an increasing compilation of empirical studies has examined leadership for creativity, to date, this line of inquiry is still in its nascent stage and lacks an overall organizing framework in which to embed creativity-conducive leadership aspects, and hence, facilitate the evaluation of leadership's role in the creative process.

The intent of this chapter is to suggest a model for examining the role of leadership in workplace creativity. Ironically, the proposed model is not a radical innovation, in and of itself, but rather an integration of previous conceptual frames for examining the advent of creativity and manners of considering leadership. What is unique about the model is that it includes an organizing framework suggesting myriad ways in which leaders may potentially shape forces central to creative action that

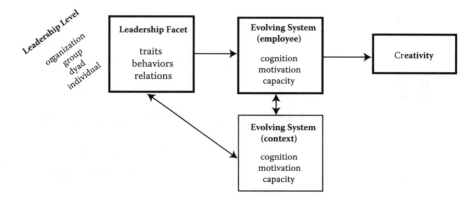

Figure 4.1 Leadership-creativity model.

include and move beyond what has been considered in existing studies. In presenting the model, the current state of creativity research will be reviewed as a means of determining how the leadership–creativity link has been examined as well as to categorize previous related studies. The final goal of the chapter is to identify gaps in our current research on creativity leadership and formulate ideas for future inquiry.

As depicted in Figure 4.1, the proposed model suggests that multiple facets of leadership come into play when influencing an "evolving system" (Gruber, 1988) of cognition, motivation, and capacity components that prevail within the organizational context (see Amabile, 1988; Ford, 1996) as well as within individuals (Gruber, 1988). Although the model acknowledges that leaders influence both contextual and individual (i.e., employee) systems, and these two systems, in turn, are likely to influence one another, the focus of the current chapter is on the individual level effects of leadership.

The model advocates attention to three issues specific to leadership when studying its relation with creativity. Figure 4.2 provides a 4 × 3 × 3 matrix incorporating these leadership aspects represented by four potential leadership levels (individual, dyadic, group, and organizational), three leader facets (traits, behaviors, and relations), and three spheres of potential leadership influence (cognition, motivation, and capacity). In sum, there are 36 cells in the matrix, each representing a combination of level, facet, and influence sphere, and each providing a unique way of examining leadership relevant to creativity. Although the matrix is not intended to be exhaustive and capture every aspect of leadership, it should prove useful for categorizing existing studies,

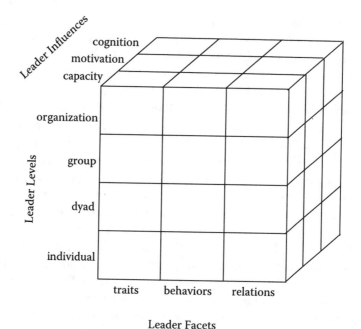

Figure 4.2 Leadership-creativity matrix.

as well as identifying gaps in our current research and potential areas for future inquiry and practice. Following is an overview of each of the three leadership issues depicted in the matrix/model and their relevance to the inquiry of the leadership–creativity link.

LEADERSHIP LEVEL

Per creativity research, noted conceptual models (Amabile, 1988; Ford, 1996; Woodman, Sawyer, & Griffin, 1993) have explicitly taken into account the multilevel nature of forces that shape creativity. Work by Drazin, Glynn, and Kazanjian (1999) is of particular import in this regard for its explicit emphasis on the specification of theory underlying the multilevel nature of the creative process. Leadership is a phenomenon with the capacity to manifest at multiple levels (Kozlowski & Klein, 2000) and as such, it is imperative for researchers exploring leadership to specify the level of analysis at which they are conceptualizing and operationalizing leadership and its effects (Yammarino, Dionne, Chun, & Dansereau, 2005) on creativity. Accordingly, the proposed model and matrix incorporate the four main levels of analysis that have been suggested in the literature (cf. Yammarino et al., 2005): the individual level (e.g., supervisor), dyadic level (e.g., interpersonal relation among two individuals), group level (e.g., work team), and the organization or collective level. Studies examining leadership–creativity associations have tended to take place "in level," investigating the influence of individually directed leadership on individual employee creativity (e.g., Madjar, Oldham, & Pratt, 2002; Oldham & Cummings, 1996; Shin & Zhou, 2003) or of group-level leadership on group-creative outcomes (e.g., Kahai, Sosik & Avolio, 1997, 2003), although possible cross-level effects of leadership have been suggested (see Woodman et al., 1993).

Although leadership at multiple levels of the organization has the capacity to influence employee creativity (Amabile, 1988; Kanter, 1988), the majority of leadership–creativity studies, to date, have confined their investigation to lower-level leaders such as work-group supervisors (e.g., Baer & Oldham, 2006; George & Zhou, 2007; Madjar et al., 2002; Oldham & Cummings, 1996; Shin & Zhou, 2003; Tierney & Farmer, 2002, 2004; Tierney, Farmer, & Graen, 1999; Zhou, 2003). Given that the work-group context is most often the "front line" for creative activity among employees, it is understandable that this research focus is popular. It has been suggested, however, that leadership resides in an embedded system within the organizational context and that examination of leaders' impacts should take into account the relevance of multiple levels (Sparrowe & Liden, 1997). As such, it is necessary to bear in mind that the associations detected among work-group leaders and employee creativity may be influenced by a broader sphere of leadership. Lower-level leaders do not operate in isolation, and their capacity and motivation to foster creativity among their employees is determined in many ways by top leaders who shape the organization's culture, structure, and processes (Amabile, 1988; Kanter, 1988). For example, although the legitimacy of creative action is determined by organizational members from different levels (Ford, 1996), top leaders often play a dominant role in establishing the prevailing institutional logic and action that signals such legitimacy (Dougherty & Heller, 1994) and shapes work-group leaders' motivation and capacity to foster their employees' creative action.

The most promising scenario for creative performance would be one in which leaders at all levels were aligned in their support of creativity. It is possible, however, that leaders' attempts to support creativity across different hierarchical levels may be more or less loosely coupled, or even contrary to one another. Leaders at upper levels may establish boundary conditions for the actions of lower-level leaders. If top leaders fail to include creative performance as a component of the organization's formal appraisal system, supervisors are less likely to attend to employee creative behaviors, thereby reinforcing the view that creativity is not supported and valued. In this sense, activities of organizational-level leadership may have a direct effect on employees' creativity as well as an indirect effect through more local levels of leadership. It is also possible that supervisors influence employee creative action in ways that are independent of those of top leadership. An example of this would be a supervisor finding ways to compensate employees for their creative efforts that fall outside of the organization's formal reward system. Conversely, supervisors can serve as obstacles for top leaders in their attempts to foster creativity at lower levels of the organization. If top leaders' efforts to promote creative action are continually thwarted by supervisors, and as a result employees refuse or repeatedly fail in creativity attempts, top leaders may alter their views on the feasibility of obtaining creativity from their work force and abandon attempts to support it.

Given its dynamic nature, it has also been noted that leadership residing at lower levels may demonstrate a "bottom-up process" by which its properties will emerge in a variant form at higher levels (Kozlowski & Klein, 2000). This intriguing notion suggests that creativity-related leadership practices at the level of the individual supervisor may manifest at more collective levels. Preliminary research (Tierney & Farmer, 2006) has explored the possibility of an emergent form of creativity leadership within work teams. Initial findings show that in work groups led by supervisors engaging in creativity-relevant behaviors, a parallel but collective form of creativity leadership is evidenced at the team level. The authors suggest that as creativity leadership on the part of the supervisor is enacted with individual team members, the overall team exposure to creativity leadership is enhanced over time and events, and the leadership form, may become embedded at a more collective level as a result of subsequent "concertive" action (Gronn, 2002) among team members.

Another way to conceptualize leadership for creativity is in terms of its proximity to focal employees. Distance serves as a useful mechanism for examining dynamics between contextual facets such as leaders and employee-related outcomes (Mowday & Sutton, 1993). A study showing that proximal contextual factors to which the employee had ongoing exposure had more impact on employee creativity than more distal factors (Shalley, Gilson, & Blum, 2000) is suggestive that the proximity of leaders should be considered when hypothesizing their impact on creative performance. Although in a general sense, more macro factors (e.g., executive leaders) are considered distal and more micro factors (work-group supervisors) considered proximal, the classification will be predicated on the focal employee's place in the organizational hierarchy.

LEADERSHIP PERSPECTIVE

Specification of the leadership perspective adopted for a study is an important step in that it shapes the kinds of research questions that can be addressed and the types of knowledge that can be generated about the leadership–creativity link. Although leadership has been defined and approached in a variety of manners, focus on a leader's personal characteristics, actions, and relations shared with employees represents traditionally presiding categorizations of leadership facets (Bass, 1990). Prior research suggests that all three aspects may come into play, in some fashion, for employee creativity.

Leader Characteristics

Personal characteristics have been recognized as fundamental to the advent of creativity (Shalley et al., 2004). If an identifiable set of attributes is required in order for an employee to perform creatively, it is plausible that a parallel set of attributes may also be necessary in order to successively lead others to create (Tierney et al., 1999). Aside from the possible development of a general creative leadership profile, adopting a leader-trait perspective for understanding creativity would also permit us to determine whether certain types of leaders are more effective with certain types of employees in fostering creative performance using an interactive framework, whereby their respective characteristics could serve to augment or complement one another. Although a comprehensive coverage of leader characteristics pertinent for creativity and innovation has been proffered (see Mumford et al., 2002), studies incorporating leader traits in their examinations of creativity are relatively few.

One interesting realm of traits that has been considered in relation to creativity leadership reflects an array of cognitive-related leader characteristics. In terms of cognitive capacity, the impact of leader general intelligence (Gibson, Fiedler, & Barrett, 1993) on follower creativity has been examined. Further, Zhou and George (2003) propose that leaders' emotional intelligence levels underscore their propensity to enable and promote creativity in a number of ways as employees engage in the various stages of the creative process. The suggested relevance of leader emotional intelligence is consistent with the notion that creativity leaders possess a level of social skill in terms of adeptness and astuteness that permits them to successfully interact with potential creators and other relevant constituents during the creative process (Mumford et al., 2002). Others have suggested that a requisite for creativity leadership is clear understanding of the steps employees undergo as part of the creative process, and of the cognitive requirements the process places on employees in their attempts to innovate (Reiter-Palmon & Illies, 2004). Basadur (2004) further notes that creativity leaders must possess an intuition or sensitivity regarding the diverse array of cognitive and creative problem-solving styles that exist among their employees, and have the ability to manage these styles through coordinating and integrating means that permit the creative potential of all employees to emerge.

Another type of cognitive capacity cited as integral for creativity leadership is the leader's personal adeptness in terms of creative problem-solving skills (Mumford et al., 2002). Possession of such skills enables the leader to adequately evaluate the creativity of employees, provide relevant creativity-related feedback regarding employee ideas and problem solutions, enables the leader to serve as a role model for creativity, and is a basis of creativity credibility in the eyes of work-group members (Mumford et al., 2002).

"Planning" is an additional form of cognitive skill relevant for creative leadership (Marta, Leritz, & Mumford, 2005). The leader's ability to read the environment, identify problem causes, as well as potential restrictions and subsequent consequences of problem solutions, are the cognitive subskills inherent in planning that facilitate creativity leaders in providing adequate structure for creativity during times of uncertainty (Marta et al., 2005). Relatedly, the ability to understand the temporal complexity inherent to creativity is a defining characteristic of creativity leadership (Halbesleben, Novicevic, Harvey, & Buckley, 2003). Temporal sensitivity should result in the leader experiencing and demonstrating greater cognitive, social, and behavioral complexity conducive to creativity (Halbesleben et al., 2003).

Finally, an additional cognitive attribute to consider is the leader's cognitive style. Numerous studies have examined employee cognitive style in relation to creativity, and correspondingly, we would anticipate that leaders characterized by an innovative cognitive style (versus an adaptive style) (Kirton, 1976) would appreciate, understand, and model creativity, amenable to the enabling and motivating of employees to create. Preliminary research (Tierney et al., 1999) in an R&D setting, however, found no relation between leader cognitive style and employee creativity.

The authors suggest that the cognitive style of leaders may have more of an impact in a different type of work setting where creative work is not routinely expected and supported.

Leading for creativity should also require a requisite set of professional and technical expertise as well (Mumford et al., 2002). A number of studies of creative productivity in R&D settings (e.g., Andrews and Farris, 1967; Farris, 1988) support the importance of those in leadership positions possessing an array of technical skills specific to the types of tasks employees conduct.

Personal motivation has been recognized as a key driver for creative performance (Amabile, 1988), and it is likely that individuals need motivation to lead others to innovate as well (Sternberg, Kaufman, & Pretz, 2003). However, few studies have explicitly considered the motivational orientation of leaders in relation to employee creativity. Farris (1988) noted that leaders effective in eliciting creativity demonstrate a certain level of enthusiasm in conducting their job. A study by Tierney et al. (1999) examined the effects of leader-intrinsic motivation for creative work on the creative performance of employees. Their results show an interactive effect such that when intrinsically motivated employees worked with intrinsically motivated supervisors, they tended to produce greater creative output. However, for employees lacking the motivation to create, working with an intrinsically motivated supervisor actually had a negative influence on their creativity.

Leader Behaviors

Where the leader-trait approach to understanding creativity prompts the question, "What are creativity leaders like?," the behavioral approach seeks to understand "What do creativity leaders do?" The majority of leadership–creativity investigations have focused on specific actions or behaviors in which leaders engage relevant to employee-creative action. As the following review will reveal, in their quest to understand how leader actions may elicit creativity, researchers, on the whole, have explored a vast and diverse array of leader behaviors. Support for many of these investigations validates the proposition that creativity leadership entails a behavioral repertoire (Hunt, Stelluto, & Hooijberg, 2004), and two recent studies (Amabile, Schatzel, Moneta, & Kramer, 2004; Tierney, 2003) have attempted to understand the gestalt of creativity leadership and its influence by conducting comprehensive qualitative field examinations. Results from both studies suggest that creativity leadership is a complex, multidimensional behavioral phenomenon.

Leader behavior-oriented studies have explored the extent to which leaders control and monitor employee work (e.g., Amabile et al., 2004; Farris, 1988; Krause, 2004; Oldham & Cummings, 1996; Stahl & Koser, 1978; Tierney, 2003; Zhou, 2003) and permit the degree of participation and involvement (e.g., Amabile et al., 2004; Choi, 2004; Pelz & Andrews, 1966) conducive to creative discovery. Although autonomy is a requirement for creative action, it is also necessary to have an adequate degree of structure that enables employees to create (Amabile, 1988). An important role for creativity leaders is the provision of such structure (Mumford et al., 2002). Accordingly, a number of studies consider the impact of various forms of leader behaviors such as providing clarification and direction on ill-defined and complex tasks (e.g., Redmond, Mumford, & Teach, 1993) and creating structure specific to dealing with the temporal complexity surrounding creative action and outcomes (e.g., Halbesleben et al., 2003). Another study examined the impact of leader-structuring activities in relation to group processes and their creative output (Marta et al., 2005).

An increasingly popular behavioral area of interest of prevailing studies has been leader "support" as it relates to employee creativity. A recent study (Amabile et al., 2004) cites that certain types of leader behaviors induce employees' perceptions of leader support that is conducive to their subsequent creativity. Mumford et al. (2002) note three main aspects of support to which creativity-effective leaders should attend: idea support, work support, and social support. They reason that for creativity to emerge and maintain in work contexts, employees must perceive and receive support in all three realms in order to be motivated and enabled to create. Related studies have explored a variety of support types on the part of leaders in creativity contexts including behaviors that fall more along the lines of socioemotional support, as well as more instrumental support forms (Amabile et al., 2004) that target technical or task aspects relevant for creativity. Although most studies tend to focus on one type or the other, it appears that, ultimately, both are requisite for creative action among employees (Amabile et al., 2004). Amabile and colleagues (e.g., Amabile, 1988; Amabile, Conti, Coon, Lazenby, & Herron, 1996; Amabile & Gryskiewicz, 1987) have considered leader support in the manner of "supervisory encouragement" that entails facilitating employees with projects, ensuring that employees develop the forms of expertise necessary for creative productivity, as well as taking steps to elicit the intrinsic motivation for creative work.

Other studies focusing more on the interpersonal support side, have found that a leader's demonstrations of empathy and consideration (e.g.,

Amabile et al., 1996; Amabile et al., 2004; Farris, 1988; Frese, Teng, & Wijnen, 1999; Marta et al., 2005; Oldham & Cummings, 1996; Stahl & Koser, 1978; Tierney, 2003) are related to creative output. A study examining the moderating influence of leader support found that when leaders engage in behaviors that are interpersonally sensitive and that elicit employee trust, employees' positive and negative moods interact in relation with employee creativity (George & Zhou, 2007).

Kanter (1988) suggests that engaging in innovative behavior in organizational contexts is a resource-laden activity and one that may be potentially risky for employees. As such, she notes that a prime role of leaders is to provide the resource support as well as the political support that will enable and motivate employees to seek innovative activities in the course of their jobs. Task-specific forms of support would also fall into this category, and studies suggest that the leader's provision of developmental feedback for employees (e.g., George & Zhou, 2007; Zhou, 2003), as well as the provision of adequate information, funding, resources, and task facilitation necessary to create (e.g., Tierney, 2003; Tierney & Farmer, 2004), link to creative performance on the part of employees. Given that creativity often emerges as a result of idea sharing or collaboration, leaders' facilitation of communication and collaboration, and the encouragement of idea sharing among peers also appears relevant for employee creativity (cf. Farris, 1988; Tierney, 2003; Tierney & Farmer, 2004). Although the political side of creative action and the leader's role in navigating employees through the process has received scant research address, a few studies have examined a subset of leader behaviors demonstrating necessary political support and advocacy for employee creativity. For example, study results have shown that when employees report that their leader is willing to support employees when they risk introducing ideas that are "unpopular" (Madjar et al., 2002), and "stand up" for employees' innovative efforts in their work (Tierney & Farmer, 2004), the level of employee creative performance is heightened.

A number of studies have considered the relevance of leader support directly linked to "work ideas," or the actual innovative activities in which employees engage (e.g., Amabile et al., 1996; Frese et al., 1999) in relation to employee creative performance. Madjar et al. (2002) found that various forms of a supervisor's support for creative action such as discussing work-related ideas for improvement or providing feedback on new ideas were associated with the level of creative performance employees exhibited in their work. Likewise, a later study (Janssen, 2005) reports that the extent to which employees' perceived influence at work associated with their innovative behavior was contingent on whether employees felt their leader provided tangible support for their innovative ideas. Baer and Oldham (2006) found that "openness-to-experience" employees were productively creative, despite operating under conditions of moderate stress, when they perceived their leader would support creativity (e.g., support new methods and ways of doing things).

Eminent creators have often benefited from the presence of role models (Mumford & Gustafson, 1988), and those in leadership positions are a likely source of such modeling for creativity and innovation (Mumford et al., 2002). The importance of a leader as a "work" model has been linked to creativity (e.g., Amabile et al., 1996), and forms of modeling behavior more specific to creative action have also been examined (e.g., Jaussi & Dionne, 2003; Tierney, 2003; Tierney & Farmer, 2002, 2004). The association between modeling for creativity and employee creative performance has been explained in terms of vicarious learning and the enhancement of employee confidence and motivation in creative attempts (Shalley & Perry-Smith, 2001; Tierney & Farmer, 2002).

To move employees toward creativity, it is vital that leaders' actions express value and expectations for creative activity and its outcomes (Amabile, 1988). Accordingly, a number of studies have attempted to capture aspects of leader behaviors that encourage creativity among employees. The provision of rewards and recognition reflects appreciation for employee creative effort and results, and studies exist showing that such acknowledgement on the part of the leader is amenable to creative productivity (e.g., Tierney, 2003; Tierney & Farmer, 2002, 2004). Other studies have found both direct effects of the leader's creative performance expectations on employee creativity (Scott & Bruce, 1994), as well as indirect effects via supportive leader behaviors and creative self-efficacy (Tierney & Farmer, 2004). Given the complex and uncertain nature of the creative process, it is also imperative that employees possess a firm sense of confidence and efficacy for creative work (Ford, 1996), and leaders are in a prime role to offer such support. A small set of studies has considered the self-efficacy-enhancing role of leaders in relation to creativity finding that leaders facilitate employees in developing a stronger sense of capacity in their ability to innovate when they engage in problem-solving activities (Redmond et al., 1993) and provide modeling and verbal encouragement for creative efforts (Tierney, 2003; Tierney & Farmer, 2002, 2004). The use of goal setting is another means of expressing creativity-related values and expectations, as well as motivational direction and focus for creative work (Shalley et al.,

2004) and studies have shown that leaders elicit creative action, in part, by encouraging employees to set creativity-specific goals (e.g., Tierney, 2003; Tierney & Farmer, 2004).

With emphasis on intellectual stimulation, vision articulation, role modeling, and transcendence of self-interest, we would expect leaders engaging in transformational leader behaviors to shape creative action at both micro (Shin & Zhou, 2003) and macro levels of the organization (Jung, Chow, & Wu, 2003; Mumford et al., 2002). Some of the earliest work testing the influence of transformational leadership on creativity-related outcomes was conducted by Keller (1992, 1995) who sought to understand how transformational leaders influenced innovative activity in R&D settings. A more recent stream of studies has considered the impact of transformational leadership on the creative processes and outcomes of groups, and on the members operating within the groups (e.g., Jung, 2001). In particular, several studies focusing on computer-mediated groups have approached their examination of leadership from a transformational perspective (e.g., Sosik 1997; Sosik, Kahai, & Avolio 1998, 1999) while taking into consideration factors such as the anonymity of group members during the creative process (Kahai, Sosik, & Avolio, 2003; Sosik, Avolio, & Kahai, 1997) and the availability of performance rewards (Kahai et al., 2003). Overall, research examining transformational leadership and creativity has provided mixed results (Mumford et al., 2002). While some studies have detected a transformational association with creative processes and outcomes (e.g. Sosik, 1997; Sosik et al., 1998), and others failed to detect such creative influence (e.g., Basu & Green, 1997; Jaussi & Dionne, 2003; Kahai et al., 2003), additional studies suggest that transformational leaders may shape creativity under conditions of employee anonymity (Sosik et al., 1999), or that engagement in a subset of transformational behaviors (e.g., inspirational motivation) may be most effective for employee and group creativity (Sosik, Avolio, & Kahai, 1998). Although limited in number, studies have found support for the impact of transformational behaviors of top leaders in terms of providing an innovation-supporting work environment (Howell & Avolio, 1993; Jung et al., 2003) and a sense of work empowerment among employees (Jung et al., 2003) conducive to creativity.

Leader Relations

The third perspective takes the stance that leadership does not exist solely within the leader (e.g., characteristics or behaviors) but is a phenomenon that resides between leader and employee. Such a perspective prompts the question, "How does the relationship a leader shares with an employee influence creative performance?" The relevance of social relations for creative performance has been noted (e.g., Perry-Smith & Shalley, 2003). Kahn (1990) explains the rationale for such relevance noting that strong attachments in the work setting provide employees with "anchoring relationships" that they need to be flexible, risk-taking, and exploratory in their work behaviors. When employees experience strong "caregiving" relationships with leaders, they deal more effectively with uncertainty and have an enhanced sense of immersion in their work conducive to creativity (Kahn, 1998).

Although the impact of the supervisor–employee relation has been investigated extensively in terms of more routine performance, studies have also begun to examine its impact on employee creative performance. A study focusing on relational sets (work and nonwork related) by Madjar et al. (2002) found that the supportive nature of the relationship with the immediate supervisor influenced an employee's creative performance on the job. The leader–member exchange (LMX) theory of leadership focuses on the differential dyadic exchanges or relationships supervisors develop with individual employees. Findings of studies adopting a relational perspective via LMX (Basu & Green, 1997; Scott & Bruce, 1994; Tierney, 1992, 2000; Tierney et al., 1999) indicate that the leader's development of a high-quality relationship with employees moves them to engage in higher levels of creative performance in their work. Given the nature of the LMX, it appears that such dyadic relations may be a natural conduit for employee creative action (Scott & Bruce, 1994; Tierney, 1992, 1999). The tendency to go "above and beyond" routine performance is a noted attribute of high LMX employees (Graen & Scandura, 1987), and they report engaging in more challenging and relevant tasks than their low LMX peers (Liden & Graen, 1980). The concept of challenge has been linked to goals and creative effort (Amabile, 1988), and employees experiencing a certain level of challenge, meaning, and relevance in their work will likely augment the effort extended toward the task necessary for creativity (Amabile, 1988). Indeed, one study found that employees involved in high LMX dyads experienced an empowering sense of impact in their work, which in turn was linked to their creative performance (Tierney, 2000). High levels of support for risk taking, resource provision, rewards, and encouragement endemic to high LMX relations are also present in work contexts receptive to creativity (Amabile, 1988). It is therefore not surprising that high LMX employees perceive that they operate in a context that is supportive of innovative work (cf. Dunegan, Tierney, & Duchon, 1992; Scott & Bruce, 1994; Tierney, 1992). Finally, given the interpersonally supportive nature of high LMX dyads, employees should experience a level of comfort, trust, and security conducive to creative action.

The association between high LMX relations and employee creativity has been evidenced in terms of both direct and indirect effects (cf. Scott & Bruce, 1994; Tierney, 1992, 2000) as well as moderating associations. Tierney et al. (1999) report that employees characterized by an adaptive cognitive style, who were not prone to creative action, engaged in higher levels of creativity when they were involved in a high LMX relationship with their supervisors. A second form of LMX moderation was detected in a study (Van Dyne, Jehn, & Cummings, 2002) examining the association between work and home strain and creative performance. Results indicate that the negative effect of both strain types on creativity was mitigated among high LMX employees, but not among low LMX employees.

THE SPHERE OF LEADER INFLUENCE

In addition to direct effects, it has been cited that leaders are also likely to indirectly influence employee performance via a variety of intervening variables (Likert, 1967). Likewise, because of the complex, social–psychological forces that characterize creative work (Amabile, 1988), it is reasonable to expect the role leaders play in the advent of creative performance to be somewhat intricate. If leaders' influence on creativity can possibly manifest in myriad ways (cf. Choi, 2004), it is important that we delve more deeply into the complex patterns that underlie the leadership–creative relationship. In particular, identification of the mechanisms by which leaders influence creative action is an important step in the evolution of our understanding of how creativity is shaped by social contextual forces. Therefore, the proposed model suggests a number of influence spheres with the potential to mediate leadership and employee creative performance.

Common to contemporary models of employee creativity (cf. Amabile, 1988; Ford, 1996; Woodman et al., 1993) is the idea that elements of cognition, motivation, and capacity come into play for creative engagement at work. Given that employees do not create in isolation, the emergence of creativity requires components of the work environment that mirror these basic facets necessary for creative action (Amabile, 1988). As central members of the work context, leaders have the potential to infuse the environment in which the employee operates with creativity-conducive elements (Amabile et al., 1996; Kanter, 1988) aligned with relevant thought, motivation, and capacity orientations (Amabile, 1988). Gruber (1988) depicts creativity as an expression of intrapersonal "evolving systems" comprised of knowledge, feelings, and purposes that are shaped, in part, by the context. His depiction lays a foundation for examining leadership's role relative to employees' evolving systems of cognition, motivation, and capacity that evoke creative action.

Leadership and Employee Cognition

At its most basic level, creativity entails the cognitive. Prominent approaches to understanding creativity have focused on the discrete cognitive stages associated with the determination of creative solutions. A more recent trend in the cognitive realm has moved researchers to consider additional components of thought that surround employee creativity that go beyond the actual cognitive problem-solving steps. This promising line of research (e.g., Drazin et al., 1999; Ford, 1996) suggests that the decision to engage in creative work entails sophisticated sensemaking activities on the part of the employee regarding a host of factors relevant to creative action in the workplace. Using available data from their work environment, employees partake in interpretive processes that impart meaning to that data. These interpretations lead employees to reach conclusions on issues pivotal to creative engagement such as the appropriateness and acceptance of creative action in the work realm and the likelihood that it will be rewarded (Ford, 1996).

Employee social cognitions and derived meanings are closely aligned with leadership (Gioia & Chittipeddi, 1991), and recent exploratory work suggests that through their behaviors, leaders can influence employee perceptions (Amabile et al., 2004) and sensemaking (Tierney, 2003) tantamount to creative performance. In settings in which creativity is anticipated and required, a crucial role of leaders is engagement in sensemaking and sensegiving activities relevant to innovation (Hill & Levenhagen, 1995). Such activities are meaningful and must take place at multiple levels of the organization. For example, social cues from work-group leaders may shape employee perceptions regarding the organization's orientation toward innovation (e.g., Amabile et al., 1996; Dunegan et al., 1992; Scott & Bruce, 1994; Tierney, 1992) that can determine whether individual creative efforts are activated or inhibited (Ford, 1996). Recent studies also suggest that leader actions at the work-group level prime employees' cognitive frames regarding the extent to which they "see" themselves as having capacity for creativity (Redmond et al. 1993; Tierney & Farmer, 2002, 2004), and the degree to which they believe their leader expects them to be actively creative in their work role (Tierney & Farmer, 2004). At upper levels of the organizational echelons, leaders may set the stage for the creative momentum of their work force through the development of a creativity-consistent vision (Amabile, 1988; Kanter, 1988) providing employees with a mental model for creative efforts and direction (Hill & Levenhagen, 1995). In addition to the provision of this mental model, leaders' public articulation of the vision in a clear and compelling manner will provide a means of sensegiving to employees (Gioia & Chittipeddi, 1991) around activities aligned with creative action (Hill & Levenhagen, 1995). Because sensemaking takes place at various levels of the organization (Drazin et al., 1999; Ford, 1996), examination of leadership from a cognitive perspective must take into account how leaders at multiple levels initiate and manage meaning relative to creative action and how these cognitive processes influence one another within this dynamic system.

Leadership and Employee Motivation

In addition to the necessity of personal motivation, the work context must also have a motivational orientation aligned with creativity before employees will engage in creative performance (Amabile, 1988). It has been suggested that contextual factors, such as leaders, predominantly shape creative performance through intrinsic motivation means (Shalley et al., 2004), and that, specifically, "motivation may be an important mediator of many social influences on creativity" (Amabile, 1996, p. 192). One of the fundamental tenets of leadership study is that leaders have a motivating influence in the workplace (Bass, 1990). Although studies have linked various aspects of leadership with motivation in a general sense, and motivation has been explicitly tied to creative performance (Amabile, 1996), there is a lack of empirical work investigating the role of leaders in the motivation–creativity association.

Motivation can manifest itself in a number of ways and in a number of forms relative to creative performance. Ford (1996) notes that motivation for creative efforts revolves around capacity beliefs, receptivity beliefs, goals, and emotion. Accordingly, leaders who offer extrinsic inducements that validate or support employee confidence trigger a "deeper involvement" in work content or process, and relay receptiveness for innovative work, which should positively impact creativity through motivational means (Amabile, 1988, 1996). This proposition is supported by two studies (Tierney & Farmer, 2002, 2004) finding that the leader's tendency to recognize and provide rewards for creativity efforts and successes enhanced employees' confidence in their creative capacity leading to creative performance. A third study (Choi, 2004) examined what was termed "psychological processes" of creative self-efficacy and creativity intentions as mediators of supportive leadership and creativity. Results show that supportive leadership influenced creative self-efficacy associated with creative performance through an open climate within groups and also led to creativity intention pursuant to employee creativity. Employees' motivational senses of impact or relevance of their task, derived from their relationship with their work-group leader, also demonstrated a mediational effect on the leadership–creative performance association (e.g., Tierney, 2000). The motivational effect of transformational leadership on creativity has been considered. In one lab study (Sosik et al., 1999), subjects working with leaders engaging in transformational behaviors experienced a motivational state of flow conducive to their creativity. The second study took place in a field setting and found that employees working with transformational supervisors reported a greater level of intrinsic motivation, which associated with their creative performance (Shin & Zhou, 2003). The authors suggest that the compilation of intellectual stimulation, role modeling, individualized consideration, and inspirational motivation inherent in transformational leadership, energizes and encourages employees to attempt the conduction of tasks and problem solving in novel ways that challenge the status quo.

Preliminary research also suggests that creativity may be as much an emotional response as a cognitive one. For example, emotional state partially determines the extent to which employees experience a sense of personal "engagement" and extended effort necessary for creative work (Kahn, 1990). Although some evidence suggests that negative mood may stimulate creativity via recognition of the need for "improvement" (cf. George & Zhou, 2002), a fair amount also points to the creativity influence of positive emotion and mood states (e.g., Higgins, Qualls, & Couger, 1992). A recent study (George & Zhou, 2007) actually makes a case for the creativity-inducing role of both mood types, finding that when employees were led in a supportive manner, both positive and negative moods jointly contributed to higher employee creative performance. Leadership's effect on employee emotions is noted explicitly in terms of actions or characteristics of immediate supervisors and implicitly through the structures, processes, and cultures (George & Brief,

1996) that top leaders create. Although an important role of leaders in the work context is the monitoring and regulation of employee emotions that will motivate and shape their creative performance (Higgins et al., 1992), empirical studies accounting for such mediating links are rare. Exceptions are two qualitative field studies in which employees working with supervisors engaging in creativity-supportive behaviors experienced a general sense of positive affect (Amabile et al., 2004) as well as a sense of "affective engagement" (Tierney, 2003) in the context of their creative productivity. In a similar manner, a third study (Madjar et al., 2002) found that employee positive-mood state mediated the relation between creativity support behaviors on the part of their supervisor and the employees' creative performance.

Leadership and Employee Capacity

As part of a personal profile for creativity, employees must possess capacity in two arenas. First, the employee must have an adequate level of skills in his or her task domain (Amabile, 1988). Such skills are considered to be the "raw materials" (Amabile, 1988, p. 131) for creativity and include a strong knowledge base, experience, as well as the requisite set of technical skills specific to the nature of the task at hand. One of the earliest premises of leadership inquiry is that organizational leaders are responsible for developing employees in the fundamentals required to carry out their basic tasks (see Bass, 1990). The establishment of creativity-requisite domain skills and knowledge within employees would entail leaders providing factual knowledge and conveying principles relevant to the paradigm, providing appropriate training, and aligning employee skills and tasks (cf. Amabile, 1988). It is also possible that the provision of appropriate task feedback, noted to influence creativity (e.g., Carson & Carson, 1993), is a mechanism by which leaders can build employee skill and knowledge. Studies (George & Zhou, 2007; Zhou, 2003) examining supervisors' provision of developmental feedback (i.e., learning, development, and performance improvement focused) to employees appears to be a crucial act in fostering employee creativity. In addition, the importance of "practice" and "immersion" in the task domain for creative performance (Weisberg, 1999) suggests that leaders permit employees time and space for task familiarization. Although the positive impact of participatory leadership on employee creativity is suggested to be a function of enhanced motivation (Oldham & Cummings, 1996), the afforded opportunity for employees to develop skills through greater task involvement may also come into play.

In addition to the more general domain skills, employees must also possess adeptness in an array of creativity-relevant skills (Amabile, 1988). Accordingly, research has suggested a number of roles leaders play in moving employees through the appropriate cognitive stages and encouraging them to "think" creatively. Specifically, members of the work environment, such as leaders, have the capacity to influence the problem construction, information gathering, information combination, and implementation stages of the creative problem-solving process (Mumford, Whetzel, & Reiter-Palmon, 1997; Redmond et al., 1993). The way the leader approaches problems with employees (Maier, 1970) and encourages them to suspend judgment (Amabile, 1988) should develop problem-solving skills influential for creativity. The leader's allotment of decision time (Mumford et al., 1997; Redmond et al., 1993) and appropriate information (Mumford et al., 1997) could also influence the employees' use of creativity skills and the degree of creativity exhibited in their solutions. At a more macro level, the implementation of information systems is a means by which top leaders can facilitate creativity problem-solving skills used by employees (Mumford et al., 1997). For example, study results suggest that in electronic meeting systems scenarios, the leader's use of a participative style results in the generation of a greater number of solutions when employees are faced with a somewhat unstructured problem (cf. Kahai, Sosik, & Avolio, 1997).

SUGGESTIONS FOR FUTURE INQUIRY

Examination of the proposed leadership–creativity framework in light of existing research suggests a number of potential directions for future research. The general dearth of empirical work focused on specific aspects of top leaders who influence employee creativity suggests that additional investigation at this level is warranted. Possible examinations may consider how executives' dispositional traits and behaviors manifest in terms of structure and processes that stimulate or discourage the presiding sensemaking, motivation to create, or use of creativity-relevant skills. For example, intellectual stimulation is a core facet of transformational leadership that ideally should discourage "habitual followership" (Graham, 1987). However, top leaders exhibit different intellectual styles dictating their orientation toward organizational problem solving that may range from creative exploration to an emphasis more aligned with speed, efficiency, and consistency (Quinn & Hall, 1983). It is likely that the former style would be more conducive to the development and use of creativity skills on the part of employees, while the latter seems more consistent with the reliance of established algorithms and procedures.

Although a decent amount of research has focused on work-group leaders in relation to creative performance, the proposed model points to a number of untapped lines of investigation that might be worthwhile. For example, high LMX relations drive employees to seek challenging and nonroutine tasks, and dyadic leaders provide resources and interpersonal support (Duchon, Green, & Tabor, 1986; Liden & Graen, 1980) consistent with the basic elements of capacity and motivation for creative behavior. These relations also implicitly encompass a reciprocal sensemaking component by which leader and employee come to a shared understanding of their relational roles (cf. Graen & Scandura, 1987). Because innovative behavior is considered part of the high LMX "coupling process" (Graen & Scandura, 1987), creative work should be seen as role-appropriate scripted behavior by high LMX behaviors. Thus, future work should further examine LMX in terms of its ability to serve as a motivating, enabling, and interpretive force for employee creativity.

There is also a need for more sophisticated understanding of the complex ways in which work-group supervisors' attributes influence employee creativity. Research on supervisor characteristics such as risk-seeking propensity, openness to experience, innovative cognitive style, and intrinsic drive for creativity may be useful in this regard. Leaders possessing these characteristics may serve as role models who influence salience and engender enthusiasm for creative achievement within their work groups. They are also more likely to build creative capacity and efficacy in employees through guidance and personal demonstration of creative behavior, and by encouraging experimentation and creative practice. An emerging area of research focuses on employee self-concept (cf. Farmer, Tierney, & Kung-McIntyre, 2003) in relation to creative performance. Given that both are functions of social influences, it may be worthwhile to consider the role leaders play in creativity-related self-concept formulation.

If creativity is partially a function of employee mood, then organizations need to identify both "enhancement mechanisms," to increase desired affect, and "suppression mechanisms," for lessening undesired affect (Cropanzano, Weiss, Hale, & Reb, 2003). An interesting research question would be if and how leaders serve to enhance creativity-consistent mood and conversely what they do to suppress it. Since there is the possibility of a contagion effect whereby leaders' moods influence the mood, affect, and processes of their work groups (Sy, Cote, & Saavedra, 2004), consideration of leader mood in future studies may be of benefit.

Recent work has brought to our attention different forms or types of creativity (e.g., Unsworth, 2001), and the need to take such differences into account in our research. Creativity leadership may "look" different depending on the type of creativity that is prevalent (Sternberg et al., 2003), and it is feasible that leading employees for various creativity types may require correspondingly various characteristics and behaviors on the part of creativity leaders. Therefore, researchers need to carefully consider the type of creativity being examined in order to more accurately formulate conclusions regarding the role of leadership for creativity.

From reviewing the body of research that has been conducted, it is apparent that a diverse and disparate set of leader behaviors has been examined in terms of creativity, including behavioral approaches that have traditionally been linked to routine employee performance. Creativity is a complex and unique form of performance, and leading for such requires a form of leadership specific to the nature of creativity (Mumford et al., 2002). Exploration into the existence and nature of a leadership profile specific to creativity could be beneficial in advancing our understanding of how individuals lead for creativity. Correspondingly, it would be useful if researchers had a measure of leadership specific to creative performance. To date, prior studies have approached leadership and its measurement in creativity studies from the perspective of existing leadership paradigms (e.g., LMX) that have related to employee routine performance. Preliminary work conducted into the nature (Tierney, 2003) and measure (Tierney & Farmer, 2003) of creativity leadership suggests that a leadership specific to creativity may exist in a superordinate, multidimensional form that relates to employee states of sensemaking, affective engagement, and creative capacity. Additional exploration into the nature of creativity leadership and its operationalization is fundamental to achieving a clear and accurate understanding of how we develop and support leaders for creativity within the workplace.

Although much of the early research examining creativity leadership took place in work contexts (e.g., R&D) and among job types (e.g., scientists) (see Elkins & Keller, 2003 for review) that supplied a "natural" setting for delineating invaluable aspects of creative work performance, we have also witnessed an emergence of studies taking place in settings that might be considered "counterproductive" for creative performance such as manufacturing sites (cf. Madjar et al., 2002; Oldham &

Cummings, 1994; Tierney & Farmer, 2002). An interesting aspect of these studies is that they highlight the fact that creativity is no longer limited to the activity domain of R&D, but that it is taking place and is required across a diversity of organizational and job types. A recent study (Tierney & Farmer, 2002) examined creative performance across two diverse organizations and found that the pattern of personal and contextual factors associated with employee creativity differed in the two setting types. Further research exploring the nature of creativity leadership in diverse work settings and among diverse job types would be instrumental in facilitating managers in their quest to foster creativity in contexts in which creative performance is increasingly relevant, but has not traditionally been the norm.

Various aspects of coworkers and teams have been examined from a creativity perspective (e.g., George & Zhou, 2001; Zhou & George, 2001; Taggar, 2002), and additional work is needed. For example, although both coworkers and supervisors have the capacity to influence employee creativity, it is not clear whether they operate in this regard in the same manner, and which is ultimately most influential. The suggestion that creativity-supportive actions of individual supervisors may somehow influence the emergence of a team level of creativity leadership (Tierney & Farmer, 2006) also should lead us to consider more closely how, and under what conditions, such emergence might take place.

In addition to addressing the varying levels, facets, and spheres of leadership in relation to creativity, future research should be directed toward delineating the ways in which employees, in their orientation toward, and participation in, creative action, shape organizational leadership over time. Failure to recognize the reciprocal association between leadership and employee creativity will result in a more static and less accurate portrayal of the dynamics surrounding the emergence of creativity in the workplace. Sorting out the nature of dynamics among leaders and employees will likely require a broader set of methods than most leadership–creativity studies have used to date. The use of qualitative means such as in-depth interviews, observational techniques, and case studies would be instrumental in providing a rich, descriptive view into the nature of creativity leadership, and longitudinal study designs will permit insight into the intricacies of creativity leadership and how it is shaped, and shapes, over time and events.

In addition to the growing need to attend to innovation, a second organizational reality is the "global face" of business with an increasing number of multinational corporations evidenced and the growing trend toward outsourcing of relevant functional activities related to innovation such as design, and research, and development. Studies considering creativity in non-U.S. settings have begun to explore how work context and personal factors come into play (e.g., Farmer et al., 2003), but few studies (for exception, see Shin & Zhou, 2003) have explicitly considered the role of leadership for creativity in such settings. As such, it appears that it may be fortuitous for researchers to explore what it means to lead for creativity from a more global perspective, and in a variety of relevant cultures.

CONCLUDING REMARKS

Leaders have traditionally been a resource organization's tap to foster a variety of outcomes necessary for corporate maintenance and survival. With the dynamic and competitive environment in which contemporary organizations operate, the notion of "creativity as a necessity" has become rapidly apparent to an increasing number and diverse type of corporations. The substantial number of leader-focused creativity studies that have taken place in the last decade reflect the recognition, by both researchers and practitioners, that leaders may be quite instrumental in advancing the creative aspirations of contemporary corporations. Although we have made impressive strides in terms of our body of knowledge regarding creativity leadership, the field of inquiry is still in a relatively nascent stage and as the current model and matrix suggest, considering research to date, there remain a number of intriguing and useful paths for further consideration.

REFERENCES

Amabile, T. M. (1988). A model of creativity and innovation in organizations. In B. M. Staw & L. L. Cummings (Eds.), *Research in Organizational Behavior, 10,* 123–167.

Amabile, T. M. (1996). *Creativity in context.* Boulder, CO: Westview Press.

Amabile, T. M., Conti, R., Coon, H., Lazenby, J., & Herron, M. (1996). Assessing the work environment for creativity. *Academy of Management Journal, 39,* 1154–1184.

Amabile, T. M. Gryskiewicz, S. S. (1987). Creativity in the R&D laboratory. *Technical Report No. 30* (May), Greensboro, North Carolina: Center for Creative Leadership.

Amabile, T. F., Schatzel, E. A., Moneta, G. B., & Kramer, S. J. (2004). Leader behaviors and the work environment for creativity: Perceived leader support. *Leadership Quarterly, 15,* 5–32.

Andrews, F. M. (1967). Supervisory practices and innovation in scientific teams. *Personnel Psychology, 20,* 497–515.

Baer, M., & Oldham, G. R. (2006). The curvilinear relation between experienced creative time pressure and creativity: Moderating effects of openness to experience and support for creativity. *Journal of Applied Psychology, 91*, 963–970.

Basadur, M. (2004). Leading others to think innovatively together: Creative leadership. *Leadership Quarterly, 15*, 103–122.

Bass, B. M. (Ed.). (1990). *Bass & Stodgill's handbook of leadership: Theory, research, and managerial applications* (3rd ed.). New York: Free Press.

Basu, R., & Green, S. G. (1997). Leader-member exchange and transformational leadership: An empirical examination of innovative behaviors in leader-member dyads. *Journal of Applied Social Psychology, 27*, 477–499.

Carson, P. P., & Carson, K. D. (1993). Managing creativity enhancement through goal setting and feedback. *Journal of Creative Behavior, 27*, 36–45.

Choi, J. N. (2004). Individual and contextual predictors of creative performance: The mediating role of psychological processes. *Creativity Research Journal, 16*, 187–199.

Cropanzano, R., Weiss, H. M., Hale, J. M. S., & Reb, J. (2003). *Journal of Management, 29*, 831–857.

Dougherty, D., & Heller, T. (1994). The illegitimacy of successful product innovation in established firms. *Organization Science, 5*, 200–218.

Drazin, R., Glynn, M. A., & Kazanjian, R. K. (1999). Multilevel theorizing about creativity in organizations: A sensemaking perspective. *Academy of Management Review, 24*, 286–307.

Duchon, D. G., Green, S., & Taber, T. D. (1986). Vertical dyad linkage: A longitudinal assessment of antecedents, measures, and consequences. *Journal of Applied Psychology, 71, 56–60.*

Dunegan, K. J., Tierney, P., & Duchon, D. (1992). Toward an understanding of innovation climate: Explaining variance in perceptions by divisional affiliation, work group interactions, and subordinate-manager exchanges. *IEEE Transactions on Engineering Management, 39*, 227–236.

Elkins, T. & Keller, R. T. (2003). Leadership in research and development organizations: A literature review and conceptual framework. *Leadership Quarterly, 14:* 587–606.

Farmer, S. M., Tierney, P., & Kung-McIntyre, K. (2003). Employee creativity in Taiwan: An application of role identity theory. *Academy of Management Journal, 46,* 618–630.

Farris, G. F. (1988). Technical leadership: Much discussed but little understood. *Research Technology Management, 31,* 12–16.

Ford, C. (1996). A theory of individual creative action in multiple social domains. *Academy of Management Review, 21*, 1112–1142.

Frese, M., Teng, E., & Wijnen, C. J. (1999). Helping to improve suggestion systems: Predictors of making suggestions in companies. *Journal of Organizational Behavior, 20*, 1139–1155.

George, J. M., & Brief, A. P. (1996). Motivational agendas in the workplace. *Research in Organizational Behavior, 18*, 75–109.

George, J. M., & Zhou, J. (2001). When openness to experience and conscientiousness are related to creative behavior: An interactional approach. *Journal of Applied Psychology, 86*, 513–524.

George, J. M., & Zhou, J. (2002). Understanding when bad moods foster creativity and good ones don't: The role of context and clarity of feelings. *Journal of Applied Psychology, 87,* 687–697.

George, J. M., & Zhou, J. (2007). Dual tuning in a supportive context: Joint contributions of positive mood, negative mood, and supervisory behaviors to employee creativity. *Academy of Management Journal.*

Gibson, F. W., Fiedler, F. E., & Barrett, K. M. (1993). Stress, babble, and the utilization of the leader's intellectual ability. *Leadership Quarterly, 4,* 189–208.

Gioia, D. A., & Chittipeddi, K. (1991). Sensemaking and sensegiving in strategic change initiation. *Strategic Management Journal, 12.* 433–448.

Graen, G. B., & Scandura, T. A. (1987). Toward a psychology of dyadic organizing. In L. L. Cummings & B. M. Staw (Eds.), *Research in Organizational Behavior, 9,* 175–208.

Graham, J. W. (1997). The essence of leadership: Fostering follower autonomy, not automatic leadership. In J. G. Hunt (Ed.), *Emerging Leadership Vistas.* Elmsford, NY: Pergamon.

Gronn, P. (2002). Distributed leadership as a unit of analysis. *Leadership Quarterly, 13,* 423–451.

Gruber, H. E. (1988). The evolving systems approach to creative work. *Creativity Research Journal, 1,* 27–59.

Halbesleben, J. R. B., Novicevic, M. M., Harvey, M. G., & Buckley, M. R. (2003). Awareness of temporary complexity in leadership of creativity and innovation: A competency-based model. *Leadership Quarterly, 14,* 433–454.

Higgins, L. F., Qualls, S. H., & Couger, J. D. (1992). The role of emotions in employee creativity. *Journal of Creative Behavior, 26,* 119–129.

Hill, R. C., & Levenhagen, M. (1995). Metaphors and mental models: Sensemaking and sensegiving in innovative and entrepreneurial activities. *Journal of Management, 6,* 1057–1074.

Howell, J. M., & Avolio, B. J. (1993). Transformational leadership, Transactional leadership, locus of control and support for innovation: Key predictors of consolidated-business-unit performance. *Journal of Applied Psychology, 78,* 891–902.

Howell, J. M., & Boies, K. (2004). Champions of technological innovation: The influence of contextual knowledge, role orientation, idea generation, and idea promotion on champion emergence. *Leadership Quarterly, 15,* 123–144.

Hunt, J. G., Stelluto, G. E., & Hooijberg, R. (2004). Toward new-wave organization creativity: Beyond romance and analogy in the relationship between orchestra-conductor leadership and musician creativity. *Leadership Quarterly, 15,* 145–162.

Janssen, O. (2005). The joint impact of perceived influence and supervisor supportiveness on employee innovative behavior. *Journal of Occupational and Organizational Psychology, 78,* 573–579.

Jaussi, K. S., & Dionne, S. D. 2003. Leading for creativity: The role of unconventional leader behavior. *Leadership Quarterly, 14,* 475–498.

Jung, D. I. 2001. Transformational and transactional leadership and their effects on creativity in groups. *Creativity Research Journal, 13,* 185–195.

Jung, D. I., Chow, C., & Wu, A. (2003). The role of transformational leadership in enhancing organizational innovation: Hypotheses and some preliminary findings. *Leadership Quarterly, 14,* 525–544.

Kahai, S. S., Sosik, J. J., & Avolio, B. J. (1997). Effects of leadership style and problem structure on work group processes and outcomes in an electronic meeting system environment. *Personnel Psychology, 50,* 121–146.

Kahai, S. S., Sosik, J. J., & Avolio, B. J. (2003). Effects of leadership style, anonymity, and rewards on creativity-relevant processes and outcomes in an electronic meeting system context. *Leadership Quarterly, 14,* 499–524.

Kahn, W. A. (1990). Psychological conditions of personal engagement and disengagement at work. *Academy of Management Journal, 33,* 539–563.

Kahn, W. A. (1998). Relational systems at work. *Research in Organizational Behavior, 20,* 39–76.

Kanter, R. M. (1988). When a thousand flowers bloom: Collective and social conditions for innovation in organizations. In B. M. Staw & L. L. Cummings (Eds.), *Research in Organizational Behavior, 10,* 169–211.

Keller, R. (1992). Transformational leadership and the performance of research and development project groups. *Journal of Management, 18,* 489–501.

Keller, R. (1995). Transformational leaders make a difference. *Research Technology Management, 38,* 41–44.

Kirton, M. J., (1976). Adaptors and innovators: A description and measure. *Journal of Applied Psychology, 61,* 622–629.

Kozlowski, S. W., & Klein, K. J. (2000). A multi-level approach to theory and research in organizations: Contextual, temporal, and emergent processes. In K. J. Klein and S. W. Kozlowski (Eds.), *Multilevel theory, research and methods in organizations: Foundations, extensions, and new directions* (pp. 3–90). San Francisco: Jossey-Bass.

Krause, D. E. (2004). Influence-based leadership as a determinant of the inclination to innovate and of innovation-related behaviors: An empirical investigation. *Leadership Quarterly, 15,* 79–102.

Liden, R. C., & Graen, G. B. (1980). Generalizability of the vertical dyad linkage model of leadership. *Academy of Management Journal, 23,* 451–465.

Likert, R. (1967). *The human organization: Its management and value.* New York: McGraw-Hill.

Madjar, N., Oldham G. R., & Pratt, M. G. (2002). There's no place like home? The contributions of work and non-work creativity support to employees' creative performance. *Academy of Management Journal, 45,* 757–767.

Maier, N. R. (1970). *Problem-solving and creativity: In groups and individuals.* Belmont, CA: Brooks/Cole.

Marta, S., Leritz, L. E., & Mumford, M. D. (2005). Leadership skills and the group performance: Situational demands, behavioral requirements, and planning. *Leadership Quarterly, 16,* 97–120.

Mowday, R. T., & Sutton, R. I. (1993). Organizational behavior: Linking individuals and groups to organizational contexts. *Annual Review of Psychology, 44,* 195–229.

Mumford, M. D., (Ed.) (2003). Special Issue: Part I Leading for innovation. *Leadership Quarterly, 14.*

Mumford, M. D., (Ed.) (2004). Special Issue: Part II Leading for innovation. *Leadership Quarterly, 15.*

Mumford, M. D., & Gustafson, S. B. (1988). Creativity syndrome: Integration, application, and innovation. *Psychological Bulletin, 103,* 27–43.

Mumford, M. D., Scott, G. M., Gaddis, B. H., & Strange, J. M. (2002). Leading creative people: Orchestrating expertise and relationships. *Leadership Quarterly, 13,* 705–750.

Mumford, M. D., Whetzel, D. L., & Reiter-Palmon, R. (1997). Thinking creatively at work: Organizational influences on creative problem-solving. *Journal of Creative Behavior, 31,* 7–17.

Oldham, G. R., & Cummings, A. (1996). Employee creativity: Personal and contextual factors at work. *Academy of Management Journal, 39,* 607–634.

Pelz, D. C., & Andrews, F. M. (1966). *Scientists in organizations.* New York: Wiley.

Perry-Smith, J. E., & Shalley, C. E. (2003). The social side of creativity: A static and dynamic social network perspective. *Academy of Management Review, 28,* 89–106.

Quinn, R. E., & Hall, R. H. Environments, organizations, and policy makers: Towards and integrated framework. In R. H. Hall and R. E. Quinn (Eds.), *Organization theory and public policy: Contributions and limitations.* Beverly Hills, CA: Sage.

Redmond, M. R., Mumford, M. D., & Teach, R. (1993). Putting creativity to work: Effects of leader behavior on employee creativity. *Organizational Behavior and Human Decision Processes, 55,* 120–151.

Reiter-Palmon, R., & Illies, J. J. (2004). Leadership and creativity: Understanding leadership from a creative problem-solving perspective. *Leadership Quarterly, 15,* 55–78.

Scott, S. G., & Bruce, R. A. (1994). Determinants of innovative behavior: A path model of individual innovation in the workplace. *Academy of Management Journal, 37,* 580–607.

Shalley, C. E., & Gilson, L. L. (2004). What leaders need to know: A review of social and contextual factors that can foster or hinder creativity. *Leadership Quarterly, 15,* 33–54.

Shalley, C. E., Gilson, L. L., & Blum, T. C. (2000). Matching creativity requirements and the work environment: Effects on satisfaction and intentions to leave. *Academy of Management Journal, 43,* 215–223.

Shalley, C. E., & Perry-Smith, J. E. (2001). Effects of social–psychological factors on creative performance: The role of informational and controlling expected evaluation and modeling experience. *Organizational Behavior and Human Decision Processes, 84,* 1–22.

Shalley, C. E., Zhou, J., & Oldham, G. R. (2004). The effects of personal and contextual characteristics on creativity: Where should we go from here? *Journal of Management, 30,* 933–958.

Shin, S. J., & Zhou, J. (2003). Transformational leadership, conservation, and creativity: Evidence from Korea. *Academy of Management Journal, 46,* 703–714.

Sosik, J. M. (1997). Effects of transformational leadership and anonymity on idea generation in computer-mediated groups. *Group and Organization Management, 22,* 460–487.

Sosik, J. J., Avolio, B. J., & Kahai, S. S. (1997). Effects of leadership style and anonymity on group potency and effectiveness in a group decision support system environment. *Journal of Applied Psychology, 82*, 89–103.

Sosik, J. M., Avolio, B. J., & Kahai, S. S. (1998). Inspiring group creativity: Comparing anonymous and identified electronic brainstorming. *Small Group Research, 29*, 3–31.

Sosik, J. M., Kahai, S. S., & Avolio, B. J. (1998). Transformational leadership and dimensions of creativity: Motivating idea generation in computer-mediated groups. *Creativity Research Journal, 11*, 111–122.

Sosik, J. M., Kahai, S. S., & Avolio, B. J. (1999). Leadership style, anonymity, and creativity in group decision support systems: The mediating role of optimal flow. *Journal of Creative Behavior, 33*, 227–257.

Sparrowe, R. T., & Liden, R. C. (1997). Process and structure in leader–member exchange. *Academy of Management Review, 22*, 522–552.

Stahl, M. J., & Koser, M. C. (1978). Weighted productivity in R&D: Some associated individual and organizational variables. *IEEE Transaction on Engineering Management, 25*, 20–24.

Sternberg, R. J., Kaufman, J. C., & Pretz, J. E. (2003). A propulsion model of creative leadership. *Leadership Quarterly, 14*, 455–474.

Sy, T., Cote, S., & Saavedra, R. (2005). The contagious leader: Impact of leader's mood on the mood of group members, group affective tone, and group processes. *Journal of Applied Psychology, 90*, 295–305.

Taggar, S. (2002). Individual creativity and group ability to utilize individual creative resources: A multilevel model. *Academy of Management Journal, 45*, 315–330.

Tierney, P. (1992). The contribution of leadership, supportive environment, and individual attributes to creative performance. Unpublished dissertation, University of Cincinnati.

Tierney, P. (1999). Work relations as a precursor to a psychological climate for change: The role of work group supervisors and peers. *Journal of Organizational Change Management, 12*, 120–133.

Tierney, P. (2000). The mediating role of psychological empowerment for employee creativity. Paper presented at the National Society of Industrial and Organizational Psychology meeting, San Diego, CA.

Tierney, P. (2003). Exploring the nature of creativity leadership and its effects: A qualitative field examination (working paper). Portland State University.

Tierney, P., & Farmer, S. M. (2002). Creative self-efficacy: Potential antecedents and relationship to creative performance. *Academy of Management Journal, 45*, 1137–1148.

Tierney, P., & Farmer, S. M. (2003). Leading for creativity: Development of the Creativity Leadership Index (CLI). Paper presented at the National Academy of Management meeting, Seattle, WA.

Tierney, P., & Farmer, S. M. (2004). The Pygmalion process and employee creativity. *Journal of Management, 30*, 413–432.

Tierney, P., & Farmer, S. M. (2006). A multi-level perspective on leading for creativity. Paper presented at the national meeting of the Academy of Management, Atlanta, GA.

Tierney, P., Farmer, S. M., & Graen, G. B. (1999). An examination of leadership and employee creativity: The relevance of traits and relationships. *Personnel Psychology, 52,* 591–620.

Unsworth, K. (2001). Unpacking creativity. *Academy of Management Journal, 26,* 289–297.

Van Dyne, L., Jehn, K. A., & Cummings, A. (2002). Differential effects of strain on two forms of work performance: Individual employee sales and creativity. *Journal of Organizational Behavior, 23,* 57–74.

Weisberg, R. W. (1999). Creativity and knowledge: A challenge to theories. In R. J. Sternberg (Ed.), *Handbook of Creativity*: 226–250. New York: Cambridge University Press.

Woodman, R. W., Sawyer, J. E., & Griffin, R. W. (1993). Toward a theory of organizational creativity. *Academy of Management Journal, 18,* 293–321.

Yammarino, F. J., Dionne, S. D., Chun, J. U., & Dansereau, F. (2005). Leadership and levels of analysis: A state-of-the-science review. *Leadership Quarterly, 16,* 879–919.

Zhou, J. (1998). Feedback valence, feedback style, task autonomy, and achievement orientation: Interactive effects on creative of performance. *Journal of Applied Psychology, 83,* 261–276.

Zhou, J. (2003). When the presence of creative coworkers is related to creativity: Role of supervisor close monitoring, developmental feedback, and creative personality. *Journal of Applied Psychology, 88,* 413–422.

Zhou, J. & George, J. M. (2001). When job dissatisfaction leads to creativity: Encouraging the expression of voice. *Academy of Management Journal, 44,* 682–696.

Zhou, J., & George, J. M. (2003). Awakening employee creativity: The role of leader emotional intelligence. *Leadership Quarterly, 14,* 545–568.

CHAPTER 5

Promoting Creativity through Feedback

Jing Zhou
Rice University

INTRODUCTION

The partnership between feedback and creativity seems to be an unlikely event. On the one hand, feedback is widely used and commonly seen in the workplace. On the other hand, creativity is usually construed as a highly desirable but often elusive phenomenon in work organizations. Because feedback is so common and creativity seems to be so uncommon, it might be difficult to imagine that organizations can actually use feedback to promote creativity. In this chapter, I review research findings in the field of organizational behavior that provide preliminary but exciting support to the notion that creativity can be enhanced through feedback.

Indeed, one of the motivational strategies and behavioral modification tools that are most frequently used in organizations is feedback (Ilgen, Fisher, & Taylor, 1979). Contemporary research has shown that feedback can have a powerful impact on individuals' creative performance (Farr & Ford, 1990; George & Zhou, 2001; Zhou, 1998a; Zhou & George, 2001). Despite the ever-increasing research interests on the relation between feedback and creativity and its potential practical significance with regard to managing for creativity in organizations, there has not been a focused effort in providing a comprehensive conceptual framework that would summarize what we know about effects of feedback on creativity, and, more importantly, what future research needs to focus on. The goal of this chapter is to fill this void.

In this chapter, I will review representative theory and research concerning feedback and creativity, propose future research directions in this area, and discuss implications of research results for management practices. More specifically, I will first explore the psychological processes (e.g., intrinsic motivation, mood states, understanding of standards, and acquisition of skills and strategies) that are responsible for the impact of feedback on creativity. Next, I will address issues related to the nature of the feedback itself (i.e., feedback valence and feedback style, developmental orientation, and person-focused versus task-focused feedback), characteristics of the feedback recipient (i.e., achievement motivation, power motivation, and emotional intelligence), and characteristics of the feedback giver (i.e., knowledge and experiences, seniority and status). Finally, I will also discuss a number of emerging issues in this area, with an emphasis on feedback delivered at multiple levels of analysis (i.e., from a single feedback giver versus aggregated from a group of people). It is the goal of this chapter to highlight research findings on the effects of feedback on creativity, stimulate more research on this topic, and inform management practitioners on what we currently know with regard to how to use feedback to enhance employee creativity, and what not to do to undermine creativity. Figure 5.1 depicts a model that describes relationships among the key variables discussed in this chapter.

The focus of this chapter is on effects of actual feedback on creativity because the complexity and richness of this topic demand a chapter's space to provide a detailed and nuanced treatment. However, research on effects of expected evaluation on creativity could also be relevant. Thus, while presenting theoretical arguments and reviewing empirical studies of actual feedback, I will briefly mention relevant studies on expected evaluation. For more detailed information on research concerning expected evaluation and creativity, the interested reader is referred to more comprehensive reviews of the creativity literature (Shalley, Zhou, & Oldham, 2004; Zhou & Shalley, 2003).

WHY MAY FEEDBACK FACILITATE CREATIVITY?

In contemporary management research, the constructs of creativity and creative performance have been used interchangeably. They are defined as employees' generation of novel and useful ideas concerning products, services, procedures, and processes at work (Amabile, 1988; Oldham & Cummings, 1996). Both novelty and usefulness are necessary conditions for an idea or solution to be judged creative. Whereas traditionally only scientists, research engineers, and artists are considered

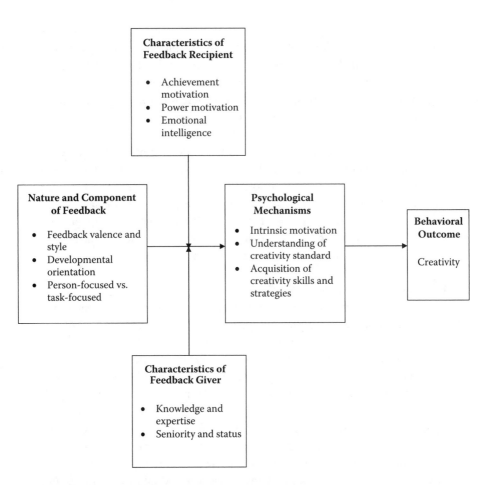

Figure 5.1 A model of effects of feedback on creativity.

creativity-relevant employees, more recently researchers have argued that creativity is desirable and possible in employees holding a wide variety of jobs. For example, an assembly line worker can exhibit creative performance by coming up with a new idea that improves the work process. As another example, a nurse can propose a new way of simultaneously dealing with the nurse shortage crisis in his or her hospital and improve the quality of patient care.

This broader and more inclusive definition of creativity is a reflection of the changing nature of work and business environment. Today, work is much less rigidly defined and specified, business competition is much more intense, and the business environment is much more uncertain. To survive, adapt, and gain competitive advantage, organizations need to fully take advantage of their employees' creative potential because employees' creative ideas can be used as building blocks for organizational innovation, change, and competitiveness (Amabile, 1988; Oldham & Cummings, 1996; Woodman, Sawyer, & Griffin, 1993). Before discussing various components of feedback and their relations with creativity, it is necessary to answer the question of why creativity-related feedback can have direct or indirect impact on employee creativity. Essentially, there are four key reasons that explain why providing employees with creativity-relevant feedback could facilitate their creativity. These reasons include (a) feedback can boost the recipient's intrinsic motivation; (b) feedback can affect employees' mood states; (c) feedback can clarify standards of creative output for the feedback recipient; and (d) feedback can facilitate the recipient's acquisition of creativity-relevant skills and strategies. Here I discuss each of these reasons.

Feedback and Intrinsic Motivation

Much of the recent research on creativity has relied on an intrinsic motivation framework (Amabile, 1996), and research concerning feedback and creativity is no exception (e.g., Zhou, 1998a). According to this framework, an individual's motivation to perform a task can be intrinsic or extrinsic in nature (Deci & Ryan, 1985). In general, an extrinsically motivated individual performs a task in order to get something else, such as contingent rewards. He or she may be able to exhibit high productivity on well-structured (algorithmic) tasks, but not on ill-structured (heuristic) tasks (McGraw, 1978) that may result in creative performance. This is because heuristic tasks require close attention and great cognitive effort to focus on the task itself and often demand adopting or creating solutions in an unconventional way.

Intrinsic motivation refers to the motivational state in which an individual is attracted to and energized by the task itself, instead of by some external outcomes that might be obtained through doing the task. In other words, the individual sees the process of doing the task as an end of itself, rather than as a means to an end (Deci & Ryan, 1985). An intrinsically motivated individual tends to be cognitively more flexible (McGraw & Fiala, 1982; McGraw & McCullers, 1979), to prefer complexity and novelty (Pittman, Emergy, & Boggiano, 1982), and to seek higher levels of challenge and mastery experience (Boggiano, Ruble, & Pittman, 1982; Pittman et al., 1982). Therefore, he or she is more likely to find many alternatives to solve a problem, to use nontraditional approaches, and to be persistent. All of these arguments suggest that an intrinsically motivated individual is more likely to exhibit high creativity.

In sum, intrinsic motivation is critical for creative work. Creativity is most likely to result from strong interests in the tasks that employees engage in, and from employees' being persistent and hard working. As described in more detail later in this chapter, appropriately designed and delivered feedback can boost individuals' intrinsic motivation, and consequently, facilitate their creative performance.

Feedback as a Source of Standard in Judging Creative Work

Another reason that feedback may boost creativity is that it can provide standards to help employees judge whether an idea or product is truly creative. Because creativity concerns with producing new and useful ideas or coming with something novel and worthwhile, it is often difficult to determine the extent to which an idea or approach is creative (Zhou, 1998b). This is especially true for employees who do not have much experience in producing creative ideas or outputs (Zhou, 2003). Hence, feedback can serve as a valuable source of information that helps the feedback recipient to learn, understand, and internalize standards for creative work (e.g., what kind of work is of high level of creativity and what kind of work is simply bizarre—unusual but not valuable or practical, which means it is of low level of creativity).

Feedback and Acquisition of Creativity Skills and Strategies

Zhou (2003) suggests that feedback facilitate the acquisition of creativity-relevant skills and strategies. Building on Amabile's (1996) notion that creativity-relevant skills and strategies are necessary ingredients for creativity and on Hayes' (1989) description of creative process (i.e., while engaging in creative activities, one needs to identify a problem, generate ideas, and evaluate and refine the ideas so that the final idea or solution is truly new and useful), Zhou suggests that possessing creativity-relevant skills and strategies increases the likelihood that one identifies the right problem, generates a variety of ideas, and uses appropriate standards to evaluate and refine the ideas. Thus, although intrinsic motivation is critical, it is not the only ingredient necessary for creativity. Especially for ordinary employees whose jobs do not revolve around creativity and who do not have a great deal of experience in generating creative ideas at work, they need to possess creativity skills and strategies in order to come up with truly new and useful ideas (Amabile, 1988, 1996; Shalley & Perry-Smith, 2001; Zhou, 2003).

THE MULTIDIMENSIONAL NATURE
OF CREATIVITY-RELATED FEEDBACK

Although it is possible to promote creativity through feedback, it would be naïve to think that this can be done easily and straightforwardly. How effectively can we use feedback in promoting creativity depends on the nature and components of the feedback itself, on the characteristics of the feedback recipient, and on the characteristics of the feedback giver. Together, these three aspects determine how successfully feedback can be used to facilitate the feedback recipient's creative performance. Now I turn to a discussion on each of these three aspects of the multidimensional feedback process.

The Nature and Components of Feedback

Feedback Valence and Style

Zhou (1998a) defines feedback valence as the positive or negative outcome of the comparison between an individual's creativity and normative or situational criteria. If the comparison indicates that the individual's ideas are more creative than the criteria, the feedback valence would be positive. If the comparison shows that the ideas are less creative than the criteria, the feedback valence would be negative.

In addition to feedback valence, Zhou (1998a) argues that creativity-related feedback has another distinct component—feedback style. The concept of feedback style is important because people do not necessarily perceive and interpret the feedback they receive in a straightforward manner. Rather, depending on the style in which a feedback is delivered, the recipient may or may not choose to listen to and respond to it. Zhou's argument concerning the joint effects of feedback valence and style is based on the intrinsic motivation framework (Amabile, 1996) mentioned earlier in this chapter.

More specifically, Zhou (1998a) defines feedback style as the manner in which feedback is delivered. Feedback style can be either informational or controlling. Feedback delivered in an informational style is not restrictive or constraining, nor does it impose the feedback giver's will or wishes on the feedback recipient. Instead, when it is used to deliver feedback, the informational style suggests that the feedback recipient is in control of his or her own behaviors and the external feedback provider's goal is simply to help the feedback recipient to learn and develop his or her creative capabilities and creative performance. Because of the nature of informational feedback, the recipient tends to feel the feedback communicated in this type of style as informative and supportive.

As a result, he or she is most likely to respond to the feedback in a positive way.

On the other hand, sometimes supervisors intentionally or unintentionally deliver feedback in a controlling style. According to Zhou (1998a), feedback delivered in a controlling style makes external constraints salient by emphasizing certain types of ideas or outcomes that the feedback recipient must obtain or certain levels of creativity the recipient must achieve. While used in delivering feedback, a controlling style emphasizes the demands of an external force to obtain certain behavioral outcomes from the feedback recipient. By making external control salient, the controlling style instills feelings of external causality in the feedback recipient. That is, the recipient is led to feel that his or her behaviors and actions are being controlled by others instead being originated from him- or herself.

Taken together, employees should respond most positively to positive feedback when it is delivered in an informational style. In this condition, employees' perceived competence and self-determination will be enhanced and supported. As a result, high levels of intrinsic motivation should be experienced (Deci & Ryan, 1985) and greater creativity should be exhibited. However, employees should exhibit relatively moderate creativity when they receive positive feedback delivered in a controlling style, or negative feedback delivered in an informational style. Finally, employees should respond negatively when negative feedback is delivered in a controlling style. In this condition, employees' perceived competence and self-determination will be diminished, low intrinsic motivation will be experienced, and low levels of creativity will be exhibited.

After reading the discussion before, one might be inclined to conclude that in order to promote creativity, we need to give people positive feedback delivered in an informational style. This is the right approach if the feedback recipient indeed has come up with ideas that are more creative than a standard. If, however, the recipient has come up with ideas that are less creative, should we still give him or her fake positive feedback for the sake of boosting creativity? Little research has examined this issue directly. Yet, to the extent that individuals need to learn standards for creativity and learn appropriate creativity-relevant skills and strategies to produce truly creative work (Amabile, 1996; Shalley & Perry-Smith, 2001; Zhou, 2003), giving fake positive feedback would jeopardize this important learning process and hence should be avoided. When one must give negative feedback, one should do so but deliver it in an informational style (Zhou, 1998a).

The value of distinguishing feedback into two components (feedback valence and feedback style) in understanding how feedback affects creativity has been validated by empirical research. In particular, Zhou (1998a) conducted an experiment to test the hypothesis that feedback valence and style would jointly affect individuals' creative performance in such a way that individuals who receive positive feedback delivered in an informational style would exhibit greater creativity, and individuals who receive negative feedback delivered in a controlling style would exhibit less creativity than individuals who receive other combinations of feedback valence and style (i.e., positive feedback delivered in a controlling style and negative feedback delivered in an informational style). Participants of the experiment worked on an in-basket task developed by Shalley (1991), in which they played the role of a personnel director of a steel company who was asked to come up with creative solutions for the problems presented in a set of memos. The participants were randomly assigned to different feedback valence by feedback style conditions: positive feedback and informational style, positive feedback and controlling style, negative feedback and informational style, and negative feedback and controlling style. Results showed that of the four experimental conditions, individuals in the positive feedback and informational style condition exhibited the greatest creativity, whereas individuals in the negative feedback and controlling style condition exhibited the least creativity, thereby supporting the hypothesis.

Previous research on expected evaluation appears to be consistent with the above results obtained in studies on actual feedback. For example, Shalley (1995) reasoned that effects of expected evaluation on creativity depend on whether the informational aspect or controlling aspect of evaluation is made salient. If the informational aspect is salient, expected evaluation would lead to enhanced creativity, much like what the cognitive evaluation theory would predict. In contrast, if the controlling aspect is made salient, expected evaluation would undermine creativity. Indeed, Shalley and Perry-Smith (2001) found that when individuals expected an upcoming evaluation to be informational, they exhibited greater creativity than when they expected the evaluation to be controlling.

Developmental Orientation

Feedback may also vary on its developmental orientation. Feedback messages that are high on developmental orientation provide employees with helpful and valuable information that enables the employees to learn, develop, and make improvements on the job (Zhou, 2003). Such feedback implies that individuals can constantly become better (e.g.. more skilled, more creative, and generally more in control of their work) by learning and improving on the job. Feedback messages that are low on developmental orientation contain little information to help employees learn to be creative and professionally grow on the job.

Prior research has shown that developmental feedback, in combination with other personal characteristics and contextual variables, facilitated employees' creative performance. For example, Zhou and George (2001) found that when office employees at a petroleum drilling equipment company experienced high levels of job dissatisfaction and continuance commitment (employees are committed to their organizations because of necessity instead of affective attachment to or identification with the organizational values and goals; Allen & Meyer, 1996), the more they received feedback high on developmental orientation from coworkers, the higher their creative performance. The researchers theorized that when an employee was dissatisfied with the job, yet perceived the cost of quitting to be too high or alternatives were just not available, he or she could either choose to be passive about the job and only work to meet the minimum standard, or choose to proactively change the unsatisfactory and unattractive work situation into something that is more interesting and attractive. If the employee received feedback from coworkers that focused on learning at work and improving work processes and methods, the employee's attention would be likely to be directed toward learning and making improvements on the job. During this process he or she would be stimulated to see things from different perspectives and come up with new and better ways of doing things.

In another study with hospital employees (e.g., nurses, pharmacists, and so forth), Zhou (2003) hypothesized that when creative coworkers were present, the more supervisors provided developmental feedback, the greater the employees exhibited creativity. Using the intrinsic motivation perspective described earlier in this chapter, Zhou reasoned that developmental feedback is likely to boost intrinsic motivation. This enhanced interest in the task itself and an orientation toward learning and improvement should allow the employees to benefit from the presence of creative coworkers. Under this joint condition, the employees would be likely to be immersed in the task and focus on skill mastery (Dweck & Leggett, 1988; Elliott & Dweck, 1988; Utman, 1997). Hence, they would find the presence of creative coworkers a particularly welcoming opportunity for them to learn and improve creativity-relevant skills. In addition, their enjoyment in the task and orientation toward learning and improvement would enable them to seek challenge and to be persistent and not afraid of making mistakes (Dweck, 1986), which are essential for their truly mastering and utilizing creativity skills and strategies. As such, when supervisors provided developmental feedback and creative coworkers were present, employees would be likely to properly acquire and use creativity-relevant skills and strategies to search for new and better ways of doing things, which would increase the chance of exhibiting high levels of creativity. Results of the study supported the hypothesis.

In a recent study focusing on the interactive effects of negative mood, positive mood, and supportive contexts on employees' creativity, the value of providing feedback with a developmental orientation was once again demonstrated. More specifically, George and Zhou (2007) found that when supervisors provided developmental feedback and positive mood was high, negative mood experienced by employees had a strong and positive relation with creativity.

Although they investigated effects of expected instead of actual assessment strategies, Zhou and Oldham (2001) found that when individuals expected an upcoming assessment to be self-administered and developmental, they exhibited greater creativity than individuals working in the expected other-administered assessment condition or individuals working in the no-developmental-assessment condition. The pattern of these results underscores the importance of developmental orientation in expected assessments, which is consistent with results obtained from studies that focused on actual feedback as reviewed above.

All in all, it appears that convergent evidence from multiple studies demonstrated that developmental feedback is an important contextual variable that works in concert with a host of other personal (e.g., job dissatisfaction and continuance commitment) and contextual variables (e.g., presence of creative role models) to facilitate creativity.

Person Focused Versus Task Focused

Another component of feedback is concerned with whether the feedback is person focused or task focused. The task versus ego involvement perspective (DeCharms, 1968; Nicholls, 1984) suggests that the focus of the feedback message can be either on the task or on the person who performs the task and who will be the recipient of the feedback. According to Nicholls (1984), task involvement refers to the situation in which individuals are less concerned with how their performance on a task may reflect the level of their personal abilities, and instead concentrate on the task itself. In contrast, ego involvement refers to the situation in which individuals feel their performance is a tool for assessing their personal abilities in comparison with others. Thus, ego-involved individuals feel the pressure to prove themselves, which distracts them from concentrating on the task itself. Moreover, the task- versus ego-involvement perspective suggests that these two psychological states can be created by external cues or instructions (e.g., DeCharms, 1968). Because task-focused feedback can maintain or boost intrinsic motivation, whereas ego- or person-focused feedback tends to diminish intrinsic motivation and subsequently creativity, Amabile (1996) argues that feedback should be task focused instead of person focused.

Characteristics of Feedback Recipient

In addition to the nature and component of the feedback itself, characteristics of the feedback recipient can influence the manner in which employees respond to the feedback. In this section, I discuss how employees' achievement motivation, power motivation, and emotional intelligence affect the employees' creative performance after they receive feedback.

Achievement versus Power Motivation

In an interesting study, Fodor and Carver (2000) found that individuals in their study responded to negative feedback differently. Individuals with achievement motivation (i.e., striving to perform well against a standard of excellence; McClelland, 1985) benefited from negative feedback, whereas individuals with power motivation (i.e., needing to exert influence on others and to experience recognition for power-oriented activities; Winter, 1973) did not benefit. More specifically, science and engineering students participated in a study in which they first completed measures of achievement motivation and power motivation. Next, the participants came up with a solution to an engineering problem, which was followed by their receiving different kinds of feedback in one of three experimental conditions (i.e., positive, negative, and no feedback). Notably, results showed that after receiving negative feedback, participants with high achievement motivation produced more creative solutions to a second engineering problem than did participants in the no-feedback condition. In contrast, participants with high power motivation did not exhibit enhanced creative performance after receiving negative feedback. On the other hand, both individuals with high achievement motivation and with high power motivation showed enhanced creativity after receiving positive feedback. As such, the Fodor and Carver study demonstrated that individuals with high achievement motivation responded positively to negative feedback by performing more creatively whereas those with high power motivation benefited only from positive feedback.

Emotional Intelligence

According to Mayer and Salovey (1997), emotional intelligence is "the ability to perceive accurately, appraise, and express emotion; the ability to access and/or generate feelings when they facilitate thought; the ability to understand emotion and emotional knowledge; and the ability to regulate emotions to promote emotional and intellectual growth" (p. 10). Synthesizing Mayer, Salovey, and their colleagues' work (e.g., Mayer & Salovey, 1997; Salovey & Mayer, 1990, Salovey, Mayer, Goldman, Turvey, & Palfai, 1995), George (2001) describes the following four primary dimensions of emotional intelligence.

The first dimension concerns individual differences in perception, appraisal, and expression of emotion in self and others. Individuals are different in their ability to accurately perceive, appraise, and express their own emotions. Some people are perfectly aware and can express the emotions and feelings they experience, whereas others are not aware or have difficulty expressing these emotions and feelings. Individuals are also different in their ability to accurate perceive, appraise, and express emotions experienced by other people.

The second dimension concerns individual differences in the ability to use emotion to facilitate cognitive processes. Research has shown that emotions are related to individuals' cognitive or thought processes. Individuals are different not only in their awareness, appraisal, and expression of emotions, but also in their ability to use emotions to benefit their cognitive and thought processes. Individuals high on this dimension are able to use the emotions they experience in functional ways. In contrast, individuals low on emotional intelligence are not able to use their emotions to facilitate cognitive processes and may even be distracted, interrupted, confused, or hindered in their cognitive processes by the emotions that they experienced.

The third dimension concerns individual differences in understanding and reasoning about emotions. Individuals who are high on this dimension are able to understand the causes and consequences of the emotions experienced by themselves or by others and how these emotions might change over time. However, individuals low on this dimension are often confused about the true causes of their or others' emotions, and they are often unaware or unable to determine the consequences of these emotions.

The fourth dimension builds upon the above three dimensions and is a higher level, and reflective meta-emotion process that is concerned with the management and regulation of emotions. Individuals high on this dimension are able to manage their emotions. For example, when they experience negative emotions they are able to repair the negative moods and restore positive moods.

The above definitions and descriptions suggest that employees with relatively high levels of emotional intelligence benefit more from creativity-related feedback than employees with low emotional intelligence. This may be especially true if the feedback is delivered in an informational style. More specifically, when employees with high emotional intelligence receive positive feedback delivered in an informational style, they should be able to accurately perceive the positive emotion that they experience to understand the fact that the positive feedback was the cause of the positive emotion and to understand the potential detrimental effect of this positive emotion (e.g., not putting forth more effort in future creative endeavor). In addition, these employees should be able to use the feedback-induced positive emotion in functional ways (e.g., engaging in divergent thinking and creative problem solving) and to manage and regulate their positive emotions so that these emotions would not let them forego future opportunities for creative performance.

On the other hand, when employees with high emotional intelligence receive negative feedback delivered in an informational style, they accurately perceive the negative emotions that they experience, understand the fact that receiving a negative feedback has caused these negative emotions, and the fact that if they let the negative emotions linger, their ability to engage in future creativity may be impaired. They also understand the fact that although the feedback is negative, it contains useful information that would help them to improve in the future. Hence, these employees are more likely to manage their negative emotions and fully take advantage of the information contained in negative but informational feedback and attempt to learn and improve their creative performance.

Characteristics of Feedback Provider

Characteristics of the feedback giver may also influence how well the feedback recipient reacts to the feedback. In general, inexperienced or noncreative individuals tend to be more strongly influenced by the feedback giver's personal characteristics because they need these as cues to judge whether or not to accept the feedback. This tendency may be especially true when they receive negative feedback.

Knowledge and Expertise

The more the feedback giver possesses knowledge and expertise, the more likely that the feedback recipient will listen to, believe in, and respond positively to the feedback. Of course, the recipient needs to be able to judge correctly whether the giver has adequate knowledge and expertise. While under many circumstances it makes sense for individuals to be especially sensitive and responsive to feedback given by people with a great deal of knowledge and expertise, in the context of creative performance this strategy may backfire. More specifically, when a person possesses a rich reservoir of knowledge and expertise in a given field, he or she may have difficulty seeing and accepting new ideas, perspectives, and approaches. As a result, his or her feedback may not be particularly helpful in encouraging, nurturing, and promoting creativity. However, if the feedback recipient is masked by the feedback giver's rich but irrelevant or even hindering knowledge and expertise, and instead accepts and responds to the feedback indiscriminately, the feedback would have a negative impact on the recipient's creative performance.

Seniority and Status

In a similar vein, the more seniority and higher status the feedback giver possesses, the more likely that the feedback recipient will respond positively to the feedback. Interestingly, this tendency can also work to the recipient's disadvantage because sometimes feedback givers with more seniority and higher status are not in the best position to provide creativity-related feedback. This may be especially true in the workplace, where those who have more seniority and higher status or more powerful position may have a vast interest in maintaining the status quo because they are already benefiting from the status quo by holding powerful positions or they may even be responsible for creating the current way of doing things. In contrast, individuals with less seniority and status might be better equipped to provide useful feedback.

To summarize, up to this point I have presented a theoretical model of feedback that includes four categories of variables, namely, the nature and components of feedback, characteristics of feedback recipients, characteristics of feedback givers, and psychological mechanisms. Although portions of this model have been tested and received initial empirical support, much research needs to be done to further test these theorized linkages in diverse settings. In addition, future research is needed to test the other portions of the model that have not been put to empirical test.

More importantly, the model has not been tested as a whole. All these provide many exciting possibilities for future research.

Emerging Research Topics
Cross-Level Feedback
Up to this point, I have essentially taken a dyadic approach in describing the multidimensional nature of the feedback process. Although this topic is not the focus of the model formulated in this chapter because of lack of research, an emerging issue is concerned with how an employee would respond to feedback if this particular feedback provided by a coworker or manager is inconsistent with aggregated feedback given by other people in the employee's group or work unit. This issue may be especially salient when one feedback giver provides negative feedback but other people as a whole provide positive feedback. For example, if Alison's fellow worker, Ron, tells her that the cost-cutting idea she proposed at their work group's weekly meeting is not very creative and that she would need to keep working on making the idea better, Alison is unlikely to accept and respond to Ron's feedback instantly and without making any judgment or comparison with feedback from other sources. If it turns out that other members of their work group praise Alison on the creativity of her idea and Ron is the only one who is critical, Alison is likely to believe the aggregated positive feedback from the rest of the group and discount Ron's negative feedback. In this instance, Ron's feedback would not facilitate Alison's creativity even if he is correct and the other group members are wrong.

This multilevel problem may not be equally salient or detrimental for all individuals. It is possible that employees with high levels of achievement motivation would be more responsive to negative feedback from one coworker even though at the same time the rest of the group provides positive feedback. In fact, employees with high levels of achievement motivation may even actively seek negative feedback in order to become more creative and to accomplish more. Employees with high levels of emotional intelligence may also be more responsive to one single coworker's negative feedback even though the rest of the group has provided positive feedback.

Feedback and Mood States
Madjar, Oldham, and Pratt (2002) found that positive mood mediated the relationship between work and nonwork creativity support and creativity. Their results suggest that mood states also serve as psycho-

logical mechanism-linking contextual factors and creativity. Because feedback is one type of contextual factor, one wonders whether mood states mediate relationships among the nature and component of feedback, the characteristics of the feedback recipient, the characteristics of the feedback giver, and creativity. Essentially, this points to the possibility of adding affect to the Psychological Mechanisms box depicted in Figure 5.1. Intuitively, we know that feedback, especially if it is very positive or very negative, tends to invoke strong affective reactions. How would these affective reactions, then, impact subsequent creativity?

Temporal Aspects of the Feedback and Creativity Relationship

Future research could also investigate the temporal dynamic of feedback and how feedback influences creativity over time. In addition, future research could examine effectiveness of the timing of providing various types of feedback and stages of the creative process. Although not focusing on actual feedback, Yuan and Zhou (forthcoming) investigated differential effects of expected external evaluation on different parts of the creative process (i.e., variation and selective retention) and the creativity of the final product. They found that expected evaluations had different effects on variation and selective retention. More specifically, during variation, individuals who expected evaluation generated fewer ideas. However, during selective retention, individuals who expected evaluation did a better job at improving the appropriateness of the ideas produced during variation. Their results suggest that at different times or stages of the creative idea production process, various types of actual feedback may have differing effects on creativity.

Finally, although the above discussion suggests' that if used appropriately, feedback can enhance employee creativity, it would be overly simplistic to believe that organizations can easily boost employees' creativity in the long run by providing them with positive feedback in an informational style once or twice. For most employees, creativity is not something that comes naturally or easily. It takes time and effort to find interesting problems or tasks for which to develop creative solutions or approaches, to develop a keen interest in one's current job, to understand standards for creative work, and to grasp creativity-relevant skills and strategies. Thus, perhaps it is safe to assume that organizations and managers need to provide consistent and repeated feedback over time in order to boost employees' creativity. In addition, researchers need to conduct rigorous research to advance our understanding of the optimal time lag between giving creativity-conducive feedback and the exhibition of creative performance by the feedback recipient.

IMPLICATIONS FOR MANAGEMENT PRACTICE

What does the current research evidence tell managers about how to use feedback to promote creativity? From the above review and discussion, we can draw a few guidelines for management practice.

Guideline 1. Compared with other combinations of feedback valence and feedback style (i.e., positive feedback delivered in a controlling style, negative feedback delivered in an informational style, negative feedback delivered in a controlling style, and no feedback), positive feedback that is delivered in an informational style leads to the highest level of creativity.

Guideline 2. If negative feedback is to be delivered, it is advisable to deliver it in an informational style.

Guideline 3. Feedback messages that contain a large dose of developmental orientation facilitate creativity.

Guideline 4. To enhance creativity, give task-focused instead of person-focused feedback.

Guideline 5. In the context of creativity, individuals with high levels of achievement motivation benefit from both positive and negative feedback, whereas those with high levels of power motivation benefit only from positive feedback.

Guideline 6. It is possible that individuals with high levels of emotional intelligence benefit from creativity-relevant feedback much more than those with relatively low levels of emotional intelligence.

Guideline 7. Individuals may be especially responsive to feedback provided by persons with more knowledge and expertise or more seniority and higher status. This tendency creates a paradox because, to the extent that persons with more knowledge and expertise or more seniority and higher status provide inaccurate or unhelpful feedback, accepting and responding to their feedback will cause more damage to creativity than inaccurate or unhelpful feedback provided by persons with less knowledge and lower status.

Guideline 8. Feedback is a socially constructed process. Employees often receive feedback from multiple sources, and feedback messages coming out of those resources can be quite inconsistent. A feedback recipient needs to be aware that the inconsistency may be the result of inaccurate feedback from some sources or simply the result of the fact that different people see the focal employee from different angles.

Guideline 9. It takes time for feedback to exert long-lasting and positive impact on creativity. Therefore, promoting creativity through feedback should not be seen as a quick fix. Instead, it should be used as a long-term managerial strategy that aims to nurture and bring out creative energy and potential in employees and should be used consistently.

To ensure that the before-mentioned guidelines are effectively followed by managers and employees so that creativity-conducive feedback can be appropriately constructed, delivered, interpreted, and acted upon, organizations need to provide training programs to their managers and employees. These training programs may teach managers and employees how to construct feedback with a high dose of developmental orientation and task focus, and how to deliver feedback in an informational style. Managers and employees also need to be trained on how to interpret feedback in a way that benefits their creativity, instead of spending too much time worrying about what the feedback says about their personal abilities (or lack of them). Moreover, they need to be aware that feedback is a socially constructed process. The extent to which a feedback message has intended positive impact on the recipient's creativity also depends on feedback messages from other sources.

CONCLUSION

Although rigorous research on the effects of feedback on creativity is still in its infancy, considerable progress has been made. Creativity-related feedback can be constructed in such a way that it becomes a valuable enabler of creativity through which managers can nurture and promote employee creativity. To maximize its positive impact and avoid potentially negative consequences, however, managers need to consider a host of organizational and personal factors in order to devise and deliver the right kind of feedback to the right kind of employees under the right circumstances.

REFERENCES

Allen, N. J., & Meyer, J. P. (1996). Affective, continuance, and normative commitment to the organization: An examination of construct validity. *Journal of Vocational Behavior, 49,* 252–276.

Amabile, T. M. (1988). A model of creativity and innovation in organizations. In B. M. Staw & L. L. Cummings (Eds.), *Research in Organizational Behavior* (Vol. 10, pp. 123–167). Greenwich, CT: JAI Press.

Amabile, T. M. (1996). *Creativity in context: Update to the social psychology of creativity.* Boulder, CO: Westview.

Boggiano, A. K., Ruble, D. N., & Pittman, T. S. (1982). The mastery hypothesis and the overjustification effect. *Social Cognition, 1,* 38–49.

DeCharms, R. (1968). *Personal causation.* New York: Academic Press.

Deci, E. L., & Ryan, R. M. (1985). *Intrinsic motivation and self-determination in human behavior.* New York: Plenum.

Dweck, C. S. (1986). Motivational processes affecting learning. *American Psychologist, 41,* 1040–1048.

Dweck, C. S., & Leggett, E. L. (1988). A social-cognitive approach to motivation and personality. *Psychological Review, 95,* 256–273.

Elliott, E. S., & Dweck, D. S. (1988). Goals: An approach to motivation and achievement. *Journal of Personality and Social Psychology, 54,* 5–12.

Farr, J. L., & Ford, C. M. (1990). Individual innovation. In M. A. West & J. L. Farr (Eds.), *Innovation and creativity at work* (pp. 63–80. New York: John Wiley & Sons.

Fodor, E. M., & Carver, R. A. (2000). Achievement and power motives, performance feedback, and creativity. *Journal of Research in Personality, 34,* 380–396.

George, J. M. (2001). Emotions and leadership: The role of emotional intelligence. *Human Relations, 53,* 1027–1055.

George, J. M., & Zhou, J. (2001). When openness to experience and conscientiousness are related to creative behavior: An interactional approach. *Journal of Applied Psychology, 86,* 513–524.

George, J. M., & Zhou, J. (2007). Dual tuning in a supportive context: Joint contributions of positive mood, negative mood, and supervisory behaviors to employee creativity. *Academy of Management Journal, 50,* 605–622.

Hayes, J. R. (1989). Cognitive processes in creativity. In J. A. Glover, R. R. Ronning, & C. R. Reynolds (Eds.), *Handbook of creativity* (pp. 135–145). New York: Plenum Press.

Ilgen, D. R., Fisher, C. D., & Taylor, M. S. (1979). Consequences of individual feedback on behavior in organizations. *Journal of Applied Psychology, 64,* 349–371.

Madjar, N., Oldham, G. R., & Pratt, M. G. (2002). There's no place like home? The contributions of work and non-work creativity support to employees' creative performance. *Academy of Management Journal, 45,* 757–767.

Mayer, J. D., & Salovey, P. (1997). What is emotional intelligence: Implications for educators. In P. Salovey and D. Sluyter (Eds.), *Emotional development, emotional literacy, and emotional intelligence* (pp. 3–31). New York: Basic Books.

McClelland, D. C. (1985). *Human motivation.* Glenview, IL: Scott, Foresman.

McGraw, K. O. (1978). The detrimental effects of reward on performance: A literature review and a prediction model. In M. R. Lepper & D. Greene (Eds.), *The hidden costs of reward.* Hillsdale, NJ: Lawrence Erlbaum.

McGraw, K. O., & Fiala, J. (1982). Undermining the Zeigarnik effect: Another hidden cost of reward. *Journal of Personality, 50,* 58–66.

McGraw, K. O., & McCullers, J. C. (1979). Evidence of a detrimental effect of extrinsic incentives on breaking a mental set. *Journal of Experimental Social Psychology, 15,* 285–294.

Nicholls, J. G. (1984). Achievement orientation: Conceptions of ability, subjective experience, task choice, and performance. *Psychological Review, 91,* 328–346.

Oldham, G. R., & Cummings, A. (1996). Employee creativity: Personal and contextual factors at work. *Academy of Management Journal, 39,* 607–634.

Pittman, T. S., Emergy, J., & Boggiano, A. K. (1982). Intrinsic and extrinsic motivational orientations: Reward induced changes in preference for complexity. *Journal of Personality and Social Psychology, 42,* 789–797.

Salovey, P., & Mayer, J. D. (1990). Emotional intelligence. *Imagination, Cognition, and Personality, 9,* 185–211.

Salovey, P., Mayer, J. D., Goldman, S. L., Turvey, C., & Palfai, T. P. (1995). Emotional attention, clarity, and repair: Exploring emotional intelligence using the Trait Meta-Mood Scale. In J. W. Pennebaker (Ed.), *Emotion, disclosure, and health* (pp. 125–154). Washington, DC: American Psychological Association.

Shalley, C. E. (1991). Effects of productivity goals, creativity goals, and personal discretion on individual creativity. *Journal of Applied Psychology, 76,* 179–185.

Shalley, C. E. (1995). Effects of coaction, expected evaluation, and goal setting on creativity and productivity. *Academy of Management Journal, 38,* 483–503.

Shalley, C. E., & Perry-Smith, J. E. (2001). Effects of social-psychological factors on creative performance: The role of informational and controlling expected evaluation and modeling experience. *Organizational Behavior and Human Decision Processes, 84,* 1–22.

Shalley, C. E., Zhou, J., & Oldham, G. R. (2004). The effects of personal and contextual characteristics on creativity: Where should we go from here? *Journal of Management, 30,* 933–958.

Utman, C. H. (1997). Performance effects of motivational state: A meta-analysis. *Personality and Social Psychology Review, 1,* 170–182.

Winter, D. G. (1973). *The power motive.* New York: Free Press.

Woodman, R.W., Sawyer, J. E., & Griffin, R. W. (1993). Toward a theory of organizational creativity. *Academy of Management Review, 18,* 293–321.

Yuan, F., & Zhou, J. (forthcoming). Differential effects of expected external evaluation on different parts of the creative idea production process and on final product creativity. *Creativity Research Journal.*

Zhou, J. (1998a). Feedback valence, feedback style, task autonomy, and achievement orientation: Interactive effects on creative performance. *Journal of Applied Psychology, 83,* 261–276.

Zhou, J. (1998b). *Managers' recognition of employee creative ideas: A social-cognitive approach.* Paper presented at The 21st century change imperative: Evolving organizations and emerging networks conference, Center for the Study of Organizational Change, University of Missouri–Columbia.

Zhou, J. (2003). When the presence of creative coworkers is related to creativity: Role of supervisor close monitoring, developmental feedback, and creative personality. *Journal of Applied Psychology, 88,* 413–422.

Zhou, J., & George, J. M. (2001). When job dissatisfaction leads to creativity: Encouraging the expression of voice. *Academy of Management Journal, 44,* 682–696.

Zhou, J., & Oldham, G. R. (2001). Enhancing creative performance: Effects of expected developmental assessment strategies and creative personality. *Journal of Creative Behavior, 35,* 151–167.

Zhou, J., & Shalley, C. E. (2003). Research on employee creativity: A critical review and directions for future research. In J. Martocchio (Ed.), *Research in personnel and human resource management, 22,* 165–217.

CHAPTER 6

Creating Roles

What Managers Can Do to Establish Expectations for Creative Performance

Christina E. Shalley

Georgia Institute of Technology

INTRODUCTION

Creativity and innovation have become increasingly valued across a variety of tasks, occupations, and industries. In our dynamic work environment, more and more managers are realizing that in order to remain competitive they need their employees to be more actively involved in their work and exhibit creative behaviors (Mumford, Scott, Gaddis, & Strange, 2002). While the importance of creative activities and the level of creativity required may differ depending on the tasks or jobs in question, there is potentially room in most jobs for employees to be more creative. Further, since individual creativity provides the foundation for organizational creativity and innovation (Amabile, 1988; Kanter, 1988; Scott, 1995; Woodman, Sawyer, and Griffin, 1993), it is important not only for employees in their jobs to generate novel and appropriate products, processes, and approaches but this also may ultimately impact firm performance and survival (Nystrom, 1990; Kanter, 1988).

Most managers would say that they would like their employees to be more creative, so why is it so difficult to get employees to actually be more creative? In this chapter, I will provide an overview of recent theory and research that has examined the issue of whether individuals perform more creatively when creativity is an expected part of their role in the organization. In particular, the expectation of creative activity can be conveyed to employees by having an actual job requirement to be creative or by assigning employees a goal to be creative in their work. Although requiring individuals to be creative in their job or setting goals for them to be creative might seem to be simple concepts, they can be very powerful in encouraging employees to actually try to be creative in their work. However, as with most things, there is more to it than just giving employees a goal to be creative or putting a line in their job description requiring some level of creative activity. What needs to be done to support creativity role expectations also is a central focus of this chapter. Thus, this chapter focuses on how to foster creative activity through role expectations and the provision of appropriate contextual supports so that the potential result of these activities will be a higher frequency of creative outcomes.

Creativity or creative performance is commonly defined in the literature as the production of new and useful ideas concerning products, processes, and services (e.g., Amabile, 1996; Ford, 1996; Oldham & Cummings, 1996; Shalley, 1991; Zhou, 1998). Creative activity is defined as the driver behind creativity, and it involves engaging in the process of trying to come up with creative outcomes (e.g., linking ideas from multiple sources, seeking out new ways to do things) (Drazin, Glynn, & Kazanjian, 1999; Mumford, 2000). Therefore, individuals could be involved in creative activities that may or may not actually result in creative outcomes. However, in order for creative performance to occur, normally it is necessary for employees to have engaged in creative activities.

WHY ARE MANAGERS NOT GETTING THE LEVEL OF CREATIVE ACTIVITY DESIRED?

Many managers do not feel that employees are being as creative as they could potentially be. This is probably because it is far easier for most employees to stick to tried-and-true methods than to experiment and attempt to come up with creative approaches to deal with different issues or problems. This is primarily because of a few main factors.

First, creativity takes a great deal of hard work. If you think about what is required in attempting to come up with novel ways of thinking about a problem, new approaches, and work processes, this can involve strenuous mental energy. For instance, cognitive effort, such as thinking outside the box, is often necessary (i.e., divergent thought processes), along with the suspension of judgment, and looking at problems in the opposite manner. By using these and other techniques, the quality of decisions or judgments should be better, yet they are not always easy to make. According to Torrance (1988), creative activities focus on identifying problems, formulating hypotheses, discussing ideas with others, and contradicting what is normally known or expected. Therefore, employees need to link ideas from multiple sources, delve into unknown areas to find better or unique approaches to a problem, or seek out novel ways of performing a task (e.g., Amabile, 1996; Drazin et al., 1999).

Second, creative work takes time (Gruber & Davis, 1988). For instance, Amabile and Gryskiewicz (1987) found that one frequently mentioned factor promoting the creativity of R&D employees was sufficient time to think creatively, to explore different perspectives, and play with ideas. Similarly, Katz and Allen (1988) found that for engineers working on new technologies, uninterrupted time was considered critical for effective performance. Also, Amabile and colleagues (2003) found that individuals under time pressure were significantly less likely to engage in creative cognitive processes. Therefore, managers need to provide enough time for employees to be creative, which can be especially difficult in our fast-paced, rapidly changing world.

This brings us to a third related issue: being creative can be very risky (Tesluk, Farr, & Klein, 1997). We know from research on decision making that people tend to avoid risks and prefer more certain outcomes (Bazerman, 1994). Since creativity does not just easily happen and evolves through a trial-and-error process that involves risk taking, failure will often occur along with potential success. If employees are risk averse or if they feel that they will be punished in some manner for failing at work, it is far easier, more efficient, and potentially more practical for them to continue performing in the same way rather than take a chance with a new, possibly better, approach. According to Ford (1996), people are likely to choose familiar behavioral options rather than more creative action because they are relatively more attractive based on past success, relative ease, and certainty. Therefore, even when the circumstances may be favorable for creative actions, they are less likely to emerge unless individuals expect that creative activity will lead to personal consequences that are more desirable relative to those expected for familiar behaviors.

That said, the following three questions can be posed. Why are some people more likely to be creative at work? How do we deal with these differences in individual's inclination to be creative? How can managers encourage all of their employees to engage in creative activities and to be more creative? The rest of the chapter addresses these three questions.

DIFFERENCES IN INDIVIDUAL'S INCLINATION
TO ENGAGE IN CREATIVE ACTIVITY

There are individual differences that may cause one employee, in general, to be more creative than another. Individual creativity is a function of personality factors, cognitive style and ability, relevant task-domain expertise, motivation, and social and contextual influences (e.g., Woodman et al., 1993). For instance, a set of core personality traits that are reasonably stable across fields has been identified (e.g., Barron & Harrington, 1981). These traits include broad interests, independence of judgment, autonomy, and a firm sense of self as creative. Furthermore, R&D scientists have identified traits such as persistence, curiosity, energy, and intellectual honesty as being important for creativity (Amabile, 1988).

Also, creative performance requires a set of skills specific to creativity (i.e., creativity-relevant skills) (Amabile, 1988). This is because creativity requires a cognitive-perceptual style that involves the collection and application of diverse information, an accurate memory, use of effective heuristics, and the ability and inclination to engage in deep concentration for long periods of time (Amabile, 1988). Therefore, creativity-relevant skills are the possession of the skill and ability to think creatively (e.g., generate alternatives, think outside the box, and suspend judgment). Exposure to different alternatives also can cause an individual to access wider categories and generate more divergent thoughts. When individuals access a variety of alternatives, example solutions, or any potentially related idea they are more likely to make connections that could lead to creativity (Amabile, Conti, Coon, Lazenby, & Herron, 1996).

Having depth and breadth of knowledge in an area also has been linked to the ability to be creative. Domain-specific knowledge generally reflects an individual's level of education, training, experience, and knowledge within a particular context (Gardner, 1993). Education provides exposure to a variety of experiences, viewpoints, and knowledge bases, and develops individuals cognitively so that they are more likely to use diverse multiple perspectives and more complicated schemas (Perkins, 1986). Education and training also can reinforce the importance of using experimentation and divergent problem-solving skills, further aiding the ability to be creative. Experience in a field also is necessary for creative success because an individual needs to have enough familiarity in the field in order to do creative work (Weisberg, 1999). That is, it would be difficult to be creative in work products or processes without having enough experience in the area to have a sense of what has historically been constituted as routine or the status quo. Although in some cases task familiarity could lead to more "habitual" performance (Ford, 1996), it also provides ample opportunities to prepare for creativity through deliberate practice of task-domain skills and activities.

Fourth, some individuals are more motivated to persevere and attempt to be creative. Creative activities require some internal, sustaining force that propels individuals to persevere in the face of challenges inherent to creative work (Amabile, 1996; Shalley & Oldham, 1997). An individual has to have the inherent interest in working hard and persevering in order to be creative. It has been argued that people will be most creative when they feel motivated primarily by the interest, enjoyment, satisfaction, and challenge of the work itself (e.g., Amabile, 1988). For instance, Glynn and Webster (1993) found significant relationships among intrinsic motivation, cognitive playfulness, and innovation intentions for a sample of highly intelligent adults. Similarly, R&D professionals have reported believing that intrinsic motivation is critical for creativity (e.g., Amabile & Gryskiewicz, 1987). Essentially, it has been proposed that individuals are likely to produce creative work when they are intrinsically motivated because they are able to concentrate their attention on the task itself, free from extraneous concerns (e.g., Amabile, 1996; Shalley, 1995).

Individuals also have to be willing to take risks and fail at times. This may not be an easy thing to do and can depend on the organizational culture. Organizations tend to have a basic orientation that motivates them to innovate or not. "Innovative orientation places a value on innovation in general, an orientation toward risk (as opposed to maintaining the status quo), a sense of pride in what members can do, and looking toward the future" (Amabile, 1988, p. 154). This highlights a point that I will discuss later in this chapter: that social and contextual factors can enable the expression of creative activity and motivate its applications.

HOW DO WE DEAL WITH INDIVIDUAL DIFFERENCES TO BE CREATIVE?

In terms of individual differences in ability to be creative, there are a variety of things that an organization can do to influence the beforementioned factors. For example, an organization can use selection devices to try to select employees who are more likely to be creative or who have higher innate creative ability. Training also can be used to increase the incidence of creative thought processes and provide educational opportunities that can enhance their task-domain expertise. For instance, Basadur, Graen, and Green (1982) demonstrated empirically that training organizational members in creative thought processes leads to positive improvements in attitudes associated with divergent thinking. Organizations also can select on task expertise and the cognitive skills needed for creativity by screening for these factors. Placement is also important so that individuals fit both the task demands and their immediate work context.

Objective job characteristics also are important for influencing an individual's motivation and attitudes toward work. By providing a context conducive to creativity, creative activity should be more likely to occur. It has been suggested that the way jobs are structured contributes to employees' intrinsic motivation and creative output at work (e.g., Oldham & Cummings, 1996; Shalley, Zhou, & Oldham, 2004). Specifically, jobs that are designed to be complex and demanding (i.e., high on challenge, autonomy, and complexity) are expected to foster high levels of intrinsic motivation. When individuals are intrinsically involved with their work, all of their attention and effort should be focused on their jobs, making them more persistent and more likely to consider different alternatives, which should lead to higher levels of creativity. On the other hand, jobs that are more simple and routinized may not motivate employees or allow them the flexibility to try new ways of doing things, to take risks, and potentially perform creatively. Furthermore, Shalley, Gilson, & Blum (2000) found that when the work environment complemented the creative requirements of the job, individuals had higher job satisfaction and lower intentions to turnover.

Finally, social influences, including the definition of work by management, coworkers, and others, are another important determinant of job attitudes (Nemeth and Staw, 1989). That is, job attitudes can depend on the social labeling of work by others as desirable or not. Further, the opinions of others such as whether one's coworkers are satisfied can affect an individual's attitudes toward work (Salancik & Pfeffer, 1978). Therefore, managers can try to influence job attitudes to be creative.

In general, I would assert that motivation is a key factor that organizations can influence. While organizations can try to select individuals who are more internally motivated to be creative, they can also do things that will influence an individuals' level of motivation at work over time because social and contextual influences in the work environment can affect both ability to be creative and motivation to be creative.

HOW CAN MANAGERS MOTIVATE EMPLOYEES TO INTENTIONALLY UNDERTAKE CREATIVE ACTION?

The key is to motivate employees so that they feel encouraged to take risks, break out of routine, safe ways of doing things, and generate novel activity. Since creative action is an iterative process, in which many ideas and alternative approaches will be produced, some of them may be creative and some will not be creative. Thus, individuals need to feel support for trying to be creative, and the sense that they will not be sanctioned for failing at times. This has sometimes been referred to as providing a culture in the unit or organization where taking risks is encouraged and employees feel psychologically safe in doing so (e.g., Edmondson, 1999).

Essentially, my premise is that if creativity is a valued outcome and employees believe this to be true, they are more likely to exhibit the behaviors that will lead to creative outcomes. How can this be accomplished besides providing encouragement and recognition when employees are creative? It can be achieved through setting goals, expectations, and job requirements to be creative so that employees do not avoid or withhold creative activities. Moreover, by setting role expectations for creativity, employees will understand what is desired of them and will be more likely to focus on these targets. Deci and Ryan (1987) suggested that behaviors are initiated through self-determined choice or because of external demands. Thus, while some behaviors are self-initiated, others can have an external driver, such as a job requirement or goal. Therefore, creative activity may occur because of an external role expectation that motivates employees to undertake such activities.

Furthermore, it is important to note that while having an organizational culture that is supportive of creative activity and valuing creative outcomes is desirable, I would argue that it is more important on a day-to-day basis for employees to know that their work unit, manager, or coworkers value creativity. For example, research has found that supportive supervisors and coworkers are beneficial for creative performance (e.g., Oldham & Cummings, 1996; Zhou, 2003). Furthermore, factors that are more proximal to employees' work life will have a stronger effect day to day on their performance than those that are more distal, and research has found support for this (Shalley et al., 2000; Unsworth, Wall, & Carter, 2005). Therefore, having creativity goals and job requirements for creativity should facilitate employees feeling more prone to frequently engage in creative activities.

Creativity Goals

One way organizations can influence the occurrence of creative activity is through goal setting. Goals influence motivation through their impact on self-regulatory mechanisms (Kanfer & Ackerman, 1989). Research on goal setting has indicated that it is an extremely effective motivational technique (Locke & Latham, 1990). The basic motivational assumption of goal setting is that goals increase attention and effort by providing clear targets toward which individuals can direct their energies. Goals serve to motivate and direct attention to important facets of a task or project and facilitate information acquisition. Goals regulate action directly by affecting what people pay attention to, how hard they work, and how long they persist on a task. Goals affect action indirectly by motivating people to discover and use task strategies that will facilitate goal achievement. Goals are more likely to be attained when people are strongly committed to the goals and are given feedback concerning their progress in relation to their goals.

Creativity goals could serve as a mechanism for inducing individuals to exhibit certain behaviors, perform at a desired level, and also as a standard against which task behavior can be evaluated. A creativity goal can be a stated standard that an individual's output should be creative (i.e., novel and appropriate) or that individuals should attempt to engage in creative activities (e.g., flexible thought, playing with ideas, environmental scanning).

A number of studies have found that when individuals know that creativity is important they are more likely to actually be creative. For instance, Speller and Schumacher (1975) found that individuals' scores on creativity tests improve if they are told that they are taking a creativity test. Additionally, it has been found that when individuals were given test instructions to "be creative" they were significantly more creative on a divergent thinking test than individuals given instructions that did not emphasize a desire for creativity (Manske & Davis, 1968). The results of these studies could be explained by the fact that the mention of a creativity test or instructions to be creative serves as a goal, priming attention and effort on trying to be creative. Priming is a process in which particular information is activated for recall. Thus, it would be expected that assigning a creativity goal, as compared to no creativity goal, would facilitate creative behavior by causing individuals to focus all of their attention and effort on generating novel, appropriate responses.

In a series of studies (e.g., Shalley 1991, 1995; Shalley & Liu, 2007), I have found that goal setting can be used to effectively enhance creativity when a creativity goal is assigned. In these studies, the presence of a creativity goal was found to have a positive, significant effect on creative behavior. This seemed to be true for both the assignment of a "do your best" and difficult creativity goal (Shalley, 1991). Also, in this study when individuals were assigned both a creativity and productivity goal, they were able to still be highly creative, suggesting that it is possible to successfully set goals for more than one aspect of performance. On the other hand, when a creativity goal was not assigned but a productivity goal was assigned, creative performance was found to be lower (Shalley, 1991). Similarly, Carson and Carson (1993) found that individuals who were assigned a creativity goal performed more creatively than those not assigned a creativity goal.

In two recent studies (Shalley & Liu, 2007), we again have found that when a creativity goal is assigned individuals will exhibit higher levels of creativity as compared to those with no creativity goal. In these two laboratory studies, we examined the effect of a creativity goal versus no creativity goal crossed by the effect of receiving no reward versus a reward (either unexpected verbal praise or an unexpected monetary reward for their initial performance on the task) on their subsequent creativity on the task. What is interesting in these two studies is that creativity goals overwhelmingly had the most significant effect on individuals' level of creativity on the task, as compared to the use of rewards.

Finally, Gilson and Shalley (2004) examined customer service technician teams' engagement in creative processes and found, among other things, that the more creative teams were those that were high on shared goals for task accomplishments. Gilson and Shalley argued that high levels of agreement among team members about what is important to the team can increase motivation, efficiency, and effectiveness (e.g., Guzzo & Shea, 1992; Shea & Guzzo, 1987). Furthermore, Gladstein (1984) proposed that when team members hold similar goals they communicate more effectively, consider more alternatives, and access more information in making a decision, which should all stimulate the creative process.

Since goals are effective in directing attention to particular facets of a task that may facilitate information acquisition, the presence of a creativity goal would be expected to influence several of the cognitive activities needed for creativity. For example, cognitive activities such as problem definition and data gathering could be aided by the directive function of a goal. Goals help determine where to search for information and how to evaluate the information obtained as to its usefulness. Assignment of a creativity goal should cause individuals to spend more time thinking about a task and trying to expand the range of potential solutions considered. Thus, providing a goal may enhance individuals' evaluation of the merits of a solution. On the other hand, individuals who are not assigned a creativity goal may explore only a few potential solution pathways before generating a final solution.

Moreover, the goal-setting process operates to focus attention and mobilize effort. Gathering diverse information should be helpful in breaking cognitive mindsets or "thinking outside the box," which is a critical component of creativity. On the other hand, if goals for creativity are not established, but there are goals assigned for other aspects of performance, creative performance has been found to be significantly less likely to occur (Shalley, 1991). Furthermore, in setting goals, managers are really cueing the individual to what is valued by the organization. For example, Amabile and Gryskiewicz (1987) found that R&D professionals cited management having set clear organizational goals as a critical factor for high creativity. On the other hand, when employees did not know what management desired because no clear goals were set, they felt that lower levels of creativity resulted. Therefore, organizations interested in encouraging more creative activity can set goals for employees to be creative.

Creative Job Requirements

Another way organizations can influence the occurrence of creativity is by making it a requirement of the job; in other words, explicitly or implicitly making it known that creativity is required in order to perform the job effectively. Specifically, job-required creativity considers whether employees perceive that creativity is necessary or required in order to perform their job effectively (Shalley et al., 2000; Unsworth et al., 2005).

You may question whether employees will actually be more creative if creativity is an actual job requirement. I would assert that by making it a job requirement, overall you will have more employees attempting creative activities that could ultimately result in creative outputs. That is, when employees are given a reason to be creative through job requirements, I would expect to see employees trying novel approaches to their work. For example, Kahn (1990) found that when designers in an architectural firm were encouraged to try new design techniques this led to their being more willing to take risks and try new things. Therefore, if employees perceive that creativity is required by their job, they potentially now have the permission and motivation to attempt to engage in creative processes, which may lead to more creative outcomes.

Job-required creativity is a component of job design that has only recently begun to be empirically examined (e.g., Shalley et al., 2000). For example, in a study of customer service technician teams (Gilson & Shalley, 2004), we found that the more team members believed that their job required creativity, the more frequently the team reported engaging in creative processes. Also, Unsworth and colleagues (2005) argued and found that job-required creativity was an important proximal determinant of employee creativity. Using a sample of health service employees they examined the role of a creativity requirement along with other work factors previously found to be predictive of creative behavior, such as empowerment, leader support, time demands, and support for innovation. They hypothesized that a creative requirement could account for the variance found in the other work factors for creative performance, and testing this with structural equation modeling, found some support for their arguments. Specifically, they found that the effect of leadership on creativity was fully mediated by a creative requirement, while the effects of empowerment and time demands were partially mediated. Support for innovation was not found to be related to either a creative requirement or employee creativity.

A related issue is that if you make creativity an explicit or implicit job requirement will employees really recognize and acknowledge that it is desired? Research has shown that employees can accurately identify when creative activity is required by their job. For instance, in one study my colleagues and I (Shalley et al., 2000) found that at least 75% of our sample of 2,870 working individuals (i.e., 2,200 people) accurately reported the level of creativity that was required in order to perform their job when their responses were compared to the creativity rating for those same jobs by the U.S. Department of Labor in its *Dictionary of Occupational Titles* (DOT). We speculated that for the remaining 25% of the sample, there may have been some misperceptions, but also factors such as the job incumbent, organizational culture, and manager's expectations may have caused an individual's job to have a higher or lower level of required creativity than the matching DOT job.

Of course, once employees know that creativity is required by the job or is a set goal for them, you still may not see more creative activity if these employees are sanctioned for failed attempts since this will quickly reduce the number of creative activities exhibited. Correspondingly, if role expectations include the desire for employees to be creative, the work context has to support these activities. Research has begun to indicate what types of contextual features of the work environment are more or less conducive to creative behaviors. Since the availability of opportunities and the absence of internal and external constraints affect the unfolding of the creative process, you need creativity-supportive conditions in the work environment. By providing those contextual features that have a positive relationship with creativity and trying to minimize those with a negative relationship, employees should be more likely to be creative.

SUPPORTIVE CONTEXTUAL CONDITIONS FOR CREATIVE ROLE EXPECTATIONS

Organizations can specifically manage creativity by ensuring that the work environment is structured to complement the creative role expectations of jobs (Shalley et al., 2000). While a complete coverage of contextual supports for creativity goes beyond this chapter, I have tried to focus on the ones that make particular sense for supporting creative role expectations. For instance, if you are going to make creativity a role expectation, employees will expect to be evaluated on this component and to receive appropriate recognition and rewards when creative activities occur or creative outcomes result.

Although it is possible that these contextual characteristics may have a negative effect on individual's intrinsic motivation to be creative, if they serve to energize and motivate individuals while providing appropriate constructive information and recognition of achievements, they should help to further stimulate creative activity. Thus, when people perceive that the contextual factors are informational, because they are expected to provide information about their personal competency and possibly behaviorally relevant information that could lead them to enhance their self-competencies in the future, this should boost their intrinsic motivation and subsequent creative activity.

If employees perceive that their manager or the organization is receptive to creative activity and they are recognized for doing so, this should stimulate creative activity. Therefore, managers need to evaluate employees on whether they are attempting to initiate creative activity and to reward both employee attempts and actual creative outcomes. Research has indicated that when individuals expect an external evaluation that will provide constructive information on how to improve their performance (i.e., supportive yet holding them accountable), this can be beneficial to their intrinsic motivation and creativity (Shalley & Perry-Smith, 2001). Research on the provision of actual feedback also has found that when informational feedback is delivered to individuals, they have higher subsequent creativity than when the same feedback is delivered in a controlling or punitive fashion (Zhou, 1998). Additionally, another study has found that providing individuals with the opportunity to self assess their own work as a strategy to help them develop their creativity-relevant skills leads to high creative performance (Zhou & Oldham, 2001). So, for example, managers could provide support for role expectations of creative activity by providing an environment where employees expect constructive feedback on their progress toward goal attainment. This may be perceived as an opportunity to learn and grow and should contribute to their inclination to engage in more creative activities.

It also is important to make it clear how performance will be measured and rewarded. If creativity is a role expectation, it should be rewarded appropriately. Employees need to know that it is okay to take risks within certain bounds, possibly fail, and that they will not be punished but rather rewarded when creative performance occurs. For instance, Abbey and Dickson (1983) found that the climate of innovative R&D units included rewards for recognition of performance and the willingness to experiment with ideas. Rewards can be monetary or nonmonetary recognition or praise. Eisenberger and Armeli (1997) have argued for the informational value of a reward for creativity. Thus, rewards should be seen as something given in recognition of an individual's competence, attempts to engage in creative activity, and actual creative accomplishments.

Further, employees rely on cues from others in their work environment to form views about their own ability to be creative (Ford, 1996). Tierney and Farmer (2002) found that employees believe they have creative capabilities (i.e., creative self-efficacy) when their supervisors work to build their self-confidence and role model activities central to creative performance. Further, this study found that creative self-efficacy influenced actual creative performance at work. Also, Farmer, Tierney, and Kung-McIntyre (2003) found that coworker expectations for an employee to be creative increased the employees' own creative role identity. In another study, Tierney and Farmer (2004) found that those employees whose supervisors held higher creativity expectations for them reported that their supervisors rewarded and recognized their creativity, used creativity goal setting, and modeled creativity in their own work. Therefore, role modeling by supervisors, and possibly coworkers, also can serve as a fundamental contextual factor for creativity.

Researchers have found that individuals viewed as highly creative have studied under highly creative types or have been exposed to creative role models (e.g., Simonton, 1984; Zuckerman, 1977). Modeling serves to clarify performance expectations and enhance skill acquisition. If individuals are capable of performing a behavior but are not currently doing it, they are more likely to perform it after a demonstration of the behavior or examples of appropriate rules and thought processes (Bandura, 1986). Modeling can help to provide the cognitive and behavioral tools needed for creativity by providing standards for organizing thought, strengthening or weakening social inhibitions concerning appropriate behaviors, and encouraging employees to be versatile (Bandura, 1986). Therefore, examples or images of desirable outcomes can foster the type of activities likely to lead to these outcomes. For example, Shalley and Perry-Smith (2001) found that individuals exposed to a creative model had higher creative performance on a subsequent task than those who were not exposed to a model. Also, Zhou (2003) found that the presence of creative coworkers had positive effects on creativity when supervisors engaged in either noncontrolling or supportive behavior, and that this effect was stronger for employees with low-creative personalities (as measured by Gough's Creative Personality Scale).

Finally, supervisory support also is important. Oldham and Cummings (1996) suggested that supportive, noncontrolling supervisors create a work environment that fosters creativity. Similarly, Andrews and Farris (1967) found that scientists' creativity was higher when their organizations were supportive and when managers listened to their employees' concerns and asked for their input into decisions affecting them. A number of studies have shown that open interactions with supervisors, encouragement, and support enhance employees' creativity and innovation (e.g., Kimberly, 1981; Madjar, Oldham, & Pratt, 2002; Oldham & Cummings, 1996; Tierney & Farmer, 2002; Tierney, Farmer, & Graen, 1999; Zhou & George, 2003). Therefore, managers should work on personally encouraging employees and developing nurturing relationships. If they are supportive and provide adequate resources for employees to be creative (e.g., Amabile et al., 1996), creative activity should be more likely to occur.

CONCLUSION

In conclusion, this chapter argues that if managers would like their employees to be more creative, they need to find ways to encourage employees to undertake creative activities. A major way to do this is by creating role expectations to be creative either by setting goals or making creative activity a job requirement. Further, organizations need to make sure that the work context supports these goals or job requirements in order to see creative activity initiated and the occurrence of creative outcomes. This chapter suggests that it is not enough for organizations to hire creative people and expect the creative performance of the unit or firm to increase. Most people are capable of some level of creativity and most employees can be motivated to be more creative at work. Also, it is not enough for organizations to emphasize that creativity is a role expectation without providing an appropriate context to support these behaviors. Although doing either of the aforementioned will probably improve the level of creative outputs occurring, doing all of them should lead to more incidences of creative activity and potentially the highest levels of creative outcomes.

REFERENCES

Abbey, A., & Dickson, J. (1983). R & D work climate and innovation in semiconductors. *Academy of Management Journal, 26,* 362–368.

Amabile, T. M. (1988). A model of creativity and innovation in organizations. In B. M. Staw & L. L. Cummings (Eds.), *Research in organizational behavior* (Vol. 10, 123–167). Greenwich, CT: JAI Press.

Amabile, T. M. (1996). *Creativity in Context.* Boulder, CO: Westview Press.

Amabile, T. M., Conti, R., Coon, H., Lazenby, J., & Herron, M. (1996). Assessing the work environment for creativity. *Academy of Management Journal, 39,* 1154–1184.

Amabile, T. M., & Gryskiewicz, S. (1987). *Creativity in the R & D Laboratory* (Tech. Rep. No. 30). Center for Creative Leadership, Greensboro, NC.

Amabile, T. M., Mueller, J. S., Simpson, W. B., Hadley, C. N., Kramer, S. J., & Fleming, L. (2003). Time pressure and creativity in organizations: A longitudinal field study (Working Paper 02-073). Harvard Business School, Cambridge, MA.

Andrews, F. M., & Farris, G. F. (1967). Supervisory practices and innovation in scientific teams. *Personnel Psychology, 20,* 497–575.

Bandura, A. (1986). *Social foundations of thought and action: A social cognitive theory.* Englewood Cliffs, NJ: Prentice Hall.

Barron, R., & Harrington, D. (1981). Creativity, intelligence, and personality. In M. R. Rosenweig & L. W. Porter (Eds.), *Annual review of psychology* (Vol. 32, 439–476). Palo Alto, CA: Annual Reviews.

Basadur, M., Graen, G. B., & Green, S. G. (1982). Training in creative problem solving: Effects of ideation and problem finding and solving in an industrial research organization. *Organizational Behavior and Human Performance, 30,* 41–70.

Bazerman, M. H. 1994. *Judgment in management decision making.* New York: Wiley.

Carson, P. P., & Carson, K. D. (1993). Managing creativity enhancement through goal setting and feedback. *Journal of Creative Behavior, 27,* 36–45.

Deci, E. L., & Ryan, R. M. (1987). The support of autonomy and the control of behavior. *Journal of Personality and Social Psychology, 53,* 1024–1037.

Drazin, R., Glynn, M. A., & Kazanjian, R. K. (1999). Multilevel theorizing about creativity in organizations: A sensemaking perspective. *Academy of Management Review, 24,* 286–307.

Edmondson, A. C. (1999). Psychological safety and learning behavior in work teams. *Administrative Science Quarterly, 44,* 350–383.

Eisenberger, R., & Armeli, S. (1997). Can salient reward increase creative performance without reducing intrinsic creative interest? *Journal of Personality and Social Psychology, 72,* 652–663.

Farmer, S. M., Tierney, P., & Kung-McIntyre, K. (2003). Employee creativity in Taiwan: An application of role identity theory. *Academy of Management Journal, 46,* 619–630.

Ford, C. M. (1996). A theory of individual creative action in multiple social domains. *Academy of Management Review, 21,* 1112–1142.

Gardner, H. (1993). *Frames of mind.* New York: Basic Books.

Gilson, L. L., & Shalley, C. E. (2004). A little creativity goes a long way: An examination of teams' engagement in creative processes. *Journal of Management, 30,* 453–470.

Gladstein, D. (1984). A model of task group effectiveness. *Administrative Science Quarterly, 29,* 499–517.

Glynn, M. A., & Webster, J. (1993). Refining the nomological net of the adult playfulness scale—Personality, motivational and attitudinal correlates for highly intelligent adults. *Psychological Reports, 72,* 1023–1026.

Gruber, H. E., & Davis, S. N. (1988). Inching our way up Mount Olympus: The evolving-systems approach to creative thinking. In R. J. Sternberg et al. (Eds.), *The nature of creativity: Contemporary psychological perspectives* (pp. 243–270). New York: Cambridge University Press.

Guzzo, R. A., & Shea, G. P. (1992). Group performance and intergroup relations in organizations. In M. D. Dunnette & L. M. Hough (Eds.), *Handbook of industrial and organizational psychology* (pp. 269–313). Palo Alto, CA: Consulting Psychologists Press.

Kahn, W. A. (1990). Psychological conditions of personal engagement and disengagement at work. *Academy of Management Journal, 33,* 692–724.

Kanfer, R., & Ackerman, P. L. (1989). Motivation and cognitive-abilities—An integrative aptitude treatment interaction approach to skill acquisition. *Journal of Applied Psychology, 74,* 657–690.

Kanter, R. M. (1988). When a thousand flowers bloom: Structural, collective, and social conditions for innovation in organizations. In B. M. Staw & L. L. Cummings (Eds.), *Research in Organizational Behavior* (Vol. 10, pp. 169–211). Greenwich, CT: JAI Press.

Katz, R., & Allen, T. J. (1988). Project performance and locus of influence in the R&D matrix. In R. Katz (Ed.), *Managing professionals in innovative organizations: A collection of readings* (pp. 469–484). Cambridge, MA: Ballinger.

Kimberly, J. R. (1981). Managerial innovation. In P. C. Nystrom & W. H. Starbuck (Eds.), *Handbook of organizational design* (pp. 84–104). New York: Oxford University Press.

Locke, E. A., & Latham, G. P. (1990). *A theory of goal setting and task performance.* Englewood Cliffs, NJ: Prentice Hall.

Madjar, N., Oldham, G. R., & Pratt, M. G. (2002). There's no place like home? The contributions of work and nonwork creativity support to employees' creative performance. *Academy of Management Journal, 45,* 757–767.

Manske, M. R., & Davis, G. A. (1968). Effects of simple instructional biases upon performance in the unusual uses test. *Journal of General Psychology, 79,* 25–33.

Mumford, M. D. (2000). Managing creative people: Strategies and tactics for innovation. *Human Resources Management Review, 10,* 313–351.

Mumford, M. D., Scott, G. M., Gaddis, B., & Strange, J. M. (2002). Leading creative people: Orchestrating expertise and relationships. *The Leadership Quarterly, 13,* 705–750.

Nemeth, C., & Staw, B. M. (1989). The trade offs of social control and innovation within groups and organizations. In L. Berkowitz (Ed.), *Advances in experimental social psychology* (Vol. 22, pp. 175–210). New York: Academic Press.

Nystrom, H. (1990). Organizational innovation. In M. S. West & J. L. Farr (Eds.), *Innovation and creativity at work: Psychological and organizational strategies* (pp. 143–162). New York: Wiley.

Oldham, G. R., & Cummings, A. (1996). Employee creativity: Personal and contextual factors at work. *Academy of Management Journal, 39,* 607–634.

Perkins, D. N. (1986). Thinking frames. *Educational Leadership, 43,* 4–10.

Salancik, G. R., & Pfeffer, J. (1978). A social information processing approach to job attitudes and task design. *Administrative Science Quarterly, 23,* 224–253.

Scott, R. K. (1995). Creative employees: A challenge to managers. *Journal of Creative Behavior, 29,* 64–71.

Shalley, C. E. (1991). Effects of productivity goals, creativity goals, and personal discretion on individual creativity. *Journal of Applied Psychology, 76,* 179–185.

Shalley, C. E. (1995). Effects of coaction, expected evaluation, and goal setting on creativity and productivity. *Academy of Management Journal, 38,* 483–503.

Shalley, C. E., Gilson, L. L., & Blum, T. C. (2000). Matching creativity requirements and the work environment: Effects on satisfaction and intentions to leave. *Academy of Management Journal, 43,* 215–223.

Shalley, C. E., & Liu, Y. (2007). *The effects of creativity goals, verbal and monetary rewards on creativity.* Working paper.

Shalley, C. E., & Oldham, G. R. (1997). Competition and creative performance: Effects of competitor presence and visibility. *Creativity Research Journal, 10,* 337–345.

Shalley, C. E., & Perry-Smith, J. E. (2001). Effects of social-psychological factors on creative performance: The role of informational and controlling expected evaluation and modeling experience. *Organizational Behavior and Human Decision Processes, 84,* 1–22.

Shalley, C. E., Zhou, J., & Oldham, G. R. (2004). The effects of personal and contextual characteristics on creativity: Where should we go from here? *Journal of Management, 30,* 933–958.

Shea, G. P., & Guzzo, R. A. (1987). Groups as human resources. In K. R. Rowland & G. R. Ferris (Eds.), *Research in personnel and human resources management* (Vol. 5, (pp. 323–356). Greenwich, CT: JAI Press.

Simonton, D. K. (1984). Artistic creativity and interpersonal relationships across and within generations. *Journal of Personality and Social Psychology, 46,* 1273–1286.

Speller, K. G., & Schumacher, G. M. (1975). Age and set in creative test performance. *Psychological Reports, 36,* 447–450.

Tesluk, P. E., Farr, J. L., & Klein, S. R. (1997). Influences of organizational culture and climate on individual creativity. *The Journal of Creative Behavior, 31,* 27–41.

Tierney P., & Farmer, S. M. (2002). Creative self-efficacy: Potential antecedents and relationship to creative performance. *Academy of Management Journal, 45,* 1137–1148.

Tierney, P., & Farmer, S. M. (2004). The Pygmalion process and employee creativity. *Journal of Management, 30,* 413–432.

Tierney, P., Farmer, S. M., & Graen, G. B. (1999). An examination of leadership and employee creativity: The relevance of traits and relationships. *Personnel Psychology, 52,* 591–620.

Torrance, R. (1988). The nature of creativity as manifest in its testing. In R. J. Sternberg (Ed.), *The nature of creativity: Contemporary psychological views* (pp. 43–75). Cambridge: Cambridge University Press.

Unsworth, K. L., Wall, T. B., & Carter, A. (2005). Creative requirement: A neglected construct in the study of employee creativity? *Group and Organization Management, 30,* 541–560.

Weisberg, R. W. (1999). Creativity and knowledge: A challenge to theories. In R. J. Sternberg (Ed.), *Handbook of creativity* (pp. 226–250). Cambridge: Cambridge University Press.

Woodman, R., Sawyer, J., & Griffin, R. (1993). Toward a theory of organizational creativity. *Academy of Management Review, 18,* 293–321.

Zhou, J. (1998). Feedback valence, feedback style, task autonomy, and achievement orientation: Interactive effects of creative performance. *Journal of Applied Psychology, 83,* 261–276.

Zhou, J. (2003). When the presence of creative coworkers is related to creativity: Role of supervisor close monitoring, developmental feedback, and creative personality. *Journal of Applied Psychology, 99,* 413–422.

Zhou, J., & George, J. M. (2003). Awakening employee creativity: Encouraging the expression of voice. *Academy of Management Journal, 14,* 545–568.

Zhou, J., & Oldham, G. R. (2001). Enhancing creative performance: Effects of expected developmental assessment strategies and creative personality, *Journal of Creative Behavior, 35,* 151–167.

Zuckerman, H. (1977). *Scientific elite: Nobel laureates in the U.S.* New York: The Free Press.

CHAPTER 7

Fostering Creativity in Groups and Teams

Paul B. Paulus

University of Texas at Arlington

INTRODUCTION

Much organizational work involves groups or teams. Meetings are often held to discuss ongoing operations and future plans. Individuals may conduct their work as part of a team. This may involve collaboration in task selection, task completion, decision making, and compensation. There appears to be a strong belief in organizations that group and team work will pay handsome dividends in terms of employee morale, motivation, and innovation (Bennis & Biederman, 1997; Kayser, 1994). This belief is often bolstered by case studies of effective groups (e.g., Ford & Gioia, 1995; John-Steiner, 2000; Sutton & Hargadon, 1996). Although some systematic reviews support the effectiveness of team-work (Kozlowski and Ilgen, 2006), others suggest that this faith in the effectiveness of teams may not always be justified (Allen & Hecht, 2004). Much research suggests that many factors in groups inhibit their productivity, creativity, and effective decision making (Paulus & Brown, 2003). Although there is some evidence for the effectiveness of work teams, many studies measure perceptions rather than actual productivity (e.g., Cohen & Ledford, 1994).

Recent research has been concerned with ways of enhancing productivity, creativity, and innovation in groups and teams. In this chapter, I will provide a brief summary perspective of this literature and then focus on the factors that influence the ways in which group and team creativity can influence organizational creativity. The main concern will be with ideational creativity since that is the type of activity that is central to many group meetings and problem-solving sessions in organizations that involve exchange of ideas (Paulus, Nakui, & Putman, 2006). Ideational creativity involves generating novel ideas related to a particular problem such as how to market a new product or develop new uses for an old product. Ideational creativity can be measured in terms of fluency (number of ideas), originality (degree of novelty), and flexibility (range of ideas) (Guilford, 1959). Most studies have focused on fluency and originality. These creative ideas can form the basis for innovations in organizations through a systematic evaluation of the most promising alternatives and their feasibility.

THE RELEVANCE FACTOR FOR LABORATORY RESEARCH ON GROUPS

Much of the work on group creativity is done with laboratory groups. So it is often suggested that this literature may have limited implications for real-world teams (Kozlowski & Ilgen, 2006; Sutton & Hargadon, 1996). Laboratory groups are short term and are typically composed of unacquainted college students. They perform tasks that may have little personal meaning. In contrast, work teams often perform a variety of tasks in meaningful organizational settings. Moreover, the team members often have a history with each other and have been selected for specific roles on the team. So it is not surprising that the team literature and the group literature are typically not well connected empirically or theoretically (Paulus & Van der Zee, 2004).

It is presumed in this chapter that many of the processes that occur in ad hoc laboratory groups are likely to play a role in work teams since these are essentially long-term groups. So even though work teams in organizations involve more complexity than ad hoc laboratory groups, they may be susceptible to the same forces that govern groups in general. Several reviews of laboratory and field research in social psychology have concluded that many laboratory phenomena are in fact replicated in field settings (Anderson, Lindsay, & Bushman, 1999; Mullen, Driskell, & Salas, 1998). One reason we do not know the extent to which this is the case is that the research approaches and questions are typically different in group and team research. Much group research is focused on understanding the social and cognitive processes that underlie group task performance. The focus of the interest is often whether groups are better than the same number of individuals in task performance or decision making. Research on work teams is focused on discovering the factors that affect team effectiveness. Typically the general utility of teams is not questioned or there are no comparisons to nonteam or individual control groups. Since work teams are an organizational reality, the main focus is on determining how to make work teams better.

Paulus and Van der Zee (2004) suggest that there is much benefit to a better integration of the literatures on groups and teamwork. The group literature suggests a variety of factors that can inhibit or facilitate teamwork. Research on work teams suggests interesting variables and ideas that deserve more careful examination in controlled group studies. Paulus and Van der Zee note that many of the factors that have been shown to be influential in laboratory groups have also been highlighted in research on work teams (cf. Paulus & Nakui, 2005). It is in this spirit that I review the implications of research on groups for organizational innovation.

COGNITIVE PROCESSES IN IDEA SHARING

Idea exchange is basically a cognitive process in which individuals share knowledge, perspectives, and beliefs, which are based on their unique experiences and education. It is presumed that with some diversity of experience and education, the group members will share a broad range of ideas. It is likely that people will be exposed to ideas or perspectives that are quite different from their own. These unique ideas may stimulate each group member to think of additional ideas. This may come about in several ways. Ideas from others may remind us of some relevant domain of knowledge or experience that can be applied. Some of our knowledge base is more readily accessible than others. For example, when brainstorming about improving one's work environment, issues of compensation and leadership will probably come to mind quite easily. Participants might think less readily about the need for training and environmental design. So one benefit of group interaction is that individuals are exposed to categories of knowledge they might otherwise not have applied to the problem (Brown, Tumeo, Larey, & Paulus, 1998). Therefore, the more unique or inaccessible the categories, the more the stimulation value to the group (Brown & Paulus, 2002). Within categories of knowledge, ideas from others may stimulate individuals to think of related ideas. As a group discusses the need for a fairer compensation system, someone may suggest the development of a more objective productivity index. Others may then think about different ways that such an index could be developed. Within categories, ideas that are more similar to one's own network of knowledge may have the most stimulation value (Dugosh & Paulus, 2005).

Diversity

There are a number of rather straightforward implications of the cognitive perspective for group-idea generation. First, some degree of diversity within a group is likely to be beneficial. This is particularly true for diversity in knowledge or expertise. Diversity in experience as reflected in age, length of tenure in a position, or cultural history may also be beneficial (Williams & O'Reilly, 1998). However, sometimes interpersonal differences may make interaction more difficult and may lead members to place less value on each other's contributions (Milliken, Bartel, & Kurtzberg, 2003). Moreover, if there is too much diversity in the knowledge bases of the group members, they may not understand each other well enough to benefit from this diversity. In this type of situation, group members who can serve as cognitive intermediaries or translators may be required to help the group tap its creative potential. Research on diversity in teams has found little benefit except when tasks are fairly complex (Bowers, Pharmer, & Salas, 2000; Webber & Donahue, 2001). In general, it appears that diversity is often associated with negative emotional reactions, and will have positive effects under limited conditions (Mannix & Neale, 2005). Diversity should be most useful on tasks that require a diversity of information or perspectives such as decision making or creativity tasks. It also appears that feelings of group members about diversity have an impact. When team members have a positive attitude toward demographic diversity, diversity is more likely related to the production of high-quality ideas (Nakui & Paulus, 2006).

Attention

Another important consideration is that group members need to carefully attend to each others' contributions. The group-interaction process can be rather overwhelming as one tries to manage generating one's own ideas, listen to the ideas of others, integrate one's knowledge base with the ideas being shared, and coordinate the timing of one's contributions with those of the other group members. A likely casualty of this process will be one's attentiveness to the ideas expressed by others. Instructions to memorize the ideas being shared by others may be helpful in increasing the attention level in some contexts such as brainstorming in pairs or on computers (Dugosh, Paulus, Roland, & Yang, 2000). However, in actual face-to-face groups, the memorization approach may simply add an extra burden to the process (Paulus & Yang, 2000; Porterfield, 2000). Other ways of insuring attention to others' ideas such as using a writing procedure in which group members read each others' ideas before adding their own (Paulus & Yang, 2000), or asking group members to take notes on ideas being exchanged, may be more effective in face-to-face groups. Of course, perceived competence or expertise of group members may also increase the degree to which group members attend to their ideas (Stasser & Birchmeier, 2003).

Incubation

When the ideas are being exchanged, individuals may be overwhelmed with all of the different perspectives. It may be quite difficult to apply one's own knowledge base effectively to all of these expressed ideas. To do so may require an incubation process in which individuals can reflect consciously or unconsciously on the exchanged information (Csikszentmihalyi & Sawyer, 1995). In our research, we have typically provided a solitary brainstorming session after the group brainstorming period to allow group members an additional opportunity to process the exchanged ideas and generate more new ideas (Dugosh et al., 2000; Paulus & Yang, 2000). Individuals who have been exposed to the ideas of others are able to generate significantly more ideas in these sessions than those who have only brainstormed alone.

Task Structure

When one is generating ideas, it is possible to get into a cognitive "rut" in that one may get stuck in a certain issue or category of knowledge. This tendency to focus on a limited range of categories is particularly likely in groups (Larey & Paulus, 1999). In fact, group members may come to the false conclusion that they have fully tapped their knowledge base both in terms of breadth of knowledge and depth of knowledge in specific areas. Of course, we do not have a simple accurate way of knowing how "empty" of ideas we really are. There may be many additional ideas and categories that we have not accessed. There are several ways that one may be able to overcome this type of rut. These involve increasing the structure of the task so that additional ideas or categories will be considered. One type of structure is to provide brief breaks during the brainstorming process. Such breaks have been shown to increase the subsequent level of idea generation (Paulus, Nakui, Putman & Brown, 2006). Exposing group members to a divergent thinking exercise during a break may be helpful in stimulating group members to again consider a broad range of categories in a subsequent session (Coskun, 2005). It has been suggested that brief breaks reduce the tendency to persist in thinking about old ideas or categories and makes it easier to consider new ones (Smith, 2003). Alternatively, breaks may simply provide additional motivation to continue the idea search process. Thus far, we do not know why such breaks are effective or how they should be dispersed in the group process (their length and number).

Another way to structure the brainstorming situation to enhance brainstorming is to provide participants with a list of topics or issues to consider as they go through the brainstorming process. A problem such as improving a corporation may have a number of different facets such as recruitment, training, compensation, resource allocation, and strategic alliances. It may be rather overwhelming for a group to consider each of these issues simultaneously. There may be a tendency to forget or ignore some of the issues in favor of others. For each of these to receive full consideration, a better strategy is to consider each of the issues in order. When groups are asked to take a sequential approach to the problem rather than a simultaneous approach, they generate many more ideas (Coskun, Paulus, Brown, & Sherwood, 2000).

SOCIAL INFLUENCES ON GROUP CREATIVITY

Although the group idea exchange process is basically a cognitive activity, it occurs in a group context and is subject to all of the social and group influences of any other group activity. Some of these influences may hinder the ability of groups to tap their cognitive potential. Others may provide additional motivational impetus to the idea-generation process.

Motivation Loss

When groups gather to combine their contributions into one group product, there may be tendency of group members to loaf or free-ride. That is, they may not exert their full effort because their individual contributions are not identifiable or they feel the efforts of others make their efforts less important for the group (Karau & Williams, 1993). When individuals are made more accountable for their individual performance, group performance is increased (Shepperd, 1993).

Production Blocking

Group interaction also has the significant liability of distracting or limiting the individual efforts of group members to contribute their ideas (production blocking, Diehl & Stroebe, 1987). Since only one member of the group can speak at one time, individuals are limited in the extent to which they can contribute ideas when they occur (Diehl & Stroebe, 1991). They may forget ideas as they wait or may be distracted rather than stimulated by the contributions of others from pursuing fruitful avenues (Nijstad, Stroebe, & Diehl, 2003).

To overcome this problem, several group-brainstorming paradigms that limit production blocking have been introduced. One involves the exchange of written ideas (Van de Ven & Delbecq, 1974) and the other relies on a computer-based brainstorming procedure (Dennis & Williams, 2003). Both of these allow individuals to be exposed to others' ideas while at the same time not hindering their ability to generate their own ideas as they occur. However, it is interesting that when electronic groups are compared to individual brainstorming, it is not always clear that the electronic interaction is beneficial. Part of the reason for that may be that electronic brainstormers do not have to pay attention to each other. They can act just as solitary brainstormers and generate ideas without regard to what others are doing. So small electronic groups (three or fewer), may perform about the same as nominal groups or sometimes slightly worse (Dennis & Williams, 2003; DeRosa, Smith, & Hantula, 2007; Pinsonneault, Barki, Gallupe, & Hoppen, 1999). Apparently, even the process of sharing ideas electronically can produce cognitive interference. Although ideas from others may be stimulating, they can also distract one from generating one's own ideas rather than simply reading those of others. However, when participants are highly motivated to perform the task and are also motivated to attend to the ideas of others, small groups of four electronic brainstormers can outperform nominal groups of four (Dugosh et al., 2000). Interestingly, when electronics groups get large (typically about eight or more) the performance of the groups increases relative to similar size nominal groups (Dennis & Williams, 2003; DeRosa et al., 2007). It is not clear why that is the case. It could be due to the enhanced stimulation produced by the large range of ideas exchange in large groups or it could be due to the fact that many of these groups are in the same room and thus may experience enhanced motivation due to the presence of other active coworkers (this is called social facilitation, Zajonc, 1980).

Social Comparison

When individuals monitor each other's idea generation, they become aware of the relative productivity of the group members. If group members care about the group product and their own status in the group, they may be motivated to do their fair share. Thus, they may try to match their performance to that of the highly productive group members. This type of upward matching is most likely if there is some sense of intragroup or intergroup competition where individual as well as group performance matters (Paulus, Dugosh, Dzindolet, Coskun, & Putman, 2002). However, if there is no strong progroup motivation or sense of competition, individuals may be tempted to free-ride or match their performance to that of the low performers in the group (Camacho & Paulus, 1995; Paulus & Dzindolet, 1993). The resulting low performance norms may then be carried over to other tasks and situations (Paulus & Dzindolet, 1993). So it is important to develop some level of group cohesion and commitment to the group goals (Gully, Devine, & Whitney, 1995) to increase the likelihood that the social comparison processes will go in an upward direction and that high productivity norms will be developed and maintained.

Information Bias

Another significant problem for the group-sharing process is the tendency of groups to focus on common information or ideas rather than unique information (Stasser & Birchmeier, 2003). This is a bit surprising since one would expect unique information to attract more attention than common information. Yet it appears the information that people have in common tends to be seen as more valid. It certainly validates one's knowledge or perspective. Since one of the main benefits of the group idea–exchange process is exposure to diverse and unique ideas, this bias to common information can be seen as inimical to group creativity. There are some ways to overcome or minimize this bias (Stasser & Birchmeier, 2003). Most importantly, practitioners need to structure group interaction in such a way that its group members are likely to share in process-unique information. The areas of expertise that are relevant to the issue being discussed should be clearly defined and members with this type of knowledge should be explicitly recruited and recognized for their expertise. It is also important to structure the interactions for effective exchange. There should be an atmosphere in the group that encourages attention to, and tolerance of, unique perspectives. Groups should also allocate sufficient time for a careful exchange of information and could consider procedures such as writing or computer technology (Jessup & Valacich, 1993).

IDEA SELECTION AFTER BRAINSTORMING

The focus of brainstorming is on generating as many ideas as possible. It is presumed that increasing the quantity of ideas will also increase the number of high-quality ideas. There is indeed considerable support for this assumption (Mullen, Johnson, & Salas, 1991). Of course, once all of these good ideas have been generated, it is often necessary in organizations to select from among these ideas the ones that should be implemented. Some ideas may be quite creative or novel but may not be very feasible because of resources or other considerations. If the group is fortunate to have generated some really good and feasible ideas, it is usually not possible to implement all of them. The selection process may be done by the group or team that generated the ideas or some external group or individual. One question to resolve is whether the decision should be made by an interacting group or set of independent evaluators or whether the group or the evaluators should be the same individuals who generated the ideas or a different set of individuals. All of these combinations occur in organizational settings and may have their specific benefits and drawbacks.

Group evaluation of alternatives should bring many different perspectives to bear on the judgment of feasibility. This may increase the chance that inappropriate alternatives are rejected (Laughlin & Hollingshead, 1995). There is some evidence that group interaction can increase the likelihood of good choices (Larey & Paulus, 1999), but Rietzschel, Nijstad, & Stroebe (2006) found no difference due to group and individual evaluation. When groups have more ideas to evaluate they are able to select more good ideas (Putman & Paulus, 2006). However, groups tend to pick the most feasible ideas rather than novel ones, and their ability to select the most novel ideas is not greater than chance (Putman & Paulus, 2006; Rietzschel et al., 2006). Consistent with the feasibility bias, groups may have a bias for ideas that are consistent with their a priori perspectives or ideas that are more common (Wittenbaum, 2000). Groups also have a tendency toward premature consensus (Janis, 1982). That is, they may not carefully evaluate all of the relevant information in making a decision. This is particularly true if the group is cohesive or has a vested interest in certain types of outcomes. If the group who generated the ideas also evaluates the ideas, this may be more a problem than if one group generates and another evaluates. Group members may be particularly fond of ideas they have generated and may not want to be critical of ideas generated by members of "our group." However, in cases where the problem addressed requires special experience or expertise, it may be difficult to have a different group that is competent to evaluate the ideas.

There are a number of guidelines that appear to enhance the effectiveness of the group decision process (see Kerr & Tindale, 2004, for a detailed review). The groups should insure that they take sufficient time to evaluate all of the alternatives adequately. They should have multiple meetings so that "second thoughts" can be added to the process. Such second meetings would also allow for the occurrence of unconscious processes, which may lead to better decisions in the case of type of complex issues that groups often face (Dijksterhuis & Nordgren, 2006). Outside evaluators or experts should be consulted to make sure that the group has considered all of the relevant issues. This is particularly important if the same group that generated the ideas also evaluates the ideas.

Innovation

Once ideas have been selected for implementation, they have to be accepted by the organization for action. This has been labeled as the innovation process (West, 2003). This is affected by a number of organizational factors. Probably the most critical is whether the organization is generally supportive of innovations.

The implementation process highlights one of the dilemmas faced by creative people or groups. It is one thing to have a great idea and another to get some corporation to implement it. There are a number of obvious reasons for this. There may simply be too many good ideas. Only the very best and ones that fit with the corporate mission can be selected (Garud, Nayyar, & Shapira, 1997). Corporations need idea people and people who are good at picking the best ideas for implementation. These two skills may be somewhat independent. The idea people need to be good divergent thinkers who are intrinsically motivated to develop the knowledge and expertise on which to base their idea-generation process. Environments that provide for much autonomy are particularly suited for these types of people (Amabile, Conti, Coon, Lazenby, & Herron, 1996). On the other hand, effective decision makers need to be good convergent thinkers. They need to be able to evaluate the shared ideas with criteria that predict that these will be worth investing with additional time and energy for their development and application. These people will need to have considerable self-confidence to make such independent decisions.

Social Context

One important factor for innovation and creativity is the social environment provided by the group or organization. It is important to have an environment that is supportive of risks and divergent ideas and that is receptive to new ideas. Many organizational environments are more concerned with conformity to organizational norms or the demands and aspirations of a leader (Nemeth, 1997). Much research has shown that exposure to dissenting or conflicting perspectives increases creative thinking (Nemeth & Nemeth-Brown, 2003). Organizations that provide a sense of psychological safety for innovative activities of their teams or groups and allow them much autonomy are more likely to benefit from the innovative potential of their employees (Amabile et al., 1996: Edmondson, 1999; West, 2003).

TEAM CREATIVITY

There are, of course, a number of layers of management in many corporations. If each of these layers has to be involved in the evaluation process, it can be rather difficult for good ideas to rise to the top. There may be only a modest correspondence between the creative potential of the employees and teams and the actual productivity of an organization (West, 2003). To increase the degree of innovation in an organization, it is important that creativity and novel perspectives are constantly being considered. To encourage such a process, many corporations have gone to a team culture with an associated flat managerial structure. It is presumed that organizing work into groups with considerable autonomy (self-managed teams) will greatly increase member motivation. Self-managed teams are given much latitude in structuring the task and the group interaction process. The team is supposed to provide its own leadership instead of relying on the direction of a superior. Teamwork should be particularly important when the tasks involve collaborative knowledge work (Janz, Colquitt, & Noe, 1997; Kozlowski & Ilgen, 2006; Paulus, 2000; Paulus, Larey, & Dzindolet, 2000).

There have been many proponents of teamwork who have sung its praises (Kayser, 1994; Tjosvold, 1991). Teams are presumed to increase organizational productivity. It is true that teams are often rated positively by their participants and supervisors. As indicated earlier, that does not mean that they are necessarily productive (Allen & Hecht, 2004; Paulus & Van der Zee, 2004). Some studies have demonstrated that self-managed teams can be more productive than other types of group work (Cohen & Bailey, 1997). However, these studies do not control for other factors that might also contribute to productivity such as compensation systems and management style. Moreover, to function effectively as a self-managed team requires considerable training (Swezey & Salas, 1992). It is not clear that the cost of training individuals to work effectively as a team in many cases outweighs the benefits for productivity (Appelbaum & Batt, 1994).

There are some reasonable guidelines for effectiveness in teams concerned with innovation (Kozlowski & Ilgen, 2006; Seta, Paulus, & Baron, 2000). Teams need to have clear objectives or goals and be committed to them. They need diversity and differences of opinion but they need to handle effectively the emotional and intellectual conflicts that may ensue. The team should have an atmosphere that is supportive of the learning processes and mistakes that are inevitable as the team attempts to develop innovations. Team members should also carefully reflect on the processes involved in the innovative process and make adjustments when necessary (West, 2003). It is important for the organization to support these innovative efforts (see Paulus and Nakui, 2005) and to provide training for effective teamwork (Salas & Cannon-Bowers, 2001).

VARIATION IN INDIVIDUAL AND GROUP ACTIVITIES

Although some tasks tend to be done mostly in groups (e.g., designing new cars) and others mostly as an individual (e.g., sculpture), many tasks could benefit from some combination of group and individual performance. A key problem that needs to be resolved for any task is the appropriate balance of group and solitary work for optimum performance. The ideal balance will likely depend on such variables as the person, situation, and task. For example, in the idea-generation situation it could be best if individuals first generate as many ideas as possible and then continue in a group to get additional stimulation when they have "run dry" individually (Baruah & Paulus, 2006). Alternatively, it may be very useful to spend some time reflecting on additional ideas after a group-sharing session. Research thus far is not clear which of these two alternative procedures is best (Paulus & Brown, 2003; Paulus, Larey, & Ortega, 1995). It is likely that some combination of these two procedures, in which there is a continual alternation between group and individual ideation, is optimal. Yet how will a group or a leader know when it is an appropriate time to switch modalities? Thus far, there is no clear evidence on this issue and it will likely depend on the type of task and type of group. However, there is some evidence that groups may be sensitive to the adequacy of their process and become motivated to change their approach during the course of their interaction. For example, there is some interesting work on groups that suggest that they may take some significant actions halfway through the process (Gersick, 1989; Gersick & Hackman, 1990). At this point, most group members seem to be sensitive to the need to restructure or reorient the activity in order to accomplish their goals. Interestingly, these groups appear to be amenable to significant interventions into their process primarily at the beginning and midpoint of their interaction time. So leadership or facilitator interventions are most likely to have an impact at these points. One reason for this is that once groups get some type of momentum (pace or style of working), they are reluctant to change it. In fact, groups that develop a fast pace or style of working (either because they have a limited time period or the problem lends itself to higher rates of activity) continue that style in subsequent sessions with different tasks, whereas groups that develop a slow style continue in this pace (Kelly & Karau, 1993; Paulus & Dzindolet, 1993). So it is particularly important that groups receive appropriate training and facilitation both prior to beginning their task and at the midpoint of their task period (Baruah & Paulus, 2006).

It might be possible for work teams to develop effective skills in managing the timing processes of their groups in an optimal fashion. This will not be an easy task. In the group creativity/innovation paradigm that would involve not only finding a balance between group and individual interaction but also between the ideation and the evaluation phases. That is, given a limited period of time, how much should be invested in the divergent phase of generating novel ideas and how much in evaluating the ideas for possible implementation? The work by Gersick suggests that most groups would begin that transition at the halfway point. However, since groups often stop generating ideas when they still have many more good ideas available (Nijstad, Stroebe, & Lodewijkz, 1999), groups may begin the evaluation process prematurely. Many of the best or most creative ideas may come after the most accessible ideas or knowledge bases have been tapped and the participants are searching for less obvious connections. With appropriate training and experience, groups may become more facile in the evaluation process so they can allocate more time to the creative phase. The use of voting procedures available in group decision support systems may help groups become more efficient in the evaluation or decision phase, but groups often do not like using electronic means for these types of activities (DeRosa et al., 2007).

LEADERSHIP IN CREATIVE GROUPS

Groups often have a leader. This leader may be appointed or elected. Since creative teams or groups may work best when they have considerable autonomy (Amabile, 1996), it is presumed that the leaders should limit the extent to which they try to control the group process. Yet, given that groups often underperform in both creative and decision-making tasks, some degree of leadership guidance may be required for groups to reach their potential. So what leadership behaviors or style should be used? Should the leader be a member of the group or an external person? These are difficult questions since leadership is complex and the literature on leadership with teams is quite limited (Day, Gron, & Salas, 2004; Kozlowski & Ilgen, 2006).

Research on leadership has evaluated many different dimensions (Bass, 1998; Chemers, 1997). One salient dimension is the extent to which the leader is directive in terms of structuring the task, setting goals, and directing the group interaction. A highly directive leader may in fact be quite useful increasing productivity when tasks are quite straightforward or there are some negative intragroup dynamics (Fiedler, 1978). However, participative leaders who emphasize the importance of individual initiative may be more appropriate for high-level intellectual tasks such as those involved in creativity and innovation. This is particularly true of self-management teams that are provided much autonomy by the organization. Manz and Sims (1987) noted that external leaders of such groups who were rated as being effective emphasized self-leadership. That is, this leader encourages the group to value high task achievement for the personal reinforcements or the reward this will provide, prompts groups members to observe and reflect on their behaviors, and suggests that the group work fully through the implications of their ideas before implementing them. In a similar vein, Burpit and Bigoness (1997) found that leaders whose behavior empowered team members by providing enhanced freedom, opportunities, and responsibilities increased rated innovation in project teams of architectural firms. Others have made a similar distinction between leaders who are structure oriented and those who focus on showing consideration (Blake & Mouton, 1985) or transactional and charismatic leaders (Bass and Avolio, 1994). Transactional leaders focus on setting goals and rewarding good performance whereas transformational leaders provide individualized monitoring and mentoring, inspire by setting high expectations and sharing a vision, and encourage innovation by challenging old assumptions and approaches (Bass & Avolio, 1994).

Which of these styles is best for creative groups or teams? Thus far, definitive evidence is lacking. Certainly one would expect leadership that emphasizes consideration, self-management, and motivation by inspiration to be most helpful for creative groups (Foels, Driskel, Mullen, &

Salas, 2000). These groups need considerable intrinsic motivation to persist in generating and evaluating novel solutions. However, groups may also benefit from the challenge provided by high goals and the structure or directive guidance from an experienced leader at crucial stages of the innovation process. So it seems likely that leaders who combine some of the best of all of these qualities might get the most out of their groups. For example, Blake and Mouton (1985) propose that team leadership that is high on concern for people and concern for productivity is ideal. This may enhance both extrinsic as well as intrinsic motivation. Alternatively, it may be that different styles are needed in different phases of the group process. A more goal-oriented or transactional style may be most helpful in leading to the production of a high quantity of ideas in a limited period of time. However, in the difficult process of carefully considering which ideas should be implemented, the inspirational and intellectual stimulating aspects of transformational style may be most helpful (Sosik, Avolio, and Kahai, 1997). This type of flexible leadership style is the focus of leader-member exchange theory, which emphasizes that leadership behaviors should be sensitive to the reactions and roles of the subordinates.

Recent developments in team leadership have also emphasized the multifaceted role of team leaders in that they may have to serve both a regulatory or task-oriented function and a developmental function (Burke et al., 2006; Kozlowski et al., in press). The task-oriented approach involves direction, monitoring, and structure-initiating behaviors. The developmental approach is more concerned with consideration, facilitation, transformation, and inspiration. From that perspective, it is likely that creative teams will need both styles of leadership at different work phases. In contrast to our reasoning about transformational and transactional leadership, during initial exploratory and divergent-thinking phases, the developmental approach seems most appropriate. When the team has to select, develop, and promote a particular innovative approach, a more task-oriented leadership may be necessary. Obviously, some research will be required to determine which speculations are correct.

Should the leader be internal or external to the group? Both types of leaders may be helpful, but they may play rather different roles (Manz & Sims, 1987). A team or group leader who is a member of the group may focus largely on the more mundane management aspects of leadership, making sure the group has the appropriate supplies and environmental support, facilitating training of newcomers, monitoring the behavior of group members, and assisting them when needed. It may be difficult to effectively play the role of an inspirational leader when one is part of a group. If one has some psychological distance from the group, it may be easier to perform the functions of transformational leadership. It helps if such leaders have some charisma in order to motivate groups to perform beyond their expectations (Bass, 1998). When one is a member of the group, there is typically pressure to conform to the group's norms and standards and not to deviate too much from the group's expectations. These group forces may make it difficult for a group member to inspire groups to go much beyond their typical level of performance.

INTERGROUP AND INTERTEAM PROCESSES

In laboratory studies, groups are typically isolated from other groups, but in organizational settings, groups may have connections with many other groups. The members of a team may be members of other teams in the organization. So a team in charge of developing innovative new directions for a corporation may consist of individuals from top management, human resources, accounting, manufacturing, and sales. This might be called a crossfunctional team since its members have multiple functions in the organization (Denison, Hart, & Kahn, 1996). Work teams in an organization are also likely to have contacts with other teams. A manufacturing team may interact with sales teams and management teams when there is some need for an exchange of perspectives or information. These teams may want to meet in their entirety or simply appoint someone to be an intermediary. Certainly much negotiation in organizations is limited to representatives of different groups or teams (Thompson, 2005).

Although interaction among different types of teams in an organization is desirable for innovation, there are a number of factors that inhibit such interactions. First, there tends to be an in-group bias in which group members see their group as superior to other groups (Hogg & Terry, 2001; Turner, 1978). This may in part reflect self-esteem motivations on the part of the group members. However, because members of different teams also may have different roles in the organization, they may have very different perspectives or very different goals (Turner & Haslam, 2001). Labor groups typically want good working conditions and as high a salary as possible, but management groups may be interested primarily in productivity and profitability. These types of discrepancies in attitudes and values among groups may make it difficult for them to work together effectively. However, some degree of competition among groups may be helpful if it increases motivation to reach high goals (Coskun, 2000).

Despite various factors that may inhibit the interteam interaction in organizations, such interactions do occur and are sometimes quite successful (Cusumano, 1997). Ancona and Caldwell (1992) studied interaction among product design teams and found that such interaction may take one of three forms. One is ambassadorial in that it is concerned with communicating with other teams in ways to promote the group and buffer it from potential negative interactions. This often involves interactions with groups who are above them in the hierarchy. A second consisted of task coordination activities related to the task including obtaining feedback and negotiation. This involves much lateral communication with other teams. A third involved scouting activities designed to obtain information from other groups about the competition, the market, and technical details. Groups tended to exhibit these activities at different times. Sometimes they focused primarily on ambassadorial activities, sometimes they were concerned with both task coordination and scouting. At other times they were somewhat isolationist in that they were involved in very little interteam activity. In general, ambassadorial and task-coordination activities are related to positive ratings by management. A focus on scouting activities was related to negative ratings of performance possibly because too much involvement in scouting delays the necessary process of decision making and implementation. In general, overall communication activity was related to more positive ratings of performance. This effect was rather weak in the later phases of group performance.

This work and that of others (West, 2003) demonstrate that innovation in organizations requires more than idea generation and selection at the level of groups. Teams have to tap other groups for information and support and persuade other groups of the value of their ideas or innovations. The best ideas may not always win out (Garud et al., 1997; Rietzschel et al., 2006). Creativity and innovation require promotion of one's ideas (Simonton, 1999; Sternberg & Lubart, 1995). Creative groups or teams in organizations face a rather daunting task. They are expected to develop novel products or ideas within a limited period of time. They have to select those that are most likely to be successful (or accepted) within and outside the organization and promote these alternatives to different decision-making groups in the organization. So group creativity in organizations involves a careful balancing of a range of activities. It is clear that the most effective groups will be active groups that do an effective job of sharing and processing information at the group and intergroup levels and promoting the resultant good ideas.

How can we create such effective teams? Are they simply "born" or can they be made or coached? Research has shown that it is feasible to train groups or teams to function more effectively (Hackman & Wageman, 2005; Oxley, Dzindolet, & Paulus, 1996; Swezey & Salas, 1992). We have found that systematic training of groups in effective brainstorming techniques does increase the quality of the ideas generated (Baruah & Paulus, 2006). There have not been any systematic studies on training creative teams in organizations that demonstrate the effectiveness of such procedures, but there are those who are quite optimistic that this is possible (Parnes, 1992; Sutton & Hargadon, 1996). Yet there are still many questions about how organizations can most effectively tap the creative potential in their employees. What combination of group and solitary activity, what type of leadership, and what type of training are necessary? The research in the past 15 years has given us much hope that some resolution of these questions is not too far away.

REFERENCES

Allen, N. J., & Hecht, T. D. (2004). The "romance of teams": Toward an understanding of its psychological underpinnings and implications. *Journal of Occupational and Organizational Psychology, 77,* 439–461.

Amabile, T. M. (1996). *Creativity in context.* Boulder, CO: Westview Press.

Amabile, T. M., Conti, R., Coon, H., Lazenby, J., & Herron, M. (1996). Assessing the work environment for creativity. *Academy of Management Journal, 39,* 1154–1184.

Ancona, D. G., & Caldwell, D. F. (1992). Demography and design: Predictors of new product team performance. *Organization Science, 3,* 321–341.

Anderson, C. A., Lindsay, J. J., & Bushman, B. J. (1999). Research in the psychological laboratory: Truth or triviality? *Current Directions in Psychological Science, 8,* 3–9.

Appelbaum, E., & Batt, R. (1994). *The new American workplace.* Ithaca, NY: ILR Press.

Baruah, J., & Paulus, P. B. (2006). *Effects of training on idea-generation in groups.* Unpublished manuscript, The University of Texas at Arlington.

Bass, B. M. (1998). *Transformational leadership: Industry, military, and educational impact.* Mahwah, NJ: Lawrence Erlbaum Associates.

Bass, B. M., & Avolio, B. J. (1994). *Improving organizational effectiveness through transformational leadership.* Thousand Oaks, CA: Sage.

Bennis, W., & Biederman, P. W. (1997). *Organizing genius: The secrets of creative collaboration.* Reading, MA: Addison Wesley.

Blake, R., & Mouton, J. (1985). *The managerial grid III.* Houston, TX: Gulf.

Bowers, C. A., Pharmer, J. A., & Salas, E. (2000). When member homogeneity is needed in work teams: A meta-analysis. *Small Group Research, 31,* 305–327.

Brown, V. R., & Paulus, P. B. (2002). Making group brainstorming more effective: Recommendations from an associative memory perspective. *Current Directions in Psychological Science, 11,* 208–212.

Brown, V., Tumeo, M., Larey, T. S., & Paulus, P. B. (1998). Modeling cognitive interactions during group brainstorming. *Small Group Research, 29,* 495–526.

Burke, C. S., Stagl, K. C., Klein, C., Goodwin, G. G., Salas, E., & Halpin, S. (2006). Does leadership in teams matter? A meta-analytic integration. *Leadership Quarterly.*

Burpitt, W. J., & Bigoness, W. J. (1997). Leadership and innovation among teams: The impact of empowerment. *Small Group Research, 28,* 414–423.

Camacho, L. M., & Paulus, P. B. (1995). The role of social anxiousness in group brainstorming. *Journal of Personality and Social Psychology, 68,* 1071–1080.

Chemers, M. M. (1997). *An integrative theory of leadership.* Mahwah, NJ: Lawrence Erlbaum Associates.

Cohen, S. G., & Bailey, D. E. (1997). What makes teams work: Group effectiveness research from the shop floor to the executive suite. *Journal of Management, 23,* 239–290.

Cohen, S. G., & Ledford, G. E. (1994). The effectiveness of self-managing teams: A quasi-experiment. *Human Relations, 47,* 13–43.

Coskun, H. (2000). *The effects of outgroup comparison, social context, intrinsic motivation, and collective identity in brainstorming groups.* Unpublished doctoral dissertation, The University of Texas at Arlington.

Coskun, H. (2005). Cognitive stimulation with convergent and divergent thinking exercises in brainwriting: Incubation, sequence priming, and group context. *Small Group Research, 36,* 466–498.

Coskun, H., Paulus, P. B., Brown, V., & Sherwood, J. J. (2000). Cognitive stimulation and problem presentation in idea generation groups. *Group Dynamics: Theory, Research, and Practice, 4,* 307–329.

Csikszentmihalyi, M., & Sawyer, K. (1995). Creative insight: The social dimension of a solitary moment. In R. J. Sternberg & J. E. Davidson (Eds.), *The nature of insight* (pp. 329–363). Cambridge, MA: MIT Press.

Cusumano, M. A. (1997). How Microsoft makes large teams work like small teams. *Sloan Management Review, Fall,* 9–20.

Day, D. V., Gronn, P., & Salas, E. (2004). Leadership capacity in teams. *Leadership Quarterly, 15,* 857–880.

Denison, D. R., Hart, S. L., & Kahn, J. A. (1996). From chimneys to cross-functional teams: Developing and validating a diagnostic model. *Academy of Management Journal, 39,* 1005–1023.

Dennis, A. R., & Williams, M. L. (2003). Electronic brainstorming: Theory, research, and future directions. In P. B. Paulus and B. A. Nijstad (Eds.), *Group creativity: Innovation through collaboration* (pp. 160–178). New York: Oxford University Press.

DeRosa, D. M., Smith, C. L., & Hantula, D. A. (2007). The medium matters: Mining the long-promised merit of group interaction in creative idea generation tasks in a meta-analysis of the electronic group brainstorming literature. *Computers in Human Behavior, 23,* 1549–1581.

Diehl, M., & Stroebe, W. (1987). Productivity loss in brainstorming groups: Toward the solution of a riddle. *Journal of Personality and Social Psychology, 53,* 497–509.

Diehl, M., & Stroebe, W. (1991). Productivity loss in idea-generating groups: Tracking down the blocking effect. *Journal of Personality and Social Psychology, 61,* 392–403.

Dijksterhuis, A., & Nordgren, L. F. (2006). A theory of unconscious thought. *Perspectives on Psychological Science, 1,* 95–109.

Dugosh, K. L., & Paulus, P. B. (2005). Cognitive and social comparison processes in brainstorming. *Journal of Experimental Social Psychology, 41,* 313–320.

Dugosh, K. L., Paulus, P. B., Roland, E. J., & Yang, H.-C. (2000). Cognitive stimulation in brainstorming. *Journal of Personality and Social Psychology, 79,* 722–735.

Edmondson, A. (1999). Psychological safety and learning behavior in work teams. *Administrative Science Quarterly, 44,* 350–383.

Fiedler, F. E. (1978). Contingency and the leadership process. In L. Berkowitz (Ed.), *Advances in experimental social psychology* (Vol. 11, pp. 59–112). New York: Academic Press.

Foels, R., Driskel, J. E., Mullen, B., and Salas, E. (2000). The effects of democratic leadership on group member satisfaction: An integration. *Small Group Research, 31,* 676–701.

Ford, C. M., & Gioia, D. A. (Eds.). (1995). *Creative action in organizations: Ivory tower visions and real world voices.* Thousand Oaks, CA: Sage.

Garud, R., Nayyar, R. R., & Shapira, Z. B. (Eds.). (1997). *Technological innovation: Oversights and foresights.* New York: Cambridge University Press.

Gersick, C. J. G. (1989). Marking time: Predictable transitions in task groups. *Academy of Management Journal, 32,* 274–309.

Gersick, C. J., and Hackman, J. R. (1990). Habitual routines in task-performing groups. *Organizational Behavior and Human Decision Processes, 47,* 65–97.

Guilford, J. P. (1959). *Personality.* New York: McGraw-Hill.

Gully, S. M., Devine, D. J., & Whitney, D. (1995). A meta-analysis of cohesion and performance: Effects of levels of analysis and task interdependence. *Small Group Research, 26,* 497–520.

Hackman, J. R., & Wageman, R. (2005). A theory of coaching. *Academy of Management Review, 30,* 269–287.

Hogg, M. A. & Terry, D. J. (2001): Social identity theory and organisational processes. In M. A. Hogg & D. J. Terry (Eds.), *Social identity processes in organisational contexts* (pp. 1–12). Hove, England: Psychology Press (Taylor & Francis).

Janis, I. (1982). *Groupthink* (2nd ed.). Boston: Houghton Mifflin.

Janz, B. D., Colquitt, J. A., & Noe, R. A. (1997). Knowledge worker team effectiveness: The role of team autonomy, interdependence, team development, and contextual support variables. *Personnel Psychology, 50,* 877–904.

Jessup, L. M., & Valacich, J. S. (Eds.). (1993). *Group support systems.* New York: MacMillan.

John-Steiner, V. (2000). *Creative collaboration.* New York: Oxford University Press.

Karau, S. J., & Williams, K. D. (1993). Social loafing: A meta-analytic review and theoretical integration. *Journal of Personality and Social Psychology, 65,* 681–706.

Kayser, T. A. (1994). *Building team power: How to unleash the collaborative genius of work teams.* New York: Irwin.

Kelly, J. R., & Karau, S. J. (1993). Entrainment of creativity in small groups. *Small Group Research, 24,* 179–198.

Kerr, N. L., & Tindale, R. S. (2004). Group performance and decision-making. *Annual Review of Psychology, 55,* 623–655.

Kozlowski, S. W. J., & Ilgen, D. R. (2006). Enhancing the effectiveness of work groups and teams. *Psychological Science in the Public Interest, 7,* 77–124.

Kozlowski, S. W. J., Watola, D., Nowakowski, J. M., Kim, B., & Botero, I. (in press). Developing adaptive teams: A theory of dynamic team leadership. In E. Salas, G. F. Goodwin, & C. S. Burke (Eds.), *Team effectiveness in complex organizations: Cross-disciplinary perspectives and approaches.* Mahwah, NJ: Lawrence Erlbaum Associates.

Larey, T. S., & Paulus, P. B. (1999). Group preference and convergent tendencies in small groups: A content analysis of group brainstorming performance. *Creativity Research Journal, 12,* 175–184.

Laughlin, P. R., & Hollingshead, A. B. (1995). A theory of collective induction. *Organizational Behavior and Human Decision Processes, 61,* 94–107.

Mannix, E., & Neale, M.A. (2005). What differences make a difference? The promise and reality of diverse teams in organizations. *American Psychological Society, 6,* 31–55.

Manz, C. C., & Sims, H. P. (1987). Leading workers to lead themselves: The external leadership of self-managing work teams. *Administrative Science Quarterly, 32,* 106–129.

Milliken, F. J., Bartel, C. A., & Kurtzberg, T. R. (2003). Diversity and creativity in work groups: A dynamic perspective on the affective and cognitive processes that link diversity and performance. In P. B. Paulus and B. A. Nijstad (Eds.), *Group creativity: Innovation through collaboration* (pp. 32–61). New York: Oxford University Press.

Mullen, B., Driskell, J. E., & Salas, E. (1998). Meta-analysis and the study of group dynamics. *Group Dynamics: Theory, Research, and Practice, 2,* 213–229.

Mullen, B., Johnson, C., & Salas, E. (1991). Productivity loss in brainstorming groups: A meta-analytic integration. *Basic and Applied Social Psychology, 12,* 3–23.

Nakui, T., & Paulus, P. B. (2006). *Effects of diversity and attitude toward diverse groups on perception and performance.* Unpublished manuscript, The University of Texas at Arlington.

Nemeth, C. J. (1997). Managing innovation: When less is more. *California Management Review, 40,* 59–74.

Nemeth, C. J., & Nemeth-Brown, B. (2003). Better than individuals? The potential benefits of dissent and diversity for group creativity. In P. B. Paulus and B. A. Nijstad (Eds.), *Group creativity: Innovation through collaboration* (pp. 63–84). New York: Oxford University Press.

Nijstad, B. A., Stroebe, W., & Diehl, M. (2003). Cognitive stimulation and interference in idea-generating groups. In P. B. Paulus and B. A. Nijstad (Eds.), *Group creativity: Innovation through collaboration* (pp. 137–159). New York: Oxford University Press.

Nijstad, B. A., Stroebe, W., & Lodewijkz, H. F. M. (1999). Persistence of brainstorming groups: How do people know when to stop? *Journal of Experimental Social Psychology, 35,* 165–185.

Oxley, N. L., Dzindolet, M. T., & Paulus, P. B. (1996). The effects of facilitators on the performance of brainstorming groups. *Journal of Social Behavior and Personality. 11,* 633–646.

Parnes, S. J. (1992). *Sourcebook for creative problem-solving.* Buffalo, NY: Creative Education Foundation Press.

Paulus, P. B. (2000). Groups, teams and creativity: The creative potential of idea generating groups. *Applied Psychology: An International Review, 49,* 237–262.

Paulus, P. B., & Brown, V. (2003). Enhancing ideational creativity in groups: Lessons from research on brainstorming. In P. B. Paulus and B. A. Nijstad (Eds.), *Group creativity: Innovation through collaboration* (pp. 110–137). New York: Oxford University Press.

Paulus, P. B., Dugosh, K. L., Dzindolet, M. T., Coskun, H., & Putman, V. L. (2002). Social and cognitive influences in group brainstorming: Predicting production gains and losses. *European Review of Social Psychology, 12,* 299–325.

Paulus, P. B., & Dzindolet, M. T. (1993). Social influence processes in group brainstorming. *Journal of Personality and Social Psychology, 64,* 575–586.

Paulus, P. B., Larey, T. S., & Dzindolet, M. T. (2000). Creativity in groups and teams. In M. Turner (Ed.), *Groups at work: Advances in theory and research* (pp. 319–338). Hillsdale, NJ: Lawrence Erlbaum Associates.

Paulus, P. B., Larey, T. S., & Ortega, A. H. (1995). Performance and perceptions of brainstormers in an organizational setting. *Basic and Applied Social Psychology, 17,* 249–265.

Paulus, P. B., & Nakui, T. (2005). Facilitation of group brainstorming. In S. Schuman (Ed.), *The IAF handbook of group facilitation* (pp. 103–114). San Francisco: Jossey-Bass.

Paulus, P. B., Nakui, T., & Putman, V. L. (2006). Group brainstorming and teamwork; Some rules for the road to innovation. In L. Thompson & H. Choi (Eds.), *Creativity and innovation in organizational teams* (pp. 69–86). Mahwah, NJ: Lawrence Erlbaum Associates.

Paulus, P. B., Nakui, T., Putman, V. L., & Brown, V. R. (2006). Effects of task instructions and brief breaks on brainstorming. *Group Dynamics: Theory, Research, and Practice, 10,* 206–219.

Paulus, P. B., & Van der Zee, K. (2004). Should there be a romance between teams and groups. *Journal of Occupational and Organizational Psychology, 77,* 475–480.

Paulus, P. B., & Yang, H. C. (2000). Idea generation in groups: A basis for creativity in organizations. *Organizational Behavior and Human Decision Processes, 82,* 76–87.

Pinsonneault, A., Barki, H., Gallupe, R. B., & Hoppen, N. (1999). Electronic brainstorming: The illusion of productivity. *Information Systems Research, 10,* 110–133.

Porterfield, R. (2000). *The effects of incubation and attention on brainstorming productivity.* Unpublished masters thesis, The University of Texas at Arlington.

Putman, V. L., & Paulus, P. B. (2006). *Brainstorming, brainstorming rules decision making.* Unpublished manuscript, The University of Texas at Arlington.

Rietzschel, E. F., Nijstad, B. A., & Stroebe, W. (2006). Productivity is not enough: A comparison of interactive and nominal brainstorming groups on idea generation and selection. *Journal of Experimental Social Psychology, 42,* 244–251.

Salas, E., & Cannon-Bowers, J. A. (2001). The science of team training: A decade of progress. *Annual Review of Psychology, 52,* 471–499.

Seta, C. E., Paulus, P. B., & Baron, R. A. (2000). *Effective human relations: A guide to people at work.* Boston: Allyn and Bacon.

Shepperd, J. A. (1993). Productivity loss in performance groups: A motivation analysis. *Psychological Bulletin, 113,* 67–81.

Simonton, D. K. (1999). *The origins of genius: Darwinian perspectives on creativity.* New York: Oxford University Press.

Smith, S. M. (2003). The constraining effects of initial ideas. In P. B. Paulus and B. A. Nijstad (Eds.), *Group creativity: Innovation through collaboration* (pp. 15–31). New York: Oxford University Press.

Sosik, J. J., Avolio, B. J., & Kahai, S. S. (1997). Effects of leadership style and anonymity on group potency and effectiveness in a group decision support system environment. *Journal of Applied Psychology, 82,* 89–103.

Stasser, G., & Birchmeier, Z. (2003). Group creativity and collective choice. In P. B. Paulus and B. Nijstad (Eds.), *Group creativity: Innovation through collaboration* (pp. 85–109). New York: Oxford University Press.

Sternberg, R. J., & Lubart, T. I. (1995). *Defying the crowd: Cultivating creativity in a culture of conformity.* The Free Press: New York.

Sutton, R. I., & Hargadon, A. (1996). Brainstorming groups in context. *Administrative Science Quarterly, 41,* 685–718.

Swezey, R. W., & Salas, E. (Eds.). (1992). *Teams: Their training and performance.* Norwood, NJ: Ablex.

Thompson, L. (2005). *The heart and the mind of the negotiator.* Upper Saddle River, NJ: Prentice-Hall.

Tjosvold, D. (1991). *Team organization: An enduring competitive advantage.* New York: Wiley.

Turner, J. C. (1978). Social comparison, similarity and ingroup favoritism. In H. Tajfel (Ed.), *Differentiation between social groups: Studies in the social psychology of intergroup relations* (pp. 235–250). London: Academic Press.

Turner, J. C., & Haslam, S. A. (2001). Social identity, organizations, and leadership. In M. E. Turner (Ed.), *Groups at work: Theory and research* (pp. 25–65). Mahwah, NJ: Lawrence Erlbaum Associates.

Van de Ven, A. H., & Delbecq, A. L. (1974). *Academy of Management Journal, 17,* 605–621.

Webber, S. S., & Donahue, L. M. (2001). Impact of highly and less job-related diversity on work group cohesion and performance: A meta-analysis. *Journal of Management, 27,* 141–162.

West, M. A. (2003). Innovation implementation in work teams. In P. B. Paulus and B. A. Nijstad (Eds.), *Group creativity: Innovation through collaboration* (pp. 245–276). New York: Oxford University Press.

Williams, K. Y., and O'Reilly, C. A. III. (1998). Demography and diversity in organizations: A review of 40 years of research. *Research in Organizational Behavior, 20,* 77–140.

Wittenbaum, G. M. (2000). Information sampling in decision-making groups: The impact of members' task-relevant status. *Small Group Research, 29,* 57–84.

Zajonc, R. B. (1980). Compresence. In P. B. Paulus (Ed.), *Psychology of group influence* (pp. 35–60). Hillsdale, NJ: Lawrence Erlbaum Associates.

CHAPTER 8

When Being Social Facilitates Creativity
Social Networks and Creativity within Organizations

Jill Perry-Smith
Emory University

INTRODUCTION

You may have heard stories of the creative genius toiling away in isolation, finally immerging with a creative breakthrough. Similarly, you may envision the creative genius as a socially awkward recluse, so immersed in deep ideas and thought that he or she relates little (or not very well) to the outside world. This caricature of creativity is not pure myth. For example, the idea of incubation, where individuals subconsciously sequester thinking on a topic until a breakthrough emerges, is widely described as being important in a creative process involving preparation, incubation, illumination, evaluation, and verification (Shalley, 1991; Wallas, 1926). In this case, creative ideas are theorized to result as part of an "aha" moment or unexpected flash (Amabile, 1996). In contrast, given the popularity of teams within organizations, you may be familiar with the general management view that it is important for people to work in teams with people representing diverse functional areas, professions, or even backgrounds for creative problem solving. The central message to this view: People need to work in teams to provide the most creative solutions. There is also a research basis for the importance of diverse information gained by teams and creativity (O'Reilly, Williams, & Barsade, 1998) as well as the conditions in which teams are creative (Gilson & Shalley, 2004).

However, these two views of the kinds of social experiences that favor creative thinking represent social extremes that are not necessarily in line with organizational reality. For example, many instances exist in organizations where *an individual* (versus a team) is faced with a challenging and complex problem that requires creative thinking. Alternatively, even in teams, individuals may be judged by their contributions (perhaps creative ones) to solving team-based problems. Further, for the everyday knowledge worker who uses unseen and unobservable inputs like intellect, their reality is largely a social one. These professionals interact with more and more people, both within and outside the firm, in highly complex and changing environments where people often move between firms. Thus, the world is becoming more connected, as people have connections both within organizations and connections that span organizations (Fleming & Marx, 2006). In contrast to the creative recluse and the team-as-everything views of creativity, certain informal social interactions can facilitate creativity in the workplace, provided that these interactions are bounded within extremes. In this chapter, I will review research suggesting that individuals should be connected but not too connected, if creativity is of interest.

In particular, social network research provides a critical basis for understanding how being socially connected relates to being creative. In contrast to a more individual focused view of behavior, a network view considers how various aspects of relationships influence or are influenced by behavior. For example, we might think about how individual characteristics such as personality influence creativity, or we might think broadly about how organizational contexts such as rewards or job complexity influence creativity. A social network approach looks specifically at how the context of social relationships influences behavior. Several recent reviews of social network research overview the importance of a social network framework for understanding a variety of behaviors within organizations and the increasing popularity of this perspective (Borgatti & Foster, 2003; Brass, Galaskiewicz, Greve & Tsai, 2004).

The advantage of a social network lens for understanding creativity is that it provides a nuanced way of understanding social interactions, consistent with the complex social reality that most workers experience. Social networks are comprised of a set of nodes (in this case, individuals) and the ties (or relationships) between nodes, although networks have been applied more broadly to study networks of schema, or cognitive networks (Schilling, 2005). A study of *social* networks within organizations encompasses questions such as what types of relationships are most helpful for a particular kind of outcome? (e.g., Granovetter, 1973; Hansen, 1999). Which positions in the broader pattern of relationships are most consequential for individuals within organizations (e.g., Brass, 1984; Krackhardt & Porter, 1985)? What is the structure of a person's ties with others that are most beneficial (e.g., Burt, 1992)? What is the overall pattern of relationships within a particular setting, such as a group, organization, or profession, that facilitates optimal performance and advancement for those within the setting (e.g., Oh, Chung & Labianca, 2004; Uzzi & Spiro, 2004)? Given these questions, the predominant outcomes of interest tend to be career advancement, overall performance, and power (see Borgatti & Foster, 2003; Brass et al., 2004, for reviews). For example, one might explore how being socially enmeshed influences ratings of job performance (Sparrowe, Liden, Wayne, & Kraimer, 2001) or how informal ties with current employees mitigate the effect of demographic variables on salaries for new hires (Seidel, Polzer, & Stewart, 2000). Creativity, however, is a distinct kind of outcome where the focus is on the generation of novel, appropriate and valued ideas and solutions (Amabile, 1983; Shalley, 1991).

The kinds of relationships represented in a network can vary from formal to informal. Formal relationships have been referred to as work-flow ties (e.g., Mehra, Kilduff, & Brass, 2001) and can be thought of as ties that are formally required to do one's job. For example, this would include ties to a boss or to others with whom a person exchanges work outputs (Brass, 1984). In contrast, I focus specifically on informal interactions within and outside of work. These are informal in that they are not specifically required as part of the job and are often the most critical interactions for creative problem solving (e.g., Hargadon & Bechky, 2006). For example, perhaps you are required to interact with your boss, subordinates, or even teammates to complete a project, but you are not required to have casual conversations about a wide range of work-related matters with Pat in accounting or Samantha in logistics. Furthermore, these associations are not necessarily specific to a particular project or problem. For example, it is not critical that your discussions with Pat or Samantha involve particular problems or projects. What is important is that you are chatting with them informally and have some level of informal relationship. In the sections that follow, I describe how informal social relationships influence creative contributions, and in particular, I have organized the literature in terms of types of relationship, which includes the interplay of relationship type and structure, position in the overall pattern of relationships, and structures of team and organizational networks.

TYPES OF RELATIONSHIPS

Relationships can be characterized in a number of different ways. In a general sense, one powerful way of thinking about network ties in addition to the content of communication, is to focus on the strength of a tie. Granovetter (1973), in his early conceptualization, described the quality of ties in terms of their strength. He suggested with this work that stronger ties are relationships characterized by some combination of high levels of emotional closeness, very frequent interaction, and reciprocated perceptions about the importance of the relationship. Subsequently, research has suggested that this notion of tie strength may be more complex. For example, while some have suggested that closeness, frequency, and duration are alternative measures representing tie strength (e.g., Hansen, 1999; Wegener, 1991), others have suggested that these are unique dimensions of tie strength that may have differential outcomes (e.g., Marsden & Campbell, 1984; Perry-Smith, 2006). In addition, recent work on negative ties (Labianca, Brass, & Gray, 1998), the extent a person is disliked, suggests another aspect of tie strength. Further, we can overlay the content of communication; in other words, are individuals exchanging advice, political support, and general communication with the strength of the tie? For simplicity, I focus on strength of relationships in terms of closeness, or more specifically, the extent a tie represents friendships versus acquaintances, although more research is needed to understand various ways of looking at types of relationships for creative outcomes.

Exactly what kinds of informal social relationships are good for creativity? The best way to begin to answer this question is to focus on relationships that are not helpful: friendships. Yes, friendship ties have many benefits such as social support, trust, and liking (Krackhardt, 1992); however, when creative and breakthrough thinking is of interest, these ties that otherwise may be helpful may be problematic. According to Granovetter's (1973) important "strength of weak tie" theory, our good friends typically know one another. For example, let's say you have strong ties with Pat and Samantha. Perhaps, you bring the two together via a simultaneous interaction with both. Since we tend to have close relationships with people who are similar to us on some dimension (Byrne, 1971), chances are good that Pat and Samantha will also find that they have something in common and will develop some kind of tie. Over time, a dense network develops where everyone knows everyone else (Granovetter, 1973). Even if people do not initially have similar views as their friends, "contagion by cohesion," where perspectives and viewpoints circulate quickly throughout a dense network (Burt, 1992), suggests that individual views on issues begin to converge over time. As a result, friendship ties are more likely to be redundant, and we are less likely to be exposed to unusual perspectives and views from interacting with friends. None of this is good for creativity (Perry-Smith, 2006; Perry-Smith & Shalley, 2003).

In contrast, the weaker acquaintance ties, the seemingly inconsequential less important relationships, may stimulate creative thinking (Perry-Smith, 2006; Perry-Smith & Shalley, 2003). These are not a person's very close friends within a company or people one interacts with very frequently. You may not have known these people for a very long time. However, these ties provide the best option for new information, unavailable through tightly knit inner circles. After all, friends tend to be connected to the same people so they tend to have similar sources and to share the same information. For example, Granovetter (1974) finds some support for the idea that some managers are more likely to find a new job through a weakly tied contact than through a strongly tied contact. More contemporary research suggests that this may depend on the status and hierarchical level of the manager. For example, there is some suggestion that for low status individuals, stronger ties may be important (Ibarra, 1992) and that the importance of weak ties for finding jobs may be particularly important for high-level managers (Granovetter, 1982).

In addition, weaker ties are less reliant on similarity in comparison to strong ties. With weaker ties, the affective component of closeness is not as primary and interactions are more infrequent. As a result, individuals may be more tolerant of the cognitive and emotional discomfort and energy associated with interacting with people who are not similar. For example, assume that Mark is a marketing manager with a joint degree in art history and marketing and you are an engineering manager. You generally like Mark, value his contributions to the organization, and occasionally go to lunch with him. However, Mark is not among your closest friends. Sometimes you find yourself losing interest in his pursuit of open discussions, and likewise, he sometimes gets frustrated with your wanting to quickly get to the bottom line and apply rigid logic. This is a stereotypical example, of course, but the point is that differences may not hinder the development of relationships but may inhibit the extent stronger ties form. As a result, weaker ties can provide the best option for connecting people who have diverse perspectives, outlooks, interests, and experiences (Coser, 1975; Granovetter, 1982). These differences have been objectively captured and observed in terms of status, levels in the organizational hierarchy, and functional area (Lin, Ensel, & Vaughn, 1981; Lincoln & Miller, 1979; Seibert, Kraimer, & Liden, 2001) but may include deeper-level differences such as ways of making decisions, gathering information, and assumptions about appropriate behavior. In contrast, strong ties are more typically between people who share similarities (Ibarra, 1992; Lincoln & Miller, 1979). Thus, weak ties are more likely to provide connections to people with diverse viewpoints and perspectives and, as previously suggested, provide access to more nonredundant information.

These ties facilitate creativity because they provide cognitive stimulation equivalent to strengthening creative "muscles" such that when persons with weaker types of ties work on unrelated problems, they are more likely to come up with creative solutions. In particular, the access to people who are different should encourage a variety of cognitive processes that may help with creative outcomes. For example, when a person's social world involves interacting with people who do not see the world in the same way, this means that he or she cannot easily make choices that are consistent with his or her group of contacts. As a result, these ties promote more autonomous thinking and making connections between ideas that may seem disconnected. This exposure may spark other creative ideas. In addition, weaker ties may facilitate the acquisition of new and varied knowledge, which may provide a broader base of possibilities for coming up with creative solutions. Consistent with these ideas, in a study of 772 artists, Simonton (1984) found that relationships that were more distant (associates versus friends or admirers versus apprentices) were more important determinants of artistic eminence. In addition, in a study of an applied research institute, I found that individuals with many acquaintance ties with other researchers were more creative (Perry-Smith, 2006). In these cases, the creativity resides with the individual, in contrast to discussions related to a particular problem where a collective synergy may occur such that the creative solution resides with the dyad or collective versus the individual (e.g., Hargadon & Bechky, 2006).

A complementary view of network ties is a structural one related to brokerage. According to Burt's (1992) seminal structural perspective, individuals can act as brokers when they are the only connection between individuals and groups. The chasm, or lack of connection between groups, has been described as a "structural hole." Here, the critical feature of the connection is that it provides a connection between otherwise disconnected groups, regardless of whether the tie connects friends or acquaintances. As such, ties that span structural holes provide important opportunities for political leverage, unique information, and power (Burt, 1992). As a result, individuals with these ties have the capacity to achieve a variety of benefits including faster promotions and larger bonuses. Particularly related to creativity, structural holes are helpful when it comes to the acceptance of ideas (Burt, 2004). In addition, managers with dense networks were found to be less likely to be adaptable and tended to not change their network in response to changes in the task environment (Gargiulo & Benassi, 2000). Dense networks can be thought of as the inverse of structural holes given that density refers to the extent individuals in a network are connected to every other person in the network (Scott, 1991).

The primary difference between the two perspectives is whether or not the structure of a person's ties (e.g., spanning structural holes) or the content of the tie (e.g., the strength or quality of the relationship) is primary. Research exploring both the strength of the tie and whether or not the tie spans a structural hole suggests that, depending on the outcome of interest, both are important (e.g., Hansen, 1999; Seibert et al., 2001). For example, Seibert and colleagues (2001) found that weak ties and structural holes were related to career success; however, weak ties related to career outcomes primarily by providing contacts to people in other functions and at higher levels whereas structural holes related to career outcomes primarily via providing access to people at higher levels. This supports the notion that it is important to understanding tie strength and network structure separately and that the mechanisms may vary, which may have differential implications depending on the outcome of interest.

When it comes to developing creative solutions and ideas, in particular, the content and quality of the relationship seems to be important, over and above the extent the relationship serves to bridge structural holes and provides political advantages. For example, I found that weaker ties were related to creativity more because of their connections to diverse perspectives, rather than the tendency to be connected to otherwise disconnected individuals (Perry-Smith, 2006). This suggests that structural notions of nonredundancy may explain less of how weak ties relate to creativity. In addition, the emotional quality of the tie also may be important. Having lots of friends at work may provide a general sense of positive affect, and some research suggests that positive affect can help creativity in some cases (George & Zhou, 2002; Isen, Daubman, & Nowicki, 1987). However, positive affect may reduce effortful processing (Kaufmann & Vosburg, 1997) and when derived from social contacts within a domain, may not help people be more creative. In particular, affective ties such as friendship ties may be more associated with social influence pressures, which can lead to conformity around accepted practices (Granovetter, 1973; Krackhardt, 1992).

Another way of thinking about the kinds of relationships that may facilitate creative thinking is to think about the characteristics of the people a person is connected to, in line with the nodal approach to network research (e.g., Lin et al., 1981). This approach focuses on the resources held by a person's contacts versus the strength of the tie or the structure of the network. Here, the quality of the relationship or the structure within a person's network ties is not explicitly considered. Instead, the interest centers on whom a person is connected to and the qualities this person possesses that may be helpful. First, for creativity in particular, relationships with people whose knowledge is very different, perhaps even to the point where it seems that the contacts have almost no work-related knowledge in common, may be important. Rodan & Galunic (2004) found that managers who were connected to managers who had different bases of knowledge than the focal manager as well as different basis of knowledge from one another were more innovative. Interestingly, the variety of knowledge sources seemed to matter more for their performance than the extent of redundant connections in their networks. This research was conducted in a Scandinavian telecommunications company, but we can also envision these results applying more broadly. For example, I would expect an engineer connected with a philosopher and three other people representing different areas of specialty to have similar experiences.

Second, connections to people who are creative may help individuals be more creative. In a study of 772 artists, Simonton (1984) suggests how the characteristics of contacts influenced the creative eminence of artists. His findings suggest that the most creative artists were those with connections to highly distinguished artists (paragons). Further, the more that an artist existed in a period with many paragons the more creative the artist, suggesting that indirect exposure to creative others plays a role in the creativity of the focal person. In a related study within a more organizationally focused context, Zhou (2003) explored how connections to creative peers related to creativity. Her results suggest an interesting twist. She focused on the presence of creative coworkers versus direct interactions with creative others, and she found that individuals were more creative when creative coworkers existed, particularly when supervisors were more encouraging of creativity by providing more developmental and helpful feedback. Interestingly, this result held more strongly for individuals who tended to not have creative personalities. This suggests that for individuals without the innate tendency to be creative (probably a large portion of the workforce in the average company), the presence and potential contact with creative others may be helpful. Interestingly, this creativity contagion is expected not because people copy and transfer a creative idea from one context to another, but via modeling processes (Baundura, 1986; Shalley & Perry-Smith, 2001; Zhou, 2003), where individuals learn creative-thought processes and behaviors that help them be more creative in general. For example, in one study (Shalley & Perry-Smith, 2001), individuals shown an example of a creative solution, which served as a creative model, were more creative when coming up with solutions to a different problem.

POSITION IN THE ORGANIZATIONAL NETWORK

Beyond with whom you have direct relationships, the overall pattern of relationships within a bounded area, such as your organization (or profession for more cosmopolitan fields), is also important for creativity. For example, consider the network of relationships reflected in Figure 8.1. Each number represents a person and the lines represent informal social ties. Up to now, I have suggested the kinds of relationships, in terms of content and ties to whom, that may facilitate creative thinking. Looking at node 144 in Figure 8.1, the prior discussion focuses on his or her seven connections to others, and we might ask ourselves are these ties to good friends, to people with diverse knowledge, or to people who are creative? However, a wide body of rigorous research suggests that in addition to focusing on direct ties, a person's position in this overall web of relationships has implications for a host of important outcomes such as promotion, advancement, and power (e.g., Blau & Alba, 1982; Brass, 1984, 1992; Cross & Cummings, 2004; Sparrowe et al., 2001).

Given a network representing the pattern of relationships among a collection of people, centrality is a helpful way of understanding a person's position in the network. Intuitively, centrality captures the extent a person is in the middle or highly immersed within the network. There are a variety of approaches to defining centrality (see Freeman, 1979, for a review), but one common approach, closeness centrality, involves a person's average social distance to every other person in the network. More formally, closeness centrality is defined as the average distance, in terms of social ties, to other members of the network (Freeman, 1979)

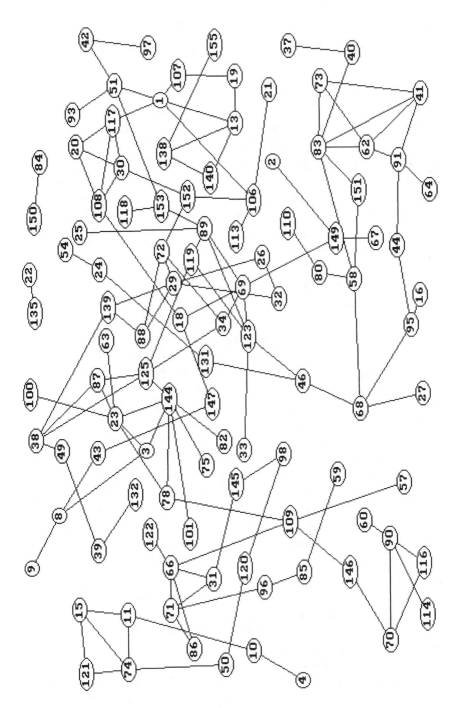

Figure 8.1 Sample network of relationships.

so that a person with high closeness centrality is able to reach the largest number of people with the fewest links. In a study within a newspaper-publishing company (Brass, 1984), individuals with central positions in the informal communications network were more likely to be promoted and were rated as being more influential. With regard to creative thinking in particular, understanding a person's centrality in the pattern of relationships is relevant for understanding how the informal social environment influences creativity. For creativity, the central message is that it is not only to whom you are connected that matters, but the pattern of indirect connections that may also be important.

That said, is it better to be very central in the overall network of relationships or on the periphery? The simple answer is: it depends. When it comes to selling ideas and gaining support for ideas, central positions may be preferred (Ibarra, 1993; Obstfeld, 2005). This makes sense given the association between centrality and power. In order to effectively advocate and gain support for an unusual solution, a more powerful person (via social connections) may be in the best position to do this. Similar positions in the overall network that provide opportunities for power via connecting otherwise disconnected subgroups also may help one better understand the context and communicate ideas in a way that they will be appreciated as more valuable (Burt, 2004). However, when it comes to contributing ideas and solutions that are also novel and creative, this may not be the case.

The relationship between network centrality and creativity has been conceptualized as a spiraling one, one that starts off positively but ultimately spirals in a negative direction (Perry-Smith & Shalley, 2003). At the positive end of the spiral, being more central in the network is proposed to lead to more creative insights. More central individuals should have more favorable perspectives and outlooks, feel very confident given their social status and be more open to taking calculated risks (Ibarra & Andrews, 1993). As an individual contributes creative thinking to the organization, associates may be more drawn to this individual due to his or her interesting ideas and ability to solve critical problems. These individuals become sought out via informal, chance conversations to help others solve problems and generate creative solutions (Hargadon & Bechky, 2006). As a result, these individuals become more central in the network and the positive self-reinforcing spiral between centrality and creativity continues, but only up to a point.

We (Perry-Smith & Shalley, 2001) further theorized that as the spiral continues and the person becomes more and more central, the person becomes so immersed in the status quo and accepted ways of doing things that it becomes cognitively difficult to see beyond this to develop new ideas and approaches. In some ways, the web of relationships and the central person's social proximity to others becomes strangling and inhibits new insights and expression. In addition, these highly central positions may be associated with more stress and knowledge overload, which may distract from creativity. At this point, centrality constrains creativity and the spiral becomes self correcting where increasing centrality leads to lower creativity.

Another perspective on whether or not one should seek to be more or less central is considering ties outside of the network or organization. Individuals with outside connections may receive fresh nonredundant information and perform the critical function of sharing information with the organization and may even import ideas from other contexts (Allen, 1984; Tushman, 1977). Within a large product design firm, Sutton & Hargadon (1996) explained how the organization's connections to a variety of different industries helped the firm act as knowledge brokers between industries. Beyond an importer or linking function, people with many ties outside of an organization are potentially exposed to approaches from other areas that may spark creative thoughts (Fleming & Marx, 2006; Perry-Smith & Shalley, 2003). In addition, relationships outside of the organization may provide important sources of social support. In a study of organizations in the Bulgarian knitwear industry (Madjar, Oldham, & Pratt, 2002), individuals receiving support for creativity from family and friends outside of their work setting were more creative because of the effect of these supportive ties on positive mood. This suggests that, in general, ties that span relevant boundaries (e.g., organization, profession) may be helpful for creativity and that not only acquaintance ties but also friendship ties may be helpful in this case.

Although it seems that ties outside of the organization are another way that individuals can be social and also creative, when a person is highly central, it may be better to have fewer outside ties. Alternatively, when a person has many outside ties, it may be best to be less central. In a study of research scientists (Perry-Smith, 2006), I found that scientists who were on the periphery of the social network (less central) but had many ties outside of the firm where highly creative. These individuals were in the beneficial position of being exposed to potentially different and interesting perspectives from outside the firm but were also not socially constrained by being highly central. However, associates with the combination of many outside ties and high centrality made the least creative contributions to the firm because outside ties in this case potentially may have distracted them from being creative. In summary, peripheral positions are helpful for creativity in combination with many outside ties. Centrality can also be helpful, assuming there are not too many outside ties and assuming that one is in the early stages of a positive creativity–centrality spiral. Otherwise, on the tail end of the spiral, increasing centrality may stifle creativity.

TEAM AND ORGANIZATIONAL NETWORKS

So far, I have discussed different ways of looking at how informal relationships can help people be more creative. For this discussion, I have assumed that a person is working alone, or has primary responsibility for a problem or task versus working collectively with a team. To clarify, although I have assumed that the work is individually focused, I have also assumed that interactions with others may influence a person's cognitive thinking and creative contributions. However, we also can think about teams in this same context. Obviously, team members are interacting with one another to complete the project or task, but interactions that are required by the work differ from the interactions that I have been focusing on so far—those discretionary, informal interactions that are not required by the job. When we think about teams, the kinds of informal interactions that team members have with one another as well as the informal interactions they have with people outside of the team can be very telling when it comes to their creativity.

Intuitively, it makes sense that team members should have reasonably close relationships with one another. According to research on teams, teams that are highly cohesive or interpersonally close have many advantages. For example, these teams have more satisfied group members and tend to have higher levels of consensus (Beal, Cohen, Burke, & McLendon, 2003; Sethi, Smith, & Park, 2001). In addition, these groups tend to be highly cooperative and committed to the group (Jehn & Shah, 1997) and tend to perform well (e.g., Balkundi & Harrison, 2006). However, in a recent study (Perry-Smith & Shalley, 2006), we found that the relationship between the closeness of the group and creativity may not be so straightforward. The results of this study suggest that groups that are not very close (weak ties with one another) were the most creative and that the closer the group, the less creative the outcome. However, this finding existed only up to a point. It seemed that moderately close groups were the least creative but that highly close groups (for example, where everyone is friends with everyone else) also were highly creative. We think this occurred because the acquaintance groups were less distracted by their closeness; as a result, they could pay more attention to unique ideas. For example, early social psychology research highlighted how cohesion could lead to group think and limit the consideration of alternative solutions (Asch, 1956; Janis, 1982). In contrast, the friendship groups may experience high levels of trust and be more satisfied with the group experience (Jehn & Shah, 1997). As a result, these groups may be more committed to group goals, allowing them to persist with difficult problems that may require creativity, and these groups also may be more willing to share diverse information and potentially new ideas.

While it is important to consider informal relationships within the team, teams are typically not socially isolated from relationships with others who are not members of the team. We can think of a team's social composition as reflecting informal ties among team members but also as including informal relationships outside of the team (Oh et al., 2004). These ties may be an important resource for teams when it comes to gaining political support, sharing appropriate knowledge, or acquiring resources (Allen, 1984; Ancona & Caldwell, 1992; Cummings, 2004; Hansen, 1999; Tushman, 1977). For example, Ancona and Caldwell (1992) found that the socially isolated teams were not very innovative. In addition, these outside connections may help diverse teams tap into broader professional affiliations and areas of specialized expertise (Murray, 2004; Reagans, Zuckerman & McEvily, 2004). As a result, these connections can be critical for teams when it comes to completing projects more quickly, working through the difficulties involved with implementation, or being more efficient.

Alternatively, individuals transfer ways of behaving and approaching problems across team boundaries so that their informal social relationships outside of the team can influence the way they approach problems and interact with their teammates (Beckman, 2006; Pettigrew, 1986). As a result, teams can be viewed as a collection of individuals, with potentially different social realities that may influence the creativity of the team (Perry-Smith & Shalley, 2006). For example, weaker connections outside of the team may enhance the tendency to think in flexible ways and come up with unique solutions, so team members with this type of exposure may bring this way of behaving within the team and act as important creative sparks that influence the creativity of others and the team.

In addition, individuals who have informal social relationships outside of the team with people representing diverse nationalities may also bring more flexible thinking into the group. Background and demographic diversity within teams is widely thought to be beneficial for creativity (see Williams & O'Reilly, 1998, for a review); it is also acknowledged that these teams also may experience a variety of internal process problems that may undermine their potential to be creative. In contrast, connections outside of the team may not necessarily be associated with similar internal process losses but may provide opportunities for creativity within the team. In particular, nationality may reflect different cultures, languages, and approaches to work (Cox, Lobel, & McLeod, 1991; Erez & Earley, 1993). Individuals with ties to people representing diverse nationalities may be more versed at being open to new ideas, adapting behaviors to fit various circumstances, and displaying greater flexibility when solving problems. When these ties exist with individuals outside of the team, this behavior can potentially be imported into the team, which should be very helpful when it comes to team processes that may help creativity like reconciling different views or paying attention to ideas that others may quickly dismiss that may have unbounded potential. Another interesting twist is whether or not it is most effective to have one individual with these kinds of connections versus many (Tushman, 1977). There is much more research needed in this area, but our early findings (Perry-Smith & Shalley, 2006) suggest that the more team members with these kinds of connections the better for creativity.

Moving from the informal social networks that individuals can bring to their teams, we also can think about how different patterns of relationships within organizations or professions affect the creativity of individuals and teams. Turning again to Figure 8.1, instead of thinking about how each person's position influences creativity, we can envision each organization as having a unique network picture that describes internal social interactions. In a study of Broadway musicals from 1945 to 1989, Uzzi and Spiro (2005) go beyond understanding the content of ties outside of the team and specifically sought to understand how the pattern of ties among artists affected the creativity of teams as well as the creativity of the entire industry. They primarily draw on Milgram's (1967) historical work on small world networks. His conclusion that the world is socially small was based on a simple experiment. He asked people in a small town to pass a letter to a randomly chosen stockbroker in Boston. He found that on average it took six contacts ("six degrees of separation") for the letter to reach the random stockbroker. His general premise was that friends tend to interact with friends, but that "small world" networks exist when at least one person in a clique is also part of another.

Subsequently (e.g., Newman, Strogatz, & Watts, 2001), small world networks have been defined as those that have dense clusters (e.g., individuals with common membership in a team) as well as individuals who connect clusters (e.g., individuals with memberships in multiple teams). Uzzi & Spiro found an inverted U-shaped relationship between the small worldliness of artists involved with productions and the creativity of these teams in terms of artistic and commercial success. They argued that moderate small worldliness provides the optimal balance of cohesion, trust, and the transfer of information within the profession. It is important to note that this study used work-required interactions since production teams were all considered fully connected by virtue of their working on the same team. In addition, this means that the small worldliness reflects the level of boundary-spanning ties within the network. Nevertheless, this idea of considering the structure of the network as a whole provides interesting implications for the kinds of global relationships organizational leaders should consider establishing to enhance the collective creativity of their organizations.

MANAGERIAL IMPLICATIONS AND FUTURE RESEARCH

In this chapter, I have reviewed how and when being social can help people be more creative. The research reviewed here suggests that bounded social contact can be good for creativity. Individuals should be connected but not too connected. For example, weaker acquaintance type ties may facilitate creative thinking, but stronger friendship ties may be less helpful. In particular, connections to people who hold different types of knowledge, who have diverse nationalities, or who are creative also are helpful. In some cases, being central in a network may help people be more creative, but being too central may be a problem. Ties outside of the network (organization or profession) may also be positive, as long as the person is not simultaneously central in the network. Being on the periphery of a network can be good, as long as the person has many outside connections. Otherwise this person may be too isolated to be creative. Lastly, organizations, communities of practice, or industries where the network of relationships between people is more "small world" in character, may be more likely to see higher creative contributions in general among associates.

These ideas offer several suggestions for organizational leaders interested in creativity. In some cases, associates designated as "creatives" such as research and development personnel are isolated from the rest of the organization. While the concept of not being too immersed in a confining culture makes sense, too much isolation, particularly with less outside professional interaction, may be problematic for their creativity. For associates who may not be designated as "creatives" but who work in dynamic and challenging environments with complex problems, there are several avenues that could be considered. For example, physical space could be used in ways to mix people up so that informal chance encounters occur that would facilitate weaker ties. Alternatively, action could be taken to move highly immersed associates, who may be highly central in the network, out of their central position and to the periphery perhaps via special assignments to a different business unit. Newer associates who may be on the periphery or may have weaker ties with more long-term associates can spark creative ideas in others. These associates could be asked to sit in on meetings at a variety of levels and encouraged to voice opinions and ask questions. Their lack of familiarity with the way things are done and their lack of immersion in the network may prompt them to raise unusual questions, even naïve ones, that may indirectly influence the thinking of others in more creative ways.

The ideas discussed herein specifically focus on creativity as the generation of ideas and solutions that are novel, appropriate, or valued (Amabile, 1983; Shalley, 1991), and how social interactions influence creative contributions at work. Although not the focus of this chapter, social interactions also play a role in moving ideas through the organization toward implementation and potentially leading to innovation. In this case, one may want to have stronger ties so that one feels more comfortable sharing unusual ideas (Albrecht & Hall, 1991) and may have an easier time convincing friends of the merits of their idea. Centrality in the network also would be important in this case. For example, Mehra et al. (2001) found that centrality in the friendship and work-flow networks were related to performance in an innovative context of a high-technology firm. In addition, bringing people together and creating more closed dense networks also may help with the potential success of an idea (Fleming & Marx, 2006; Obstfeld, 2005). In particular, in a study within an engineering division of an automotive manufacturer (Obstfeld, 2005), individuals with a strategic orientation around bringing together previously disconnected people were more likely to be involved with implemented innovations. Additionally, networks have provided an important explanation for the diffusion of innovations (e.g., Rogers, 1983). This interplay between creativity and innovation has interesting implications for being social and how informal social interactions affect both.

In general, it is important to create a climate where associates are comfortable taking risks and feel the freedom and support necessary to come up with creative contributions. Many cases exist within organizations where a standard and plain solution will not satisfy the complexities of the problem. For example, although creativity has often been described as a necessary precursor to innovation, creative thinking is also needed throughout the process to overcome difficulties and barriers associated with implementation or commercialization (Ford, 1996; Perry-Smith & Vincent, forthcoming). While there are many ways to create organizational climates that can help people be more creative, thinking about creativity from a social perspective, and in particular using a social network lens, offers several possibilities for encouraging creativity within organizations while at the same time raising a variety of interesting questions for future research.

REFERENCES

Albrecht, T. L., & Hall, B. J. (1991). Facilitating talk about new ideas: The role of personal relationships in organizational innovation. *Communication Monographs, 58,* 273–288.

Allen, T. J. (1984) *Managing the flow of technology: Technology transfer and the dissemination of technological information within the R&D organization.* Cambridge, MA: M.I.T. Press.

Amabile, T. M. (1983). The social psychology of creativity: A componential conceptualization. *Journal of Personality and Social Psychology, 45,* 357–377.

Amabile, T. M. (1996). *Creativity in Context.* Boulder, CO: Westview Press.

Ancona, D. G., & Caldwell, D. F. (1992). Demography and design: Predictors of new product team performance. *Organization Science, 3,* 321–341.

Asch, S. E. (1956). Studies of independence and conformity: A minority of one. *Psychological Monographs, 70,* 1–70.

Balkundi, P., & Harrison, D. A. (2006). Ties, leaders, and time in teams: Strong inference about network structure's effects on team viability and performance. *Academy of Management Journal, 49,* 49–68.

Baundura, A. (1986). *Social foundations of thought and action: A social cognitive theory.* Englewood Cliffs, NJ: Prentice-Hall.

Beal, D. J., Cohen, R. R., Burke, M. J., & McLendon, C. L. (2003). Cohesion and performance in groups: A meta-analytic clarification of construct relations. *Journal of Applied Psychology, 88,* 989–1004.

Beckman, C. M. (2006). The influence of founding team company affiliations on firm behavior. *Academy of Management Journal, 49,* 741–758.

Blau, J. R., & Alba, R. D. (1982). Empowering nets of participation. *Administrative Science Quarterly, 27,* 363–379.

Borgatti, S. P., & Foster, P. C. (2003). The network paradigm in organizational research: A review and typology. *Journal of Management, 29,* 991–1013.

Brass, D. J. (1984). Being in the right place: A structural analysis of individual influence in an organization. *Administrative Science Quarterly, 29,* 518–539.

Brass, D. J. (1992). Power in organizations: A social network perspective. *Research in Politics and Society, 4,* 295–323.

Brass, D. J., Galaskiewicz, J., Greve, H. R., & Tsai, W. (2004). Taking stock of networks and organizations: A multilevel perspective. *Academy of Management Journal, 47,* 795–817.

Burt, R. S. (1992). *Structural holes.* Cambridge, MA: Harvard University Press.

Burt, R. S. (2004). Structural holes and good ideas. *American Journal of Sociology, 110,* 349–399.

Byrne, D. (1971). *The attraction paradigm.* New York: Academic Press, Inc.

Coser, R. (1975). The complexity of roles as a seedbed of individual autonomy. In L. Coser (Ed.), *The idea of social structure: Papers in honor of Robert K. Merton* (pp. 237–263). New York: Harcourt Brace.

Cox, T. H., Lobel, S. A., & McLeod, P. L. (1991). Effects of ethnic group cultural differences on cooperative and competitive behavior on a group task. *Academy of Management Journal, 34,* 827–847.

Cross, R., & Cummings, J. N. (2004) Ties and network correlates of individual performance in knowledge-intensive work. *Academy of Management Journal, 47,* 928–937.

Cummings, J. (2004). Work groups, structural diversity, and knowledge sharing in a global organization. *Management Science, 50,* 352–364.

Erez, M., & Earley, P.,C. (1993). *Culture, self-identity, and work.* New York: Oxford University Press.

Fleming, L., & Marx, M. (2006). Managing creativity in small worlds. *California Management Review, 48,* 6–26.

Ford, C. (1996). A theory of individual creative action in multiple social domain. *Academy of Management Review, 21,* 215–239.

Freeman, L. C. (1979). Centrality in social networks: Conceptualizations and clarifications. *Social Networks, 1,* 215–239.

Gargiulo, M., & Benassi, M. (2000). Trapped in your own net? Network cohesion, structural holes, and the adaptation of social capital. *Organization Science, 11,* 183–196.

George, J. M., & Zhou, J. (2002). Understanding when bad moods foster creativity and good ones don't: The role of context and clarity on feelings. *Journal of Applied Psychology, 87,* 687–697.

Gilson, L. L., & Shalley, C. E. (2004). A little creativity goes a long way: An examination of teams' engagement in creative processes. *Journal of Management, 30,* 453–470.

Granovetter, M. S. (1973). The strength of weak ties. *American Journal of Sociology, 6,* 1360–1380.

Granovetter, M. S. (1974). *Getting a job: A study of contacts and careers.* Cambridge, MA: Harvard University Press.

Granovetter, M. S. (1982). The strength of weak ties: A network theory revisited. In P. V. Marsden & N. Lin (Eds.), *Social structure and network analysis* (pp. 105–130). Beverly Hills, CA: Sage.

Hansen, M. T. (1999). The search-transfer problem: The role of weak ties in sharing knowledge across organizational subunits. *Administrative Science Quarterly, 37,* 422–447.

Hargadon, A. B., & Bechky, B. A. (2006). When collections of creatives become creative collectives: A field study of problem solving at work. *Organization Science, 17,* 484–500.

Ibarra, H. (1992) Homophily and differential returns: Sex differences in network structure and access in an advertising firm. *Administrative Science Quarterly, 37,* 277–303.

Ibarra, H. (1993). Network centrality, power, and innovation involvement: determinants of technical and administrative roles. *Academy of Management Journal, 36,* 471–501.

Ibarra, H., & Andrews, S. B. (1993). Power, social influence, and sense making: Effects of network centrality and proximity on employee perceptions. *Administrative Science Quarterly, 38,* 277–303.

Isen, A. M., Daubman, K. A., & Nowicki, G. P. (1987). Positive affect facilitates creative problem solving. *Journal of Personality and Social Psychology, 32,* 1122–1131.

Janis, I. L. (1982). *Groupthink: Psychological studies of policy decisions and fiascoes.* Boston: Houghton Mifflin.

Jehn, K. A., & Shah, P. P. (1997). Interpersonal relationships and task performance: An examination of mediating processes in friendship and acquaintance groups. *Journal of Personality and Social Psychology, 72,* 775–791.

Kaufmann, G., & Vosburg, S. K. (1997). "Paradoxical" mood effects on creative problem-solving. *Cognition and Emotion, 11,* 151–170.

Krackhardt, D. (1992). The strength of strong ties: The importance of philos in organizations. In N. Nohria & R. C. Eccles (Eds.), *Networks and organizations: Structure, form, and action* (pp. 216–239). Cambridge, MA: Harvard University Press.

Krackhardt, D., & Porter, L. W. (1985). When friends leave: A structural analysis of the relationships between turnover and stayers' attitudes. *Administrative Science Quarterly, 30,* 242–261.

Labianca, G., Brass, D. J., & Gray, B. (1998) Social networks and perceptions of intergroup conflict: The role of negative relationships and third parties. *Academy of Management Journal, 1,* 55–67.

Lin, N., Ensel, W. M., & Vaughn, J. C. (1981). Social resources and strength of ties. *American Sociological Review, 46,* 393–405.

Lincoln, J. R., & Miller, J. (1979). Work and friendship ties in organizations: A comparative analysis of relational networks. *Administrative Science Quarterly, 24,* 181–199.

Madjar, N., Oldham, G. R., & Pratt, M. G. (2002). There's there no place like home? The contributions of work and nonwork creativity support to employees' creative performance. *Academy of Management Journal, 45,* 757–767.

Marsden, P. V., & Campbell, K. E. (1984). Measuring tie strength. *Social Forces, 63,* 482–501.

Mehra, A., Kilduff, M., & Brass, D. J. (2001).The social networks of high and low self-monitors: Implications for workplace performance. *Administrative Science Quarterly, 46,* 121–146.

Milgram, S. (1967). The small world. *Psychology Today, 2,* 60–67.

Murray, F. (2004). The role of academic inventors in entrepreneurial firms: Sharing the laboratory life. *Research Policy, 33,* 643–659.

Newman, M. E. J., Strogatz, S. H., & Watts, D. J. (2001). Random graphs with arbitrary degree distributions and their applications. *Physical Review E, 64,* 1–17.

Obstfeld, D. (2005). Social networks, the tertius lungens orientation, and involvement in innovation. *Administrative Science Quarterly, 50,* 100–130.

Oh, H., Chung, M., & Labianca, G. (2004). Group social capital and group effectiveness: The role of informal socializing ties. *Academy of Management Journal, 47,* 860–875.

O'Reilly, C., Williams, K., & Barsade, S. (1998). Group democracy and innovation: Does diversity help? *Research on Managing Teams, 1,* 183–207.

Perry-Smith, J. E. (2006). Social yet creative: The role of social relationships in facilitating individual creativity. *Academy of Management Journal, 49,* 85–101.

Perry-Smith, J. E., & Shalley, C. E. (2003). The social side of creativity: A static and dynamic social network perspective. *Academy of Management Review, 28,* 89–106.

Perry-Smith, J. E., & Shalley, C. E. (2006). *Team creativity: The role of informal interactions.* Paper presentation at the 2006 Academy of Management Annual Meeting, Atlanta, Georgia.

Perry-Smith, J. E., & Vincent, L. (Forthcoming). The benefits and liabilities of multidisciplinary commercialization teams: How professional composition and social networks influence team processes. In M. Thursby (Ed.), *Advances in the study of entrepreneurship, innovation, and economic growth.*

Pettigrew, T. F. (1986). Intergroup contact theory. *Annual Review of Psychology, 49,* 65–85.

Reagans, R., Zuckerman, E., & McEvily, B. (2004). How to make the team: Social networks vs. demography as criteria for designing effective teams. *Administrative Science Quarterly, 49,* 101–133.

Rodan, S., & Galunic, C. (2004). More than network structure: how knowledge heterogeneity influences managerial performance and innovativeness. *Strategic Management Journal, 25,* 541–562.

Rogers, E. M. (1983). *Diffusion of innovations.* New York: The Free Press.

Schilling, M. A. (2005). A "small world" network model of cognitive insight. *Creativity Research Journal, 17*(2,3), 131–154.

Scott, J. (1991). *Social network analysis: A handbook.* Thousand Oaks, CA: Sage.

Seibert, S. E., Kraimer, M. L., & Liden, R. C. (2001). A social capital theory of career success. *Academy of Management Journal, 44,* 219–237.

Seidel, M. L., Polzer, J. T., & Stewart, K. J. (2000). Friends in high places: The effects of social networks on discrimination in salary negotiations. *Administrative Science Quarterly, 45*(1), 1–27.

Sethi, R., Smith, D. C., & Park, C. W. (2001). Cross-functional product development teams, creativity, and the innovativeness of consumer products. *Journal of Marketing Research, 38,* 73–85.

Shalley, C. E. (1991). Effects of productivity goals, creativity goals, and personal discretion on individual creativity. *Journal of Applied Psychology, 76,* 179–185.

Shalley, C. E., & Perry-Smith, J. E. (2001). Effects of social-psychological factors on creative performance: The role of informational and controlling expected evaluation and modeling experience. *Organizational Behavior and Human Decision Processes, 84,* 1–22.

Simonton, D. K. (1984). Artistic creativity and interpersonal relationships across and within generations. *Journal of Personality and Social Psychology, 46,* 1273–1286.

Sparrowe, R. T., Liden, R. C., Wayne, S. J., & Kraimer, M. L. (2001). Social networks and the performance of individuals and groups. *Academy of Management Journal, 44,* 316–325.

Sutton, R. I., & Hargadon, A. (1996). Brainstorming groups in context: Effectiveness in a product design firm. *Administrative Science Quarterly, 41,* 685–718.

Tushman, M. L. (1977). Special boundary roles in the innovation process. *Administrative Science Quarterly, 22,* 587–605.

Uzzi, B., & Spiro, J. (2005). Collaboration and creativity: The small world problem. *American Journal of Sociology, 111,* 447–504.

Wallas, G. (1926). *The art of thought.* New York: Harcourt Brace Jovanovich.

Wegener, B. (1991). Job mobility and social ties: Social resources, prior job, and status attainment. *American Sociological Review, 56,* 60–71.

Williams, K. Y., & O'Reilly, C. A. (1998). Demography and diversity in organizations: A review of 40 years of research. In *Research in Organizational Behavior* (pp. 77–140). Greenwich, CT: JAI Press.

Zhou, J. (2003). When the presence of creative coworkers is related to creativity: Role of supervisor close monitoring, developmental feedback, and creative personality. *Journal of Applied Psychology, 88,* 413–422.

CHAPTER 9

Climates and Cultures for Innovation and Creativity at Work

Michael A. West
Aston Business School

Andreas W. Richter
Instituto de Empresa Business School

INTRODUCTION

At the root of the growth of our species from our primitive beginnings to the recent stunning advances in technology, communication and social complexity have been creativity and innovation—the development and implementation of ideas for improved processes, products, or procedures (Drazin & Schoonhoven, 1996). So how can we create organizations that enable people to deploy their creativity in ways that lead to progress and new understanding? In this chapter, we explore what psychological and management research suggests are the values, attitudes, and shared meanings that characterize the cultures and climates of innovative organizations. What is it about the climates and cultures of these places where we work that influences us to be creative and innovative in our work?

We make sense of this domain of social science research by distinguishing between creativity and innovation. Creativity can be seen as the development of new ideas, while innovation implementation is the application of those new ideas in practice (West, 2002a). Creativity, we propose, requires individuals with creative characteristics, who feel free from threat and pressure, and work in a supportive environment. Innovation requires diversity (of knowledge particularly), integration of people's knowledge and efforts, external challenge or demand, and practical support for innovation. We also suggest that understanding the organizational cultures or climates that promote creativity and innovation requires a consideration of effects at the individual, team, and organizational levels.

We suggest that creative, innovative organizations are places where there is a firm and shared belief among most members in an appealing vision of what the organization is trying to achieve. There is a high level of interaction, discussion, constructive debate, and influence among the members of the organization as they go about their work. Trust, cooperative orientations, and a sense of interpersonal safety characterize interpersonal and intergroup relationships. Members of the organization, particularly those at the upper echelons (and there are few echelons) are consistently positive and open to members' ideas for new and improved ways of working, providing both encouragement and the resources for innovation. Finally, such organizations operate in situations where the demands on them are high; they are under strong external pressure but members see this positively as a challenge rather than an impossible burden.

In order to justify these assertions, we begin by examining briefly what is meant by organizational culture and by organizational climate. We then turn to examine how climates (since this is the most discernible element of culture) influence individuals, groups, and whole organizations to innovate. But we focus most strongly on team creativity and innovation, since groups of people are primarily responsible for implementing change in organizations rather than individuals or organizations (West, 2002a). We also focus most on the implementation of creative ideas in organizations, since it is implementation that determines the value of creative ideas in practice (West, 2002b). Finally, we examine organizational climate as a factor predicting innovation at the level of organizations.

ORGANIZATIONAL CULTURE AND CLIMATE

Organizations can be described much as we might describe to our friends the experience we had in visiting a distant foreign country. We might talk about the dress, laws, physical environment, buildings, nightlife, recreational activities, language, humor, food, values, and rituals. Similarly, organizations can be described in terms of their cultures—meanings, values, attitudes, and beliefs. Surface manifestations of culture include

Hierarchy	Number of levels from the head of the organization to the lowest level employee
Pay levels	High or low, whether there is performance-related pay, and what the differentials are between people at different grades
Job descriptions	How detailed or restrictive they are and what aspects they emphasize such as safety, or productivity, cost saving or quality
Informal practices such as norms	Management and nonmanagement employees sit at separate tables in the canteen; dress is strictly formal, there are uniforms, or dress is casual
Espoused values and rituals	An emphasis on cooperation and support versus cut-and-thrust competition between teams; cards, gifts, and parties for those leaving the organization or such events are not observed
Stories, jokes, and jargon	Commonly told stories about a particular success or the failings of management; humor about the sales department, for example; and jargon or acronyms (most government departments have a lexicon of acronyms and jargon and the language is often impenetrable to outsiders)
Physical environment	Office space, canteens, restrooms; are all spaces clean, tidy and comfortable, or is it only the areas on public display? Are there decorations such as plants and paintings and good facilities such as water fountains?

The meanings of all these aspects taken together tell us about the underlying culture of the organization, that is, shared meanings, values, attitudes, and beliefs (Schein, 1992). Managers have been particularly interested in how to "manage" culture and considerable resources have been spent trying to "shape" organizational cultures and create "a service culture," "an open culture," or "an innovation culture," to name but three examples.

Central to most, if not all, models of organizational behavior are perceptions of the work environment, referred to generally as "organizational climate" (Rousseau, 1988). Organizational climate has occupied a pivotal role in the organizational sciences dating from Lewin's classic work on motivation in the 1950s (Lewin, 1951) and was formalized through the human relations movement of the 1960s (e.g., Argyris, 1958). Primarily understood as the intervening variable between the context of an organization and the responses and behavior of its members, the concept has inspired many descriptions and operationalizations. Climate refers to the perceptions of the work environment and the term climate can designate descriptions and perceptions at the individual, group, or organizational level of analysis. Individual perceptions of the work environment are usually termed psychological climate, and when shared to a level sufficient for aggregation to the group or organizational level are labeled group or organizational climate.

At the broadest level, organizational climate describes how organizational members experience organizations and attach shared meanings to their perceptions of this environment (James & James, 1989). Schneider (1990) suggests that organizational climate perceptions focus on the processes, practices, and behaviors that are rewarded and supported in an organization. Most also agree that individuals interpret these aspects of the organizational environment in relation to their own sense of well being (James, James, & Ashe, 1990). But what are the dimensions of climate?

Individuals can describe the organizational environment both in an overall global sense, as well as in a more specific, targeted manner. In relation to the global organizational environment, James and his colleague (James & James, 1989) describe four dimensions of global organizational climate, which have been identified across a number of different work contexts:

1. Role stress and lack of harmony (including role ambiguity, conflict and overload, subunit conflict, lack of organizational identification, and lack of management concern and awareness)
2. Job challenge and autonomy (as well as job importance)
3. Leadership facilitation and support (including leader trust, support, goal facilitation and interaction facilitation, and psychological and hierarchical influence)
4. Work group cooperation, friendliness, and warmth (as well as responsibility for effectiveness; James & McIntyre, 1996)

James suggests that individuals develop a global or holistic perception of their work environment (e.g., James & Jones, 1974), which could be applied to any number of contexts and industries.

What is the difference between climate and culture? First, it is important to recognize that the two concepts are metaphors borrowed from quite different domains, so comparing them is rather like comparing the color of a car with the characteristics of its engine. The first is anthropological and implies an outsider's perspective—or at least the perspective of an insider skilled in discerning elements of culture. The second is meteorological and relies on the perspectives of organizational members to report on climatic conditions (it rains a lot here in England; people are supportive in this organization). Climate is often described as members' surface experiences and perceptions, while culture shapes (almost unseen) are taken for granted and even unconscious assumptions about

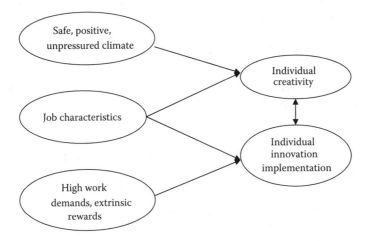

Figure 9.1 Aspects of climate and culture influencing individual creativity and innovation implementation.

how to behave in the organization and the meaning of events. What aspects of culture or climate therefore influence levels of creativity and innovation in organizations at three different levels of analysis: individual, group or team, and organizational?

INDIVIDUAL CREATIVITY AND INNOVATION

Creativity can be seen as the development of new ideas, while innovation implementation is the application of those new ideas in practice. Creativity, we suggest, requires individuals with creative characteristics, who feel free from threat and pressure, and work in a supportive environment. Innovation requires groups and organizations with shared vision, knowledge diversity, integration of efforts and skills, external challenge or demand, and practical support for innovation. Figure 9.1 shows the aspects of climate and culture that we argue most influence individual creativity and innovation.

The innovation process begins with the creativity of individuals, so the generation of a new idea is a cognitive process located within individuals, albeit fostered by interaction processes, for example, in teams (Mumford & Gustafson, 1988). Creative cognitions occur when individuals feel "free from pressure, safe, and positive" (Claxton, 1997). Experimental manipulations of stress levels in experiments support this conclusion since they show that high levels of stress lead to a reliance on habitual solutions. Prince (1975) considers the corollary of this and argues that on the basis of applied work in organizations focused on increasing creativity, speculation in work settings (a critical creative process) makes us feel vulnerable because we tend to experience our workplaces as unsafe (a finding also reported by Nicholson and West, 1988, in a study of the experience of work among U.K. managers). Questioning the person who comes up with an idea too closely, joking about the proposal (even in a light way), or simply ignoring the proposal can lead to the person feeling defensive, which tends to "reduce not only his speculation but that of others in the group." Prince (1975) goes on, "The victim of the win–lose or competitive posture is always speculation, and therefore idea production and problem solving. When one speculates he becomes vulnerable. It is easy to make him look like a loser." Moreover, psychological threats to face or identity are also associated with more rigid thinking, and time pressure increases rigidity of thinking on work-related tasks such as selection decisions.

While some theories of creativity and flow suggest that creative work is primarily sustained by intrinsic motivation (Amabile, 1988), emerging research evidence suggests that *extrinsic rewards* can complement intrinsic motivation. Rewards appear to be counterproductive only if they serve to displace attention from the task toward the reward. There is evidence that extrinsic rewards can encourage individual innovation implementation (Eisenberger & Cameron, 1996).

The characteristics of work roles (discernible in job descriptions and in practice) also influence both creativity and innovation implementation. Oldham and Cummings (1996) found five *job characteristics* predicted levels of individual innovation at work: *skill variety, task identity, task significance, autonomy,* and *task feedback*. Skill variety refers to the degree to which a job requires different activities in order for the work to be carried out and the degree to which the range of skills and talents of the person working within the role is used. Thus, a nurse working with the elderly in their homes may need to use her professional skills of dressing wounds, listening, counseling, being empathic, and appraising the supports and dangers in the person's home. Task identity is the degree to which the job represents a whole piece of work. It is not simply adding a rubber band to the packaging of a product, but being involved in the manufacture of the product throughout the process, or at least in a meaningful part of the process. Significance of the task in terms of its impact upon other people within the organization, or in the world at large, has an influence on creativity. Monitoring the effectiveness of an organization's debt collection is less significant than addressing the well-being of elderly people in rural settings, and may therefore evoke less creativity. Autonomy refers to the freedom, independence, and discretion for the people performing tasks, in determining how to do their work and when to do it. When people receive feedback on their performance, they are more likely to become aware of the "performance gaps." Consequently, they are more attuned to the need to initiate new ways of working in order to fill the gaps. Of course, this also implies they have clear job objectives.

Human beings minimize effort in their activities and therefore some external stimulus is necessary to prompt the extra effort required to innovate. Among individual health workers we have found in a number of studies that *high work demands* are significant predictors of individual innovation (Bunce & West, 1995, 1996; West, 1989). Indeed, studies of work role transitions show that changing role objectives, strategies, or relationships is a common response to the demands of new work environments (West, 1987a, 1987b). Andrews (1979) too found that moderate time pressure was generally associated with higher creativity among R&D scientists. Similar, yet even more complex, findings on the relationship between perceived time pressure and employee creativity were noted in a study of 170 employees of a manufacturing company (Baer & Oldham, 2006). The authors discovered that this relationship followed an inverted U-shaped function for those employees who received high support for creativity and scored high on openness to experience. Thus, when perceived time pressure was intermediate, employees high on both support and openness rated higher on creativity by their supervisors than those who received less support, displayed less openness to experience, or both. Of course, excessive work demands can have detrimental effects also on stress levels, absenteeism, and turnover.

GROUP CREATIVITY AND INNOVATION

In order to understand how the climate in a team or group affects creativity and innovation we consider the external environment or climate of the group in relation to the level of demand or uncertainty the group faces. Then we examine the internal climate of the group focusing on shared vision, participation in decision making, managing conflict and minority dissent constructively, intragroup trust and safety, support for innovation, and "reflexivity" (taking time out to review team performance and then making changes accordingly).

The external context of the group's work, be it organizational climate, market environment, or environmental uncertainty, is likely to have a highly significant influence both on its creativity and innovation implementation. Borrill and colleagues (2000) recently explored innovation in 100 U.K. primary health-care teams. Innovations reported by the teams were blind rated by external raters who were experts in the domain of primary health care. The external demands of the health-care environment were assessed using a U.K. government index of health and illness for each local area (the Jarman Index). Perceived levels of participation by team members were also measured using the Team Climate Inventory (Anderson & West, 1998). Where levels of participation in the team were high, team innovation was also high, but only in environments characterized by high levels of ill health, with associated strong external demands on the health-care professionals. These findings suggest that if the environment of teams is demanding and uncertain, it is likely that they will innovate in order to reduce the uncertainty and level of demand.

Innovation implementation involves changing the status quo, which implies resistance, conflict, and a requirement for sustained effort. A team that attempts to implement innovation is likely to encounter resistance and conflict among others in the organization, and therefore sustained effort is required to overcome these disincentives to innovate. But, effort itself is aversive—like most species, we strive to achieve our goals while expending the minimum effort necessary. So the effort required to innovate has to be motivated, at least partly, by external demands.

Table 9.1 shows the key group climate factors that enable the team to translate the effects of task characteristics and the effects of diversity of knowledge into the generation and implementation of ideas for new and improved products, processes, services, or ways of working. We consider each of these factors on the following pages.

Clarifying and Ensuring Commitment to Shared Vision

Ensuring clarity of and commitment to shared team objectives or vision is a sine qua non for integrating knowledge diversity to meet task requirements for teamwork. In the context of group innovation, ensuring clarity of team objectives is likely to facilitate innovation by enabling focused development of new ideas, which can be filtered with greater precision than if team objectives are unclear. Pinto and Prescott (1987), in a study of 418 project teams, found that a clearly stated mission was the only factor that predicted success at all stages of the innovation process (conception, planning, execution, and termination). Research evidence from studies of the top management teams of hospitals (West & Anderson,

Table 9.1   Group Climate Factors for Innovation

Clarifying and ensuring commitment to group vision

Participation in decision making

Managing conflict and minority influence constructively

Supporting innovation

Developing intragroup safety and trust

Reflexivity

1996) and of primary health-care teams (Borrill et al., 2000) provides clear support for the proposition that clarity of and commitment to team goals is associated with high levels of team innovation.

Participation in Decision Making

Participation in teams can, under appropriate conditions, lead to high levels of creativity. Group members can be motivated to perform at higher levels of creativity by social comparison processes (providing group members and teams with a comparison standard) and providing feedback on individual performance (Paulus, Dzindolet, Poletes, & Camacho, 1993; Paulus, Larey, Putman, Leggett, & Roland, 1996).

Sharing ideas with others in a team (via sustained participation) can also increase the chances of producing quite novel ideas, but this requires that group members attend to one another's ideas (Paulus, 2000). Recent research evidence suggests that enhanced creativity can occur as a result of group participation not just during but also after group meetings (Paulus & Yang, 2000).

There are obvious reasons for supposing that participation will be linked to team innovation. To the extent that information and influence over decision making are shared within teams, and there is a high level of interaction among team members, the cross fertilization of perspectives, which can spawn creativity and innovation (Cowan, 1986; Mumford & Gustafson, 1988; Pearce & Ravlin, 1987; Porac & Howard, 1990), is more likely to occur. More generally, high participation in decision making means less resistance to change and therefore greater likelihood of innovations being implemented. When people participate in decision making through having influence, interacting with those involved in the change process, and sharing information, they tend to invest in the outcomes of those decisions and to offer ideas for new and improved ways of working (Kanter, 1983; King, Anderson, & West, 1992). Studies of teams in oil companies, health care, a TV program production organization, and top management support this proposition (Borrill et al., 2000; Burningham & West, 1995; Carter & West, 1998; Poulton & West, 1999; West, Patterson, & Dawson, 1999).

Managing Conflict and Minority Dissent Constructively

Many scholars believe that the management of competing perspectives is fundamental to the generation of creativity and innovation (Mumford & Gustafson, 1988; Nemeth & Owens, 1996; Tjosvold, 1998). Such processes are characteristic of task-related or information conflict (as opposed to conflicts of interest, emotional or interpersonal conflict—see De Dreu & De Vries, 1997) and arise primarily from a common concern with quality of task performance in relation to shared objectives. Information conflict is evidenced by appraisal of, and constructive challenges to, the group's task processes and performance. In essence, team members are more committed to performing their work effectively and excellently than they are either to bland consensus or to personal victory in conflict with other team members over task-performance strategies or decision options. Yet task conflict might relate to innovation in a nonlinear fashion such that moderate levels stimulate innovation, while high levels are detrimental (De Dreu, 2006).

Dean Tjosvold and colleagues (Tjosvold, 1982, 1998; Tjosvold & Field, 1983; Tjosvold & Johnson, 1977; Tjosvold, Wedley, & Field, 1986) have presented cogent arguments and strong supportive evidence that such constructive (task-related) controversy in a cooperative group context improves the quality of decision making and creativity. Constructive controversy is characterized by full exploration of opposing opinions and frank analyses of task-related issues. It occurs when decision makers believe they are in a cooperative group context; where mutually beneficial goals are emphasized, rather than in a competitive context; where decision makers feel their personal competence is confirmed rather than questioned; and where they perceive processes of mutual influence rather than attempted dominance.

In a study that focused more directly on innovation (though not in teams), faculty members and employees of a large educational institution reported that when they discussed their opposing views openly, fully, and forthrightly, they developed innovative solutions to problems. But when they discussed issues competitively, or from only one point of view, and were unable to integrate the differing views of colleagues, they were frustrated and developed poor quality and low novelty solutions (Tjosvold & McNeely, 1988).

An important perspective on conflict and creativity is offered by minority influence theory. This theory is concerned with how dissenting minorities can influence and persuade majorities. Minority dissent occurs when a minority in a group publicly opposes beliefs, attitudes, ideas, procedures, or policies supported by the majority of the group (McLeod, Baron, Marti, & Yoon, 1997). A number of researchers have shown that minority consistency of arguments over time is likely to lead to change in majority views in groups (see, e.g., Maass & Clark, 1984). The experimental evidence suggests that while majorities bring about attitude change through public compliance prior to attitude change (i.e., the individual first publicly conforms to the majority view prior to internalizing that view), minority influence works in the opposite direction. People exposed to a confident and consistent minority change their private views prior to expressing public agreement. Minority influence researchers have labeled this process as "conversion." Research on minority influence suggests that conversion is most likely to occur where the minority is consistent and confident in the presentation of arguments. Moreover, it is a behavioral style of persistence that is most likely to lead to attitude change and innovation (Nemeth & Owens, 1996).

De Dreu and De Vries (1997) suggest that a homogeneous workforce in which minority dissent is suppressed will evidence low levels of creativity, innovation, individuality, and independence (De Dreu & De Vries, 1993; see also Nemeth & Staw, 1989). Disagreement about ideas within a group can be beneficial and some researchers even argue that team task or information-related conflict is valuable, whether or not it occurs in a collaborative context, since it can improve decision making and strategic planning (Cosier & Rose, 1977; Mitroff, Barabba, & Kilmann, 1977; Schweiger, Sandberg, & Rechner, 1989). This is because task-related conflict may lead team members to reevaluate the status quo and adapt their objectives, strategies, or processes more appropriately to their situation (Coser, 1970; Nemeth & Staw, 1989; Roloff, 1987; Thomas, 1979). From the perspective of systems theory, the concept of *requisite variety* suggests that disagreement and variety are necessary for systems to adapt to their environment and perform well (Ashby, 1956).

In a study of newly formed postal work teams in the Netherlands, De Dreu and West found that minority dissent did indeed predict team innovation (as rated by the teams' supervisors), but only in teams with high levels of participation (De Dreu & West, 2001). It seems that the social processes in the team necessary for minority dissent to influence the innovation process are characterized by high levels of team-member interaction, influence over decision making, and information sharing. This finding has significant implications for our understanding of minority dissent in groups operating in organizational contexts.

Overall, therefore, task-related (as distinct from emotional or interpersonal) conflict within a psychosocially safe environment, and minority dissent in a participative environment will lead to innovation by encouraging debate and consideration of alternative interpretations of information available leading to integrated and creative solutions.

Supporting Innovation

Innovation is more likely to occur in groups where there is support for innovation, and where innovative attempts are rewarded rather than punished (Amabile, 1983; Kanter, 1983). Support for innovation is the expectation, approval, and practical support of attempts to introduce new and improved ways of doing things in the work environment (West, 1990). Within groups, new ideas may be routinely rejected or ignored, or attract verbal and practical support. Such group processes powerfully shape individual and group behavior (for reviews see, e.g., Hackman, 1992) and will encourage or discourage team members to introduce innovations. In a longitudinal study of 27 hospital top management teams, support for innovation emerged as a powerful group process predictor of team innovation (measured by independent evaluations of implemented innovations; West & Anderson, 1996). Further studies in TV production teams (Carter & West, 1998), primary health-care teams, and community mental-health teams (Borrill et al., 2000) have strongly supported this finding (see also Agrell & Gustafson, 1996).

Developing Intragroup Safety and Trust

Intragroup safety refers to the sense of psychological or psychosocial safety that group members feel in the presence of their fellow group members and especially during whole group interactions. It includes the related concepts of group affective tone, safety climate, and conflict acceptance, which are described later this chapter. Groups that consistently develop intragroup safety, it is proposed, by encouraging positive group affect, constructive management of conflict, and creating a climate within which it is safe to learn, will be both more creative and more innovative.

George (1996) uses the term *group affective tone* to refer to

... consistent or homogeneous affective reactions within a group. If, for example, members of a group tend to be excited, energetic and enthusiastic, then the group itself can be described as being excited, energetic and enthusiastic. As another example, if members of a group tend to be distressed, mistrustful and nervous, then the group also can be described in these terms. (p. 78)

George believes that a group's affective tone will determine how innovative (and effective) the group will be. Relevant to this belief is evidence that when individuals feel positive, they tend to connect and integrate divergent stimulus materials—they are more creative (Cummings, 1998; Isen & Daubman, 1984; Isen, Daubman, & Nowicki, 1987; Isen, Johnson, Mertz, & Robinson, 1985); see interrelatedness among diverse stimuli; and use broader, inclusive categories (Isen & Daubman, 1984; Isen et al., 1987). How does this affect group or team behavior? George suggests that if all or most individuals in a work group tend to feel positive at work (the group has a "high positive affective tone"), then their cognitive flexibility will be amplified as a result of social influence and other group processes. As a result of these individual- and group-level processes, the group will develop shared (and flexible) mental models. In effect, groups with a high positive affective tone will be creative.

Jehn (1995) found that norms reflecting the acceptance of conflict within a group, promoting an open and constructive atmosphere for group discussion, enhanced the positive effect of task-based conflict on individual and team performance for 79 work groups and 75 manager groups. Members of high-performing groups were not afraid to express their ideas and opinions. Such a finding further reinforces the notion that safety may be an important factor in idea generation or creativity. Indeed, Tjosvold (1998) makes a strong case, based on his considerable research, that the management of conflict in a cooperative context will lead to a greater sense of integration and safety among the parties. Safety is the *consequence* of the management of diversity in views rather than the cause. If we operate in situations where there is no diversity or there is no conflict, we never have the opportunity to discover safety in our psychosocial environment. In one study in the service sector (West & Wallace, 1991), cohesiveness in primary health-care teams predicted levels of team innovation.

Similarly, there is evidence that teams differ in the extent to which they create a climate of safety within which it is possible to engage in group learning. Edmondson (1996) demonstrated differences between teams in a study of hospital patient care, finding significant differences across work groups in their management of medication errors. In some groups, members openly acknowledged and discussed their medication errors (giving too much or too little of a drug, or administering the wrong drug) and discussed ways to avoid their occurrence. In others, members kept information about errors to themselves. Learning about the causes of these errors as a team and devising innovations to prevent future errors were only possible in groups of the former type.

Reflexivity

West has argued elsewhere (West, 1996; West, 2000) that team reflexivity will also predict group innovation (as well as effectiveness). Team reflexivity is "the extent to which team members collectively reflect upon the team's objectives, strategies and processes as well as their wider organizations and environments, and adapt them accordingly" (West, 1996, p. 559). There are three central elements to the concept of reflexivity: *reflection, planning,* and *action* or *adaptation.* Reflection consists of attention, awareness, monitoring, and evaluation of the object of reflection. Planning is one of the potential consequences of the indeterminacy of reflection, since during this indeterminacy, courses of action can be contemplated, intentions formed, plans developed (in more or less detail) and the potential for carrying them out is built up. High reflexivity exists when team planning is characterized by greater detail, inclusiveness of potential problems, hierarchical ordering of plans, and long-, as well as, short-range planning. The more detailed the implementation plans, the greater the likelihood that they will manifest in innovation (Frese & Zapf, 1994; Gollwitzer, 1996). Indeed the work of Gollwitzer suggests that innovation will be implemented almost only when a team has articulated implementation intentions. This is because planning creates a conceptual readiness for and guides team members' attention toward relevant opportunities for action and means to implement the innovation. Action refers to goal-directed behaviors relevant to achieving the desired changes in team objectives, strategies, processes, organizations, or environments identified by the team. In a variety of studies, links between reflexivity and team innovation and effectiveness have been demonstrated (Borrill et al., 2000; Carter & West, 1998; West et al., 1999).

These then are the key external and internal climate factors that we believe research and theory suggest will influence team members to innovation: shared vision, high levels of safe, supportive participative interaction in teams, constructive management of conflict and dissent, reflexivity and strong support for innovation combined with an external environment that creates demands for innovation. But what of organizations as a whole?

ORGANIZATIONAL CREATIVITY AND INNOVATION

Amabile's componential model of creativity and innovation (Amabile, 1988, 1997) provides a link between the work environment, individual and team creativity, and organizational innovation. The simplified schematic model in Figure 9.2 illustrates the major elements of the theory.

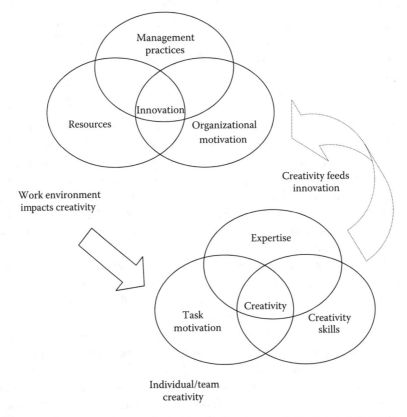

Figure 9.2 The impact of the organizational environment on creativity. (Adapted from Amabile, T. M., *California Management Review, 40,* 39–58, 1997.)

The organizational work environment is conceptualized as having three key characteristics. *Organizational motivation to innovate* describes an organization's basic orientation toward innovation, as well as its support for creativity and innovation. *Management practices* include the management at all levels of the organization, but most importantly the level of individual departments and projects. Supervisory encouragement and work-group support are two examples of relevant managerial behavior or practices. *Resources* are related to everything that an organization has available to support creativity at work. Amabile proposes that the higher the concurrent levels of these three aspects of the organizational environment, the more the innovation in organizations, as indicated by the intersection of the three upper circles.

The central statement of the theory is that elements of the work environment will impact individual and team creativity by influencing expertise, task motivation, and creativity skills (see Figure 9.2). The influence of intrinsic task motivation on creativity is considered essential. Even though the environment may have an influence on each of the three components, the impact on task motivation is thought to be the most immediate and direct. Furthermore, creativity is seen as a primary source of organizational innovation.

Amabile's componential theory of creativity and innovation (Amabile, 1988) offers a detailed and specific conceptual model from which a corresponding and useful questionnaire to assess the work environment for creativity was derived (Amabile, 1995): *KEYS: Assessing the climate for creativity* provides a validated instrument to fulfill this purpose (Amabile, Conti, Coon, Lazenby, & Herron, 1996). The model and the instrument focus on individuals' perceptions of relevant organizational dimensions and their influence on creativity.

In a study examining whether and how the work environments of highly creative projects differed from the work environments of less-creative projects, Amabile and colleagues found that five dimensions consistently differed between high-creativity and low-creativity projects (Amabile et al., 1996). These were challenge, organizational encouragement, work-group support, supervisory encouragement, and organizational impediments (see Table 9.2 for details).

Challenge is regarded as a moderate degree of workload pressure that arises from the urgent, intellectually challenging problem itself (Amabile, 1988; Amabile et al., 1996). The authors carefully distinguish challenge from excessive workload pressure, which is supposed to be negatively related to creativity, and suggest that time pressure may add

Table 9.2   The Conceptual Categories, KEYS Scales, and Sample Items of the Work Environment for Creativity

CONCEPTUAL CATEGORIES OF WORK ENVIRONMENT	SCALES FOR ASSESSING PERCEPTIONS OF WORK ENVIRONMENT (KEYS SCALE)	SAMPLE ITEM	
Encouragement of creativity	Organizational encouragement	People are encouraged to solve problems creatively in this organization	(+)
	Supervisory encouragement	My supervisor serves as a good working model	(+)
	Work-group support	There is free and open communication within my work group	(+)
Autonomy or freedom	Freedom	I have the freedom to decide how I am going to carry out my projects	(+)
Resources	Sufficient resources	Generally, I can get the resources I need for my work	(+)
Pressures	Challenging work	I feel challenged by the work I am currently doing	(+)
	Workload pressure	I have too much work to do in too little time	(−)
Organizational impediments to creativity	Organizational impediments	There are many political problems in this organization	(−)

Note: (+) indicates stimulants to creativity; (−) indicates obstacles to creativity. Table adapted from "Assessing the Work Environment for Creativity," by T. M. Amabile et al., 1996, *Academy of Management Journal, 39,* 1154–1184. (With permission.)

to the perception of challenge in the work if it is perceived as a concomitant of an important, urgent project. This challenge, in turn, may be positively related to intrinsic motivation and creativity.

Organizational encouragement refers to several aspects within the organization. The first is encouragement of risk taking and idea generation—a valuing of innovation from the highest to the lowest levels of management. The second refers to a fair and supportive evaluation of new ideas; the authors underline this by referring to studies that showed that whereas threatening and highly critical evaluation of new ideas was shown to undermine creativity in laboratory studies, in field research, supportive, informative evaluation can enhance the intrinsically motivated state that is most conducive to creativity. The third aspect of organizational encouragement focuses on reward and recognition of creativity. In studies, Amabile and colleagues showed that reward perceived as a bonus, a confirmation of one's competence, or a means of enabling one to do better, more interesting work in the future, can stimulate creativity, whereas the mere engagement in an activity to obtain a reward can be detrimental toward it (see Amabile et al., 1996). In support of this proposition, a more recent study by Farmer, Tierney, and Kung-McIntyre (2003) with Taiwanese employees from eight organizations revealed that employees' perceptions of the organization's valuing of creativity were strongly related to supervisors' ratings of employee creativity. The final aspect refers to the important role of collaborative idea flow across the organization, participative management, and decision making in the stimulation of creativity. Work-group support indicates the encouragement of activity through the particular work group. The four aspects thought to be relevant for this are team member diversity, mutual openness to ideas, constructive challenging of ideas, and shared commitment to the project. Whereas the former two may influence creativity through exposing individuals to a greater variety of unusual ideas, the latter two are thought to increase intrinsic motivation. In a study with 265 employees of three organizations in the Bulgarian knitwear industry, Madjar, Oldham, and Pratt (2002) found that work support from both colleagues and supervisors positively predicted employee creativity. Similarly, Zhou (2003) found in two field studies of a university and a for-profit hospital that when creative coworkers were present, supervisor monitoring was reduced, and employee creativity higher.

Supervisory encouragement stresses the aspects of goal clarity, open supervisory interactions, and perceived supervisory support. Whereas goal clarity might have an effect on creativity by providing a clearer problem definition, Amabile et al. (1996) argue that open supervisory interactions as well as perceived supervisory support may influence creativity through preventing people from experiencing fear of negative criticism that can undermine the intrinsic motivation necessary for creativity. In a study with 290 R&D employees of 46 Korean companies, transformational leadership predicted supervisors' ratings of follower creativity (Shin & Zhou, 2003). This relationship was particularly strong if employees displayed high levels of conservation, a value favoring propriety and harmony in interactions with others.

In reporting the last of the five factors, organizational impediments, Amabile et al. (1996) refer to a few studies indicating that internal strife, conservatism, and rigid, formal management structures represent obstacles to creativity. The authors suggest that because these factors may be perceived as controlling, their likely negative influence on creativity may evolve from an increase in individual extrinsic motivation (a motivation through external factors but not the task itself) and a corresponding decrease in the intrinsic motivation necessary for creativity. However, research on impediments to creativity is, in comparison to research on stimulants of creativity, still comparatively limited.

In conclusion, the practical usefulness of the inventory can be seen as considerable, which was further indicated in a subsequent study during an organization's downsizing, where the *KEYS* scales sensitively pictured changes in the organization's work environment relevant to creativity (Amabile & Conti, 1999).

What other aspects of the culture or climate of an organization influence levels of creativity and innovation? Below we briefly consider aspects of climate and culture that we have not already discussed above in relation to individuals' and teams' work environments. These include aspects of hierarchical structure/culture and organization size and age. Companies operating in uncertain environments will require flexible, decentralized, and informal work practices with little hierarchy (organic rather than mechanistic forms of organizing) in order to respond effectively through innovation. Collaborative idea development across an organization is often cited as a precondition for organizational innovation (Kanter, 1983; Zaltman, Duncan, & Holbek, 1973). There is support for the notion that high centralization and strong hierarchy are negative predictors of innovation (Burns & Stalker, 1961), and Lawrence and Lorsch's (1967) case studies showed that tightly coupled interdepartmental relationships fostered new product development in organizations. However, research also suggests that centralization may also be necessary to ensure innovation implementation. Zaltman et al. (1973) call this the innovation dilemma. Decentralization at local level is necessary for creative ideas to be developed but centralization may be required for the effective implementation of those ideas in the wider organization. The failure of many organizations to innovate may be a consequence of a failure to recognize this inherent tension.

However, in large organizations, decentralization and specialization are not sufficient to ensure innovation. Integration across groups, departments, and specializations is also necessary for communication and sharing of disseminated knowledge, and this requires some centralization or else the sophisticated development of team-based structures. The resolution of the dilemma may therefore be *team-based organizations*. Teams provide the sources for ideas (especially cross-functional teams) while the team-based organization also offers simultaneously centralized and distributed decision-making structures that enable successful innovation

(Mathieu, Marks, & Zaccaro, 2001). Indeed, the extent of team-based working in organizations appears to be a good predictor of innovation.

ORGANIZATIONAL SIZE AND AGE

Large organizations have difficulty changing their forms to fit changing environments. Yet organizational size has been a positive predictor of both technological and administrative innovations. Innovative agility is more a characteristic of smaller organizations (Rogers, 1983). Size may be a surrogate measure of several dimensions associated with innovation such as resources and economies of scale. More recent research examining all 35 U.S. firms that produced microprocessors between 1971 and 1989 showed that smaller organizations were more likely to be the sources of innovation.

The longer human social organizations endure, the more their norms become embedded and the more resilient their traditions become to change. Consequently, mature organizations will have more difficulty innovating and adapting. Evidence from both U.K. and U.S. studies suggests that younger organizations (years since start up) are likely to innovate in products, production technology, production processes, work organization, and people management.

CONCLUSIONS

Findings across a range of levels and sectors make it clear that innovation only occurs where there is strong cultural support for efforts to introduce new and improved products and procedures. At the same time, opportunities to develop and implement skills in the workplace and to innovate are central to the satisfaction of people at work (Nicholson & West, 1988), while innovation is vital to the effectiveness of organizations in highly demanding and competitive environments.

This review has argued that creative, innovative organizations are those where employees perceive and share an appealing vision of what the organization is trying to achieve—one, therefore, that is consistent with their values. Innovative organizations have vigorous and enjoyable interactions and debates between employees at all levels about how best to achieve that vision. Conflicts are seen as opportunities to find creative solutions that meet the needs of all parties in the organizations rather than as win–lose situations. People in such organizations have a high level of autonomy, responsibility, accountability, and power—they are free to make decisions about what to do, when to do it, and with whom to do it. Trust, cooperativeness, warmth, and humor are likely to characterize interpersonal and intergroup interactions. There is strong practical support for people's ideas for new and improved products, ways of working, and ways of managing the organization. Senior managers are more likely than not to encourage and resource innovative ideas, even when they are unsure of their potential value (within safe limits). Such organizations will almost certainly find themselves in uncertain, dynamic, and demanding environments, whether this is due to competition, scarcity of resources, changing markets or legislation, or to global and environmental pressures. After all, that is why innovation has always occurred—humans have adapted their organizations and ways of working to adapt to the changing environments they find themselves in. That is how we have developed so astonishingly as an animal species. Continuing to encourage organizational cultures and climates that promote organizational creativity, and thereby human well-being, is how we can continue this process.

REFERENCES

Agrell, A., & Gustafson, R. (1996). Innovation and creativity in work groups. In M. A. West (Ed.), *The handbook of work group psychology* (pp. 317–344). Chichester, England: Wiley.

Amabile, T. M. (1983). The social psychology of creativity. A componential conceptualization. *Journal of Personality and Social Psychology, 45*, 357–376.

Amabile, T. M. (1988). A model of creativity and innovation in organizations. In B. M. Staw & L. L. Cummings (Eds.), *Research in organizational behavior* (Vol. 10, pp. 123–167). Greenwich, CT: JAI.

Amabile, T. M. (1995). *KEYS: Assessing the climate for creativity*. Greensboro, NC: Center for Creative Leadership.

Amabile, T. M. (1997). Motivating creativity in organizations: On doing what you love and loving what you do. *California Management Review, 40*, 39–58.

Amabile, T. M., & Conti, R. (1999). Changes in the work environment for creativity during downsizing. *Academy of Management Journal, 42*, 630–640.

Amabile, T. M., Conti, R., Coon, H., Lazenby, J., & Herron, M. (1996). Assessing the work environment for creativity. *Academy of Management Journal, 39*, 1154–1184.

Anderson, N., & West, M. A. (1998). Measuring climate for work group innovation: Development and validation of the team climate inventory. *Journal of Organizational Behavior, 19*, 235–258.

Andrews, F. M. (1979). *Scientific productivity*. Cambridge: Cambridge University Press.

Argyris, C. (1958). Some problems in conceptualizing organizational climate: A case study of a bank. *Administrative Science Quarterly, 2*, 501–520.

Ashby, W. R. (1956). *An introduction to cybernetics*. London: Methuen.

Baer, M., & Oldham, G. 2006. The curvilinear relation between experienced creative time pressure and creativity: Moderating effects of openness to experience and support for creativity. *Journal of Applied Psychology, 91*, 963–970.

Borrill, C. S., Carletta, J., Carter, A. J., Dawson, J., Garrod, S., Rees, A., Richards, A., Shapiro, D., & West, M. A. (2000). *The effectiveness of health care teams in the national health service.* Birmingham: Aston Centre for Health Service Organisation Research.

Bunce, D., & West, M. A. (1995). Changing work environments: Innovative coping responses to occupational stress. *Work and Stress, 8,* 319–331.

Bunce, D., & West, M. A. (1996). Stress management and innovation interventions at work. *Human Relations, 49,* 209–232.

Burningham, C., & West, M. A. (1995). Individual, climate and group interaction processes as predictors of work team innovation. *Small Group Research, 26,* 106–117.

Burns, T., & Stalker, G. M. (1961). *The management of innovation.* London: Tavistock.

Carter, S. M., & West, M. A. (1998). Reflexivity, effectiveness and mental health in BBC-TV production teams. *Small Group Research, 29,* 583–601.

Claxton, G. L. (1997). *Hare brain, tortoise mind: Why intelligence increases when you think less.* London: Fourth Estate.

Coser, L. A. (1970). *Continuities in the study of social conflict.* New York: Free Press.

Cosier, R., & Rose, G. (1977). Cognitive conflict and goal conflict effects on task performance. *Organizational Behavior and Human Performance, 19,* 378–391.

Cowan, D. A. (1986). Developing a process model of problem recognition. *Academy of Management Review, 11,* 763–776.

Cummings, A. (1998, April). *Contextual characteristics and employee creativity: Affect at work.* Paper presented at 13th Annual Conference, Society for Industrial Organizational Psychology, Dallas, TX.

De Dreu, C. K. W. (2006). When too little or too much hurts: Evidence for a curvilinear relationship between task conflict and innovation in teams. *Journal of Management, 32,* 83–107.

De Dreu, C. K. W., & De Vries, N. K. (1993). Numerical support, information processing, and attitude change. *European Journal of Social Psychologie, 23,* 647–662.

De Dreu, C. K. W., & De Vries, N. K. (1997). Minority dissent in organizations. In C. K. W. De Dreu & E. Van De Vliert (Eds.), *Using conflict in organizations* (pp. 72–86). London: Sage.

De Dreu, C. K. W., & West, M. A. (2001). Minority dissent and team innovation: The importance of participation in decision-making. *Journal of Applied Psychology, 68,* 1191–1201.

Drazin, R., & Schoonhoven, C. B. (1996). Community, population, and organization effects on innovation: A multilevel perspective. *Academy of Management Journal, 39,* 1065–1083.

Edmondson, A. C. (1996). Learning from mistakes is easier said than done: Group and organizational influences on the detection and correction of human error. *Journal of Applied Behavioral Science, 32,* 5–28.

Eisenberger, R., & Cameron, J. (1996). Detrimental effects of reward: Reality or myth? *American Psychologist, 51,* 1153–1166.

Farmer, S. M., Tierney, P., & Kung-McIntyre, K. (2003). Employee creativity in Taiwan: An application of role identity theory. *Academy of Management Journal, 46,* 618–630.

Frese, M., & Zapf, D. (1994). Action as the core of work psychology: A German approach. In H. C. Triandis, M. D. Dunnette, & L. M. Hough (Eds.), *Handbook of industrial and organizational psychology* (2nd ed., Vol. 4, pp. 271–340). Palo Alto, California: Consulting Psychologists Press.

George, J. M. (1996). Group affective tone. In M. A. West (Ed.), *Handbook of work group psychology* (pp. 77–94). Chichester, England: John Wiley.

Gollwitzer, P. M. (1996). The volitional benefits of planning. In P. M. Gollwitzer and J. A. Bargh (Eds.), *The psychology of action: Linking cognition and motivation to behaviour* (pp. 287–312). New York: Guilford Press.

Hackman, J. R. (1992). Group influences on individuals in organizations. In M. D. Dunnette & L. M. Hough (Eds.), *Handbook of industrial and organizational psychology* (Vol. 3, pp. 269–313). Palo Alto, CA: Consulting Psychologists Press.

Isen, A. M., & Daubman, K. A. (1984). The influence of affect on categorization. *Journal of Personality and Social Psychology, 47,* 1206–1217.

Isen, A. M., Daubman, K. A., & Nowicki, G. P. (1987). Positive affect facilitates creative problem solving. *Journal of Personality and Social Psychology, 52,* 1122–1131.

Isen, A. M., Johnson, M. M. S., Mertz, E., & Robinson, G. F. (1985). The influence of positive affect on the unusualness of word association. *Journal of Personality and Social Psychology, 48,* 1413–1426.

James, L. A., & James, L. R. (1989). Integrating work environment perceptions: Explorations into the measurement of meaning. *Journal of Applied Psychology, 74,* 739–751.

James, L. R., James, L. A., & Ashe, D. K. (1990). The meaning of organisations: The role of cognition and values. In B. Schneider (Ed.), *Organisational climate and culture* (pp. 40–129). San Francisco: Jossey-Bass.

James, L. R., & Jones, A. P. (1974). Organisational climate: A review of theory and research. *Psychological Bulletin, 81,* 1096–1112.

James, L. R., & McIntyre, M. D. (1996). Perceptions of organizational climate. In Kevin R. Murphy (Eds.), *Individual differences and behavior in organizations.* San Francisco: Jossey-Bass.

Jehn, K. A. (1995). A multimethod examination of the benefits and detriments of intragroup conflict. *Administrative Science Quarterly, 40,* 256–282.

Kanter, R. M. (1983). *The change masters: Corporate entrepreneurs at work.* New York: Simon & Schuster.

King, N., Anderson, N., & West, M. A. (1992). Organizational innovation: A case study of perceptions and processes. *Work and Stress, 5,* 331–339.

Lawrence, P. R., & Lorsch, J. W. (1967). *Organization and environment: Managing differentiation and integration.* Boston: Harvard Business School.

Lewin, K. (1951). *Field theory in social science.* New York: Harper.

Maass, A., & Clark, R. D. (1984). Hidden impacts of minorities: Fifty years of minority influence research. *Psychological Bulletin, 95*(3), 428–450.

Madjar, N., Oldham, G. R., & Pratt, M. G. (2002). There's no place like home?: The contributions of work and non-work sources of creativity support to employees' creative performance. *Academy of Management Journal, 45,* 757–767.

Mathieu, J. E., Marks, M. A., & Zaccaro, S. J. (2001). Multiteam systems. In N. Anderson, D. S. Ones, H. K. Sinangil, & C. Viswesvaran (2001). *Handbook of industrial, work and organizational psychology, Volume 2: Organizational psychology* (pp. 289–313). London: Sage.

McLeod, P. L., Baron, R. S., Marti, M. W., & Yoon, K. (1997). The eyes have it: Minority influence in face-to-face and computer-mediated group discussion. *Journal of Applied Psychology, 82*(5), 706–718.

Mitroff, J., Barabba, N., & Kilmann, R. (1977). The application of behaviour and philosophical technologies to strategic planning: A case study of a large federal agency. *Management Studies, 24,* 44–58.

Mumford, M. D., & Gustafson, S. B. (1988). Creativity syndrome: Integration, application and innovation. *Psychological Bulletin, 103,* 27–43.

Nemeth, C., & Owens, P. (1996). Making work groups more effective: The value of minority dissent. In M. A. West (Ed.), *Handbook of work group psychology* (pp. 125–142). Chichester, England: Wiley.

Nemeth, C., & Staw, B. M. (1989). The trade offs of social control and innovation within groups and organizations. In L. Berkowitz (Ed.), *Advances in experimental social psychology* (Vol. 22, pp. 175–210). New York: Academic Press.

Nicholson, N., & West, M. A. (1988). *Managerial job change: Men and women in transition.* Cambridge: Cambridge University Press.

Oldham, G. R., & Cummings, A. (1996). Employee creativity: Personal and contextual factors at work. *Academy of Management Journal, 39,* 607–634.

Paulus, P. B. (2000). Groups, teams and creativity: The creative potential of idea-generating groups. *Applied Psychology: An International Review, 49,* 237–262.

Paulus, P. B., Dzindolet, M. T., Poletes, G., & Camacho, L. M. (1993). Perception of performance in group brainstorming: The illusion of group productivity. *Personality and Social Psychology Bulletin, 19,* 78–89.

Paulus, P. B., Larey, T. S., Putman, V. L., Leggett, K. L., & Roland, E. J. (1996). Social influence process in computer brainstorming. *Basic and Applied Social Psychology, 18,* 3–14.

Paulus, P. B., & Yang, H. (2000). Idea generation in groups: A basis for creativity in organizations. *Organizational Behavior and Human Decision Processes, 28,* 76–87.

Pearce, J. A., & Ravlin, E. C. (1987). The design and activation of self-regulating work groups. *Human Relations, 40,* 751–782.

Pinto, J. K., & Prescott, J. E. (1987). Changes in critical success factor importance over the life of a project. *Academy of Management Proceedings, New Orleans,* 328–332.

Porac, J. F., & Howard, H. (1990). Taxonomic mental models in competitor definition. *Academy of Management Review, 2,* 224–240.

Poulton, B. C., & West, M. A. (1999). The determinants of effectiveness in primary health care teams. *Journal of Interprofessional Care, 13,* 7–18.

Prince, G. (1975) Creativity, self and power. In I. A. Taylor & J. W. Getzels (Eds.), *Perspectives in creativity* (pp. 249–277). Chicago: Aldine.

Rogers, E. M. (1983). *Diffusion of innovations* (3rd ed.). New York: Free Press.

Roloff, M. E. (1987). Communication and conflict. In C. R. Berger & S. H. Chaffee (Eds.), *Handbook of communication science* (pp. 484–534). Newbury Park, CA: Sage.

Rousseau, D. M. (1988). The construction of climate in organizational research. In C. L. Cooper & I. T. Robinson (Eds.), *International review of industrial and organizational psychology* (Vol. 3, pp. 139–158). Chichester, England: Wiley.

Schein, E. H. (1992). *Organizational culture and leadership* (2nd ed.). San Francisco, California, Jossey Bass.

Schneider, B. (1990). The climate for service: An application of the climate construct. In B. Schneider (Ed.), *Organizational climate and culture* (pp. 383–412). San Francisco: Jossey-Bass.

Schweiger, D., Sandberg, W., & Rechner, P. (1989). Experimental effects of dialectical inquiry, devil's advocacy, and other consensus approaches to strategic decision making. *Academy of Management Journal, 32,* 745–772.

Shin, S. J., & Zhou, J. (2003). Transformational leadership, conservation, and creativity: Evidence from Korea. *Academy of Management Journal, 46,* 703–714.

Thomas, K. W. (1979). Organizational conflict. In S. Kerr (Ed.), *Organizational behavior* (pp. 151–184). Columbus, OH: Grid Publishing.

Tjosvold, D. (1982). Effects of approach to controversy on superiors' incorporation of subordinates' information in decision making. *Journal of Applied Psychology, 67,* 189–193.

Tjosvold, D. (1998). Co-operative and competitive goal approaches to conflict: Accomplishments and challenges. *Applied Psychology: An International Review, 47,* 285–342.

Tjosvold, D., & Field, R. H. G. (1983). Effects of social context on consensus and majority vote decision making. *Academy of Management Journal, 26,* 500–506.

Tjosvold, D., & Johnson, D. W. (1977). The effects of controversy on cognitive perspective-taking. *Journal of Education Psychology, 69,* 679–685.

Tjosvold, D., & McNeely, L. T. (1988). Innovation through communication in an educational bureaucracy. *Communication Research, 15,* 568–581.

Tjosvold, D., Wedley, W. C., & Field, R. H. G. (1986). Constructive controversy, the Vroom-Yetton Model, and managerial decision-making. *Journal of Occupational Behaviour, 7,* 125–138.

West, M. A. (1987a). A measure of role innovation at work. *British Journal of Social Psychology, 26,* 83–85.

West, M. A. (1987b). Role innovation in the world of work. *British Journal of Social Psychology, 26,* 305–315.

West, M. A. (1989). Innovation among health care professionals. *Social Behaviour, 4,* 173–184.

West, M. A. (1990). The social psychology of innovation in groups. In M. A. West & J. L. Farr (Eds.), *Innovation and creativity at work: Psychological and organizational strategies* (pp. 309–333). Chichester, England: Wiley.

West, M. A. (1996). Reflexivity and work group effectiveness: A conceptual integration. In M. A. West (Ed.), *Handbook of work group psychology* (pp. 555–579). Chichester, England: Wiley.

West, M. A. (2000). Reflexivity, revolution and innovation in work teams. In M. Beyerlein (Ed.), *Product development teams: Advances in interdisciplinary studies of work teams* (pp. 1–30). Stamford, CT: JAI Press.

West, M. A. (2002a). Sparkling fountains or stagnant ponds: An integrative model of creativity and innovation implementation in work groups. *Applied Psychology: An International Review, 51,* 355–387.

West, M. A. (2002b). Ideas are ten a penny: It's team implementation not idea generation that counts. *Applied Psychology: An International Review, 51,* 411–424.

West, M. A., & Anderson, N. (1996). Innovation in top management teams. *Journal of Applied Psychology, 81,* 680–693.

West, M. A., Patterson, M. G., & Dawson, J. F. (1999). A path to profit? Teamwork at the top. *Centrepiece, 4,* 6–11.

West, M. A., & Wallace, M. (1991). Innovation in health care teams. *European Journal of Social Psychology, 21,* 303–315.

Zaltman, G., Duncan, R., & Holbek, J. (1973). *Innovations and organizations.* London: Wiley.

Zhou, J. (2003). When the presence of creative coworkers is related to creativity: Role of supervisor close monitoring, developmental feedback, and creative personality. *Journal of Applied Psychology, 88,* 413–422.

CHAPTER 10

Creative Organizing to Enable Organizational Creativity

The Case of Sustained Product Innovation

Deborah Dougherty and J. Neill Tolboom

Rutgers, the State University of New Jersey

INTRODUCTION

The purpose of this chapter is to articulate three deep structures for defining work and work relationships that enable sustained innovation and the creative mindset that underpins it. Sustained product innovation is organizational creativity in action, since it both generates creative organizational outcomes and relies on creative organizational processes. The ability to create a stream of new products and services is essential to many organizations, since new products are the primary means through which they adapt to changing markets, technologies, and competitive imperatives. Organizations that are capable of sustained product innovation can enhance the quality of their products and production processes, discover new synergies among their resources, leverage investments in technologies that cannot be recouped with one new product, and feel out potential market places or business opportunities, to mention a few of the important outcomes (Helfat & Eisenhardt, 2004; Leonard, 1998; Tushman & O'Reilly, 1997). Not surprisingly, given its importance, the work of innovation has been detailed extensively, and what people *ought* to do to more effectively generate new products or services is well established (e.g., Bacon, Beckman, Mowery, & Wilson, 1994; Cooper, 1998; Dougherty, 2006; Wheelwright & Clark, 1992). Despite the wide diffusion of innovative best practices, organizations continue to struggle with effective innovation (Adams, 2004), so something is still missing in all these best practices.

We suggest that the missing ingredient is organizing that expressly enables people's *collective* ability to carry out the activities of innovation and to invoke a creative mindset. "Collective" refers to the fact that new products cannot be generated by individuals working alone, since new products synthesize the expertise of engineers, production specialists, scientists, logistics, marketing, market research, sales, and so on. Product innovation is also an organization-wide activity, since people must manage organizational resources of technology, production, and sales to support multiple products. We propose three approaches to organizing that together constitute creative organizing. These approaches are "deep structures," or underlying logics shared by organization members that order their everyday thinking and acting, not recipes or blueprints for structures. Deep structures for organizing comprise the organizational archetype defined by Greenwood and Hinings (1988) as an interpretive scheme that is made up of understandings and linked assumptions. These shared understandings give meaning to experience and guide imagination (Bartunek, 1984).

We develop deep structures for three aspects of work roles and relationships: (a) defining the work of the organization and breaking that work up into jobs for people to do; (b) grouping or departmentalizing those jobs into coherent, sensible units around the core activities of the organization; and (c) coordinating and integrating the work of the various units. The bureaucratic organizational form is based on well-known deep structures, and the contrast between our new deep structures and these familiar ones helps to highlight the differences (Blau, 1956; Thompson, 1967). Bureaucratic work is defined as the efficient execution of a clearly defined task carried out by a clearly delineated "office" or "function," through jobs that are themselves precisely defined. Bureaucratic work is departmentalized by functional specialty, and each department is separated from others so that it can be made as efficient as possible without worrying about ramifications on other parts. Bureaucratic work is integrated by abstracted standards that represent optimal operation. Integration occurs primarily through hierarchy, with each level charged to monitor subordinates' compliance with standards, and to handle any exceptions that arise. Scholars have argued that bureaucratic deep structures of organizing cannot accommodate the activities of sustained product innovation, but disagree over what might comprise new deep structures (Burns & Stalker, 1961/1994; Dougherty, 2001; Nord & Tucker, 1987).

To preview our proposed deep structures for creative organizing, the first is that people in innovative organizations understand their work as a professional practice, and their jobs as professional practitioners who both "set" and solve the problems they address. Everyone understands the practice of the enterprise as a whole-value creation, and their own work as a practice that contributes to that value being created. The second is to differentiate practice into separable problems of value creation. Each problem encompasses the entire flow of value creation, but brackets out a particular kind of problem that focuses attention on particular scope of knowing and doing and is organized into a community of practice. The third is to integrate work by standards that are enacted in, and represent, practice.

However, to understand how these deep structures for work relationships enable organizational creativity for innovation, it is first necessary to understand the work of sustained product innovation itself and the creative mindset that these activities require. To be optimal, an organization—especially its deep structures—should be tailored to the activities and mindsets it seeks to foster and systematize. In the next section, we synthesize the huge literature on what people ought to do to innovate into three sets of activities and creative mindsets that describe the content of what needs to be organized. These activities and mindsets are the "design specs" for what the deep structures need to address. In the following section, we elaborate our new deep structures for how work in innovative organizations is defined and translated into jobs, how the jobs are departmentalized or grouped into sensible units, and how the units are integrated. We conclude with some ideas for managing a change from a noninnovative bureaucratic approach to work and work relationships to one that develops and reinforces these three deep structures for innovative and creative work and work relationships.

INNOVATIVE ACTIVITIES AND THE CREATIVE MINDSETS NECESSARY FOR SUSTAINED PRODUCT INNOVATION

Creative Integrity Necessary to Integrate Market–Technology Knowledge

The work of product innovation is inherently integral since each activity is framed by other activities and needs to be done with reference to other activities, not apart from them. The integrality of innovation operates on several levels. At the product level, "product integrity," according to Clark and Fujimoto (1991), means that the various elements of a product must fit with each other and with customer needs, so development tasks such as design, manufacturing, and marketing must be executed in parallel. People must jointly solve problems, which requires that they understand constraints in other departments and anticipate others' problems (Clark & Fujimoto, 1991). But projects are intertwined with each other and the organization as a whole over time. Even microscopic technology choices for a specific project may define the costs of whole new generations of technology, according to Iansiti (1998), who argues that this high degree of simultaneous activity requires an underlying pattern of consistency in processes, strategies, abilities, and skills across the firm.

This integrity can be sorted out into two core issues: market-technology linking activities and the creative mindset necessary to pull together all this knowledge. New products are the manifestation of organizational knowledge about technologies and markets (Leonard, 1998). Products are created by integrating knowledge of the organization's internal capabilities (e.g., skills, technologies, marketing know-how) with external opportunities (e.g., customer needs, emerging markets and technologies). To design a product, people need particular knowledge of (a) user needs, priorities, and values even though the market may be evolving and customers cannot articulate what they want; (b) the scientific and engineering know-how necessary to achieve particular design attributes; and (c) the fit between various operating subsystems to produce the requisite levels of volume and quality (Bacon et al., 1994). The requisite knowledge creation goes well beyond the project level since no organization can operate manufacturing, selling, distribution, logistics, or R&D systems for each product. Each product must fit with existing systems, while managers of each system must anticipate emerging trends to accommodate new kinds of products over time. These organizational systems need to be linked with relevant knowledge in universities, professional associations, and industry groups to keep organization members apprised of dynamics and altering opportunities. Business managers must track market trends, usually by participating actively in those markets and accumulating the intelligence gained from ongoing experimentation.

Market–technology linking requires a certain way of seeing knowledge and knowing. This new product knowledge is not simply stored information or systematic principles that have been learned in school, but rather is generated in action. People must know how to continually know about external opportunities and internal abilities, know what to know, and know what to do with all this knowledge. Developing and integrating all this knowledge requires the ability to both create and connect elements of a viable product package together from inside and outside the firm, and to create and connect firm-wide resources with multiple products over time. People must generate unique, situated knowledge in a systematic, coherent, and reliable manner.

A creative mindset enables people to gather up and assimilate large amounts of complex and ambiguous knowledge, and shape it into multiple product concepts and business models. This creative mindset for product integrity is based on personal integrity, or the recognition that people require the "space" to think, reflect, and muddle through. This creative mindset involves freedom to set and solve problems and to allocate time to incubation, freedom from rigid time constraints so people can venture into new areas, and intrinsic motivation. With a creative mindset, people can try new combinations of knowledge components and incubate new ideas.

Freedom is a critical element of creative thought because it gives people the ability to focus on one idea for a prolonged period of time. To step outside the daily routines of their everyday living and traverse unscripted paths is an important pathway to creative thinking (Amabile, Barsade, Mueller, & Staw, 2005; Amabile, Conti, Coon, Lazenby, & Herron, 1996; Csikszentmihalyi, 1996). The freedom to "experience flashes of intense living" (Csikszentmihalyi, 1997) provides moments during which individuals are at their most creative. Research has also shown that creative ideas normally require a period of incubation before they become fully developed (Amabile et al., 1996). This period of incubation can involve time spent thinking about the problem or even time spent thinking about something else (Tolboom, 2005). Studies have shown that the human brain may be subconsciously working on problems even when it is actively doing something else. The individual may not be aware that he is thinking about the problem (Snyder, Mitchell, Ellwood, Yates, & Pallier, 2004), which may explain why sleep can enhance learning and creative problem solving (Strickgold & Walker, 2004). Intrinsic motivation is critical to creative thought as well because creative people love what they do and do what they love (Amabile, 1997). Creativity has also been linked to a positive affect (Amabile et al., 2005).

Numerous processes, procedures, and best practices have been devised to help people generate all this knowledge, especially at the project level (e.g., quality function deployment, lead user analysis, technology maps and portfolios, procedures for phase reviews, concurrent engineering, and design for assembly). But these discussions of what ought to happen are barren unless we can articulate how to achieve them. The deep structures of the innovative organization must somehow enable the personal integrity that is necessary for this creative mindset, so that the organization can achieve the product integrity required by sustained innovation.

Creatively Collaborating across the Organization

People cannot develop large amounts of complex knowledge unless they also organize the work in a way that supports all this knowing. To create and integrate all this knowledge, people must be able to quickly form multifunctional teams from around the organization, and move in and out of teams easily and readily over time (Orlikowski, 2002). These multifunctional teams operate at different levels. Some develop new products, some work on enhancing organizational resources and systems to support future products, and some work on rethinking the product and business conceptual frames. Organizations need specialization more than ever because of the demands for knowledge outlined before, but the specialties must easily integrate their knowledge into coherent products.

The requisite collaboration is creative because it goes far beyond the simple addition of teams to the organization. This challenge calls for fundamentally different ways of seeing work roles and work relationships between individuals and between units. As Burns and Stalker (1961/1994, p. 93) pointed out, people need to be able to see their own work "... in the light of the implications of [their] decisions for the rest of the firm's activities." They cannot see their role apart from others as the bureaucratic deep structure for specialization emphasizes since they must apply their expertise to the joint problem of emergent product development. At the level of the project team, the work of each specialty proceeds in parallel. Designs are being developed as manufacturing is being created and logistics and marketing plans set out (Clark & Fujimoto, 1991). Thus the specialty work of one unit must proceed by taking into account the work of another (Cooper, 1998). Iansiti (1993, p. 139) suggests that individuals need "T-shaped" skills, which means that people have both a deep understanding of their specific area and an "... intimate understanding of the potential systemic impacts of their particular tasks." People need to shape their specialized knowledge to fit the problem at hand, rather than insist that the problem appear in a certain way (Leonard, 1998).

Work units such as manufacturing, computer support, human resources, or marketing need the same T-shaped skill to see their unit's work in terms of its contributions to the larger whole. For example, not all the individual innovation teams can be expected to figure out how to redesign the computer system, reengineer the engineering change orders, train the sales people, or fix the evaluation procedure to support their new product. These are systemic issues that the computer support team, engineering department, sales department, or human resources should take charge of in a way that supports the collective process of value creation. Moreover, these work units must enable the people assigned to them to work effectively on various project teams, but also to keep their specialty knowledge up to date. The organization overall, therefore, needs organizing structures and processes to facilitate connections from plant to plant, business to business, lab to plant, and so on. Strategic managers need to assure that products draw on competencies, and continually revise the administrative procedures to accommodate new activities (Dougherty, 2001; Galbraith, 1995; Helfat & Eisenhardt, 2004).

Collaborating also enables the creative mindset, which in turn fosters a creative collaborative community. Studies indicate when people are encouraged and enabled to build relationships outside their day-to-day contacts, they have access to a greater constellation of knowledge, and can develop a more holistic view that gives them a better understanding of the creative needs of the organization. The availability of new and varied cognitive material has been found to be directly related to increased creativity (Amabile et al., 1996). Community interaction and collaboration increase this storehouse of cognitive material. Novel pieces of knowledge may fit together with existing pieces to create new knowledge. By understanding the processes throughout the organization, the people increase their expertise and therefore are in a better position to incorporate new pieces of knowledge into their creative ideas.

However, as is the case with creative market and technology knowledge generation, simply adding project management techniques and teams will not address the underlying challenge. As well, we have relatively few useful insights for structuring the organization as a whole to enable all these collaborations. Textbooks still emphasize the either-or options of functional versus product versus geographic when most large organizations must organize around multiple dimensions of departmentalization at once. More integrative theories tend to be rather vague and whimsical: the hybrid (Barney & Hesterly, 2006), N-form (Hedlund, 1994), spider plant (Morgan, 1993), or shamrock (Handy, 1990) theories of organizing, for example, while perhaps "out of the box," do not convey much knowledge.

Creatively Controlling Organization-Wide Innovation Activities

Sustained product innovation means that people are always working on multiple projects that potentially move in different directions, and they are reinventing underlying capabilities in technology, production, and operations to support future innovation needs. The possibility of flying apart at the seams, both individually and organizationally, is ever present, since the sense of coherence and synergy required to meet the first two challenges can be easily dissipated by so many activities of knowing and doing. A system of control must bound and frame work roles and responsibilities for both individuals and work units. People need to know what they will be held accountable for, and how that accountability will be assessed.

Even for the simplest of jobs no one can specify in advance exactly what is to be done, what the role of the person is, and what the rights and responsibilities of the employee and the employer are. These can be worked out only in the continuing day-to-day relations. The work of innovation exacerbates these challenges of defining roles and responsibilities because it is that much more indeterminate. Burns and Stalker (1961/1994, p. 122) found that innovative work was "experienced by the individual manager as an uneasy, embarrassed, or chronically anxious quest for knowledge about what he should be doing, or what is expected of him, and similar apprehensiveness about what others are doing." Without some way to make sense of this work relationship, both individual workers and work units will fixate on specifying—and delimiting—their rights and responsibilities.

The requisite control for innovation is creative because the standards cannot be rigid or fixed ahead of time, but people need standards nonetheless. Innovators must be able to assess their progress: How are we doing? Are we going in the right direction at the right pace? Should we drop this activity in favor of another? They need standards. But the assessment is ambiguous, uncertain, and collective. The standards cannot dictate the particulars of the work since innovation requires experimentation (Leonard, 1998) and improvisation (Moorman & Miner, 1998). The standards must allow those particulars to be enacted as the work proceeds by mutual adjustment (Mintzberg, 1991; Thompson, 1967) in which processes of work are defined collectively as the work unfolds. The standards must also evolve through mutual adaptation in which one activity might be reinvented (e.g., manufacturing) to accommodate simultaneous change in another (Leonard, 1998).

Research also indicates that the mindset for creative control involves setting boundaries on the process. Once the problem is clearly understood, if the process tightly defines where the people should look for a solution then the participants become bored quickly and lose motivation. On the other hand, if the process gives people no outer boundaries, then the deluge of information and possibilities can lead to paralysis. Creative control processes can help to set clear expectations for creative problem solving (Csikszentmihalyi, 1996). Organizational processes should allow for both minimum and maximum time boundaries for creative projects. While clear maximum time boundaries have been found to enhance creative thought (Csikszentmihalyi, 1997), the opposite is also true. Creative ideas that are developed too quickly may benefit from further incubation. Supervisors should avoid interrupting and changing the goals of people who are deeply involved in the creative process as this breaks the creative flow (Amabile et al., 2005; Csikszentmihalyi, 1997). Supervisors should be trained to sense when people are immersed in this creative flow.

But how to create an organizing system that provides the necessary levels of control, for both individual and organizational integrity, without being too controlling remains unanswered. Obviously the organization needs good decision-making systems, good leadership, an entrepreneurial culture that also emphasizes respect and dignity—one could go on for pages with all these clichés. Indeed, the challenges suggest that people in innovative organizations must be all knowing, able to interact with anyone at any time, and omniscient, which are impossible to achieve. To figure out how to address these challenges, we ask, how can organizations develop and organize all this knowledge? How can they define all these tasks, assign them across the organization, and coordinate and control them? How can they assure that the people feel more commitment and take more responsibility without making them "chronically anxious"?

DEEP STRUCTURES FOR THE CREATIVE ORGANIZING OF SUSTAINED INNOVATION

Table 10.1 summarizes the deep structures for defining, differentiating, and integrating work that we propose would enable the creative work of innovation, both the innovative activities and the creative mindsets. The table outlines how each deep structure enables all three sets of activities and mindsets so that all work together. In this section, we describe each

Table 10.1 Deep Structures for Innovative Organizing, and How They Enable the Creative Work of Innovation

Activities of Sustained Product Innovation	DEEP STRUCTURES		
	Defining Work As Professional Practice: Specifically as practice of value creation via long-term, problem-solving relationships with customers	Differentiating Work into Distinct Problems in Value Creation: Products, capabilities, business management, strategic management; each organized into a community of practice	Integrating Work via Enactable Standards of Practice: Common experience of doing that reflect practice across all communities
Creatively generating and integrating market-technology knowledge	Knowing in doing Invokes complex constellation of knowledge Know how to know Freedom to act	Each problem area focuses needs for knowing, context for practice incubation	Standards represent aspects of knowledge, providing vivid objectives for all Provides boundaries
Creatively collaborating across the organization	Work defined as a collective activity Invokes collective sensemaking Connects outward to gather more insights	Communities bound collaboration Communities enhance interaction skills	Standards enable heedful interrelating by providing a joint representation
Creatively controlling innovation activities across the organization	Professional norms shape roles, responsibilities Emphasizes skill basis of work Job is broad but not diffused	Problems of work are framed and narrowed People learn to rely on community Can implement processes to further map roles	Standards provide clear guidelines Standards can absorb new meaning by being enacted

deep structure and then in the final section suggest some ways to implement all three deep structures together.

Understanding Work as Practice

First, to enable sustained innovation, we suggest that work needs to be understood collectively as professional practice (Schon, 1983), not as a set of discrete, clearly defined jobs. The idea of work as professional practice is a familiar one since many people are professionals even though they work in organizations (e.g., architects, researchers, teachers, managers, equipment repair personnel, computer experts). In professional or occupational practice, the practitioner "sets" the problem she or he will address by defining the decisions to be made, the ends to be achieved, and the means that may be chosen (e.g., how to set a building into a site, teach an idea, figure out a computer problem—see Barley, 1996; Schon, 1983). The problem thus defined is then solved over time as the practitioner applies a complex body of professional knowledge, skills, and experience to a particular context.

The term "practice" has a variety of meanings, however, so it is necessary to first sort them out. "Best practice" refers to a recipe-like set of processes and procedures for carrying out a complex activity in the most effective or efficient manner (e.g., best practices for performance evaluation, logistics, or inventory control). Best practice captures the sense of work complexity and its flow over time, but it also implies codification and routine. "Practice" is also used more generically to refer to the various activities that people do, the social relations people engage in, or even as a synonym for social structure. We use the term more specifically as a way to define and describe work and jobs, drawing on the sense of the term of practice that has developed in recent years to define "knowledge work," and the exercise of a profession or occupation in an active, hands-on, problem-solving manner (Brown & Duguid, 1991). Defining work as practice highlights the spontaneous, improvisational ways through which people get things done (Miner, Bassoff, & Moorman, 2001), the "in-the-doing" (Barley, 1996) or action-based nature of knowledge they employ, and the collective nature of complex work in the sense that it is carried out by a community of practice (Lave & Wenger, 1991). Work as practice also highlights the ongoing creation of the work itself that comprises "institutional work" of creating, maintaining, and redoing social worlds (Lawrence & Suddaby, 2006).

We suggest that the innovative organization ideally defines work in terms of a certain kind of practice: the practice of value creation. People create value by developing and maintaining long-term working relationships with customers to understand their problems, and by using the firm's capabilities to solve these problems effectively. People see themselves as part of the overall flow of value creation that the firm is engaged in: creating wholesome meals, building quality consumer durables, or applying skills in textile science to solve customers' problems in materials. The practice-centered (Dougherty, 1992) image of value creation plays a crucial role in organizing because it gives people a clear, sharp view of their common enterprise and common objectives. Everyone knows what they are all working toward and why. These rich, concrete, and shared understandings of practice become the foundation for new product generation because they provide a common understanding of "what we know and can do." People can more easily "see" the tacit, practice-based knowledge that they have and that they need to develop further to innovate. They see their own specific specialty as the practice of applying that specialty to the practice of value creation for the organization.

Understanding work of the organization and one's own work as professional practice helps to meet all three challenges of organizational creativity as outlined in Table 10.1. First, work as practice provides another way to see knowledge and knowing since practice invokes the complex constellation of know-that, know-how, and experience that professionals like architects, civil engineers, or equipment-repair personnel use in their work (Lave & Wenger 1991). For example, Dougherty (1992) finds that the ability to creatively envision or "visceralize" the product in the user's hands helps people to understand various product attributes that are necessary in priority order, link up the emerging knowledge, and consider alternate product packages. Practitioners are more likely to visceralize readily. Leonard (1998) suggests that connecting individual projects to the organization's knowledge base also helps to frame all the knowledge work. People working on a specific project can get lost in the many problems of design and development, and need a "project guiding vision" that clarifies what the project is adding to the knowledge base of the firm. At the organization level, a vivid shared understanding of "what we do here" works like an organizational identity, providing a sense of the collective self that shapes the myriad efforts to generate situated knowledge of markets and technologies (Fiol, 1991).

It is not that practitioners possess more knowledge than functional specialists, but rather that practitioners *know how to know*. Practice reflects the emergent connections of principles to details of a particular context rather than the formulaic use of abstract knowledge, and emphasizes how doing the task is structured by the constantly changing conditions of work. Practice enables a holistic conceptualization of work so people can more readily generate a view of the whole task and their role in that task. Practice also embodies knowing by doing, so how knowledge is generated in the first place is literally part of the job. According to Brown and Duguid (1991), service technicians develop their understanding of the work in the authentic activity of doing work. Everybody does not know everything, but most people have some experience in common because of the emphasis on doing. Individuals have a background of experience in a specialty and in a market context; they all have some substantive knowledge of how the products are made and some applied knowledge of how products are used.

Work as practice provides for some of the creative mindset necessary for innovation work as well. Professional practitioners can generate freedom because they have the authority to determine their own work and how to approach it, within the bounds of professional norms. This deep structure also sets the stage for incubation since people can "step out" to reflect and muddle on their own as needed, because the norms of professional practice mean that the others will cover. Obviously there will always be a tension between incubation and getting the work done, but this deep structure provides a basis for working on that tension rather than ignoring it.

Understanding work as practice also invokes a community of practice, which is how this deep structure for defining work helps to meet the challenge of collaboration. As Cook and Brown (1999) explain, only individuals can carry out particular tasks, but knowledge of acceptable practice is possessed by the community of practice. Practitioners are effective in part because they can access the larger body of know-that and know-how in the community. By virtue of being part of a community and working in that community, practitioners are more skilled at and more attuned to social interrelations such as the narrations, storytelling, and the ongoing social constructions through which collaborations occur (Brown & Duguid, 1991). When they work together on an innovation project or organization-wide task force, practitioners can more readily negotiate a shared frame of reference for the work, and a common language for the task. Then each person applies his or her own expertise to the commonly appreciated task.

Finally, work as practice enables creative control through the professional norms of practice. Understanding work as a practice emphasizes the application of skills and know-how, reliance on situated judgment, and responsibility for the whole task rather than separate pieces. Practitioners take control of their own work, have the integrity to not let "good enough" serve, and take responsibility for fitting it into the work of others. The job of a professional practitioner is "broad" in the sense that it encompasses a good deal of the activity, yet it is specific in the sense that the job holder understands clearly what she or he is expected to do. Individual practitioners will be more or less attentive to their responsibilities, more or less adept at and motivated by their practice, of course, so this way of understanding work does not automatically solve the myriad problems of commitment and responsibility. Instead, work as practice is an alternate structuring device that enables much more creative organizing than does work as a discrete, precisely defined set of activities. Effective management is still necessary.

Differentiation of Work into Communities of Practice on Problems of Innovation

Building on Dougherty (2001, 2006), we suggest that the overall practice of the organization's work be differentiated into autonomous communities of practice, each of which takes charge of discrete problems in innovation management. Each problem area is a "lateral slice" of value creation that reflects a different kind of situation and set of problems in creating value, designing and managing products, and working with customers. Differentiating work by problems of practice recognizes the entire process of value creation, thus preserving the inherent integrity of the work of innovation. This differentiation is a qualitatively different kind of "break" in the complex whole of work that is not based on functional specialty, steps in value creation, or market segment. Rather, work is sorted by kind of problem and situation, which assures that setting and solving the problems of designing and launching products are at the heart of organizing. Differentiation of the kinds of problems to be worked on draws attention to all of them, and makes dealing with all of them comprehensible. Differentiation by problem to be set and solved also emphasizes the situated, context-bound nature of the work.

Finally, differentiation into communities enables people to build the broader sets of work relationships beyond their everyday contacts and provides for ongoing collaboration within the community even with strangers (Orlikowski, 2002). It also frames the problems to sustain creativity in a clear yet broad way, so people are neither overwhelmed nor bored, and thus able to be creative. Such differentiation enables "iterative organizing," suggested by Yang and Dougherty (1993) as a project-structuring process. They found that effective innovators could shift readily from work within their functions to creative problem solving across functions as unanticipated problems came up. The product is collectively conceived of in a comprehensive way, so people could work separately on their own tasks for the overall development (e.g., in manufacturing, sales development, engineering). However, when problems came up, the whole team could iterate to the collective problem and work it out in a way that fit the needs of all the functions. They could anchor jointly on a particular problem and solve it by taking the constraints of the other functions into account. With this collective work, individuals can step out occasionally and reflect on their part.

The literature suggests four categories of problems in value creation that can be separated out and organized into different communities of practice: (a) working on new products, (b) managing the businesses to leverage innovation, (c) managing the capabilities to support and lead innovation, and (d) developing the strategic processes to move the whole organization ahead (see Dougherty, 2006, for a summary). Perhaps the most obvious category is the new product development practice. Product practitioners, who come from all functions, work on creating new products, managing product lines, and developing new opportunities. They are skilled at forming multifunctional teams; defining product concepts; determining customer needs for a product in priority order; assessing and solving technical problems in a product's design; and managing joint problem solving in the design, manufacture, and delivery of the product. The business management practice deals with the problem of making a profit by bundling firm resources to fit with market, technology, and competitive trends, overseeing product portfolios and platforms to maintain the right mix, and tracking dimensions of value for the particular business. Business practitioners are skilled at knowing the business well enough to forecast their resource needs well, so that their colleagues managing these organizational capabilities can allocate resources and invest in the competencies. They also reconfigure the business unit structurally to accommodate new products, and organize and manage systems that integrate the various tasks in product development.

The third and fourth categories of problems around which communities of practitioners form are strategic. One is the competency management practice, or the management of technology, production, operations, and marketing capabilities across the firm to support the businesses and the products. These practitioners are skilled at identifying and developing deep expertise in the technological, operational, and marketing knowledge bases necessary for long-term value creation; keeping competencies connected with the businesses and product efforts to disseminate new capabilities and learning about new ways of defining value; and encouraging creativity and ongoing development of skills. They concentrate on developing the competencies to produce customer value now and in the future. Finally, the strategic community of practice deals with the problems of forming and reaffirming the corporate identity for value creation; converting that identity into standards for action that make sense in the other practices; making long-term investments in competencies; and creating decision-making systems to move resources to the right place and connect the various practices over time. Strategic practitioners evaluate opportunities and manage the organizational processes and procedures to assure that connections are working and that the standards fit the work.

This deep structure for differentiation also helps people with the challenges of so much to know by focusing them on a particular kind of problem to be set and solved with market–technology knowledge at different scopes of organizational action, thus bounding the work. Each community of practice has a kind of market or technology knowledge to create and integrate. For example, both the product development and the technology competency community develop technology knowledge, but different kinds in different ways. Product developers work on identifying specific technical solutions for a given need, while technology practitioners work on mastering basic technological capabilities to match emerging industry needs. Both practices are part of the work of innovation but occur at different levels around different activities, so can work separately. Each community also focuses on a particular context of practice, so as people become experienced within a community they know more and more about what to know and how to know. The differentiated communities of practice frame the relevant whole and each person's role in that whole.

Differentiation by community of practice helps with creative collaboration because each community bounds the arenas of collaboration for much of the work that most people do, but also provides relationships with a dispersed community that can provide a large constellation of knowledge. By emphasizing the practices of work, the communities encourage people to see their work outward in terms of its contribution to value creation, not in its own terms. People who work on designing and developing new products are located around the organization in a variety of specialties, such as process and product engineers, marketing, sales, and logistics. These people may all report to different bosses within their own specialty, for example, at a particular plant, in central R&D, in business unit sales, or in a venture unit. But they are all members of the product development community of practice, and all see their role as getting products designed and developed properly and quickly. A person's particular job might be to bring new products into the plant to enhance capacity utilization, or to develop new materials in R&D, or to make sales more efficient. Available members of the community are pulled into a particular product team from around the company.

Finally, communities of practice facilitate the control of work by framing the problems to be solved, not by controlling individuals and individual action. People need not be chronically anxious about what they are to do or what is expected of them, since they know their jobs as members of a community of practice. Each one is charged with an understandable, sensible realm of responsibility, and given the sensible yet clear expectations that foster the creative mindset. Because they are part of a community of practice, and because the process itself is extensively mapped out across the organization with clear demarcations of what needs to get done and who is accountable for what when, people know what to do when they get together even though they do not know each other. Members of a community are also trained in this practice as processes are updated even though they report to different bosses in different units. Indeed, organizing work around core problems to be set and solved provides a great deal of control in general because it assures that the necessary issues are dealt with.

Integrating Communities of Practice

People in innovative organizations integrate by standards, but those standards are enacted in practice. They work toward specific, vivid, clear standards for practice and then rethink those standards in the work. These sensible, "see-able," achievable standards are there leading the way, so to speak, helping to frame the kinds of actions people might take in their particular situations of practice. They coordinate their work by focusing on *"what we have been doing,"* a common experience rather than a common cognition (Orlikowski, 2002; Weick & Roberts, 1993), and on standards that represent this experience: delivery, quality, and product cost to customers. Each standard connotes action for specialists and product teams. Integration by common experience and standards for action is very different from integration by standardizing thoughts and action. Enacting standards in practice provides fluidity yet constancy, while matching activities to standards provides only stability, and no sense for continually emerging customer needs or technologies.

As outlined in Table 10.1, this deep structure for control helps people generate knowledge for innovation because the standards help represent business opportunity or customer value, thus enabling effective product and business conceptualization, which in turn enables knowledge generation. People do not have to spend time translating generic standards of operations into meaningful indicators of practice for their own units since the standards already represent sensible practice. This deep structure facilitates coordination because the standards help people to construct a vivid, collectively sensible representation of the joint situation of innovation, which in turn promotes heedful interrelating (Dougherty & Takacs, 2004). Heedful interrelating is that which is done with heed or with care and thoughtfulness. It depends on how richly yet coherently all parties can see the joint situation, so they can figure out their own contribution to that situation. People do not have to negotiate specific roles, role expectations, task goals, and decision criteria among all the players every time collaboration is called for, nor worry that some people may change their outcome objectives later on, as they do in noninnovative organizations. The practiced skills people have in working with customers, invoking common frames of reference, and applying their expertise to solving problems keep them focused on common issues, make individuals' roles clear and simple to understand, and provide the clarity of purpose that underlies creativity.

Enactable but straightforward standards of practice serve as clear guidelines for controlling work. For example, "target price" and "target cost" are routine standards, but they do not have to be abstract numbers that are imposed on the businesses in a firm. Rather, each business can enact the standards based on the actual working relationships with customers experienced in each business. These common standards represent the value creation process in simple terms that people across the organization can enact in their own situations. These standards are not "owned by" senior managers and sensible only to them; they make sense to every community. However, by enacting these standards in a particular situation, the standards absorb new meaning about the working relationship with customers, and this new meaning becomes part of the next interaction between groups that the standards help mediate.

Integration by enacted standards also fits with research. Dougherty (2006) suggests that people in innovative organizations need a well-developed sense for situated judgment. "Situated" refers to being engaged in the intricate details of an activity to appreciate the complex, tacit issues involved (Brown & Duguid, 1991); "judgment" refers to the ability to size up unstructured situations and make decisions based on less than perfect data (Vickers, 1965). Rather than confine "high velocity decision making" (Eisenhardt, 1990) to senior managers, everyone needs to be skilled at real time information gathering, tapping into counselors, and collaborative decisions. Successful new product teams can create the requisite commitment to the complex work by locating accountability collectively in the team. Such collective accountability makes people more comfortable taking on broader responsibilities because they feel they can share it with others as well as count on others—once again, incubation and reflection possibilities are "baked in" to the structuring. Westley (1990) proposes that including middle managers in "strategic conversations" involves people across the organization in articulating directions and framing rules of action. Such inclusion both energizes and informs people. Strategic conversation is a good metaphor for the vertical negotiating and framing necessary to generate the coherent sense of the business and its objectives, to clarify the meaning of these objectives for particular activities, and to rethink them over time.

Finally, this deep structure for integration highlights the very important role that senior managers play in controlling the creatively innovative organization, and in organizing overall. Senior managers are the ones who generate specific, vivid standards that sensibly represent the practice overall in all specific communities of practice, and then oversee their ongoing enactment and reenactment. The strategic community of practice interacts with people in the other communities of practice to frame their enactment of these standards to fit the various situations of work they encounter. Senior managers also articulate processes and procedures that map out necessary activities and connections in the innovative firms, and they take charge of constructing and reconstructing these important processes over time. Indeed, this careful attention to organizing is a big part of the practice of the strategic community of practice. This attention to the process is reinforced by a wide variety of procedures for decision making, operations review, process evaluations, assessments of customer satisfaction, product-development processes, planning, and so on.

DISCUSSION

Despite whimsical myths about intrepid champions working alone, it is well established that ongoing product innovation requires organization-wide activity. As Jelinek and Scoonhoven (1990) point out, people in innovative organizations always know what their job is, who their boss is, and where to go for resources—that is, they are organized. However, their organizational structures and processes are adjusted easily to fit specific work, and are understood as tools to be changed rather than as means for marking out turf or controlling behavior of others. In this chapter, we have summarized three deep structures for defining work, differentiating that work around core innovation problems to be set and solved, and integrating the work over time that we think enable the kind of organizing for sustained product innovation described by Jelinek and Schoonhoven, Leonard, and others. These innovative deep structures about work and work relations differ fundamentally from the familiar bureaucratic structures, which is why we suggest they constitute creative organizing. Together they add up to a qualitatively different kind of work organization where boundaries, definitions, rules, and standards enable continued creativity among members of the organization as they accomplish the work of innovation.

To make creative use of these deep structures, it is necessary to consider how they can be institutionalized in established organizations, or indeed in a newly formed organization. We summarize some insights from research regarding the transformation to a creative organization, but all of these inferences must be explored and tested further in subsequent research. These insights come from large, long-established organizations in mature industries where processes of transformation can be relatively slow (Dougherty, 2001). They may not apply to "high-technology" organizations that must transform rapidly in swiftly changing industries.

One key is to emphasize work as practice, which happens most easily, we suggest, when managers organize work and workers around problems in value creation to be solved. The real break from the noninnovative work relations begins with the formal institution of multifunctional teams for managing new product development, which includes granting the teams authority over all the design choices and product strategy and the freedom to work out these choices. Research suggests that working on teams for new products gives people a strong sense of accomplishment and the wherewithal to get the work done creatively. People know that they cannot do the work alone within a single function, and a properly organized team approach provides them with the resources, freedom, and opportunity for accomplishment that are essential for creativity.

As more and more teams are in operation, people from across the organization who work on new products see themselves as members of a product community of practice. Product development is differentiated as a realm of responsibility and handed over to the product community to take charge of within general strategic parameters. New product development is indeed a professional practice in its own right, with standards, processes and procedures, and professional associations. If managers begin to organize product development as a community of practice, the organization as a whole can implement the wide array of processes and procedures that have already been designed to enable innovation practice at the product level including phase reviews; concurrent engineering techniques; new market analyses, such as lead-user analysis, quality function deployment, multifunctional team customer visits; and technology-management techniques such as platform development (Cooper, 1998; Griffin & Hauser, 1993; Wheelright & Clark, 1992).

Once a consumer-products firm implemented a product-development community of practice in a business unit, the rest of the value creation work was slowly but surely evolving into communities of practice as well. Manufacturing had still been organized as a discrete function managed for reduced costs. However, product teams increasingly bumped up against a lack of flexibility and forward-looking capital investment. They began to attack these fundamental infrastructure problems in manufacturing, not because they wanted to invade that turf, but because these problems had to be solved if they were to get their new products out the door on time. This bottom-up pressure for improved manufacturing capability pushed manufacturing people to see themselves more as practitioners in charge of an organizational capability rather than as keepers of a separate function. The shift of manufacturing as a community of practice was enabled further by changes in top-down corporate investment strategies. For years, corporate research had been run in separate units for tax purposes, so new insights and machinery were not easily implemented into the plants operated by the separate businesses. But the company began to put together world-wide task forces for bits of technology that many units could share (e.g., pasta-making equipment). Like with product innovation work, there are numerous management techniques and processes to enable technology and manufacturing to be organized as communities of practice (Iansiti, 1998). Once the work is understood as a practice, these techniques make more sense and can be implemented easily.

An industrial products firm also started the transformation with product teams, and then formed separate business units to help people see the end-to-end flow of product creation and delivery to customers to meet needs. The company had been organized as one large functional unit until the early 1990s. Once businesses began to operate as communities of practice working in their markets, they began to need resources they could not afford alone. In this firm, the problem of developing complex, long-term technology and manufacturing capability was not apparent until different businesses saw that they could not afford the technology development alone, and that they could share basic technologies.

The last community to sort itself out fully from the old hierarchy in our data was the strategic management community. The changes in product teams and manufacturing and technology into communities of practice pushed senior managers to take up certain organizational problems such as developing organization-wide standards for innovativeness, implementing HR practices to support teams, developing the information technology infrastructure to enable the greater communication necessary, and so on. The strategic community is essential because it provides the shared understandings of the business that reflect fundamental value creation and enables others to work as practitioners. These strategic articulations focus on specific practices that have broad, fundamental implications for customers, and therefore invoked rich images of the whole flow of value creation in people's minds. With these images in mind, people can socially construct specific and realistic innovations for particular situations.

CONCLUSION

The creative organizing necessary for organizational creativity is not simply more of some aspects of bureaucratic organizing and less of others (e.g., more coordinating devices, fewer levels). It comprises a very different way of understanding the work of the organization and the jobs people hold, how that work is differentiated into core activities, and how these activities are integrated. These deep structures enable organizations to implement the more manifest organizing devices that are recommended for innovation and creativity. Our contribution is to articulate these underlying understandings of work and work relations that enable both collective innovation and a creative mindset.

REFERENCES

Adams, M. (2004, March) *Comparative performance assessment study findings*. Presentation at the Comparative Performance Assessment Conference, PDMA Foundation, New Orleans.

Amabile, T. (1997). Motivating creativity in organizations: On doing what you love and loving what you do. *California Management Review, 40*, 39–58.

Amabile, T., Barsade, S., Mueller, J., & Staw, B. (2005). Affect and creativity at work. *Administrative Science Quarterly, 50,* 367–403.

Amabile, T., Conti, R., Coon, H., Lazenby, J., & Herron, M. (1996). Assessing the work environment for creativity. *Academy of Management Journal, 39,* 1154–1184.

Bacon, G., Beckman, S., Mowery, D., & Wilson, E. (1994). Managing product definition in high-technology industries: A pilot study. *California Management Review, 36,* 34–56.

Barley, S. (1996). Technicians in the workplace: Ethnographic evidence for bringing work into organization studies. *Administrative Science Quarterly, 41,* 404–441.

Barney, J., & Hesterly, W. (2006). Organizational economics: Understanding the relationship between organizations and economic analysis. In S. Cregg, C. Hardy, T. Lawrence, & W. Nord (Eds.), *The Sage handbook of organizational studies* (2nd ed., pp. 111–148). London: Sage.

Bartunek, J. (1984). Changing interpretive schemes and organizational restructuring: The example of a religious order. *Administrative Science Quarterly, 29,* 355–372.

Blau, P. (1956). *Bureaucracy in modern society.* New York: Random House.

Brown, J. S., & Duguid, P. (1991). Organizational learning and communities of practice. *Organization Science, 2,* 40–57.

Burns, T., & Stalker, G. M. (1994). *The management of innovation.* Cambridge: Oxford University Press. (Original work published 1961)

Clark, K., & Fujimoto, T. (1991). *Product development performance.* Boston: Harvard Business School Press.

Cook, S. D., & Brown, J. S. (1999). Bridging epistemologies: The generative dance between organizational knowledge and organizational knowing. *Organization Science, 10*(4), 381–400.

Cooper, R. (1998). *Product leadership.* Reading MA: Perseus Books.

Csikszentmihalyi, M. (1996). *Creativity: Flow and the psychology of discovery and invention.* New York: Harper Perennial.

Csikszentmihalyi, M. (1997). *Finding flow: The psychology of engagement with everyday life.* New York: Basic Books.

Dougherty, D. (1992). A practice-centered model of organizational renewal through product innovation. *Strategic Management Journal, 13,* 77–92.

Dougherty, D. (2001). Re-imagining the differentiation and integration of work for sustained product innovation. *Organization Science, 12*(5), 612–631.

Dougherty, D. (2006). Organizing for innovation in the 21st century. In S. Clegg, C. Hardy, T. Lawrence, & W. Nord (Eds.), *The Sage handbook of organization studies* (2nd ed., pp. 598–617). London: Sage.

Dougherty, D., & Takacs, C. H. (2004). H. Takacs 2004 Heedful interrelating in innovative organizations: Team play as the boundary for work and strategy. *Long Range Planning, 37,* 569–590.

Eisenhardt, K. (1990). Speed and strategic choice: How managers accelerate decision making. *California Management Review, 32,* 1–16.

Fiol, M. (1991). Managing culture as a competitive resource: An identity-based view of sustainable competitive advantage. *Journal of Management, 17,* 191–211.

Galbraith, J. (1995). *Designing organizations.* San Francisco: Jossey-Bass.

Greenwood, R., & Hinings, C. R. (1988). Organizational design types, tracks, and the dynamics of strategic change. *Organization Studies, 9*(3), 293–316.

Griffin, A., & Hauser, J. (1993). The voice of the customer. *Marketing Science, 12*, 1–27.

Handy, C. (1990). *The age of unreason.* Boston: Harvard Business School Press.

Hedlund, G. (1994). A model of knowledge management and the N-form corporation. *Strategic Management Journal, 5*(5), 73–90.

Helfat, C., & Eisenhardt, K. (2004). Inter-temporal economies of scope, organizational modularity, and the dynamics of diversification. *Strategic Management Journal, 25*(13), 1217–1232.

Iansiti, M. (1993, May–June). Real world R&D: Jumping the product generation gap. *Harvard Business Review,* pp. 138–147.

Iansiti, M. (1998). *Technology integration.* Boston: Harvard Business School Press.

Jelinek, M., & Schoonhoven, C. (1990). *The innovation marathon: Lessons from high technology firms.* Oxford, Basil Blackwell.

Lave, J., & Wenger, E. (1991). *Communities of practice.* Cambridge: Cambridge University Press.

Lawrence, T., & Suddaby, R. (2006). Institutions and institutional work. In S. Clegg, C. Hardy, T. Lawrence, & W. Nord (Eds.), *The Sage handbook of organization studies* (2nd ed., pp. 215–254). London: Sage.

Leonard, D. (1998). *Well-springs of knowledge: Building and sustaining the sources of innovation* (2nd ed.). Boston: Harvard Business School Press.

Miner, A. S., Bassoff, P., & Moorman, C. (2001). Organizational improvisation and learning: A field study. *Administrative Science Quarterly, 46*, 304–337.

Mintzberg, H. (1991). The structuring of organizations. In H. Mintzberg and J. Quinn (Eds.), *The strategy process* (pp. 330–350). Englewood Cliffs, NJ: Prentice Hall.

Moorman, C., & Miner, A. (1998). Organizational improvisation and organizational memory. *The Academy of Management Review, 23*(4), 698–723.

Morgan, G. (1993). *The art of creative management.* London: Sage.

Nord, W., & Tucker, S. (1987). *Implementing routine and radical innovations.* Lexington, MA: Lexington Books.

Orlikowski, W. (2002). Knowing in practice: Enacting a collective capability in distributed organizing. *Organization Science, 13*(3), 249–273.

Schon, D. (1983). *The reflective practitioner.* New York: Basic Books.

Snyder, A., Mitchell, J., Ellwood, S., Yates, A., & Pallier, G. (2004). Nonconscious idea generation. *Psychological Reports, 94*(3), 1325–1330.

Strickgold, R., & Walker, M. (2004). To sleep, perchance to gain creative insight? *Trends in Cognitive Sciences, 8*, 191–192.

Thompson, J. (1967). *Organizations in action.* New York: McGraw Hill.

Tolboom, J., (2005). Networking, sabbath and idea generation. (Working paper). Rutgers University.

Tushman, M., &. O'Reilly, C. (1997). *Winning through innovation.* Boston: Harvard Business School Press.

Vickers, G. (1965). *The art of judgment.* New York: Basic Books.

Weick, K., & Roberts, K. (1993). Collective mind in organizations: Heedful interrelating on flight decks. *Administrative Science Quarterly, 38,* 357–381.

Westley, F. (1990). Middle managers and strategy: Micro-dynamics of inclusion. *Strategic Management Journal, 11,* 337–351.

Wheelwright, S., & Clark, C. (1992). *Revolutionizing product development.* New York: Free Press.

Yang, E., & Dougherty, D. (1993). Product innovation management: More than just making a new product. *Creativity and Innovation Management, 2,* 137–155.

CHAPTER 11

CREATIVITY AND SENSEMAKING AMONG PROFESSIONALS

Robert Drazin
Emory University

Robert K. Kazanjian
Emory University

MaryAnn Glynn
Boston College

INTRODUCTION

Researchers studying innovation and creativity in organizations have accorded professionalism an important theoretical role. This literature has developed almost exclusively within the meta-theoretical framework of structural-functionalism (Gouldner, 1970; Morgan, 1980; Parsons, 1951; Wagner & Berger, 1985). Parsons (1939, 1951) provides a classic definition of functional analysis. He argued that the professions are institutionalized role structures that function to provide an adaptive capacity for the larger social system, and that professionals are socialized role incumbents motivated more by achievement and a collectivity orientation than possible remuneration or other self-interests. He maintained that these normative aspects of professional structure continue to ensure the contribution of professionals in the area of creativity and innovation. Professionals use their base of knowledge and their networks of contacts with other professionals to generate creative ideas in their employing organizations (Amabile, 1983).

In this chapter, we argue that researchers studying professionals, creativity, and innovation should consider adopting an approach other than the structural-functional paradigm. We suggest instead that researchers approach the problems of creativity using the lens of sensemaking (Drazin, Glynn & Kazanjian, 1999; Weick, 1995). After raising and making explicit the assumptions about professionals and creativity held by structural functionalists, we introduce a sensemaking approach that focuses on conflict between the frames of reference held by different professional groups as a central element. According to Goffman (1974), individuals pose to themselves the question, "What is it that is going on here?" Their answer determines how they will engage in that situation. What is central to meaning or sensemaking is that a professional (a) develops an intrasubjective cause-and-effect frame of events, actions, and consequences; (b) places him- or herself in this frame; and (c) takes action according to this frame as events unfold. Frames organize meaning, motivation, and subsequent involvement in creative tasks. Frames can be idiosyncratic to professional communities and subcommunities. This places professionals with differing worldviews in contest with each other. Ultimately the form of creativity that emerges can be seen as a negotiated order between professionals with opposing views.

A sensemaking perspective emphasizes how professionals (and their work groups) come to understand their environment and how these understandings lead to cognitive frames that emphasize vested interest as the drivers of action and behavior. Conflict among sensemaking communities becomes the underlying phenomenon of interest, and organizations become the arenas in which this conflict is played out. Most importantly, creativity and innovation comes about not from the contributions of single professionals groups, but rather from the political actions of multiple professional communities espousing their point of view (Gibbons, 2004).

THE STRUCTURAL-FUNCTIONAL PERSPECTIVE ON CREATIVITY: DESCRIPTION AND CRITIQUE

Social and organizational theories are constructed based upon the implicit and explicit assumptions about human behavior held by the researcher. These assumptions govern what questions we ask, the models we create, and the approach we use to test our models (Wagner & Berger, 1985). Recently, several major analytical schemes have been proposed for clustering these assumptions into paradigms, or schools of thought (Morgan, 1980; Strasser, 1976). Conflicts between these assumption bases have been shown to be at the heart of central debates in the organization theory literature (Astley & Van De Ven, 1983).

Two schools of thought stand out in these debates. First, structural functionalism has clearly dominated the sociological and management literature (Benson, 1977; Gouldner, 1970). According to this perspective, a given social structure, such as a profession, can best be analyzed as a component of a larger social field. The structure is presumed to be in a functional or contributory relationship to a larger social system in which it is embedded. That is, the structure contributes to the well-being of the overall system through the outputs it produces. Structural functionalism emphasizes a deterministic orientation; behavior is orderly, rational, and constrained by externalities. Outcomes dominate as criteria of action, and change occurs primarily through a division of labor into creative and productive roles that are assumed to integrate harmoniously (Parsons, 1951).

The sensemaking paradigm argues instead that individuals and groups struggle to make sense of their environments. Different groups may have opposing viewpoints based on their own intersubjective sensemaking. The conflicting groups have to negotiate final outcomes in the organization. The organization itself is considered to be a negotiated order and tension pervades the organization as different sensemaking groups continuously introduce new ideas designed to support their unique point of view.

The sociological literature on professionals per se has not escaped this debate and indeed has actually been a focus of this controversy (Benson, 1973; Bucher & Strauss, 1961; Day & Day, 1977; Forsyth & Danisiewicz, 1985; Freidson, 1970; Heydebrand & Noell, 1973; Klegon, 1978; Larson, 1977). However, the study of the professions and their role in processes of innovation and creativity continues to be dominated by a structural-functional viewpoint. Underlying assumptions of the structural-functional perspective are so deeply ingrained that they often function as unquestioned axioms, guiding research in this area in an uncritical manner. These assumptions need to be examined, and their continued utility for the development of creativity theory assessed.

Two fundamental assumptions of social structure characterize the structural-functionalist approach to the role professionals play in innovation and creativity. The first assumption is that professional communities are basically homogeneous with respect to their value system. All professionals are expected to be trained and socialized to provide for the better good of the organizations with which they work. Their contribution consists of developing and applying knowledge to resolve organizational problems in a creative manner. Certainly, this assumption could be seen as fundamentally inaccurate, resulting in the masking of many important features of professional life (Bucher & Strauss, 1961; Freidson, 1986). Instead, professions should be viewed as internally differentiated, consisting of multiple communities or segments that participate in a wide variety of tasks and activities, and that adhere to correspondingly diverse communal systems of norms and values.

Second, we might further question the structural-functional assumption that professionals are socialized role incumbents leading an altruistic life, devoted primarily to knowledge development and serving clients. Alternatively we could maintain that the underlying motivations of professionals are primarily ones of power, status, and access to and control over a knowledge domain (Freidson, 1986). It is the conflict of interest that accompanies professional differentiation that has significant consequences for the innovation process (Freidson, 1986; Rosenberg, Tonkins, & Day, 1981). When innovations are implemented in professional organizations a redefinition of the professional's tasks, rights, and authority can take place. To the extent that these changes result in the relative advantaging of one segment of the profession over another, conflicts of interest are likely to result (Heydebrand & Noell, 1973). Creativity might instead be seen as a mostly political act, taking place in a network of partisan interactions (Benson, 1977), and invoked by professionals to advance, maintain, or defend their claims to legitimate control over a technical domain. The ultimate pattern of diffusion that obtains represents a politically renegotiated social order (Day & Day, 1977; Freidson, 1986; Pettigrew, 1973).

The issue of intraprofessional differentiation can be addressed in somewhat more detail. Within any professional setting a minimal social structure can be shown to exist. Professionals differ with respect to professional association and specialty group membership, types of journals read, the institutional settings in which professional practice occurs, types of professional activities (i.e., teaching, practice, research). and demographic characteristics (age, degree type, institutions attended, etc.). However, a more complex, and perhaps more consequential, form of diversity exists that needs to be addressed—a diversity more commonly associated with the schisms and fractures that characterize most professional groups. This diversity reflects what Benson (1975) calls a "depth structure"—one associated with divergent political interests.

These differences have important behavioral and career implications for those who identify with a given segment. Identification with one segment may preclude membership in another, at least practically if not socially. Segment membership allows individual professionals to maintain power and legitimacy through subgroup affiliation and membership (Freidson, 1986). Work activities, employment opportunities, income streams, publication patterns, and other very real issues are tied to segment choice. It is these career interests that often put both intra- and interprofessional groups at odds with each other. The creative actions of one group, taken to establish or advance their own political position, may relatively disadvantage other groups. At stake are issues of some consequence, including access to client groups, employment positions, funding, prestige and status within the profession, and legitimation of control over a professional domain. Segments and intersegment interactions are the focal point of change in a profession (Rosenberg et al., 1981).

Structural-functional perspectives dominate most of the current literature on creativity. Beginning in the early 1980s and into the 1990s, creativity researchers extended their models beyond the study of individuals (Ford, 1996; Woodman, Sawyer, & Griffin, 1993) to include the effects of group or team level variables (see Amabile, 1988, for an account of the social-psychological approach to creativity). Several studies found that contexts characterized by the availability of opportunities and the absence of constraints enabled creativity in individuals (Amabile, 1988; Amabile & Gryskiewicz, 1987; Oldham & Cummings, 1996). Settings in which creativity is valued and rewarded (Mumford & Gustafson, 1988) and where required resources are available were found to foster creativity (Amabile, 1988; Glynn, 1996). These findings on context led to a number of structural-functional studies that investigated the effect of group-level constructs on creativity. Group-level characteristics related to leader style, cohesiveness, group tenure, and degree of cooperation have been found to be antecedents to creativity (King & Anderson, 1990) and have been related to the effectiveness of research teams (Payne, 1990). Group diversity has been found to be a determinant of recognition, effectiveness, and the publication records of professional R&D teams (Andrews, 1979).

Only recently, and in a very few cases, have organizational level variables been incorporated in models of creativity. Factors such as organizational policies, structures and climate (Burkhardt & Brass, 1990; Tushman & Nelson, 1990), and organization-wide training of individuals (Basadur, Graen, & Scandura, 1986; Wheatley, Anthony & Maddox,

1991) have been linked to creative output. The most comprehensive theoretical model to include organizational level creativity is offered by Woodman and colleagues (1993) who link culture, resources, technology, strategy, and rewards to creativity. What all of these models have in common is that their core assumption base is functional in character.

In these studies, creativity is almost always regarded as an important *outcome* to the social system, and independent variables are considered as factors to be manipulated to improve these outcomes. Rousseau (1985, pp. 25–26) terms this approach to building multilevel theories as functionalist-reductionist. Functionalist and reductionist arguments together allow the researcher to specify a theory that allows for the functional contribution of lower members of a hierarchy to the goals of higher levels. Typically, creativity is treated as the dependent variable, with the focus being on the creative outputs of the organization. For example, Amabile (1988, p. 126) defines creativity as the production of novel and useful ideas by an individual or small group of individuals (including professionals) working together. Similarly, Oldham and Cummings (1996) define creativity as products, ideas, or procedures that are (a) novel or original and (b) relevant and useful. Ford (1996) views creativity as output oriented with the outputs being novel and valuable. Finally, Woodman and colleagues define creativity as the creation of a valuable, useful new product, service, idea, procedure, or process by individuals working together in a complex social system (1993, p. 293). Following functionalist traditions, the research question posed explicitly or implicitly in most creativity studies is: How do you increase creativity in organizations?

SENSEMAKING AND CREATIVITY: AN ALTERNATIVE APPROACH

The interpretive or sensemaking perspective is a useful approach to understanding organizational processes (Goffman, 1974; Weick, 1995). Although functionalist perspectives dominate organizational research (Gioia & Pitre, 1990), a sensemaking view has made significant headway (Burrell & Morgan, 1979). Sensemaking research has examined such diverse topics as issue and agenda formation (Dutton & Jackson, 1987; Dutton & Dukerich, 1991), strategy formation in top management teams (Porac, Thomas, & Baden-Fuller, 1989), change management (Gioia & Chittipeddi, 1991; Poole, Gioia, & Gray, 1989), and technology diffusion (Barley, 1986). Some researchers have examined the general innovation process using a sensemaking framework (Dougherty, 1992, 2004; Hill & Levenhagen, 1995; Ring & Rands, 1989), but we know of only limited work that applies an interpretive framework specifically to the study of creativity (Ford, 1996; Ford & Gioia, 1995).

One goal of theory building in the interpretive perspective is to describe organizational life. The focus is less on understanding how to manipulate a system to achieve desired goals, as it is to understand the process through which individuals and organizations develop systems of meaning and how these systems of meaning lead to the emergence of a stream of organization behavior over time. Thus, the interpretive perspective fits well with the goals of describing creative processes. In an interpretive framework, the central research question becomes: How does the process of creativity unfold in organizations?

We define creativity as a process rather than an outcome. This distinction is not new in the literature on creativity or the general literature on organizational behavior (Mohr, 1982; Perry-Smith, 2003). For example, creativity has been defined as an individual cognitive process that involves multiple stages. The process that individuals engage in generates creative outcomes; in effect, creativity as a process is a necessary but not sufficient condition for creativity as an outcome. The mainstream literature on creativity assumes that this process takes place, but does not examine it explicitly. Instead, this literature examines the relationship between context and outcomes using a variance analysis framework, implemented primarily as regression or ANOVA analysis of the effects of individual variables on a dependent variable (Mohr, 1982).

At the individual level we define creativity as the psychological engagement of an individual in a creative act (Ford, 1996). A creative act occurs when an individual cognitively and behaviorally attempts to produce creative outcomes. For example, a professional may choose to be creative on part of a project on which she or he is currently working. In the act of creativity, he or she may collect data, consult past solutions, ruminate on alternatives, incubate over ideas, and propose ideas. The ideas may be considered by others as creative or not, but the process of generating those ideas can logically be called creativity.

Creativity is a choice to engage in the cognitive and behavioral aspects of producing ideas and as such can vary from person to person and situation to situation. A professional may choose minimal engagement by proposing simple solutions that may not be novel or useful—a behavior Ford (1996) refers to as habitual action. Alternatively, that professional may choose to engage in a full manner, using all of his or her knowledge and abilities to produce creative outcomes. The process of engagement or disengagement varies over time. The actions of an individual can be represented as an ebb and flow of engagement from moment to moment and from day to day.

As detailed below, creative processes at the organizational level are not simple aggregations of individual creativity (Taggar, 2002). Creativity at the organizational level is a process that varies over time, but is a result of a negotiated order between professional groups that are responsible for creativity. Understanding the distinction between individual creativity and higher-level creativity requires the introduction of the level of analysis our model deals with.

A sensemaking perspective on creativity also reverses other functionalist assumptions. Although researchers recognize, as in the functionalist view, that individuals are the center of organizational life, they are accorded a different role than in the traditional perspective. Individuals have agency; they are seen as having an important role in subjectively interpreting and shaping their environments (Weick, 1979). In the functionalist perspective, individuals are acted upon rather than being actors. Because individuals develop and maintain subjective interpretations of their roles in organizations, a different model of higher levels of organizational analysis emerges (Weick, 1995). Instead of the traditional levels of analysis of individual, group, and organization, sensemaking researchers consider (a) an individual (or intrasubjective) level, (b) an intersubjective level that represents shared frames of reference that may transcend formal groups or subunits, and (c) a collective level that represents the unfolding of change across intersubjective levels.

The Individual Level: Developing Sensemaking Frames

When professionals are confronted with an ambiguous set of events, they struggle to make sense of their situation (Weick, 1979). According to Goffman (1974), individuals pose a question to themselves that is something like "What is it that is going on here?" The answer determines how an individual engages in that setting. Meaning, or sense, develops about the situation that allows the individual to act in some rational fashion; thus meaning, or sensemaking, is a primary generator of individual action.

The meanings that are applied to situations have variously been called frames (Bateson, 1972; Goffman, 1974), enactments (Weick, 1979), schemata (Poole et al., 1989), and cognitive maps. What is central to all these definitions is that an individual (a) develops an intrasubjective cause-and-effect map of stimuli, actions, and consequences, (b) places him- or herself in this map, and (c) takes actions according to his or her map as events unfold. Actions and events that either happen to an individual or are self-initiated are real. Professionals who are engaged in a creative process develop prototypes, test designs, and survey clients; as a result, they develop cognitive frames about these events that represent individual and social constructions of the meaning attached to that reality (Ford, 1996). For example, a test of a critical component that is part of a larger project could be regarded by a professional as a task worthy of creative engagement; alternatively, the same test could be viewed as having a negative effect on creativity (the test is "make work" imposed by management that takes away from other creative endeavors). At the individual level of analysis, experience is organized in the individual's mind and he or she ascribes meaning and causality to that experience.

The organization of perception and experience requires more than mere cognitive constructions; frames organize meaning, motivation, and subsequent involvement and action. During any experience of work activity, an individual not only obtains a sense of what is going on, but also a sense of how much to be involved. According to Goffman (1974) all primary frames involve normative expectations of the extent to which an individual engages in the activity organized by the frame. This involvement can range from complete boredom and abstention, to full engagement in the activities at hand. Thus frames, and the process of framing, can have substantial impact on the extent to which an individual engages in a process of creativity. Negative scripting can result in disengagement from creative work and a consequent focus on habitual routine, while positive scripting can denote opportunities for creative effort (Ford, 1996).

The Intersubjective Level: The Construction of Shared Meaning

An individual's development of his or her frame of reference does not take place in social isolation. The creation of an individual's structure of meaning involves exploration with others who are engaged directly or indirectly in the same endeavors (Perry-Smith, 2006). Third-party sensemaking is a mode of creating meaning in an ambiguous or stressful setting (Volkema, Farquhar, & Bergmann, 1996). When a person faces an equivocal situation he or she reduces that equivocality by seeking out the interpretations of others, typically those involved in a similar occupation or profession. Schemata, scripts, and categorization may diffuse through conversations with others (Poole et al., 1989). By seeking the advice of others, and by giving advice in return, sensemaking is shared throughout an organizational field. An individual can be influenced by members of the same occupation who partake in the same work, third parties in related work, or even through networks of weaker ties (Granovetter, 1973). When interdependence is high, as in large-scale creative projects, a collective mind can emerge from collective interaction (Weick & Roberts, 1993). Through these interactions, undertaken to create in an individual a reliable framing of events, a universal sense of what makes sense arises. As individuals engage in interaction to reduce their own sense of confusion they in turn reciprocally reduce the confusion of others. When sensemaking changes from the self-referential "I" to the more inclusive "we," then a shared or intersubjective meaning arises (Hargadon & Bechky, 2006; Weick, 1995).

In this manner, an intersubjectively determined understanding of the process of creativity arises. This understanding transcends the group or project team level and may apply to the entire organization or to major professional communities within the organization. It provides answers to the questions: How should we be creative? What does creativity mean to this organization?

Individual frames of reference become interlocked into intersubjective frames that have enduring properties. These intersubjective frames have been referred to as organizational memory (Walsh & Ungson, 1991), organization mind (Sandelands & Stablein, 1987), collective mind (Weick & Roberts, 1993), and organizational intelligence (Glynn, 1996). As mutual understandings emerge concerning principal classes of sensemaking frames, then so, too, does the culture of a particular social group (Goffman, 1974, p. 27). By assuming sharing of mental maps, and convergence in belief systems, interpretive researchers define an intersubjective level of analysis that differs from traditional conceptualizations.

The Collective Level: Negotiated Order among Differing Communities

For the most part, interpretive researchers regard intersubjectively shared frames of reference as constitutive of the frame of an entire organization. However, sensemaking is informed by beliefs that are embedded in job categories, the professions, ideologies, and paradigms, as well as within a single organization (Weick, 1995, p. 133). As Goffman (1974) noted, even though two actors share a similar set of experiences, their frames of reference may differ based on their positions with respect to that activity. Professional communities of different beliefs are expected to argue their positions to influence the development of intersubjective meaning (Gibbons, 2004; Walsh & Fahey, 1986; Walsh, Henderson & Deighton, 1988; Weick, 1995). Sensemaking is not neat, tidy, and polite, but rather marked by divergent and often antagonistic competing frames of reference. Adopting a sensemaking perspective does not imply that there will be no differences in opinion; specifically, there may even be conflict over those differences.

How do opposing frameworks emerge? Different professions and segments within a profession involve different, though potentially overlapping, experiences and consequently different senses of what these experiences mean. The context in which individuals are embedded include their profession, the tasks they are asked to perform, their level in the organizations, their career histories, and the patterns of interaction and interdependence that places some groups in closer proximity than others. The very nature of their work implies tension and contradiction (Weick, 1995). Creative acts, undertaken in large-scale organizations, lead to tension between innovation and control (Weick, 1995, p. 72). Opposing frameworks imply a natural dialectic that occurs when groups are in opposition to each other (Huff, 1988).

The work of Dougherty (1992) is instructive to an account of opposing interpretive frameworks. Dougherty argues that innovation often requires the insights of multiple "thought worlds." Thought worlds are the interpretive schemes of different communities of specialists, where these communities literally think differently from each other. Each community values different information and models and cannot readily share information or make decisions. Dougherty (1992) argues that at best each thought worldviews the other as esoteric or at worst, meaningless.

In her study, Dougherty argues that functional departments represent different thought worlds. She lists four competing thought worlds: technical, field, manufacturing, and planning. Organizations can also be viewed as collections of diverse subcultures that subscribe to different systems of meanings. This suggests that there is no one monolithic culture, but rather an intermingling of often opposing subcultures of departments or occupations. These subcultures compete over the control of work, access to power and resources, and credit. The inevitable clashes between these subcultures are resolved through adaptation and negotiation. Similar clashes can occur at the margins of worldviews of any professional community or subcommunity.

Inherent in large-scaled creative projects is a conflict of sensemaking between multiple professionals and managerial communities. Each community uses past frameworks and prior knowledge developed from their career histories to make sense of their current assignments (Thomas & McDaniel, 1990). In professionally based organizations, dual-career ladders differentiate the career histories of project managers and professional staff. Professional staff have a vested interest in developing reputations of creativity in science and engineering in their own communities or subcommunities, while project managers have vested interests in developing reputations of creativity in bringing projects to successful completion, on time and within budget. It is the context of each group's work that informs differences in their thought worlds. Differences in task are supported by differences in interaction patterns. Each subcommunity has higher within-group contact than contact across groups. The task differences of each group are supported by interaction patterns that reinforce one belief system over the other.

As a result of these differences, what makes sense to one community may not make sense to another community. Each in turn proposes creative solutions that they understand and that advance their own discipline (Aguilar, 1967). Ambiguity over the relative authority of different communities in a single creative project is a manifestation of deeper conflict between multiple occupational subcultures (Barley, 1986). The issue is fundamentally one of the separation of position from expertise (Barley, 1986). Because they face different task settings and develop different views of what makes sense in the accomplishment of creative tasks, professional groups are likely occasionally to have opposing views of what constitutes creativity. These views clash in concrete settings, each group representing its opinions to the other in the form of an argument that contains its unique model of what kind of creativity makes sense. These arguments reveal to the other parties the sensemaking perspectives each holds. Although one outcome might be mutual accommodation (Poole et al., 1989), another might be that each party sees the other as not making any sense (Dougherty, 1992).

In studies of individual and organizational creativity, much has been written of tensions within organizations that reject or select creative action (Ford, 1996; Woodman et al., 1993) or that encourage persistence versus change (March, 1981). Our model suggests that an alternative struggle can occur within organizations; there may not simply be a clash over *whether or not* an organization should act creatively, but also over *which* creative domain-specific frame may prevail to direct organizational action. Our sensemaking perspective clearly suggests the feasibility of a political approach to mapping creative processes within organizations; it is a view of creativity that has largely been overlooked in the literature.

Our sensemaking perspective indicates that in addition to the motivational and contextual factors that have been associated with creativity (e.g., Amabile, 1983; Ford, 1996; Woodman et al., 1993), cognitive frames are key to creative effort. Such frames direct a creative approach to defining as well as solving project and organizational problems. In our view, these frames operate at multiple levels in the organization, both for individuals who may develop personal or idiosyncratic creativity schemas and for intersubjective interactions (at the dyadic or group levels) where consensually validated schemas are constructed and negotiated.

CONCLUSION AND RESEARCH DIRECTIONS

The critique of the structural-functional perspective on innovation and professionals offered in this chapter does not imply the abandonment of research traditions in this area, but rather a restructuring of the approach we should take to designing and conducting research. We need to consider how new research should be shaped that will reflect and integrate the perspectives of the sensemaking paradigm into a functionalist approach. The remainder of this chapter suggests two possible avenues for advancement and raises questions relevant to each that the prospective creativity researcher can consider.

Theory Building

A conceptual synthesis that combines sensemaking and structural-functional perspectives together in an enriched theory of professionals and innovation is proposed here as a direction for future research on professionals and creativity. This synthesis draws on the essential differences in professional motivations that the two theoretical perspectives advocate and seeks to show how a broader view on the dynamics of professional life over time could accommodate both motivations. The motivational basis of the structural-functional argument is that professionals have institutionalized the values of their profession, especially with respect to the growth of knowledge through technology and innovation. To ignore these values, their legitimating role and grounding in conflicting bases of knowledge would ignore all the training and socialization that professionals undergo. However, to ignore conflicting worldviews, which sensemaking emphasizes, and the examination of the conditions under which professionals use, ignore, or distort their values for personal gain would ignore the realities of day-to-day professional life. These motivations are not incompatible and may be examined at different times in the lives of a professional or the development of a profession.

Recent research suggests that industry and organization change is marked by long periods of convergence and incrementalism, followed by relatively brief periods of radical reorientation and metamorphosis (Tushman & Anderson, 1986; Tushman & Romanelli, 1985). Convergence consists of fine-tuning, through refinement and extension of existing knowledge bases; reorientation consists of frame-breaking change that sets the industry into upheaval. Reorientations can be precipitated by the emergence of new technologies, the introduction of deregulation or the appearance of major economic or political shifts. A similar metamorphosis model might hold for the professions as well. During relatively tranquil periods of convergence, the structural-functional model of creativity may be more applicable during periods of innovative turbulence when professional communities and subcommunities are most likely to clash; the sensemaking model may be more descriptive of professional behavior.

Research Methods

To date, most research on creativity has been conducted either with individuals or small groups in the laboratory or through surveys (see Shalley, Zhou and Oldham, 2004, for a recent review). A sensemaking perspective points to the need for longitudinal, qualitative case studies that examine, detail, and incorporate the perspectives of multiple participants and describe the unfolding dynamics of the creative process in organizations. Researchers in the ethnographic tradition (Eisenhardt, 1989; Glaser & Strauss, 1967; Yin, 1989, 1993) have described ways of developing grounded theory, where traveling between data and conceptualization is an iterative process. We believe that such qualitative research would be instrumental in discovering how sensemaking underwrites the creative process in organizations.

A creative way of conducting qualitative research on creativity might be to employ the techniques of participant observation, where researchers use their own creative experiences in organizational roles to inform their theoretical perspective. In organizational studies, participant observation has been used in roles as diverse as machinist (Roy, 1959), Disneyland worker (Van Maanen, 1990), university committee member (Gioia & Chittipeddi, 1991), and college professor. Whyte (1984, p. 29) notes that "[s]ome of the most valuable studies of organizational behavior have been made by participant observers." What may be unique to creativity research is the pairing of roles of creator with theoretician, perhaps to their mutual benefit.

The goals of these efforts should be to identify the various occupational and professional groups in the organization, to delineate the frames of reference and motivations of each group, and to determine what types of creativity and innovation would advance or hinder each group. Given this understanding, the field research can then observe how the process of creativity unfolds. Who advances what creative proposals? Which professional groups support or protest each proposal? How does the organization adjudicate this process? By mapping out these processes, we will understand better how sensemaking impacts the course of creativity.

REFERENCES

Aguilar. F. (1967). *Scanning the business environment*. New York: Macmillan.

Amabile, T. M. (1983). *The social psychology of creativity*. New York: Springer-Verlag.

Amabile, T. M. (1988). A model of creativity and innovation in organizations. In B. M. Staw & L. L. Cummings (Eds.), *Research in organizational behavior* (Vol. 10, pp. 123–167). Greenwich, CT: JAI Press.

Amabile, T. M., & Gryskiewicz, S. S. (1987). *Creativity in the R&D laboratory* (Tech. Rep. No. 10). Greensboro, NC: Center for Creative Leadership.

Andrews, F. M. (1979). *Scientific productivity*. Cambridge, England: Cambridge University Press.

Astley, W. G., & Van De Ven, A. H. (1983). Central perspectives and debates in organization theory. *Administrative Science Quarterly, 28*, 245–273.

Barley, S. (1986). Technology as an occasion for structuring: Evidence from observations of CAT scanners and the social order of radiology departments. *Administrative Science Quarterly, 31*, 78–108.

Basadur, M., Graen, G. B., & Scandura, T. A. (1986). Teaching effects on attitudes toward divergent thinking among manufacturing engineers. *Journal of Applied Psychology, 71*, 612–617.

Bateson, G. (1972). *Steps to an ecology of mind*. New York: Ballantine Books.

Benson, J. K. (1973). The analysis of bureaucratic-professional conflict versus dialectic perspectives. *The Sociological Quarterly, 14*, 376–394.

Benson, J. K. (1975). The interorganizational network as a political economy. *Administrative Science Quarterly, 20*, 229–249.

Benson, J. K. (1977). Organizations: a dialectic view. *Administrative Science Quarterly, 22*, 1–21.

Bucher, R., & Strauss, A. (1961). Professions in process. *American Journal of Sociology, 66*, 325–334.

Burkhardt, M. E., & Brass, D. J. (1990). Changing patterns or patterns of change: The effects of change in technology on social network structure and power. *Administrative Science Quarterly, 35*, 1–8.

Burrell, G., & Morgan, G. (1979). *Sociological paradigms and organizational analysis*. London: Heinemann.

Day, R. A., & Day, J. V. (1977). A review of the current state of negotiated order theory: An appreciation and critique. *Sociological Quarterly, 18*, 126–142.

Dougherty, D. (1992). Interpretive barriers to successful product innovation in large firms. *Organization Science, 3*, 179–202.

Dougherty, D. (2004). Innovation, creativity, and discovery in modern organizations. *Academy of Management Review, 29*, 301–322.

Drazin, R., Glynn, M. A., & Kazanjian, R. K. (1999). Multi-level theorizing about creativity in organizations: A sense-making perspective. *Academy of Management Review, 24*, 286–308.

Dutton, J. E., & Dukerich, J. M. (1991). Keeping an eye on the mirror: Image and identity in organizational adaptation. *Academy of Management Journal, 34*, 517–554.

Dutton, J. E., & Jackson, S. E. (1987). Categorizing strategic issues: Links to organizational action. *Academy of Management Review, 12*, 76–90.

Eisenhardt, K. M. (1989). Building theory from case study research. *Academy of Management Review, 14*, 532–550.

Ford, C. M. (1996). A theory of individual creativity in multiple social domains. *Academy of Management Review, 21*, 1112–1134.

Ford, C. M., & Gioia, D. A. (1995). *Creativity in organizations: Ivory tower visions and real world voices.* Newbury Park, CA: Sage.

Forsyth, P. B., & Danisiewicz, T. J. (1985). Toward a theory of professionalization. *Work and Occupations, 12*, 159–176.

Freidson, E. (1970). *Profession of medicine: A study of the sociology of applied knowledge.* New York: Harper & Row.

Freidson, E. (1986). *Professional powers.* Chicago: University of Chicago Press.

Gibbons, D. (2004). Friendship and advice networks in the context of changing professional values. *Administrative Science Quarterly, 49*, 238–259.

Gioia, D. A., & Chittepddi, K. (1991). Sensemaking and sense giving in strategic change initiation. *Strategic Management Journal, 12*, 433–448.

Gioia, D. A., & Pitre, E. (1990). Multiparadigm perspectives on theory building. *Academy of Management Review, 4*, 584–602.

Glaser, B. G., & Strauss, A. L. (1967). *The discovery of grounded theory.* Chicago: Aldine Publishing Co.

Glynn, M. A. (1996). Innovative genius: A framework for relating individual and organizational intelligences to innovation. *Academy of Management Review, 21*, 1081–1111.

Goffman, E. (1974). *Frame analysis.* Cambridge, MA: Harvard University Press.

Gouldner, A. W. (1970). *The coming crisis in western sociology.* New York, Basic Books.

Granovetter, M. S. (1973). The strength of weak ties. *American Journal of Sociology, 78*, 1360–1380.

Hargadon, A. B., & Bechky, B. A. (2006). When collections of creatives become creative collectivities: A field study of problem solving at work. *Organization Science, 17*, 484–302.

Heydebrand, W., & Noell, J. (1973). Task structure and innovation in professional organizations. In W. Heydebrand (Ed.), *Comparative organizations: The results of empirical research.* Englewood Cliffs, NJ: Prentice-Hall.

Hill, R. C., & Levenhagen, M. (1995). Metaphors and mental models: Sensemaking in innovative and entrepreneurial activities. *Journal of Management, 21*, 1057–1074.

Huff, A. S. (1988). Politics and argument as a means of coping with ambiguity and change. In L. R. Pondy, R. J. Boland, & H. Thomas (Eds.), *Managing ambiguity and change.* New York: John Wiley.

CREATIVITY AND SENSEMAKING AMONG PROFESSIONALS **279**

King, N., & Anderson, N. (1990). Innovation in working groups. In M. A. West & J. L. Farr (Eds.), *Innovation and creativity at work* (pp. 81–100). Chichester, England: Wiley.

Klegon, D. (1978). The sociology of professions: an emerging perspective. *Sociology of Work and Occupations, 3,* 259–283.

Larson, M. S. (1977). *The rise of professionalism.* Berkeley, CA: University of California Press.

March, J. G. (1981). Footnotes to organizational change. *Administrative Science Quarterly, 26,* 563–577.

Mohr, L. B. (1982). *Explaining organizational behavior.* San Francisco: Jossey-Bass.

Morgan, G. (1980). Paradigms, metaphors and puzzle solving in organization theory. *Administrative Science Quarterly, 25,* 605–622.

Mumford, M. D., & Gustafson, S. B. (1988). Creativity syndrome: Integration, application, and innovation. *Psychological Bulletin, 103,* 27–43.

Oldham, G. R., & Cummings, A. (1996). Employee creativity: Personal and contextual factors at work. *Academy of Management Journal, 39,* 607–634.

Parsons, T. (1939). The professions and social structure. *Social Forces, 17,* 457–468.

Parsons, T. (1951). *The social system.* Glencoe, IL: Free Press.

Payne, R. (1990). The effectiveness of research teams: A review. In M. A. West & J. L. Farr (Eds.), *Innovation and creativity at work* (pp. 101–122). Chichester, England: John Wiley.

Perry-Smith, J. E. (2003). The social side of creativity: A static and dynamic social network perspective. *Academy of Management Review, 28,* 89–102.

Perry-Smith, J. E. (2006). Social yet creative: The role of social relationships in facilitating individual creativity. *Academy of Management Journal, 49,* 85–107.

Pettigrew, A. M. (1973). *The politics of organizational decision-making.* London: Tavistock.

Poole, P., Gioia, D., & Gray, B. (1989). Influence modes, schema change, and organizational transformation. *Journal of Applied Behavioral Science, 25,* 271–289.

Porac, J. F., Thomas, H., & Baden-Fuller, C. (1989). Competitive groups as cognitive communities: The case of Scottish knitwear manufacturers. *Journal of Management Studies, 26,* 397–416.

Ring, P. S., & Rands, G. P. (1989). Sensemaking, understanding, and committing: Emergent interpersonal transaction processes in the evolution of 3M's microgravity research program. In A. H. Van de Ven, H. L. Angle, & M. S. Poole (Eds.), *Research on the management of innovation.* New York: Harper & Row.

Rosenberg, D., Tonkins, C., & Day, P. (1981). A work role perspective on accountants in local government departments. *Accounting, Organization and Society, 7,* 123–137.

Rousseau, D. M. (1985). Issues of level in organizational research. In B. M. Staw & L. L. Cummings (Eds.), Research in organizational behavior (Vol. 17, pp. 1–37). Greenwich, CT: JAI Press.

Roy, D. F. (1959). Banana time: Job satisfaction and informal interaction. *Human Organization, 18,* 158–168.

Sandelands, L. E., & Stablein, R. E. (1987). The concept of organization mind. In S. Bacharach & N. DiTimaso (Eds.), *Research in the sociology of organizations* (Vol. 5, pp. 135–161). Greenwich, CT: JAI.

Shalley, C. E., Zhou, J., and Oldham, G. R. (2004). The effects of personal and contextual characteristics on creativity: Where should we go from here? *Journal of Management, 30,* 933–958.

Strasser, H. (1976). *The normative structure of sociology: Conservative and emancipatory themes in social thought.* Boston: Routledge & Kegan Paul.

Taggar, S. (2002). Individual and group ability to utilize individual creative resources: A multi-level model. *Academy of Management Journal, 35,* 315–334.

Thomas, J., & McDaniel, R. (1990). Interpreting strategic issues: Effect of strategy and the information-processing structure of top management teams. *Academy of Management Journal, 33,* 286–306.

Tushman, M. L., & Anderson, P. (1986). Technological discontinuities and organizational environments. *Administrative Science Quarterly, 31,* 439–465.

Tushman, M. L,. & Nelson, R. R. (1990). Introduction: Technology, organizations, and innovation. *Administrative Science Quarterly, 35,* 1–8.

Tushman, M. L., and Romanelli, E. (1985). Organizational evolution: A metamorphosis model of convergence and reorientation. In L. Cummings and B. Staw (Eds.), *Research in organizational behavior.* Greenwich, CT: JAI Press.

Van Maanen, J. (1990). The smile factory. In P. J. Frost, L. F. Moore, M. R. Louis, C. C. Lundberg, & J. Martin (Eds.), *Reframing organizational culture* (pp. 58–76). Newbury Park, CA: Sage Publications.

Volkema, R. J., Farquhar, K., & Bergmann, T. J. (1996). Third-party sensemaking in interpersonal conflicts at work: A theoretical framework. *Human Relations, 49,* 1437–1454.

Wagner, D. G., & Berger, J. (1985). Do sociological theories grow. *American Journal of Sociology, 70,* 137–158.

Walsh, J., & Fahey, L. (1986). The role of negotiated belief structures in strategy making. *Journal of Management, 12,* 325–338.

Walsh, J., Henderson, C., & Deighton, J. (1988). Negotiated belief structures and decision performance: An empirical investigation. *Organizational Behavior and Human Decision Processes, 42,* 194–216.

Walsh J., & Ungson, G. (1991). Organizational memory. *Academy of Management Review, 16,* 57–91.

Weick, K. E. (1979). *The social psychology of organizing.* Reading, MA: Addison-Wesley.

Weick, K. E. (1995). *Sensemaking in organizations.* Thousand Oaks, CA: Sage.

Weick, K. E., & Roberts, K. H. (1993). Collective mind in organizations: Heedful interrelating on flight decks. *Administrative Science Quarterly, 38,* 357–381.

Wheatley, W. J., Anthony, W. P., & Maddox, E. N. (1991). Selecting and training strategic planners with imagination and creativity. *Journal of Creative Behavior, 25,* 52–60.

Whyte, W. F. (1984). *Learning from the field.* Beverly Hills, CA: Sage.

Woodman, R. W., Sawyer, J. E., & Griffin, R. W. (1993). Toward a theory of organizational creativity. *Academy of Management Review, 18,* 293–321.

Yin, R. K. (1989). *Case study research: Design and methods.* Newbury Park, CA: Sage.

Yin, R. K. (1993). *Applications of case study research.* Newbury Park, CA: Sage.

CHAPTER 12

Creativity and Organizational Change
Linking Ideas and Extending Theory

Richard W. Woodman

Texas A & M University

INTRODUCTION

It seems quite logical that creativity occurring within the work setting and processes of organizational change would be related. How best to conceptualize such relationships? The major theme of this chapter is that the arenas of organizational creativity and organizational change can inform each other. The literature on organizational change is vast; the literature focused on individual-level creativity is equally large, but the literature on *organizational* creativity is much smaller. A notable feature of these literatures, however, is how little they overlap. Organizational scientists engaged in research and writing on organizational change pay little attention to creativity within the work setting. Few scholars focused on creativity have much to say about broader processes of change within organizations. In the world of change management, there is likewise little focus on truly creative products, processes, situations, or persons.

In this chapter, I will explore potential areas of overlap and attempt to identify ways in which the two areas might inform each other to their mutual advantage. First, some definitions of organizational creativity, organizational change, and innovation (a closely related term) will be provided. Next, perspectives that link creativity and organizational change will be identified. The potentially useful areas of overlap will be divided into three categories: implications for research on organizational change, implications for research on organizational creativity, and implications for change management practice.

SOME DEFINITIONS

Organizational creativity refers to the creation of a valuable, useful new product, service, idea, procedure, or process by individuals working together in a complex social system (Woodman, Sawyer, & Griffin, 1993). This is the organizational analogue of commonly accepted definitions of individual creativity (e.g., Barron, 1969). A closely related term, innovation, is typically described as the adoption of a product, service, procedure, and so on that is new to the organization so adopting (cf. West & Farr, 1990). What separates definitions of creativity from definitions of innovation in much of the literature is the aspect of "invention" or first-time use. Innovation, in an organizational sense, can thus include the adoption of ideas, products, procedures, and so on invented elsewhere. Organizational change (the broadest of the terms) is such a commonly used construct in the organizations literature that often no attempt is made to define it. For our purposes here, however, a parallel definition should be useful. Struckman and Yammarino (2003) have recently developed such a definition after reviewing how the topic of *change* is handled in a variety of fields including biology, social psychology, environmental science, and physics. They propose that, in the organizational sciences, organizational change can be defined as a managed system, process, or behavioral response over time or all three to a trigger event. The parallelism of these three definitions—creativity, innovation, and change—provides a framework to explore linkages among them.

PERSPECTIVES LINKING CREATIVITY AND CHANGE

There are at least two distinct ways to conceptualize the linkages between creativity and organizational change. We can view them in a stage model fashion that describes the process of change in the organization (e.g., Amabile, 1988). From the stage model perspective, creativity could be viewed as the incubation or idea stage, innovation as the implementation or action portion of the process, and the change itself as the end result or final stage in this process. Alternatively, we might view organizational change as the total process that includes stages related to creativity and innovation. Historically, much of the literature relating creativity to organizational change (as well as much of the traditional innovation literature) has taken a stage model approach either explicitly or implicitly.

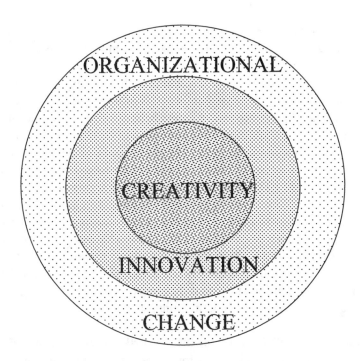

Figure 12.1 The domains of organizational change, innovation, and creativity.

However, I think that this is not the most useful way to view the fundamental relationship between creativity and change. I propose that a *domain model*, as shown in Figure 12.1, provides richer insight into relationships among creativity, innovation, and change. From this perspective, organizational creativity is seen as a "special case" of organizational change. Further, from the domain perspective, we can view creativity as nestled within the construct of innovation (which has a broader meaning than creativity), which in turn is nestled within the broader construct of change. Thus, only some organizational changes represent true innovations—the introduction of some new product, process, idea, service, or procedure into the organization. On the other hand, all innovation is a change. Similarly, only some organizational changes involve creativity, although all organizational creativity is, of course, change.

All of this is more than a game of semantics. Viewing organizational creativity as a special case of organizational change suggests that similar processes underlie both creativity and change that, in turn, suggests new ways that exploration of organizational creativity (and indeed, individual-level creativity) might inform change models and theories. At the same time, perhaps the much more extensive literature about organizational change might add to the rather sketchy amount of work on organizational creativity.

A further advantage of the domain approach to linking creativity and change stems from an increased ability to identify where, in the broader organizational change process, creative behaviors and outcomes might be most needed. An additional notion that will be explored is that this linkage could have implications for the practice of change management. By definition, all organizations need the ability to change, adapt, and innovate. Whether all systems need true creativity seems to be somewhat more debatable. Nevertheless, processes leading to change in general appear quite similar to organizational processes leading to creative outcomes. Further, both research on resistance to change (e.g., Cummings & Worley, 2005, pp. 157–159; Piderit, 2000) and research that explores barriers to organizational creativity (cf. Kilbourne & Woodman, 1999) seem to suggest similar individual differences and situational antecedents as potential stumbling blocks in the process.

IMPLICATIONS FOR RESEARCH ON ORGANIZATIONAL CHANGE

There are a number of implications for further development of research on organizational change stemming from knowledge about organizational creativity and the creativity of individuals. I make no attempt to provide an exhaustive list of creativity theories that might inform the organizational change arena, but rather provide a few illustrative examples.

Milgram (1990) identified four categories of "giftedness" in an attempt to clarify the diversity of abilities that contribute to individual creativity. The category of *general intellectual ability* refers to the ability to solve problems logically and to think in an abstract manner. The category of *specific intellectual ability* refers to intellectual ability in a given arena such as mathematics or music. The category of *general creative thinking* identifies the general ability to generate solutions to problems that are both unique and of high quality. Finally, the category of *specific creative talent* refers to domain-specific creative ability such as the ability to produce valuable, original products in specific areas such as physics, art, business, and so on. To illustrate the potential value of extending such a categorization scheme, in Table 12.1, I have listed Milgram's categories of individual giftedness and suggested organizational analogues for each. For example, the organizational analogue of Category I is the general capacity of the organization to change while Category II represents the capacity to change in specific ways. The general capacity to

Table 12.1   Categories of Giftedness and Their Organizational Analogues

CATEGORIES OF GIFTEDNESS (MILGRAM, 1990)	INDIVIDUAL	ORGANIZATION
I	General intellectual ability	General capacity to change, adapt
II	Specific intellectual ability	Capacity to change in specific ways
III	General creative thinking	General capacity to create
IV	Specific creative talent	Capacity to create in specific domains

change will be a function of culture, flexible organizational design, talent, time, slack resources, and so on. The capacity to adapt or change in specific ways (e.g., redesign jobs) will require domain-specific skills and knowledge in addition to the necessary resources, favorable context (e.g., culture, structure), and commitment. Similarly, Category III, when viewed from the perspective of the organization, refers to the general capacity to create while Category IV identifies the ability or capacity of the organization to innovate or create in specific domains. Thus, two of Milgram's four categories find analogues that focus on the broader issue of organizational change, while the remaining two suggest counterparts in the organizational creativity arena. In total, this schema logically supports the notion of meaningful linkage between the domains of change and creativity.

Milgram designed his model of giftedness (which included ability levels and different types of learning environments in addition to the giftedness categories discussed here) to be both heuristic (i.e., generative of theory and research) and practical. In a practical vein, he suggested that a deeper understanding of creativity-related abilities allowed curriculum and instructional strategies to be tailored to the individual developmental needs of schoolchildren, among others. Similarly, contrasting the general capacity of organizations to change, the capacity to change in specific domains, the general capacity to create, and the capacity to create in specific domains suggests the potential to develop a richer understanding of organizational change, and illuminates possible linkages between the domains of change and creativity that may be of both heuristic and practical value.

A further example of creativity theory with implications for organizational change research is found in Epstein's work on generativity theory and creativity. Generativity theory asserts that "ongoing behavior is generated as the probabilities of a large number of behaviors [that] are continuously subjected to a number of simple transformation functions which are presumed to have physical reality in the nervous system" (Epstein, 1990, p. 116). In contrast with most learning theories of behavior, generativity theory treats behavior as fluid, probabilistic, and potentially novel. An example from animal studies illustrates the meaning of the foregoing statements. Many readers are, no doubt, familiar with the famous box-and-banana experiments with chimpanzees. In these studies (first performed by Wolfgang Kohler in 1917; see Kohler, 1925), chimps are placed in a room with a banana hung just out of reach and supplied with a box of sufficient size to allow the banana to be reached if the box is moved below it. While many chimps will quickly (or eventually) lose interest in acquiring the banana, some percentage of them demonstrate sufficient "insight" to recognize that moving the box will allow the banana to be grasped by jumping from the top of the box. These experiments demonstrated the ability of chimps to *transform* previously established behavior (i.e., jumping to seize a banana, moving boxes and other objects around) into novel behavior that solves a problem. When human beings exhibit similar novel, problem-solving behavior in a situation new to them, we often describe their behavior as "creative."

Amazingly enough, Epstein has demonstrated that pigeons, faced with a similar problem, can also generate novel behaviors from repertories of learned behaviors. Pigeons learned to (a) open a small portable door, (b) move a box, (c) climb, (d) peck a banana when it was within reach, and (e) refrain from jumping at or flying to a banana when it was out of reach. These birds never saw any of these objects (box, banana, or portable doorway) together at the same time while they were learning these behaviors. Here are Epstein's words to describe the behavior of a pigeon so trained: "The banana was placed out of the bird's reach, and the box was placed behind the door. In just under four minutes, the bird managed to retrieve the box from behind the door, push it to the right place, climb, and peck the banana" (Epstein, 1990, p. 138). Pigeons that have not acquired the behaviors mentioned before, however, cannot solve this problem; they do not have the appropriate behavioral repertoires to generate the problem-solving behavior. Epstein does not, of course, necessarily consider the pigeon's behavior as creative or insightful; rather he would describe this outcome as a demonstration that previously established behavior manifests itself in new situations in lawful, predictable ways. That is, novel behavior can be described by a set of transformation functions that predict continuous and probabilistic changes in behavior.

Similar experiments were done with humans by N. R. F. Maier in the 1920s. He developed what is now called the "two-string" or "pendulum" problem (cf. Maier, 1931). In this experiment, two strings were suspended from a high ceiling and objects (e.g., a pair of pliers) placed on a table near the strings. Subjects were tasked with tying the ends of the string together. However, individually neither string can reach the other, nor can the subject stretch far enough with his or her arms to pull the strings together. The solution is to construct a pendulum, using one of the heavy objects tied to one of the strings. The subject can then set one string in motion using this weight, pull the other string to the center of the room, catching the first string as it swings within reach and tying the two strings together. Many people have trouble solving this problem. (Human beings, it appears, do not perform a great deal better than chimpanzees on problems of this type.) However, if Maier "set one of the strings in motion" for his subjects they typically would easily solve the problem.

Epstein (1990) extrapolated generative theory to human beings using the experimental procedure developed by Maier. He was able to demonstrate that he could develop transformation functions that would predict novel, problem-solving behavior in this instance by observing behavioral patterns of tying objects to the strings, attempting to pull one string to the other, swinging the strings, and so on. Tying an object to the string makes swinging the string more likely; swinging the string makes connecting them more likely. As with the animal studies, Epstein concluded that the novel behavior can be modeled as a transformative function of previously demonstrated behaviors.

Epstein further explains that he avoids using the language of creativity when discussing "generative phenomena." He sees a major problem with creativity stemming from the usefulness criterion—that is, it is impossible to avoid value judgments when describing, in particular, some product as creative. The product must necessarily be judged, thus suggesting that some admittedly original or novel products might be rejected, that is, judged to lack value. Epstein would thus suggest that the creative product is often a poor index of the creative process—in itself a rather novel viewpoint. However, this observation seems to address a fundamental problem in organizational change and organizational creativity. There is certainly a social judgment dimension to the valuing and accepting of change goals in the organization. Similarly, the valid recognition of employee creative products and behavior on the part of the organization's management is a crucial component in fostering organizational creativity (Dailey & Mumford, 2006; Zhou & Woodman, 2003). Indeed, Csikszentmihalyi argued that ". . . creativity is not an attribute of individuals but of social systems making judgments about individuals" (1990, p. 198).

Generativity theory may provide an exciting avenue to reconceptualize the organizational behaviors involved in effective organizational change processes. Perhaps organizational change may be meaningfully modeled as the transformation of established processes, underlying behaviors and thinking, and so on into novel processes that effectively solve problems facing the system. This line of inquiry is intriguing and would seem to hold promise to enrich our theories of organizational change.

Creativity researchers have often found it useful to conceptualize creativity as consisting of four components: (a) the creative process, (b) the creative product, (c) the creative person, and (d) the creative situation (Brown, 1989). Some confusion in the literature was eliminated when scholars more carefully identified the component of creativity that was under investigation in a particular study. In addition, a focus on the creative situation (cf. Amabile, 1983) has proven particularly valuable in extending creativity theory and research into organizational contexts. Perhaps most importantly from my perspective, an interactionist explanation of, first, individual creativity (cf. Woodman & Schoenfeldt, 1989, 1990) and later, organizational creativity (Woodman et al., 1993) has been developed that allows these components to be meaningfully dealt with in a holistic fashion. Creative behavior, as with other forms of behavior, is powerfully modeled as an interaction between person and situation. An interactionist model of creative behavior allowed the cognitive, personality, and social psychology explanations of creativity to be combined into a single, unifying perspective. Similarly, an interactionist model of *organizational* creativity provided a theoretical framework that not only included the components of process, product, person, and situation but also allows these to be addressed simultaneously at the individual, group, and organizational levels. Models and theories of organizational change might benefit from the interactional, cross-level perspectives that we find in theories of organizational creativity (cf. Amabile, 1988; Woodman et al., 1993).

While both person and situation are typically taken into account in organizational change theory, there remains an uncomfortable dichotomy between micro and macro theory development in the organizational sciences in general and the field of organizational change in particular. Micro change theory, heavily focused on individual behavior and grounded in the psychological sciences, is typically the province of organizational behavior (OB) and organizational development (OD) scholars; more macro change theory, perhaps more cognizant of context and situation and grounded in organizational sociology and economics, is often the domain of organizational training (OT) and strategy scholars. While each arena (i.e., micro and macro) typically pays "lip service" to both person and situation when dealing with behavior, much of the writing and research tilts heavily one way or the other.

The interactionist perspective, which by definition recognizes the importance of both individual differences and context, has been demonstrated to be of great value in organizational creativity research (e.g., Gilson, Mathieu, Shalley, & Ruddy, 2005; Kurtzberg, 2005; Shalley, Gilson, & Blum, 2000; Zhou & George, 2001). Cross-level, interactionist research could inform the organizational change arena much more than it has to date.

IMPLICATIONS FOR RESEARCH ON ORGANIZATIONAL CREATIVITY

Similar to the problem addressed immediately above, the leading theories of organizational creativity have been advanced by behavioral scientists (e.g., Amabile, 1988; Woodman et al., 1993) grounded in social psychology and interactional psychology. Consistent with the arguments above, I think these theories do a good job of crossing levels of analysis and encompassing explanatory variation stemming from both person and situation. Nevertheless, it is still a fair assessment to suggest that macro theories in organizational change have yet to fully inform theory development on organizational creativity. For example, Van de Ven and Poole (1995) have advanced a well-received typology consisting of four basic theories to explain developmental change processes in organizations. These theories posit different sequences of change events, identify different change motors, and operate at different organizational levels. *Life-cycle theory* suggests that change is imminent within the organization and there exists some underlying logic or program of change that will regulate organizational changes and move the system toward some end that is predetermined by the current state of the organization. Life cycle theory presupposes stages with each stage of development being a necessary precursor for succeeding stages. *Teleological theory* explains organizational change in terms of a purpose or goal that can be considered, in a very real sense, as the "final cause" for the change. The organization is a purposeful entity that envisions an end state, takes action to reach it, and is capable of monitoring its progress and making corrective adaptations as it proceeds. In *dialectical theory,* the organization is seen as existing in a pluralistic world buffeted by external events and forces, and conflicting internal values that compete for control. Conflict or opposition comes, thus, both from within and outside of the system. Change occurs when opposing forces or values gain sufficient power to challenge the status quo. Finally, *evolutionary theory* suggests that organizational change proceeds through a continuous cycle of variation, selection, and retention similar to biological evolution. Different forms of organizations emerge, perhaps by chance; organizations are selected by the tournament for scarce resources, and retained by forces that preserve successful organizational forms and organizational practices. Similar to the dynamic observed biologically, while the survival of individual organizations cannot be predicted, populations of organizations persist and evolve through time as described by the evolutionary theory of organizational change.

What would be the implications of applying these four perspectives to explanations of organizational creativity? In Table 12.2, I identify potential "creativity motors" and contrast them with the change motors developed by Van de Ven and Poole (1995). Possible creativity motors called up by this imagery include the notion, from the life-cycle perspective, that the organization creates in order to advance from stage to stage along the programmatic development path that is laid out. In the teleological theory, the organization creates in much the same manner as individuals who can be considered to socially construct the reality that surrounds them in order to satisfy their needs. This socially constructed creativity is in the service of the goals that the system is pursuing. In dialectical theory, creativity is a function of the dialectical tensions experienced by the system. The organization creates in order to relieve the

Table 12.2   Change and Creativity Motors Suggested by Development Theories of Organizational Change

THEORY (VAN DE VEN & POOLE, 1995)	CHANGE MOTOR	CREATIVITY MOTOR
Life-cycle theory	Preconfigured program	Stage advancement
Teleological theory	Goal enactment	Social construction
Dialectical theory	Confrontation and conflict	Dialectical tension
Evolutionary theory	Competitive selection	Biological imperative

tensions and to reestablish equilibrium. Finally, from the perspective of evolutionary theory, creativity in the organization might be considered as a biological imperative in the service of the survival of the system. This table is highly speculative, and is intended merely to be illustrative of how such a rich theoretical tapestry might inform the further development of theory on organizational creativity.

Some further examples from the extensive literature of change theory are suggestive as well. For example, Weick and Quinn (1999) divide change theories into those dealing with *episodic* change and those dealing with *continuous* change. Episodic change is intentional and goal directed, discontinuous, and relatively infrequent. From this perspective, change represents a divergence from some equilibrium state occasioned by the organization's failure to adapt to a changing environment. In contrast, continuous change is ongoing and grounded in the notion that small, incremental adjustments are constantly necessary for effective organizing. Change represents a pattern of continuous adjustments to work processes, organizational practices, and social relationships. These perspectives, extended into the world of organizational creativity, might suggest some intriguing theoretical perspectives. Perhaps all organizations must engage in episodic creation from time to time in order to survive. As a special case of organizational change, creativity is not called for in the day-to-day operations of the firm but is occasioned by serious disruptions in organizational equilibrium. Continuous creation, on the other hand, is called for by certain organizational environments and missions (e.g., an R&D operation, an advertising agency). Thus some systems (or some subsystems of the organization) employ creative processes on a continuous basis; some engage with creativity on an episodic basis. These observations would seem to be well grounded in the reality of organizations. Whether this dichotomy could lead to theory development of a substantial nature remains to be explored.

Another potentially insightful dichotomy was advanced some time ago by Porras and Robertson (1987). They suggested that theories within the organization development arena can be meaningfully divided into two categories: change process theory and implementation theory. Change process theory attempts to explain the dynamics through which individuals, groups, and organizations change. Implementation theory focuses on the specific intervention activities needed to carry out effective planned change. Change process theories have a more scholarly, "basic science" feel to them; implementation theories in OD are clearly focused on change management practice. The two types of theory are linked in

OD—a change process theory might describe the fundamental nature of the system to be changed and, as such, should inform the approaches used for change (implementation theory). This dichotomy has no naturally occurring counterpart in the theories so far developed dealing with organizational creativity, but perhaps it should. Certainly theories about creativity in the organizational setting have a focus on the creative process. Perhaps the field could gain as well from some further theorizing about how organizations can be managed and designed in order to facilitate creative behavior and outcomes. For example, Woodman (1995) has suggested that the high payoff strategy in managing organizational creativity is to manage context. That is, the best the organization can hope to achieve is to increase the probability of creative behavior by adding things to the situation that facilitate creativity and removing things from the situation that serve as barriers to creativity. These rudimentary notions (there is more to them than described here) and some excellent work focused on applying knowledge of creativity to organizations (e.g., Amabile, 1995; Fong, 2006; Ford, 1995) perhaps contain the beginnings of an "implementation theory" for organizational creativity. Porras and Robertson (1987) were of the opinion that implementation theory in OD is more strongly developed than change process theory. Certainly the reverse would be true for the organizational creativity arena. Imperfect though our knowledge may be, we still have a much better understanding of the basic dynamics of creative behaviors, processes, and outcomes than we do about how to harness this knowledge in the service of individual and organizational goals.

The role of the individual in changing organizations has been much explored. Woodman and Dewett (2004) have taken the flip side of this perspective and developed a theoretical lens through which to examine the ways that organizations change their employees. They posit that socialization processes, organizational training, organizational change programs, and managerial interactions with employees are among the most important sources or antecedents of individual change and development in organizations. Further, they suggest that changes in individual behavior patterns and individual characteristics (such as job knowledge, job attitudes, and job motivation) induced by the organization are moderated by the *changeability* of individual characteristics and behaviors, the *depth* of the changes, and the *time* needed for the change process. This line of inquiry, too, would seem to have implications for organizational creativity. Similar to notions of developing an implementation theory for organizational creativity discussed above, it could be of value to develop theory explaining how and why individual and group creative potential or capacity might be developed (or reduced) by the organization.

IMPLICATIONS FOR CHANGE MANAGEMENT

The parallelism, shown in Table 12.1, between creativity theory and change theory suggests some interesting implications for change management. Specifically, thinking about contrasting the general capacity of the organization to change, to change in specific ways, the general capacity to create, and to create in specific domains could lead to further refinement of change management practice. Most obviously, organizational interventions focused specifically on any one of these four arenas might differ from approaches to the others in a variety of important ways—actors, strategies, implementing techniques, follow-up evaluation methods (Woodman, Bingham, & Yuan, in press), and so on.

The difficulty in linking organizational diagnosis with needed actions represents a serious challenge for effective change management. Clearly, the importance of valid diagnosis as a precursor for organizational change is well understood. Still, careers have been wrecked (and sometimes made) as change managers make or fail to make this linkage effectively. It is a tricky business. Despite a wealth of popular business press books with suggestions for managers about how to take effective action based on valid data, in reality prescriptive approaches to this linkage tend not to work very well (Woodman & Pasmore, 2002). Knowing what to do, even when we have valid information about the current situation, attitudes toward change, and so on, remains more art than science. Table 12.1 suggests that needed insight might be developed from this framework. Organizational intervention strategies and techniques that are effective for improving the general capacity to change might be very different, for example, from approaches to be used when change is more tightly focused on specific domains. Further, a major theme introduced here is that underlying processes of organizational change and organizational creativity are related. Change management practice could be improved by developing theory (including implementation ideas) that would guide the recognition of needed creative behaviors and outcomes. When does planned change need to focus on true creativity in addition to addressing change in general? As mentioned earlier, seldom does change management practice really deal with creative persons, products, situations, or processes. Yet sometimes (perhaps more frequently than not), changes in the ability of the system to develop and nurture creative behavior and processes should be a significant change target. The capacity to create is a potential change lever that the organizational change and development field is largely ignoring.

Similar to the reasoning discussed before, Unsworth (2001) recently suggested that creativity research in organizations has suffered by typically treating creativity as a unitary construct. Unsworth suggested a matrix of creativity types: responsive, expected, contributory, and proactive. These four types are arrayed along two dimensions: the type of problem being addressed (ranging from closed—the problem is presented to the problem solver, to open—the participant must find or invent the problem) and the driver for engagement in the creative process (ranging from external—the problem solver is required to engage in the process, to internal—the problem solver is driven by internal desires to be creative, solve the problem, attain a goal). As such, *responsive creativity* applies when there is a required solution to a specified problem (closed problem, external driver). *Expected creativity* represents a required solution to a discovered problem (open problem, external driver). *Contributory creativity* is a volunteered solution to a specified problem (closed problem, internal driver), while *proactive creativity* refers to a volunteered solution to a discovered problem (open problem, internal driver). Congruent with the logic of Table 12.1, Unsworth suggests that there may be differences in applicable theory, differences in key antecedents to creativity, and indeed differences in underlying processes depending on the nature of the problem being addressed creatively and the underlying motivations of the problem solver (creator). I do not view Unsworth's suggestions about processual differences to be a refutation of my basic premise, from the domain perspective, that there are fundamental similarities between processes of change and creativity. Rather, I see her suggestions as mapping onto the dimensionality of Table 12.1. That is, a theoretical framework that allows recognition of underlying variability in situations adds understanding and insight. Use of such theoretical frames can only enhance effective change management in practice.

Yet another set of ideas with implications for change management is captured by the work on "creative environments." There is a tradition of research on individual creativity that has examined the effect of environment on the creativity of gifted (and other) individuals (cf. Harrington, 1999). This line of inquiry suggests the importance of supportive social systems, the importance of opportunities to learn and create, the importance of rewards that are relevant for creative persons, the importance of access to sources of needed information, and the like. The research on creative environments or "climate for creativity" has been extended into organizations (e.g., Amabile, 1996; Isaksen, Lauer, Ekvall, & Britz, 2000–2001). A reasonably large amount of data has been accumulated with regard to contextual factors that can enhance or constrain creativity in the work setting. As argued earlier, it is through the management of these contextual factors that the organization can have the greatest impact on creative behavior and outcomes (Woodman, 1995; Woodman et al., 1993). Change managers, organizational scientists, and organizations grapple with many parallel problems developing work cultures and settings that are conducive to change (Pasmore, Woodman, & Simmons, in press). Resistance to change must be diagnosed, understood, and overcome. Expectations that constrain the willingness and ability of individuals, teams, and departments to change must be examined and altered. Structures, rules, rigid procedures, and other situational aspects impeding change must be challenged and redesigned, and so on. As with other areas of overlap identified in this chapter, it would appear that research and writing devoted to understanding creative environments and "creative situations" would have direct implications and insights for change management. This is particularly true to the extent that the change efforts include not only improving the capacity of the organization to change, but also include enhancing the capacity of the organization to create (see Table 12.1).

CONCLUDING COMMENTS

Extant research and theories devoted to (a) organizational change and (b) individual creativity are extensive. In contrast, the literature on organizational creativity, which brings together ideas from these two areas, is in its infancy. If we take a domain perspective, arguing that fundamental linkages and relationships exist between processes of change and creativity in organizational settings, then the potential benefits from examining the overlap in these areas seem promising. In fact, upon starting down this path, one quickly discovers numerous intriguing ways that theory and research in each arena might inform the other. In terms of this potential insight, I have examined some of the (a) implications for research on organizational change stemming from creativity theory and research, (b) implications for research on organizational creativity stemming from theory and research on organizational change, and finally (c), implications for change management stemming from creativity research and writing.

In the final analysis, similarities and dissimilarities, congruities and incongruities, between the creative process and organizational change processes, between the situations supporting change and the situations nurturing creativity, and so on, are all empirical questions. The possible answers appear promising.

REFERENCES

Amabile, T. M. (1983). *The social psychology of creativity*. New York: Springer-Verlag.

Amabile, T. M. (1988). A model of creativity and innovation in organizations. In B. M. Staw & L. L. Cummings (Eds.), *Research in organizational behavior* (Vol. 10, pp. 123–167. Greenwich, CN: JAI Press.

Amabile, T. M. (1995). Discovering the unknowable, managing the unmanageable. In C. M. Ford & D. A. Gioia (Eds.), *Creative action in organizations* (pp. 77–82). Thousand Oaks, CA: Sage.

Amabile, T. M. (1996). *Creativity in context*. Boulder, CO: Westview Press.

Barron, F. (1969). *Creative person and creative process*. New York: Holt, Rinehart & Winston.

Brown, R. T. (1989). Creativity: What are we to measure? In J. A. Glover, R. R. Ronning, & C. R. Reynolds (Eds.), *Handbook of creativity* (pp. 3–32). New York: Plenum Press.

Csikszentmihalyi, M. (1990). The domain of creativity. In M. A. Runco & R. S. Albert (Eds.), *Theories of creativity* (pp. 190–212). Newbury Park, CA: Sage.

Cummings, T. G., & Worley, C. G. (2005). *Organization development and change* (8th ed.). Cincinnati, OH: South-Western College Publishing.

Dailey, L., & Mumford, M. D. (2006). Evaluative aspects of creative thought: Errors in appraising the implications of new ideas. *Creativity Research Journal, 18,* 367–384.

Fong, C. T. (2006). The effects of emotional ambivalence on creativity. *Academy of Management Journal, 49,* 1016–1030.

Ford, C. M. (1995). A multi-domain model of creative action taking. In C. M. Ford & D. A. Gioia (Eds.), *Creative action in organizations* (pp. 330–354). Thousand Oaks, CA: Sage.

Epstein, R. (1990). Generativity theory and creativity. In M. A. Runco & R. S. Albert (Eds.), *Theories of creativity* (pp. 116–140). Newbury Park, CA: Sage.

Gilson, L. L., Mathieu, J. E., Shalley, C. E., & Ruddy, T. M. (2005). Creativity and standardization: Complementary or conflicting drivers of team effectiveness? *Academy of Management Journal, 48,* 521–531.

Harrington, D. M. (1999). Conditions and settings/environment. In M. A. Runco & S. R. Pritzker (Eds.), *Encyclopedia of creativity* (Vol. 1, pp. 323–340). San Diego, CA: Academic Press.

Isaksen, S. G., Lauer, K. J., Ekvall, G., & Britz, A. (2000–2001). Perceptions of the best and worst climates for creativity: Preliminary validation evidence for the situational outlook questionnaire. *Creativity Research Journal, 13,* 171–184.

Kilbourne, L. M., & Woodman, R. W. (1999). Barriers to organizational creativity. In R. Purser & A. Montuori (Eds.), *Social creativity in organizations* (pp. 125–150). Cresskill, NJ: Hampton Press.

Kohler, W. (1925). *The mentality of apes.* London: Routledge & Kegan Paul.

Kurtzberg, T. R. (2005). Feeling creative, being creative: An empirical study of diversity and creativity in teams. *Creativity Research Journal, 17,* 51–65.

Maier, N. R. F. (1931). Reasoning in humans. II. The solution of a problem and its appearance in consciousness. *Journal of Comparative Psychology, 12,* 181–194.

Milgram, R. M. (1990). Creativity: An idea whose time has come and gone? In M. A. Runco & R. S. Albert (Eds.), *Theories of creativity* (pp. 215–233). Newbury Park, CA: Sage.

Pasmore, W. A., Woodman, R. W., & Simmons, A. L. (in press). Toward a more rigorous, reflective and relevant science of collaborative management research. In A. B. Shani, N. Adler, S. A. Mohrman, W. A. Pasmore, & B. Stymne (Eds.), *Handbook of collaborative management research.* Thousand Oaks, CA: Sage.

Piderit, S. K. (2000). Rethinking resistance and recognizing ambivalence: A multidimensional view of attitudes toward an organizational change. *Academy of Management Review, 25,* 783–794.

Porras, J. I., & Robertson, P. J. (1987). Organization development theory: A typology and evaluation. In R. W. Woodman & W. A. Pasmore (Eds.), *Research in organizational change and development* (Vol. 1, pp. 1–57). Greenwich, CT: JAI Press.

Shalley, C. E., Gilson, L. L., & Blum, T. C. (2000). Matching creativity requirements and the work environment: Effects on satisfaction and intentions to leave. *Academy of Management Journal, 43,* 215–223.

Struckman, C. J., & Yammarino, F. J. (2003). Organizational change: A categorization scheme and response model with readiness factors. In W. A. Pasmore & R. W. Woodman (Eds.), *Research in organizational change and development* (Vol. 14, pp. 1–50). Oxford, UK: Elsevier Science.

Unsworth, K. (2001). Unpacking creativity. *Academy of Management Review, 26,* 289–297.

Van de Ven, A. H., & Poole, M. S. (1995). Explaining development and change in organizations. *Academy of Management Review, 20,* 510–540.

Weick, K. E., & Quinn, R. E. (1999). Organizational change and development. In J. T. Spence, J. M. Darley, & D. J. Foss (Eds.), *Annual review of psychology* (Vol. 50, pp. 361–386). Palo Alto, CA: Annual Reviews.

West, M. A., & Farr, J. L. (1990). Innovation at work. In M. A. West & J. L. Farr (Eds.), *Innovation and creativity at work* (pp. 3–13). Chichester, England: John Wiley & Sons.

Woodman, R. W. 1995. Managing creativity. In C. M. Ford & D. A. Gioia (Eds.), *Creative action in organizations* (pp. 60–64). Thousand Oaks, CA: Sage.

Woodman, R. W., Bingham, J. B., & Yuan, F. (in press). Assessing organization development and change interventions. In T. G. Cummings (Ed.), *Handbook of organization development and change.* Thousand Oaks, CA: Sage.

Woodman, R. W., & Dewett, T. (2004). Organizationally relevant journeys in individual change. In M. S. Poole & A. H. Van de Ven (Eds.), *Handbook of organizational change and innovation* (pp. 32–49). Oxford, UK: Oxford University Press.

Woodman, R. W., & Pasmore, W. A. (2002). The heart of it all: Group- and team-based interventions in organization development. In Waclawski, J. & Church, A. H. (Eds.). *Organization development: A data-driven approach to organizational change* (pp. 164–176). San Francisco, CA: Jossey-Bass.

Woodman, R. W., Sawyer, J. E., & Griffin, R. W. (1993). Toward a theory of organizational creativity. *Academy of Management Review, 18,* 293–321.

Woodman, R. W., & Schoenfeldt, L. F. (1990). An interactionist model of creative behavior. *Journal of Creative Behavior, 24,* 279–290.

Woodman, R. W., & Schoenfeldt, L. F. (1989). Individual differences in creativity. In J. A. Glover, R. R. Ronning, & C. R. Reynolds (Eds.), *Handbook of creativity* (pp. 77–91). New York: Plenum Press.

Zhou, J., & George, J. M. (2001). When job dissatisfaction leads to creativity: Encouraging the expression of voice. *Academy of Management Journal, 44,* 682–696.

Zhou, J., & Woodman, R. W. (2003). Managers' recognition of employees' creative ideas: A social-cognitive model. In L. V. Shavinina (Ed.), *International handbook on innovation* (pp. 631–640). New York: Erlbaum.

SECTION III

Normative Implications of Organizational Creativity Research

CHAPTER 13

Why be Creative

A Review of the Practical Outcomes Associated With Creativity at the Individual, Group, and Organizational Levels

Lucy L. Gilson

University of Connecticut

INTRODUCTION

When asked to list outcomes that result from creativity, one immediately thinks of paintings by Picasso, Matisse, and Mondrian, a concert piece composed and played by Mozart or Philip Glass, or a new foreign language learned perfectly by a gifted child. When we think of creative outcomes within an organizational framework, we think of a marketing manager developing a new slogan for an ad campaign, a scientist trying out different drug combinations, or even an employee reorganizing the way parts are labeled and stored in their work area. However, while these could all be considered creative outcomes in and of themselves, it is hard to ascertain whether practical outcomes follow the creative ones. For instance, practical outcomes could encompass the following: Did the employee's novel approach to the work area, the new ad slogan, or the new drug combination result in improved job or organizational performance, higher levels of customer satisfaction, increased employee job satisfaction, or increased efficiency on the production line?

Predominantly, the creativity literature has focused its attention on creativity as the outcome of interest and less attention has been given to what happens as a result of an employee, group of employees, or even an organization exhibiting creative performance. In part, this is attributable to the assumption that creativity will result in positive outcomes (James,

Clark, & Cropanzano, 1999; Mumford, 2003). However, is this really the case?

The value of creativity is rarely debated with theorists going so far as to suggest that the quality of human life is greatly influenced by the creative contributions of individuals (Mumford & Gustafson, 1988). To this end, a vast number of organizations are placing a premium on creativity as a driver of success. Given this, it is important to take stock in what we know regarding the practical outcomes associated with creativity.

A recent article in *The Economist* (Frymire, 2006) argued that the biggest challenge facing organizations today is not finding or hiring cheap workers, but rather hiring individuals with "brainpower (both natural and trained) and especially the ability to think creatively" (p. 11). In essence, the argument put forth in this article is that if companies want to succeed in the global economy, they need individuals who have the talent to develop new ideas, as well as novel and useful approaches to their work. *The Economist* is not alone in this claim. Over the last twenty-five years, academic and practitioner interest in creativity has flourished, during which time a great deal of attention has been focused on what creativity means in a organizational environment and what leads employees and teams to be creative at work. Given this, we now know, as outlined in several earlier chapters in this volume, that individual differences, management practices, feedback from leaders and coworkers, social networks, and the organizational climate, along with many other factors can either stifle or enhance creativity at work (e.g., Amabile, 1996; Gilson & Shalley, 2004; Gough, 1979; Scott & Bruce, 1994; Tierney & Farmer, 2002; Zhou, 1998). That said, a great deal of the theoretical and empirical work in the creativity arena opens by stating that creativity should significantly increase performance, be a driver of team effectiveness, and be positively associated with organizational change and success. For example:

> "Creativity is a necessary requirement for organizational effectiveness" (Basadur, Taggar, & Pringle, 1999, p. 75).
>
> "Creative activity is essential in the current business environment. Creativity is a necessary step in the innovation process, contributing to the long-term productivity and effectiveness of the workplace" (Carson & Carson, 1993, p. 36).
>
> "Organizations in today's turbulent and competitive economy need creativity from their employees if they are to survive and be successful" (James, Chen, & Goldberg, 1992, p. 545).

"Considerable evidence now suggests that employee creativity can make a substantial contribution to an organization's growth and competitiveness" (Baer & Oldham, 2006, p. 963).

"People's creative efforts make an important contribution to organizational performance" (Redmond, Mumford, & Teach, 1993, pp. 120–121).

"In recent years, employee creativity and corporate innovation have emerged as prime factors in accomplishing company goals and, ultimately, in maintaining a profitable business" (Scott, 1995, p. 65).

What these quotations all suggest is that there is almost unanimous agreement on the value of creativity for the greater organizational good. That said, it is interesting to note that while expounding on the organizational level benefits of creativity, most of the research associated with the above quotes deals with creativity at the individual and group level of analysis. In addition, most of this work uses creativity as the outcome variable of interest. Accordingly, before beginning my discussion on the practical outcomes associated with creativity, I shall first take a step back and discuss creativity as a multilevel construct and what creativity means at the individual, group, and organizational levels. In particular, when conceptualizing creativity at different levels there may be different outcomes associated with being creative. In the remainder of this chapter, I will review the empirical findings between creativity and practical outcomes across all levels of analysis.

CREATIVITY AS A MULTI-LEVEL CONSTRUCT

Creativity, the development of novel and useful ideas, processes, and outcomes, has been conceptualized and theoretically modeled as one of the few multi-level constructs (Drazin, Glynn, & Kazanjian, 1999). Creativity is truly a multi-level construct in that creativity as both a process and an outcome is meaningful at different levels of analysis (Chen, Mathieu, & Bliese, 2004). For example, as an outcome creativity refers to the production of novel and useful products or services by an individual, group, or organization. In contrast, creative processes refer to the steps taken or creative acts that result in an outcome. Creative processes can also be undertaken at all three levels of analysis. Furthermore, creativity appears to be both isomorphic and homologous. Creativity is isomorphic because the structure of the construct does not change across levels. The core notion of coming up with something novel or trying new things traverses and retains its meaning regardless of whether the analysis is at the individual, group, or organizational level. Thus, individuals can develop a new product or means to complete their work, as can a group or organization. Regardless of the entity of interest, being creative means essentially the same thing. Creativity is also a homologous construct in that similar relationships hold across levels of analysis (Chen, Bliese, & Mathieu, 2005). The X → Y relationships hold such that the predictors of individual creativity are the same as those for group creativity. For example, individual and group goals have been found to predict creativity (Gilson & Shalley, 2004; Shalley, 1991).

While the preceding paragraph focused on the multilevel nature of creativity as the outcome or dependent variable, an interesting set of theoretical and empirical questions remains unanswered when creativity is conceptualized as the predictor. Specifically, given that creativity at the individual, group, and organizational levels of analysis has similar predictors, does each level have the same relationship with outcomes? Starting at the organizational level and working downward, creativity has been described as a means to ensure that organizations remain flexible, competitive, able to successfully implement and embrace change, and ultimately succeed in an increasingly complex and rapidly changing global economy. In other words, creativity is the cornerstone of organizational effectiveness (Amabile, 1996; Woodman, Sawyer, & Griffin, 1993). At the group or team level, it has been argued that creativity is a vital component of team effectiveness and viability. Teams that are able to generate new ideas and come up with different perspectives regarding how their work should be done are the most likely to succeed, thrive, and have high levels of customer satisfaction (Gilson, Mathieu, Shalley, & Ruddy, 2005; Hackman & Morris, 1975; Stein, 1974; Tagger, 2002; Tesluck, Farr, & Klein, 1997). Finally, at the individual level, employees who are willing and able to come up with new ideas and try new ways of going about their work are thought to be more satisfied, less stressed, have better health and welfare, and are deemed to be the most successful and sought after by employers (e.g., Frymire, 2006; Runco, 1995; Stokols, Clitheroe, & Zmundzinas, 2002). So, what do we know to date about the practical outcomes associated with creativity?

INDIVIDUAL OUTCOMES

At the individual level of analysis, the practical outcomes considered in concert with creativity encompass both performance and affective variables.

Performance

Starting with performance where the research is somewhat sparse, findings do however suggest a positive association. For example, in a study of undergraduate psychology students in the United Kingdom, Chamorro-Premuzic (2006) found significant positive correlations between creative thinking and academic performance. Further, he found that after accounting for student scores on the Big Five personality test, creative thinking made an incremental contribution to their final thesis grades. Similarly, Powers and Kaufman (2004) reported a significant, albeit small, positive correlation between creativity and the verbal, quantitative, and analytical scores of 342 individuals taking the Graduate Record Examination (GRE). In an excellent review of the creativity training literature, Scott, Leritz, & Mumford (2004) concluded that "creativity training works" (p. 382). Specifically, they conducted a meta-analysis on 70 studies and found that across populations, settings, cognitive levels, and participant demographics, well-designed and delivered creativity training was positively related to divergent thinking, problem solving, performance, attitudes, and behaviors. Their results further suggest that domain-specific training that is realistic, focuses on component skills, and allows for feedback is most strongly correlated with improved performance. Finally, using a sample of elementary school teachers, Milgram and Feldman (1979) found that creative activity in the classroom was significantly related to classroom effectiveness and teacher job satisfaction.

While the results reviewed above all appear to support a positive relationship between creativity and performance, it is somewhat of a conceptual leap to generalize between undergraduate thesis work, training course performance, and GRE scores to on-the-job performance. However, what these results do suggest is that on a purely cognitive level, there appears to be an association between creativity and performance. Thus, at the individual level of analysis, a great deal of work remains to be done in examining whether creative processes and outcomes result in improved performance as conceptualized in an organizational setting. This is not, however, a simple question because what is considered to be high performance is not uniform across jobs or organizations. For a real estate agent the number of houses sold would be a performance metric of interest whereas for a customer service associate, wait time to speak to an attendant may be the metric used to judge superior performance. Would creativity have the same relationship with both of these performance outcomes? What if the performance metric for a scientist at a nuclear plant is safety or accident reduction? Both of these outcomes are associated with reducing variance whereas creativity is usually conceptualized as a variance-increasing process (Gilson et al., 2005; Taylor & Greve, 2006) — would creativity still be positively associated with employee performance?

Innovation

Another form of performance is innovation that is broadly defined as the adoption, implementation, and incorporation of new ideas or practices (Amabile, 1996; Scott & Bruce, 1996; Woodman et al., 1993). Creativity is often described as more of the cognitive generation and selection of ideas, whereas innovation is the behavioral implementation of something new (West, 2002). Using this divide, it follows logically that creativity (i.e., the generation of new ideas, processes, or products) is a necessary prerequisite for innovation. To this end, researchers have found significant positive associations between suggestion generation and implementation (Axtell, Holman, Unsworth, Wall, & Waterson, 2000; Scott & Bruce, 1994). Work by Axtell and colleagues demonstrated that individual (i.e., self-efficacy) and job characteristics (i.e., autonomy) were strongly related to the generation of suggestions. Thus, employees who had the latitude in their jobs to make their own decisions and believed that they were capable of doing so, were more likely to try new product improvements or approaches to their work. However, when it came to implementing some of these suggestions, group and organizational factors were found to be more relevant. Here, the notion is that while an individual can come up with an idea, it takes others along with organizational support to implement the idea. Hence, participative safety and support for innovation were stronger predictors of innovation.

Innovation is also said to involve risk (Janssen, van de Vliert & West, 2004) and therefore individuals who promote creative ideas with the goal of improving performance often meet with resistance from supervisors and coworkers who are threatened by change or content with the status quo (Janssen, 2003). Given this, the implementation of creative ideas can often result in frustration, increased conflict, and less satisfactory relationships at work (Janssen, 2003), which are all affective outcomes.

Affective Outcomes

Moving away from performance to affective outcomes, several researchers have considered the relationship between creativity and job satisfaction. In a 1995 study, Runco administered an extensive battery of creative personality tests to a number of artists who all worked in creative jobs within a large organization. The goal of this work was to examine whether for artists (e.g., sculptors, illustrators, painters, and writers), having a creative personality and working in a climate conducive to creative productivity affected job satisfaction. Given that most artists work alone, not much was known about how artists would respond in an organizational setting. In this work, Runco found that creativity was a key contributor to job satisfaction. However, when he further delved into the various dimensions of creative personality his results suggested that those individuals who described themselves as the most original were in fact the least satisfied. Using a sample of supervisory and office workers, Stokols and colleagues (2002) found that perceived support for creativity at work was positively related to job satisfaction and further had a mitigating effect on levels on job stress. In addition, support for creativity mediated the relationships between environmental distractions (such as outside noise and privacy) and social relations (supportive and nonsupportive communications with supervisors and coworkers) on job satisfaction and stress. However, while this study examines support for creativity and affective outcomes it does not take into account whether or not the employees surveyed were actually creative at work.

When examining the relationship between creativity and job satisfaction, most researchers have incorporated the notion of "fit" between the individual and the job or work environment. Using data from three organizations in two different industries, Livingstone, Nelson, and Barr (1997) studied whether the fit between an individual's desired and current work environment for creativity, as well as the fit between an individual's ability to be creative and the creative demands of the work environment would affect job satisfaction, strain, commitment, and performance. While a very complex pattern of results emerged, one of the most robust findings was that when there was a fit between the demands for creativity placed on an individual by the work environment and the individual's abilities to be creative, lower levels of strain and higher levels of job satisfaction ensued. Similarly, it has been argued that the lack of fit between an individual's preference for creativity and the creative climate of the organization can be perceived as stressful (Nicholson & West, 1988).

Job-Required Creativity: At the individual level of analysis, another area that has received attention when considering affective outcomes is the role of job-required creativity. In effect, Runco's aforementioned study (1995) that was designed to specifically examine the relationships between creativity and the job satisfaction of artists is one of the first studies of job-required creativity. Job-required creativity considers how important creativity is for successful performance of the job in question. For instance, some jobs, like those of package designers in a consumer products company, will have very high levels of job-required creativity, whereas individuals working in inventory control in the same company will have much lower levels of job-required creativity. That is not to say that the inventory-control jobs will not allow for some level of creativity. In fact, it has been argued that creativity is possible in all jobs, but that creative processes and outcomes can range from minor adaptations to major breakthroughs (Kirton, 1976; Shalley, Gilson & Blum, 2000; Unsworth, 2001).

Combining both fit and job-required creativity and using a large sample of employed individuals across a wide range of occupations, Shalley and her colleagues (2000) found that when individuals worked in jobs where their perceived creativity requirement matched those of the job (as rated by the *Dictionary of Occupational Titles*), they were more satisfied and less likely to be considering leaving their jobs. The notion of job-required creativity (Shalley et al., 2000; Unsworth, Wall & Carter, 2005) and job complexity (Oldham & Cummings, 1994; Scott & Bruce, 1994) suggest that there are facets of a job that when considered in concert with creativity can be drivers of employees' well-being.

To date, research has considered satisfaction, stress, and intentions to turnover, but there is every liklihood not to believe that when individuals are in jobs that either match their personal characteristics or there is convergence with their job expectations, higher levels of commitment, positive affect, and organizational citizenship behaviors should follow. It is interesting to note that while academics have not considered the relationships between creativity and commitment, the practitioner press has spent a great deal of time arguing that employee engagement should result in increased levels of creativity (i.e., Richman, 2006; Woodruffe, 2006). The arguments put forth here are that when employees are engaged by their jobs or organizations they will be more likely to try different approaches to their work because they care about the future of the organization. However, I believe that the reverse causality also could hold. When employees are encouraged, supported, and allowed to try novel approaches to their work and take risks, greater job ownership should ensue that will ultimately result in increased levels of commitment.

Negative Outcomes

While researchers have focused on the positive performance and affective outcomes associated with creativity, care needs to be given, and research should also examine the "dark" side of creativity. In a theoretical article on groups and creativity, James and colleagues (1999) suggest that creativity also can be associated with negative behaviors such as theft, sabotage, and exploitation. The authors explain that novel approaches to work do not necessarily have to be for the "good" of one's coworkers or the organization. In fact, creativity could just as easily be used to slow down work on the production line or hinder a new product getting to market. To this end, work by Policastro and Gardner (1999) has found that creative work can be associated with a disrupted family life, and Runco and Charles (1997) argue that there is a positive association between creativity and alcohol abuse—neither of which is a positive individual level outcome!

Conclusion

My intent here is not to leave the individual section of this chapter on a negative note, but rather to make sure that some space is given to a topic that is more often than not neglected. That said, the research that has examined creativity and individual level outcomes has for the most part found positive associations with performance, innovation, job satisfaction, and a reduction in strain. However, taken as a whole the relationships between individual creativity and outcomes are not direct, but rather appear to be predicated upon a fit or congruence between an individual and the job and/or the individual's job and the organization. Therefore, there are many avenues for future inquiry. For example, given that a climate supportive of creativity can reduce the effects of strain and help increase job satisfaction, an interesting extension is whether the results would hold for individuals with differing levels of creative ability or personality correlates that have been found to predict creativity (see work by Gough, 1979; Jabri, 1991). In other words, when an individual is required to be creative and the climate is supportive of creativity, is there a stronger relationship with job satisfaction (or commitment) for more creative rather than less creative individuals? Furthermore, what is the functional form of the relationship between creativity and performance? Is being creative once or on one task enough to enhance performance, or do individuals have to be creative in multiple facets of their jobs to see a positive relationship with performance? Given that at this point in time we know more about creative outcomes, creative personalities, and creative jobs, it is now time to turn our attention to how these factors predict performance, innovation, employee behaviors, and affect.

GROUP LEVEL OUTCOMES

In their 1997 review of the group process literature, Cohen and Bailey included thirteen studies on new product development project teams. New product development is usually tightly coupled with creativity and the studies all considered the processes used by these teams to develop new products; however none of them included any measures of productivity or objective performance, thereby making it impossible to ascertain whether there was a relationship between group creativity and outcomes. Luckily, the landscape is not quite so bleak when other types of teams are considered (i.e., top-management teams, empowered work teams). Also, since the publication of this review article, some progress has been made, the results of which will be discussed here in more detail. However, much of the work on teams and creativity has been theoretical, with articles describing the potential relationships between creativity and group outcomes (e.g., Paulus, 2000; West, 2002). That said, an initial perusal of the empirical literature suggests that while at the individual level there is research that links creativity to both affective and performance outcomes, at the team level I could find no studies that have examined creativity and affective outcomes (i.e., team satisfaction, satisfaction with team members, commitment). Therefore, the remainder of this section will focus on the associations of creativity, performance, innovation, and customer satisfaction and conclude with a call for research that examines creativity in concert with group affective outcomes.

Performance

As previously mentioned, creativity has been conceptualized and measured as both a process and an outcome (Drazin et al., 1999). At the team level, research has primarily focused on the association between creative processes and performance. For example, in a study of empowered teams of service technicians, Gilson and colleagues (2005) hypothesized and found that when members encouraged one another to try new things even when they were not sure whether they would work, welcomed change, and were willing to try creative solutions to difficult problems, they had higher levels of objective performance than those teams who were not supportive of creative processes. In this research, the performance metric was a composite measure that encompassed aspects of equipment reliability and team expenditure to budget. The results of this study add to our knowledge of team creativity and practical outcomes in several different ways. First, the measures of creativity and performance used in this work make the results highly generalizable across different types of teams, organizational settings, and even industries. Second, as discussed with regard to individuals, teams of service technicians are not performing jobs that are usually associated with high levels of creativity. Therefore, finding that teams that were supportive of creative processes had higher levels of objective performance has wide-ranging implications to both researchers and managers.

Innovation

At the team level, the relationship between innovation and performance has been examined by West and Anderson (1996) in a sample of top-management teams in U.K. hospitals. In their study, the authors primarily sought to determine whether team processes (i.e., participation, setting objectives) predicted innovation. Here, they found that the proportion of innovative members in a team was associated with innovation radicalness (extent to which a change in status quo would result from the innovation). In addition to multiple dimensions of innovation, the study also asked hospital managers to rate whether the innovations would benefit administrative efficiency, patient care, and staff well-being—practical outcomes. Examining the practical outcomes in more detail reveals some interesting associations between them and the innovation dimensions, as well as a measure of support for innovative team processes, and the development of new ideas. Specifically, support for innovation, overall innovation, and the radicalness of a team's innovations were all positively associated with administrative efficiency. This relationship suggests that teams who perceive there is support (time and resources) for them to be innovative, who have more radical ideas, along with a greater number of innovations also are rated by managers as being more efficient in their work.

Customer Satisfaction

In addition to performance and efficiency, customer satisfaction is another key measure of success within many organizations. Customers who frequent hotels, restaurants, hardware stores, auto dealerships, public libraries, and even some government agencies are frequently asked to evaluate the service they receive. The relationship between creativity and customer satisfaction appears to be somewhat complex. For instance, in their study of 90 service technician teams, Gilson and colleagues (2005) found no direct relationship between team creativity and results from three months' worth of customer satisfaction surveys. Similarly, in their study of hospital top-management teams, West and Anderson (1996) found that neither measures of patient care (external customers) nor staff well-being (internal customers) were significantly associated with support for innovation, overall innovation, or innovation radicalness. However, there were significant positive relationships between innovation magnitude (consequences as a result of the innovation), staff well-being, and patient care. Taken together these findings suggest that creativity may not have a direct effect on customer satisfaction. This supports the contention made by Sutton (2002) that creativity may be best utilized as a "back room" function or sheltered away from customers, especially in settings where creativity is not expected or the norm. Sutton argued that creative people may be hesitant to try things in front of others. Similarly, Gilson and colleagues (2005) suggested that teams may not try new things in front of customers for fear that the attempt will be perceived as experimentation or as if the team does not know what it is doing. In support of this, Gilson and her colleagues did find that when teams employed both creative processes and utilized standardized work practices, these two seemingly conflicting processes interacted with one another to positively influence customer satisfaction. Specifically, teams that were high on both creativity and used high levels of work standardization (i.e., routinized problem-solving procedures, documented work processes) had the highest customer satisfaction ratings.

Affective Outcomes

In the introduction to this section, I mentioned that I could find no research that has directly linked creativity to affect at the group level of analysis. However, some interesting results have been found in the brainstorming literature that may be applicable to the study of group creativity. Brainstorming, like creativity, is frequently defined as the generation of novel ideas or is referred to as a means to fuel creativity through the generation of ideas (Osborn, 1957). When considering the success of brainstorming in groups, researchers have consistently found, contrary to popular belief, that individuals working alone generate a greater number of ideas as well as higher-quality ideas than do groups of individuals working together (cf. Paulus, 2000). Similarly, individuals are better able than teams to integrate creative and divergent experiences into their idea generation (Taylor & Greve, 2006). However, of particular note here is that individuals working in groups are *more* satisfied and pleased with the ideas they generate than are individuals working alone. This finding has led to the suggestion that a benefit of group brainstorming is not the number or quality of ideas generated, but rather the affective outcomes associated with the technique and process (Sutton & Hargadon, 1996). Specifically, in a qualitative study of design teams, Sutton and Hargadon (1996) concluded that brainstorming techniques are not particularly efficient; however, they are effective because they are positively associated with both user and client satisfaction. In addition, Paulus and colleagues (Paulus, Larey & Ortega, 1995) have found that individuals enjoy brainstorming in groups.

The results from the brainstorming literature may shed light on why there are so few published studies on group creativity and outcomes. There may be a great deal of research on the topic with no significant results; hence, the work never appeared in any journals. However, the brainstorming results also suggest that researchers need to consider affective outcomes. If individuals working in creative groups are happier, more satisfied, and ultimately more committed to their work, group, and organization, this could have important implications for employee engagement and customer satisfaction. The relationship between creativity and affect at the team level of analysis is obviously still wide open. Given the earlier discussion on creativity as a multi-level construct that is homologous, the argument can be made that because individuals are more satisfied when they are creative, groups of individuals also should be more satisfied when they are creative. However, the results at the individual level are mostly based on a fit between the individual and his job or his organization. Would this be the same at the team or group level?

Negative Outcomes

As with individual level creativity, it would be remiss of me to end this section without a cautionary warning along with a call for research that examines the negative side of group creativity. James and colleagues (1999) developed a theoretical model that described how group creative processes and outcomes may result in theft, sabotage, and the undermining of group and organizational goals. Both the notions of groupthink and group norms could result in very cohesive groups that develop and employ creative processes that undermine the good of the organization and its customers, but may result in very satisfied group members. Therefore, along with examining affective outcomes, group creativity researchers should start to consider whether there are different antecedents to creative processes and outcomes that result in negative rather than positive outcomes. Or, are there differences in the creative processes or outcomes themselves that affect whether outcomes are beneficial or detrimental? What is it that leads creative groups to the dark side?

In conclusion, research has started to examine the relationship between team creativity and performance but there is still a great deal left to be done. One area in particular that is very relevant today is the relationship between creativity and performance in different types of teams. For example, virtual teams are becoming more and more prevalent (Martins, Gilson, & Maynard, 2004) and work by Nemiro (2002) on virtual-project teams has found that the already fine line between creativity and innovation is even more blurred in this setting. In her discussion, Nemiro suggests that because the process of communication is different in virtual teams, idea generation becomes interwoven with development, evaluation, refinement, and implementation. Therefore, many questions remain as to the relationship of creativity, innovation, performance, and let us not forget, affect in virtual teams.

ORGANIZATIONAL LEVEL OUTCOMES

At the organizational level of analysis most examples of creativity and practical outcomes are based on case studies or in-depth analysis of a single organization. In his *Harvard Business Review* article on the Matsushita Electric Company, Nonaka (1991) discusses how at the organizational level creativity is really synonymous with knowledge creation, which enables organizations to be more flexible and able to quickly respond to changing environmental conditions or customer demands. For example, Nonaka describes how Japanese companies use cryptic expressions, silly slogans, and metaphors to keep employees thinking of ways to do things differently, ways to adapt what they do, and means to embellish upon what is currently being done—all to ultimately improve customer satisfaction and firm performance. However, it is interesting to note that the impetus for new knowledge creation at the organizational level begins with individuals being committed to continually re-create their jobs or work environment. In other words, to harness organizational level outcomes that result from creativity we, in effect, have to go full circle and start by focusing on individuals. Interestingly, the arguments put forth also stress that creativity is needed from *all* employees, not only those who work in jobs that require high levels of creativity. This is the same premise discussed earlier under individual outcomes—

every job, to some degree allows a level of creativity, and when there is a match between individuals who possess creativity relevant attributes and an environment that is supportive of trying new things, creativity along with positive outcomes (at all levels of analysis) will ensue. Finally, Nonaka introduces the concept of trust. Specifically, he discusses how employees at all corporate levels, from all functional areas, need to have access to company information so that they have the necessary tools and knowledge to be creative. Trust is an outcome that has not received attention in concert with creativity and raises the proverbial chicken-and-egg question. Given that metaphors and clichés are argued to help foster creativity, I feel that using one is appropriate here! However, a question for future researchers and managers to ponder is: Does creativity or knowledge creation build trust between employees and their organization or does trust from the organization result in employees who are more willing to try new approaches to their work and share what they come up with? In other words, should trust be considered as an antecedent or outcome to creativity? Finally, would creativity engender trust at the individual and group levels of analysis as well?

Related to trust is the concept of leadership that has frequently been suggested to play a key role in stimulating employee and group creativity as well as performance. In a study on the effects of leadership on performance, Howell and Avolio (1993) found that support for innovation (defined as support for creativity and tolerance of differences) moderated the relationship between leadership behaviors and performance. Using a sample of senior managers from a financial institution in a turbulent and unstable environment, they found that transformational leaders had higher levels of unit performance when subordinates described their work environments as innovative.

Innovation

At the organizational level, there is a fairly extensive literature on innovation. The focus of this work has been on empirically establishing the multidimensionality of innovation, the antecedents to innovation, and the organizational and environmental factors that moderate the effects of innovation (cf. Damanpour, 1991; Janssen et al., 2004). Similar to the creativity research that has examined individual characteristics that result in creative processes or outcomes, the innovation literature has predominantly sought to determine organizational characteristics (e.g., managerial tenure, slack resources, formalization, vertical integration) that determine innovation and as such, innovation is the "end product" of interest (Anderson, De Dreu, & Nijstad, 2004). The innovation literature has supported the assertion that new products that are essentially extensions to current offerings are positively associated with financial returns. However, new products that are radically different are associated with either very high or very low financial gains (variance) due to the risk associated with this level of change from the status quo (cf. Taylor & Greve, 2006). In a study conducted in the comic book industry, Taylor and Greve (2006) indeed found that creativity and innovation resulted in increased performance variance. Further, they found that having a deep understanding and knowledge in a particular area of expertise was a stronger predictor of variance behavior than simply having individuals who represented different specialty areas working together. Thus, they demonstrate an often discussed but previously untested linkage between knowledge combinations, creativity, and performance. Extrapolating this finding to previous discussions on the positive and negative aspects of creativity, at the organizational level, it thus appears that creativity is associated with performance variance, which can mean either financial gains or losses.

CONCLUSIONS

Creativity exists along a continuum ranging from incremental adaptations to radical breakthroughs (Kirton, 1976). At the individual level of analysis, researchers have taken this into consideration when considering affective outcomes. Specifically, here it has been argued that individuals range in their creative abilities, and jobs range in their levels of required creativity and that when the two complement each other, higher levels of positive affect ensue (Livingstone et al., 1997; Scott & Bruce, 1994; Shalley et al., 2000). In contrast, at the group level of analysis, researchers have focused their attention on more objective outcomes finding that creativity is positively related to performance (Gilson et al., 2005; West & Anderson, 1996). The findings in the brainstorming literature would suggest that creative processes may be positively related to member affect. However, whether creativity is positively related to individual or group affect is an area for future research.

In 2003, Mumford noted that the creativity literature has shown an "apparent lack of interest in the effects of creativity" (p. 117). Mumford credits this lack of interest to universal assumptions that creativity is good and motivational. Similarly, the innovation literature almost universally states that the adoption of an innovation is intended to contribute to the performance or effectiveness of an organization (Damanpour, 1991). However, for research to be of practical value we need to better understand whether creativity *is* good and motivational and *will* result in improved performance and organizational effectiveness.

In the beginning of this chapter, I highlighted a series of quotations all extolling some rather grandiose benefits associated with creativity. While I tend to agree with Mumford's viewpoint, I also think that the notion of variance (Taylor & Greve, 2006) may be limiting the amount of work published on creativity and outcomes. By its very nature, creativity involves risk—coming up with a novel approach to work or a new outcome that is a break with the status quo that may or may not work. If it works, the creative process or outcome can have either a minor impact on performance if the change is incremental or a massive effect if the new product or process is radically different. However, note that I said an "impact on performance," which implies that the association could be either positive or negative. This "unknown" component has probably kept many researchers away from measuring practical outcomes both intentionally and unintentionally. Furthermore, the notion of time may play a critical role here as creativity is an iterative process and given that refinements and adaptation may be necessary to see the effect on practical outcomes, what is creative may be constantly evolving. However, that creativity can lead to performance enhancement as well as detriments is actually a very exciting line of inquiry. Specifically, what factors at the individual, group, organizational, and even environmental levels influence whether creativity results in performance detriments, maintenance, or increases? In conclusion, "why be creative" remains a fascinating question that should keep both researchers and managers busy for at least another couple of decades.

REFERENCES

Amabile, T. M. (1996). *Creativity in context*. Boulder, CO: Westview Press.

Anderson, N., De Dreu, C., & Nijstad, B. (2004). The routinization of innovation research: A constructively critical review of the state-of-the science. *Journal of Organizational Behavior, 25*, 147–174.

Axtell, C. J., Holman, D. J., Unsworth, K. L., Wall, T. D., & Waterson, P. E. (2000). Shopfloor innovation: Facilitating the suggestion and implementation of ideas. *Journal of Occupational and Organizational Psychology, 73*, 311–322.

Baer, M., & Oldham, G. (2006). The curvilinear relations between experienced creative time pressure and creativity: Moderating effects of openness to experience and support for creativity. *Journal of Applied Psychology, 91*, 963–970.

Basadur, M., Taggar, S., & Pringle, P. (1999). Improving the measurement of divergent thinking attitudes in organizations. *Journal of Creative Behavior, 33*, 75–111.

Carson, P. P., & Carson, K. D. (1993). Managing creativity enhancement through goal setting and feedback. *Journal of Creative Behavior, 27*, 36–45.

Chamorro-Premuzic, T. (2006). Creativity versus conscientiousness: Which is a better predictor of student performance? *Applied Cognitive Psychology, 20*, 521–531.

Chen, G., Bliese, P., & Mathieu, J. (2005). Conceptual framework and statistical procedures for delineating and testing multilevel theories and homology. *Organizational Research Methods, 8*, 375–409.

Chen, G., Mathieu, J. E., & Bliese, P. D. (2004). A framework for conducting multi-level construct validation. *Research in Multi-Level Issues, 3*, 273–303.

Cohen, S. G., & Bailey, D. E. (1997). What makes teams work: Group effectiveness research from the shop floor to the executive suite. *Journal of Management, 23*, 239–290.

Damanpour, F. (1991). Organizational innovation: A meta-analysis of effects of determinants and moderators. *Academy of Management Journal, 34*, 555–590.

Drazin, R., Glynn, M., & Kazanjian, R. (1999). Multilevel theorizing about creativity in organizations: A sensemaking perspective. *Academy of Management Review, 24*, 286–307.

Frymire, B. (2006, October 7). The search for talent; Business and society. *The Economist, 8498*, 11.

Gilson, L. L., Mathieu, J. E., Shalley, C. E., & Ruddy, T. M. (2005). Creativity and standardization: Complementary or conflicting drivers of team effectiveness. *Academy of Management Journal, 48*, 521–531.

Gilson, L. L., & Shalley, C. E. (2004). A little creativity goes a long way: An examination of teams' engagement in creative processes. *Journal of Management, 30*, 453–470.

Gough, H. G. (1979). A creative personality scale for the Adjective Check List. *Journal of Personality and Social Psychology, 37*, 1398–1405.

Hackman, J. R., & Morris, C. G. (1975). Group tasks, group interaction processes, and group performance effectiveness: A review and proposed integration. In L. Berkowitz (Ed.), *Advances in experimental social psychology, 8*, 45–99. San Diego, CA: Academic Press.

Howell, J. M., & Avolio, B. J. (1993). Transformational leadership, transactional leadership, locus of control, and support for innovation: Key predictors of consolidated business-unit performance. *Journal of Applied Psychology, 78*, 891–902.

Jabri, M. (1991). The development of conceptually independent subscales in the measurement of modes of problem solving. *Educational and Psychological Measurement, 51*, 975–983.

James, K., Chen, J., & Goldberg, C. (1992). Organizational conflict and individual creativity. *Journal of Applied Social Psychology, 22*, 545–566.

James, K., Clark, K., & Cropanzano, R. (1999). Positive and negative creativity in groups, institutions, and organizations: A model and theoretical extension. *Creativity Research Journal, 12*, 211–226.

Janssen, O. (2003). Innovative behavior and job involvement at the price of conflict and less satisfactory relations with co-workers. *Journal of Organizational and Occupational Psychology, 73*, 287–302.

Janssen, O., van de Vliert, E., & West, M. (2004). The bright and dark side of individuals and group innovation: A special issue introduction. *Journal of Organizational Behavior, 25*, 129–145.

Kirton, M. (1976). Adaptors and innovators: A description and measure. *Journal of Applied Psychology, 61,* 622–629.

Livingstone, L. P., Nelson, D. L., & Barr, S. H. (1997). Person-environment fit and creativity: An examination of supply-value and demand-value ability versions of fit. *Journal of Management, 23,* 119–146.

Martins, L. L., Gilson, L. L., & Maynard, M. T. (2004). Virtual teams: What do we know and where do we go from here? *Journal of Management, 6,* 805–835.

Milgram, R. M., & Feldman, N. O. (1979). Creativity as a predictor of teacher's effectiveness. *Psychological Reports, 45,* 899–903.

Mumford, M. D. (2003). Where have we been, where are we going: Taking stock in creativity research. *Creativity Research Journal, 15,* 107–120.

Mumford, M. D., & Gustafson, S. B. (1988). Creativity syndrome: Integration, application, and innovation. *Psychological Bulletin, 103,* 27–43.

Nemiro, J. E. (2002). The creative process in virtual teams. *Creativity Research Journal, 14,* 69–83.

Nicholson, N., & West, M. A. (1988). *Managerial job change: Men and women in transition.* New York: Cambridge University Press.

Nonaka, I. (1991). The knowledge-creating company. *Harvard Business Review, 69,* 96–104.

Oldham, G. R., & Cummings, A. (1996). Employee creativity: Personal and contextual factors at work. *Academy of Management Journal, 39,* 607–634.

Osborn, A. F. (1957). *Applied Imagination* (1st ed.). New York: Scribner.

Paulus, P. B. (2000). Groups, teams, and creativity: The creative potential of idea-generating groups. *Applied Psychology: An International Review, 49,* 237–262.

Paulus, P. B., Larey, T. S., & Ortega, A. H. (1995). Performance and perceptions of brainstormers in an organizational setting. *Basic and Applied Social Psychology, 17,* 249–265.

Policastro, E., & Gardner, H. (1999). From case studies to robust generalizations: An approach to the study of creativity. In R. J. Sternberg (Ed.), *Handbook of creativity* (pp. 213–225). Cambridge, MA: Cambridge University Press.

Powers, D. E., & Kaufman, J. C. (2004). Do standardized test penalize deep-thinking, creative or conscientious students? Some personality correlates of Graduate Record Examination test scores. *Intelligence, 32,* 145–153.

Redmond, M. R., Mumford, M. D., & Teach, R. (1993). Putting creativity to work: Effects of leader behavior on subordinate creativity. *Organizational Behavior and Human Decision Processes, 55,* 120–151.

Richman, A. (2006). Everyone wants an engaged workforce: How can you create it? *Workspan, 49,* 36–39.

Runco, M. (1995). The creativity and job satisfaction of artists in organizations. *Empirical Studies of the Arts, 13,* 39–45.

Runco, M. A., & Charles, R. E. (1997). Developmental trends in creative potential and performance. In M. A. Runco (Ed.), *The creativity research handbook* (pp. 115–154). Cresskill, NJ: Hampton.

Scott, G., Leritz, L. E., & Mumford, M. D. (2004). The effectiveness of creativity training: A quantitative Review. *Creativity Research Journal, 16,* 361–388.

Scott, R. K. (1995). Creative employees: A challenge to managers. *Journal of Creative Behavior, 29,* 64–71.

Scott, S. G., & Bruce, R. A. (1994). Determinants of innovative behavior: A path model of individual innovation in the workplace. *Academy of Management Journal, 37,* 580–607.

Shalley, C. E. (1991). Effects of productivity goals, creativity goals, and personal discretion on individual creativity. *Journal of Applied Psychology, 76,* 179–185.

Shalley, C. E., Gilson, L. L., & Blum, T. C. (2000). Matching creativity requirements and the work environment: Effects on satisfaction and intent to turnover. *Academy of Management Journal 43,* 215–224.

Stein, M. K. (1974). *Stimulating creativity.* New York: Academic Press.

Stokels, D., Clitheroe, C., & Zmuidzinas, M. (2002). Qualities of the work environment that promote perceived support for creativity. *Creativity Research Journal, 14,* 137–147.

Sutton, R. I. (2002). The weird rules of creativity. *Harvard Business Review, 80,* 94–103.

Sutton, R. I., & Hargadon, A. (1996). Brainstorming groups in context: Effectiveness in a product design firm. *Administrative Science Quarterly, 41,* 685–718.

Taggar, S. (2002). Individual creativity and group ability to utilize individual creative resources: A multilevel model. *Academy of Management Journal, 45,* 315–330.

Taylor, A., & Greve, H. R. (2006). Superman or the fantastic four? Knowledge combinations and experience in innovative teams. *Academy of Management Journal, 49,* 723–740.

Tesluk, P. E., Farr, J. L., & Klein, S. R. (1997). Influences of organizational culture and climate on individual creativity. *The Journal of Creative Behavior, 31,* 27–41.

Tierney, P., & Farmer, S. M. (2002). Creative self-efficacy: Potential antecedents and relationship to creative performance. *Academy of Management Journal, 45,* 1137–1148.

Unsworth, K. L. (2001). Unpacking creativity. *Academy of Management Review, 26,* 289–297.

Unsworth, K. L., Wall, T. D., & Carter, A. (2005). Creative requirement: A neglected construct in the study of creativity? *Group & Organization Management, 30,* 541–560.

West, M. A. (2002). Sparkling fountains or stagnant ponds: An integrative model of creativity and innovation implementation in work groups. *Applied Psychology: An International Review, 51,* 255–424.

West, M. A., & Anderson, N. R. (1996). Innovation in top management teams. *Journal of Applied Psychology, 81,* 680–693.

Woodman, R. W., Sawyer, J. E., & Griffin, R. W. (1993). Toward a theory of organizational creativity. *Academy of Management Review, 18,* 293–320.

Woodruffe, C. (2006). Employee engagement—the real secret of winning a crucial edge over your rivals. *The British Journal of Administrative Management, 28,* 28–29.

Zhou, J. (1998). Feedback valence, feedback style, task autonomy, and achievement orientation: Interactive effects on creative performance. *Journal of Applied Psychology, 83,* 261–276.

CHAPTER 14

CREATIVITY THAT WORKS

Andrew Hargadon
University of California–Davis

INTRODUCTION

Just about everyone has heard Edison's formula for creativity: 1 percent inspiration and 99 percent perspiration. But it deserves mention once more in reflecting on what we know about creativity and how we pursue it. In short, creativity researchers have, by and large, spent 99 percent of their time trying to understand the creative insight, or "eureka" moment and little, if any, on everything else. In this chapter, I would like to remind scholars and practitioners alike that creativity depends on a host of other behaviors, mindsets, and practices that fall outside the traditional focus. These factors set the stage, work backstage, and clean up after the main event that most people have come to view as creativity.

Creativity involves the generation of novel, valuable, and nonobvious solutions (Amabile, 1983, 1988). It is a process that Jevons (1877, in Albert & Runco, 1999, p. 25; see also Becker, 1995) eloquently called "divergence from the ordinary grooves of thought and action," and reflects our appreciation for the difficulty of breaking free of the cognitive, emotional, and behavioral bounds of what is appropriate or even possible. My purpose is not to diminish the importance of creative insight, the ability to break free of tradition, but instead to recognize its dependence on other, less glamorous but equally critical practices. To do so, I will draw on examples of creativity from the historic to the modern and from the momentous to the mundane. What follows is an illustrative (and by no means exhaustive) set documented with the hope that in reading it, you will recognize these and other factors that also contribute to, enable, and in other ways support creativity. For clarity, I present these practices as advice, grounded in theory, of the creative practices that do the work.

DO NOT CREATE ... CONNECT

When it comes to generating a creative solution, sometimes the best approach is to avoid creating something new and, instead, focus on connecting old ideas. The lightbulb that famously went off over Thomas Edison's head in 1878 was already 30 years old. Edison's original patent application for the electric light was rejected (reported in the January 18, 1879 issue of *Scientific American*), because "Edison's invention was an infringement upon that of John W. Starr, of Cincinnati, who filed a caveat for a divisible light in 1845" (Conot, 1979; Israel, 1998). Edison's contribution was not inventing the electric light, but in combining it with improvements in generators, wiring, materials, and business models.

Edison was not alone in pursuing a recombinant form of creativity. Henry Ford did not invent mass production so much as connect elements of technologies in use, some for almost a century, in other industries. In armory production, he found the technologies of interchangeable parts; in canneries, granaries, and breweries, he found the technologies of continuous-flow production; in the meatpacking plants of Chicago, the assembly line; and in the emerging electric industry, the electric motor (Hargadon, 2003; Hounshell, 1984). Ford (Gordon, 2001, p. 103) once even testified: "I invented nothing new. I simply assembled into a car the discoveries of other men behind whom were centuries of work.... Had I worked fifty or ten or even five years before, I would have failed. So it is with every new thing." In 1972, Ray Tomlinson wrote the first electronic mail application by combining the code of an existing *intra*-computer messaging application with an *inter*-computer file-transfer protocol (Segaller, 1998). As Tomlinson describes: "It seemed like an interesting hack to tie these two together to use the file-transfer protocol to send the email to the other machine. So that's what I did. I spent not a whole lot of time, maybe two or three weeks, putting that together and it worked."

The notion of creativity as connecting old ideas is not itself new. Schumpeter (1934, pp. 65–66) defined innovation as the "carrying out of new combinations" and Weick (1979, p. 252) defined creativity as "putting new things in old combinations and old things in new combinations."

Psychologists, sociologists, economists, and historians have long recognized creativity as a recombinant process. Bethune (1837) considered it the ability to "originat[e] new combinations of thought" and William James (1880) called it "the most unheard-of combinations of elements" (quoted in Albert & Runco, 1999, pp. 25–26; see also Becker, 1995). People create novel insights by importing and recombining schemas and scripts learned in other contextual domains—in other words, people do not think out of the box, they think in other boxes (Hargadon & Fanelli, 2002).

When someone challenges us to be creative or to solve a problem in organizations, our first reaction is often to see this as a test, an opportunity to prove our individual creative talents. But that does more harm than good. Approaching creativity from a perspective of connecting existing ideas means responding to new problems by asking: What do I already know that might solve this problem? Where should I look to find other existing solutions? Whom can I bring in to help solve this problem? Rather than withdrawing, reach out and connect to other people and their ideas.

ATTEND TO YOUR NETWORKS

When creativity is seen as a recombinant and not inventive process, the focus shifts from aspects of creative individuals—their personalities, motivations, abilities, even childhoods—to aspects of their external network. Who you are becomes less important than who you know because those social networks provide access to the range of existing ideas out there. So a second creative practice is the construction and maintenance of a wide-ranging external network.

Most of us spend our time within relatively small worlds in which the people, ideas, and objects we work with tend to work with each other as well (e.g., your friends know each other, see the same movies, and read the same books). Within these small worlds, in the language of social network theory, we are strongly tied to others. These small worlds create communities with shared knowledge similar to Burt's (1983, p. 180) description of actors who "know one another, are aware of the same kinds of opportunities, have access to the same kind of resources, and share the same kinds of perceptions." Yet the ability to see creative possibilities before others requires a different set of network connections—weak ties—that span multiple worlds.

Weak ties are those network ties that expose us to people, ideas, and objects that are not already connected to our existing networks. Weak ties create more diverse social networks because they expose you to the people, ideas, and objects of many different small worlds. Such diverse networks have many surprising benefits (Baker, 2000). At work, scientific research has shown that diverse networks are associated with finding jobs, higher pay, faster promotion, greater influence, and more effectiveness. At home, similar research has shown that diverse and robust networks are associated with better health, longer life, and even fewer colds. In the pursuit of creativity, then, we should pay close attention to the networks that connect us to others.

Individuals and organizations that span otherwise disconnected groups—that have many weak ties—are called brokers. Such brokers have an advantage in the creative process since "non-redundant contacts are linked only through the central player, [brokers] are assured of being the first to see new opportunities created by the needs in one group that could be served by skills in another group" (Burt, 1992a, p. 70). Thomas Edison was one such broker and the role these weak ties can play in the creative process is evident in the inventions of his Menlo Park laboratory, which consulted to clients in a range of industries from the telegraph to the telephone, from gas lighting to arc lighting, and from railroads to iron mining.

The Menlo Park laboratory, in operation between 1876 and 1881, produced over 400 patents, and while so much attention has gone to Edison (and his childhood), in fact much of the laboratory's success depended on its network. Edison and his colleagues used their knowledge of electromagnetic power from the telegraph industry where they first worked to transfer old ideas that were new to the lighting, telephone, phonograph, railway, and mining industries (Hughes, 1989; Millard, 1990). Edison's products often reflected blends of existing, but previously unconnected, ideas that his engineers picked up as they worked in these disparate industries. The phonograph blended old ideas from products Edison's engineers had developed for the telegraph, telephone, and electric motor industries, as well as ideas developed by others, that they had learned about while working in those industries.

Modern-day Edisons attempting to recreate the magic of Menlo Park would better set the stage for their own creative pursuits by attending to the diversity of their external networks—to the different worlds that they have access to—in order to provide access to the raw materials for the creative process. Ask yourself: What does our world look like? What other worlds are out there? Where have others faced the same problems we are facing in our organization and industry? How can we build bridges to those other worlds—to learn about them, find opportunities to help them, and find opportunities for them to help us?

BUILD THE INTERNAL NETWORK

For managing creativity in large organizations, the networks that connect the organization to the outside world(s) around them are not the only ones that matter—internal networks are equally important. The structures that organizations build to deal with many diverse external environments conspire to make unexpected internal connections between them nearly impossible. As one IBM executive was quoted as saying, "We don't talk to the people in the other operations. They have become the competition. There is no sharing of information and limited cooperation" (Crow, 1995, p. 47). The boundaries between divisions, groups, and even project teams can make it difficult, if not downright dangerous to your career, to move across. Yet many businesses have grown precisely because of their ability to take the ideas developed in one market and apply them to another.

Hewlett-Packard grew to prominence in just this way. What began in 1937 as two Stanford engineering graduates in a garage, making precision audio oscilloscopes, became a multibillion-dollar business because they soon expanded their technologies to other test and measurement devices, and ultimately branched into computers, medical devices, printing, and telecommunications. Lew Platt, one of HP's CEOs, explained this recombinant path in the 1994 Hewlett-Packard Annual Report by saying:

> We have a terrific advantage when we combine our areas of expertise. A lot of innovative solutions are coming from HP in telecommunications and in the medical business because of the combined strengths of HP's computing, communications, and measurement business.

But what enabled HP to make these valuable combinations was its unique culture that put engineering above politics and an internal network that connected those engineers regardless of their business affiliations. Indeed, much of HP's expertise emerged through their next-bench design process, where engineers would create products by solving the problems of their colleagues at the next bench. Unfortunately, in 1999, executives at HP decided to spin out most of the noncomputer-related businesses, forming Agilent to develop and manufacture test and measurement equipment and components for electronics, communications, life sciences, and semiconductors. What HP gained in market valuation by separating computers and printers from their other endeavors is easier to calculate than what it lost in the ability to generate creative ideas by connecting otherwise disparate markets and applications.

Other companies have also built networks that foster a next-bench design environment, or in other ways connect people across the organization. IDEO product development, a design consulting firm, creates robust internal networks by building each project team anew, by holding regular project brainstorms that bring people from outside the team in to work on current problems, and by having weekly "show-and-tell" meetings that bring larger studios together to learn what everyone is working on (for more detail on IDEO's practices, see Hargadon and Sutton, 2000). Larger firms do not have the luxury of bringing all of their employees into a single room, and as a result have adopted more formal means for identifying and fostering valuable internal networks. 3M creates formal centers around promising technologies and charters these groups with injecting their ideas into the products and services of the many business units under 3M (for more detail, see Hargadon, 2003). 3M augments this practice with a strong emphasis on managerial job rotations. The promotion paths of 3M's managers move diagonally across divisions rather than vertically within any one and, as a result, managers acquire a broad set of weak ties that span the entire organization, making them more willing and able to tap creative solutions wherever they reside within the firm.

Building robust internal networks is the responsibility of the architects of the firm's internal structure—but it is also the responsibility of each individual within an organization. As pointed out earlier, an individual's pay, promotion, and perceived effectiveness are positively associated with the diversity of his or her own social network. It is not only in the best interests of the organization to foster wide-ranging networks that connect individual employees, it is in everyone's interests. The creative potential of individuals and groups within organization hinges on the networks that connect them across the organization because these internal networks connect, in turn, to the people, ideas, and artifacts of the broader markets through which those organizations move.

LEARN WHAT IS ALREADY OUT THERE

Diverse external and internal networks set the stage for individual- and group-level creativity by providing access to a wide range of old ideas—the raw materials for new creative acts. But such networks will not tell you what you are missing or where to look for it. The next step is using those networks to learn what is out there. Take advantage of your connections to many different markets to learn about the people, the ideas, and the artifacts that reside within each. Edison's instructions about how to start a new project were clear: "First, study the present construction. Second, ask for all past experiences ... study and read everything you can on the subject" (Millard, 1990, p. 9). Today, some of the most creative organizations, like IDEO and Design Continuum, do the same thing. They spend the first part of every project collecting related products and information, and, perhaps most important, observing users to learn what is already out there.

The designers at IDEO, for example, seem obsessed with learning about materials and products they have no immediate use for. At lunch one day, my colleague, Robert Sutton, and I watched two engineers take apart the napkin container to look at the springs inside. Another time, we brought a new digital camera to a brainstorming session, and the meeting was delayed for 10 minutes while engineers took apart our new toy to see how it was designed and manufactured. IDEO designers also visit the local Ace Hardware store to see new products and to remind themselves of old ideas, as well as take field trips to places like the Barbie Hall of Fame, an airplane junkyard, and a robot wars competition.

When Design Continuum was hired to improve the tools and techniques used in knee surgery, its engineers went to a convention for surgeons where they recreated the surgical process in a way that allowed them to watch and talk with users. One of their engineers (unpublished data) described the scene:

> We wanted to observe the procedures, so we had a cadaver lab, which was actually in a swank hotel. One room was the lecture room and the other held 12 cadavers. They had the room chilled down to 50°, had the cadavers in there and had a guard 24 hours a day making sure so nobody accidentally walked in. We just wanted to see how doctors used the tools, the little blocks and stuff they use for doing the procedures.

The result? Designers learned that surgeons had developed elaborate habits to make up for what one described as the "missing third arm"; this inspired them to develop a new surgical tool that allowed doctors to hold, rotate, and operate on the kneecap. Similarly, when Design Continuum was asked to develop an innovative kitchen faucet for a client that had worked in the industry for decades, the project team undertook a massive benchmarking exercise, not just to learn about kitchen faucet valves, but also about valves used in products like automobiles, medical products, and toys. The final design delighted the client whose engineers had assumed, after so many years in the business, that they knew everything there was to know about valves.

Being creative means collecting—not eschewing—the many existing ideas already out there. Thomas Edison once said the same thing, in a different way: "To invent, you need a good imagination and a pile of junk" (Words of Wisdom 4U). And while it's easy to see how imagination adds value to "junk," it may be as important to understand how that pile of junk adds value to one's imagination. Dean Simonton argues that the thought processes that generate new ideas by recombining old ones shape how people approach their environment. Those who are more engaged in exploring new combinations are often more attuned to the world around them:

Those people who make their minds accessible to chaotic combinatory play will also make their sense more open to the influx of fortuitous events in the outside world. Both the retrieval of material from memory and the orientation of attention to environmental stimuli are unrestricted (Simonton, 1995, p. 470).

Rather than believing they have seen it all, or at least seen all that is worth seeing, those in the habit of finding unexpected connections begin to recognize in each new person they meet, each new idea they hear, and each new object they find, the potential for new combinations with others. As CEO Gian Zaccai (personal communication) put it, such experience "frees you from the dogma of any one industry." The more worlds you move through, the more you are able to see and exploit the ideas of each as they emerge and evolve in their own settings. When you come across an idea that does not look immediately promising, do not just ignore it. Play with it, in your mind and when possible with your hands, figure out how and why it works, learn what is good and bad about it, and start spinning fantasies about new ways to use it. Then bring it back to the office and find a way to share it with your colleagues.

REMEMBER WHAT YOU HAVE ALREADY LEARNED

But even the ideas learned are easily forgotten. In fact, cognitive psychologists have shown that the biggest hurdle to solving problems often is not ignorance. It is that people cannot find what they have learned at the moment they need it (Reeves & Weisberg, 1994). Organizational memories are even tougher to maintain and use. Companies lose what they learn when people leave. Geographic distance, political squabbles, internal competition, or bad incentive systems may result in ideas not being spread as much as they could be.

Another set of practices that sets the stage for the "aha" moment involves those that help individuals and organizations to remember what they already know. In some cases, this is as simple as keeping old products, prototypes, hardware, and drawings lying around. At IDEO, for example, designers put plastic parts, toys, prototypes, drawings, and sketches on display in their offices. One engineer, Dennis Boyle, had a collection that included 23 battery-powered toy cars and robots, 13 plastic hotel keys collected during trips, a flashlight powered by squeezing the handle, an industrial pump, 11 prototypes of a portable computer, 14 prototypes of a computer docking station, 6 computers in various stages of disassembly, 15 binders from past projects, a pile of disk drives, a collection of toothpaste tubes, a toy football with wings, a pair of ski goggles he had designed, 4 humorous plaques awarded for past projects (e.g., "under-the-gun" award for working under pressure), a Frisbee that flies under water, and dozens of other products and parts. He portrayed this collection as "a congealed process—three-dimensional snapshots of the ideas from previous projects" and it was treated in many ways as a small shrine to the past. IDEO even institutionalized the practice (and principle) of keeping memories alive. In six IDEO studios, designers assembled, and now add to and constantly talk about, a shared collection of over 400 materials and products. This "Tech Box" contains things like tiny batteries, switches, glow-in-the dark fabric, high-strength materials from NASA, flexible circuit boards, springs, and electric motors.

It is harder to keep ideas alive when they are not embedded in tangible objects. The people who designed knowledge-management systems for Andersen Consulting and McKinsey originally thought that lists of best practices, reports, and "decks" of PowerPoint presentations would be a complete, one-stop shopping experience. Consultants would be able to solve problems just by reading through databases. But people quickly found these systems were most useful as annotated "yellow pages," to find out who to talk to about how the knowledge was really used and might be used again. So McKinsey formed its Rapid Response Team to remember who knows what—to link people to other people, rather than to stored information. Generally speaking, spreading information about who knows what is a powerful way to keep ideas alive. Thomas Edison was renowned for his ability to remember how old ideas were used and—as importantly—by whom. The most respected people at IDEO are part pack rat (because they have great private collections of stuff), part librarian (because they know who knows what), and part good Samaritan (because they go out of their way to share what they know and to help others).

To remember the many ideas people see and learn about in their past wanderings, devote resources to capturing those ideas and to celebrating and sharing them across the larger organization. Shelves of project binders, drives filled with old code, servers holding past Powerpoint presentations rarely work as intended—because storing and remembering are different acts. Find ways to keep old ideas alive by posting them on walls, on shelves, and in display cases where they are not only visible but honored. Establish areas where people can post, share, and talk about other ideas—interesting new technologies or market opportunities, or simply examples of cool practices in wildly different fields.

THINK IN OTHER BOXES

Creativity gurus everywhere implore individuals and groups to "think outside the box" by questioning what you know and the implicit boundaries that prevent you from venturing into new territory. Yet, essentially, this advice is next to impossible. Research by cognitive psychologists into the problem-solving process suggests that people understand new situations only in terms of old ones they are already familiar with (Gentner and Gentner, 1983; Gentner and Markman, 1997; Reeves and Weisberg, 1993, 1994). Paraphrasing the art historian E. H. Gombrich (1961, p. 4), "There's no such thing as an immaculate perception." This thought process is described as analogical reasoning, and occurs when an individual recognizes similarities in the new situation to others that he or she has faced in the past. People do not think out of the box—they think in other boxes.

Schon (1983, 1993) recognized this process in the work of architects and designers, describing the role of "seeing-as" in problem solving as creating solutions through the use of generative metaphors, which describe one phenomenon as another and relate two phenomenon that were "initially perceived, named, and understood as very different things" (1983, p. 185). He distinguishes such generative metaphors from other forms of metaphor in that they create "new perceptions, explanations, and inventions" (1983, p. 185). In a similar fashion, Neustadt and May (1986) describe how political leaders use metaphors to define and solve policy problems by framing current situations in terms of past ones.

There is no guarantee, however, that individuals will use their past knowledge, let alone the appropriate past knowledge, to generate novel and creative solutions. The same mechanisms that allow individuals to make sense of novel situations in terms of old ones often encourage them to recall more recent, more familiar, or more traditional ideas. Problem solvers are more likely to mindlessly misinterpret new situations as familiar old ones, or ignore them altogether, than to see them as opportunities for creative insights (Lave, 1988; Weick, 1995). To do otherwise requires *mindfully* defining situations in new ways that trigger new searches for solutions (Schank & Abelson, 1977).

Such mindful redefinitions of problematic situations require having a repertoire of diverse problems and solutions to draw upon—and the willingness to play with them. Take the example of Design Continuum designers conceiving the Reebok Pump shoe. They did so by first seeing the shoe as something else—in this case an inflatable splint that might help prevent ankle injuries. Confronted with the physical difficulties of turning a shoe into an inflatable splint, they then reenvisioned the inflatable splint as an IV bag, common in hospital settings. As a result, the project team was able to create a shoe that housed an inflatable insert capable of providing a form-fit—and providing their client, Reebok, with a highly creative and differentiating product in the market. The same analogical reasoning takes place in other firms as well. At McKinsey, a senior partner (pers. comm.) described how such analogies were fundamental to her work,

> I've done product market strategies in the chemicals world, in the medical device world, in the foods business. And you begin to see how challenges are parallel. It's often helpful, in working with clients, to bring those analogies out and say 'Gee, by the way, this problem you're facing is the same one we faced when working with frozen foods.'

And to this day we screw in lightbulbs because one of Edison's lab assistants saw the similarity between problems keeping the newly developed lightbulbs in their sockets and the screwtop cap of a kerosene can (Conot, 1979, p. 187).

Thinking in other boxes means actively seeking out new ways of seeing the problems that you are confronting. That means asking, how is this problem like others I have seen before? But it also means continually exploring the situation in which the problem presents itself—are you really dealing with the true problem, or simply one of its symptoms? Try to see past the surface details that came with the original description of the project. What essential elements does this problem share with other, more distant, experiences?

DO NOT WORK ALONE

The focus of creativity research, and particularly in industrial applications, is dominated by an obsession with the particular individuals and moments when ideas seemingly appeared—like the proverbial lightbulb—out of nowhere. The notion that a single name and date can identify the moment of invention reflects this obsession with the "aha" moment. As the economic historian Nathan Rosenberg (1979, p. 25) has argued, our misconceptions about the innovation process stem from this insistent focus on invention:

> The public image of technology has been decisively shaped by popular writers … mesmerized by the dramatic story of a small number of major inventions—steam engines, cotton gins, railroads, automobiles, penicillin, radios, computers, etc.… Indeed, not only our patent law but also our history textbooks and even our language all conspire in insuring that a single name and date is attached to each invention.

Worse than simply an incomplete and inaccurate account of what happened, these stories distort our ideas of how to pursue creativity, how to manage it, even how to make sense of it when it happens again. In reality, creativity is a team sport. As Edison's long-time assistant, Francis Jehl, once said, "In reality, Edison was a collective noun and meant the work of many men" (Conot, 1979, p. 469). The same is true today, and so another set of practices that fosters creativity in organizations is the active construction of collectives—small groups—within which creativity can flourish.

The role of collective creativity is evident, for example, in the initial development of new artistic styles in painting such as the impressionist movement in the 1860s and the Fauve movement of the early 1900s. While history gives prominence to individual artists—the impressionists Renoir, Monet, and Cezanne and Fauve's Matisse, Gauguin, and Mondrian—art historians have documented the artists' circles in which these individuals were embedded and in which their individual contributions were often indistinguishable (cf. Diehl, 1975; Farrell, 1982). For instance, Farrell (1982) described the artistic circle of early impressionists who, in splitting from the dominant styles of the art world, worked closely to develop their emerging style and to jointly construct an environment of support and motivation for their creative efforts. Later, when the new movement was established, these artists made efforts to distinguish themselves as individuals but, in the early days, they worked so closely together that their paintings were often indistinguishable. When two paintings were on display in a gallery much later, Monet could not say which was his and which was Renoir's without looking at the signature. Many such works of art, Farrell argues, and particularly those of the early stages of new movements should be viewed as the product of the circle and not the individual artist. These collectives—when formed early in the creative process—foster a shared belief in the cause and its chances for success just when it is needed most, when the ideas (and people) are attempting to go against the established ways of doing things.

In 1951, the psychologist Solomon Asch wondered just how effective individual judgment really was in the face of social pressures to conform. He brought groups of students together in a single room to purportedly test their visual judgment. The students were all shown a card with a line drawn on it, and then a card with three different lines, and they were asked which line was the same length as on the first card. The trick was that seven of the eight students were in cahoots with the experimenter and gave a uniform and false answer. It turned out that almost three-quarters of the subjects bent to the will of the group at least some of the time, and about a third who went along with the groups' (wrong) answers a majority of the time. In later studies, Asch found no real differences in the effects of the group size. Whether it was three or sixteen people, the individual pressures to conform remained the same. This was just a line—there were no friendships involved, no departmental budgets on the line, and no installed customer base to cut into. Yet people found it painful to go against the majority.

For our purposes, however, Solomon Asch found out something else. He found that the easiest way to get somebody to go against the larger group was to give the individual a group of his or her own. Adding one more independent subject to the group—from one to two—makes the effect of the group pressures disappear. When subjects had one other person who agreed with them, they were able to stand against the larger group. Asch also found that this collective deviance was a fragile thing. Take one of the partners away in the middle of experiments and the other often began conforming again.

In this way, collectives encourage individuals to think differently together. When you work with others who are visibly engaged in and passionate about their work, you feel better about it yourself. The moment you find yourself engaged in the creative process is the moment to seek out others to enlist in the same cause. Who else is interested in working on these problems? Who else sees these problems? Who shares your discontent with the status quo. Now is not the time for individual heroics, but rather for creating the collective efforts that will enable your ideas, in combinations with others, to make a difference.

JUST BUILD IT

A good idea for a new product or business practice is not worth much by itself. It needs to be turned into something that can be tested and, if successful, implemented as a routine part of what a company does, makes, or sells. So quickly turning imaginative ideas into real services, products, processes, and business models is a critical step in the creative process. "The real measure of success," Edison believed, "is the number of experiments that can be crowded into 24 hours" (Millard, 1990, p. 40).

At places like IDEO and Design Continuum, almost immediately after thinking of a promising concept, development teams build a prototype of the idea, show it to users, test it for workability, then revise it and improve it, repeating the sequence again and again. These prototypes can be anything from crude mock-ups to finely machined working parts. IDEO designers in the Boston office built a full-sized foam model of an Amtrak train to test ideas about seating, layout, and signage. To make more refined prototypes, IDEO's machine shop uses sophisticated computerized milling machines and other tools. IDEO's machinists can take a rough sketch and quickly turn it into a working model.

Testing prototypes is a way of life at the incubator idealab! as well. Most idealab! companies started as cheap experiments that cost between $10,000 and $250,000. These were often prototype Web sites, opened temporarily to find out how many people would visit and if customers would spend money to buy the product or service offered. For example, when CEO Bill Gross and his team had the idea of selling cars online—not just using the Internet to send customers to a dealer, but selling cars directly to customers like Dell sells computers—they did not spend a lot of time planning. Instead, they quickly assembled a group to try the new idea out. They did not build a fancy Web site that linked dealers and could handle a lot of traffic; they just built something simple that worked well enough to test the idea. Gross hired a CEO for the emerging company for 90 days and told him his job was to sell one car. The plan was that if a customer bought a car, idealab! would buy it from a dealer, and then sell it to the customer at about a $5,000 loss. The test site got 1,000 hits and sold four cars the first day. This experiment led to the founding of CarsDirect.com.

Putting a concept to the test not only helps determine whether it has commercial value, it also teaches you lessons that you might be able to use later, even when that first idea turns out to be a complete flop. Such failures can help to avoid repeating mistakes in other projects—Bill Gross claims that he learns at least as much from business ideas that did not fly, like Ideanet.com, as from ones that did, like eToys. Failures can also help because a failed idea in one context can be a useful solution somewhere else. Edison's laboratory once had a contract to design a new telegraph cable that would span the Atlantic Ocean. The group tried to insulate the wires with a carbon putty material; the cable worked on the lab bench, but short circuited when tested in water. Eventually, they figured out it failed because water pressure transformed the putty from an insulator to a conductor. They remembered and, a few years later, tried the carbon putty again in another application. The result was an inexpensive, effective, and reliable microphone that helped make the telephone commercially feasible.

As soon as possible, turn an idea into a model—a cardboard, string, glue, Play-Doh, or duct tape model that you can hold and play with; a Powerpoint model of a Web site that you can show others; an Excel spreadsheet that can run through various financial simulations. It does not need to be perfect—by the time it is, it is too late to learn anything from it. Focus on what you want to learn from any one model and build just what you need to be confident in the answers you find.

SHARE THE PIE

"Creativity is not the product of single individuals, but of social systems making judgments about individuals' products" (Csikszentmihalyi, 1999, p. 314). These judgments are far from detached—they are reflections of the extent to which others will converge around the new ideas. We measure the creative value of works by Albert Einstein, Pablo Picasso, and Martha Graham by some intuitive combination reflecting their deviation from what came before and the convergence that followed. While the former process involves a sort of social destruction, a taking down of established thought and action, the latter involves social construction, the building up of new thoughts and actions first by an individual or small group and later by larger groups. These processes firmly place creativity in the ability of people to convince others to join their new ventures.

So one of the final creative acts is stepping back from your idea and figuring out how to make it inviting for others. This begins with ownership of the very ideas. As Florence Luscomb once said, "There is no end to what you can accomplish if you don't care who gets the credit" (Wise-Quotes.com) But it moves beyond simply credit for the idea—it also means designing the final creation in ways that allow others to benefit from its success.

Too often, we think that a good idea will sell itself—and so we devote most of our efforts toward making the best idea possible. Yet Ralph Waldo Emerson's famous advice, "Build a better mousetrap, and the world will beat a path to your door," is misleading. The world tends not to beat a path to your door, no matter how good you think your idea. As Hope (1996) describes, since the patent office opened in 1828 it has issued some 4,400 patents for mousetraps and yet only 20 or so have made any money (the most successful, the spring trap, was patented in 1899). A better mousetrap, like anything else, succeeds only when those who envision the idea convince others to join in their new venture—as investors, suppliers, employees, retailers, customers, and even competitors—all of whom, in turn, bring their own contributions and connections with them. The revolutionary impacts we see from creative efforts are often the result of the community that adopted the initial, well-intentioned, but underdeveloped ideas. Case in point is Emerson's now-famous quote. In actuality, he never said that. The quote originated some seven years after Emerson's death. Emerson said "if a man has good corn, or wood, or boards, or pigs, to sell ... you will find a broad, hard-beaten road to his house" (Hope, 1996, p. 90). Emerson was not talking about creativity but rather about selling a good product. It became so much more only when others joined in the process.

Truly creative efforts are those that trigger radical shifts in established worlds. These shifts are not random. They are the result of conscious actions on the part of entrepreneurs to piece together the people and ideas of distant worlds in new ways and conscious decisions on the part of each of those participants to join in. Edison's lightbulb succeeded where his predecessors' did not because he built a new community around his original innovations—a community of suppliers, investors, engineers, even technicians.

These efforts are not focused on selling your idea once it is already completed but rather on designing the idea in ways that make it possible for others to easily embrace and adopt. The first commercial computer, the ENIAC, was introduced in 1951 and was widely seen as the wave of the future. It was going to replace the punched-card systems of machines (and people) that had previously performed computing calculations (Yates, 1999). At the time, IBM was successfully manufacturing those punched-card calculators and a prime candidate for disruption. Instead, IBM's response, the IBM 650, would rapidly overtake Univac, maintaining IBM's leadership position in the marketplace. The IBM 650 was not nearly as powerful as these pioneering computers. Indeed, despite sharing its technical DNA with these more powerful computers, it was considered more of an extension of existing punch-card equipment. One Univac sales manager stated, the IBM 650 "... slipped right in to the existing punched card processing scheme. It was punched cards in, it was punched cards out, and it was just like a bigger calculator for them."

As a result, the IBM 650 served as a stepping stone for insurance firms moving from their existing punched-card systems to new computers—and by the time those customers were ready, so was IBM:

> IBM provided an easy migration path from the tabulator era into the computer era. Insurance executives could draw on their existing models for technology and its use in insurance operations, as well as for business relations with the vendor. Adopting a 650 computer provided gains in speed and reduced growth in clerical staff, without requiring them to undertake extensive reconfiguration of their processes. (Yates, 1999, p. 20)

As historian Joanne Yates suggests, IBM succeeded by taking a revolutionary technological innovation and, through its design, presenting it to customers as an incremental innovation in technology and use.

When you have got a good idea, step back and ask yourself how this idea will, in its current form, encourage others to get involved. Whose support is critical for this idea to succeed? How will they respond? Does it build on their strengths—or threaten their weaknesses? Can you change the idea just enough to win their support? If not, then where else can you find support? Sometimes, the better mousetrap is the one that others can adopt the most easily.

KNOW WHERE (AND WHEN) TO BE CREATIVE

Perhaps the most important question about creativity is whether to pursue it at all. From the strategic choices of the executive management team to the decisions of managers in the trenches of new product and process development, individuals and entire organizations constantly face this choice. Ultimately, it comes down to a trade-off between exploiting your existing routines, competencies, and knowledge to survive today and creating new ones to thrive tomorrow. This distinction between exploration and exploitation comes from the early organizations of the oil industry, who had to balance both the short-term certainties of extracting oil from known fields with the long-term need to explore for new fields. The two pursuits conflicted in everything from goals to performance measures to cultures and were often divided into two distinct divisions: exploitation and exploration. James March and colleagues have since developed this distinction between exploration and exploitation as an underlying tension within all organizations (see, for example, Levitt and March, 1988; March, 1991).

As a result, one of the most important aspects of creativity is knowing when it is appropriate. Much of the discussion around exploitation and exploration revolves around the competency trap—the unwillingness of people, once they are good at one task, to abandon it for another at which they are not, in the short term, as proficient (even when the long term promises greater gains). This trap underlies most organized hostility toward new and creative efforts, because any such novelty involves exactly these performance sacrifices in others. And yet on the other side, a willingness to try every new idea that comes down the road creates the opposite problem—an *incompetency* trap in which people, with visions of vast improvements, ignore the short-run costs of each new idea they embrace. Before gaining competency at any one new practice, they are seduced by another.

The challenge to creativity here is understanding when and where to be creative, and the set of practices that support practical creativity entail strategically allocating your creative efforts across the range of opportunities. It is wise to adopt, formally or informally, a Pareto analysis of the creative opportunities at hand. Vilfredo Pareto was an Italian economist who, in 1906, noticed that 20 percent of Italy's population owned 80 percent of its land. This balance became known as Pareto's Principle and describes how a small minority of (vital) inputs are responsible for the large majority of (important) effects. Pareto's Principle is very useful because it focuses our attention and efforts on those few critical inputs that most influence the outcome. We could spend our day exploring new ways to tie our shoes, to little effect in our organizational performance. Indeed, I have the distinct honor of having designed one of the most innovative and expensive power adaptors ever to power a portable computer. I am confident in suggesting that not one more computer was sold because of that adaptor, in the same way that not one deli sandwich was ever sold because of the pickle that came with it. It is important to ask: Which pieces of a problematic situation, when solved, will have the most significant impact on the overall problem? Trying to cost-reduce a process or product? Ask which elements account for the vast majority of the costs and direct your problem-solving efforts there. Trying to change your own work habits? Ask which activities account for 80% of your time but only 20% of your accomplishments—and focus your creative energies toward how you might reduce, delay, or stop doing them entirely.

SUMMARY

In the preceding pages, I have attempted to catalog a set of activities that, while not directly (or at least traditionally) associated with the "aha" moment of creativity, nevertheless play a critical role in the creative process. These practices set the stage, work backstage, and clean up after the main event that most people have come to view as creativity. I do not mean to deny the role played by individuals and their moments of insight, but rather to recognize how those individuals and moments depend on often-neglected others without which the creative process would grind to a halt.

REFERENCES

Albert, R. S. & Runco, M. A. (1999). A history of research on creativity. In R.J. Sternberg (Ed.), *Handbook of creativity* (pp. 16–34). New York: Cambridge University Press.

Amabile, T. M. (1983). *The social psychology of creativity.* New York: Springer-Verlag.

Amabile, T. M. (1988). A model of creativity and innovation in organizations. In B. M. Staw and L. L. Cummings (Eds.), *Research in organizational behavior* (Vol. 10, pp. 123–167). Greenwich, CT: JAI Press.

Amabile, T. M. (1995). *Creativity in context.* Boulder, CO: Westview Press.

Asch, S. E. (1951). Effects of group pressure upon the modification and distortion of judgments. In H. Guetzkow (Ed.), *Groups, leadership, and men* (152–162). Pittsburgh: Carnegie Press.

Baker, W. E. (2000). *Achieving success through social capital.* San Francisco: Jossey-Bass.

Becker, M. (1995). Nineteeth century foundations of creativity research. *Creativity Research Journal, 8,* 219–229.

Burt, R. S. (1983). Range. In R.S. Burt and M.J. Minor (Eds.), *Applied network analysis* pp. 176–194. Beverly Hills, CA: Sage.

Burt, R. S. (1992a). The social structure of competition. In N. Nohria and R.G. Eccles (Eds.), *Networks and organizations* (pp. 57–91). Cambridge, MA: Harvard University Press.

Burt, R. S. (1992b). *Structural holes: The structure of competition.* Cambridge, MA: Harvard University Press.

Csikszentmihalyi, M. (1999). Implications of a systems perspective for the study of creativity. In R.J. Sternberg (Ed.), *Handbook of Creativity* (pp. 313–335). New York: Cambridge University Press.

Conot, R. E. (1979). *A streak of luck.* New York: Seaview Books.

Crow, R. (1995). Institutionalized competition and its effects on teamwork. *Journal for Quality and Participation, 18,* 47.

Diehl, G. (1975). *The Fauves.* In J. L. Hochmann (Coll. Ed.), *Library of great art movements.* New York: Harry N. Abrams, Inc.

Farrell, M. P. (1982). Artists' circles and the development of artists. *Small Group Behavior,13*(4), 451–474.

Gentner, D., & Gentner, D. R. (1983). Flowing waters or teeming crowds: Mental models of electricity. In D. Gentner & A. Stevens (Eds.), *Mental models* (pp. 99–130). Hillsdale, NJ: Lawrence Erlbaum Associates.

Gentner, D., & Markman, A. B. (1997). Structure mapping in analogy and similarity. *American Psychologist, 52*(1), 45–56.

Gombrich, E. H. (1961). *Art and illusion: A study in the psychology of pictorial representation.* Princeton: Princeton University Press.

Gordon, J. S. (2001). *The business of America: Tales from the marketplace — American enterprise from the settling of New England to the breakup of AT&T.* New York: Walker Publishing.

Hargadon, A. B. (2003). *How breakthroughs happen: The surprising truth about how companies innovate.* Cambridge: Harvard Business School Press.

Hargadon, A. B., & Fanelli, A. (2002). Action and possibility: Reconciling dual perspectives of knowledge in organizations. *Organizational Science, 13*(3), 290–302.

Hargadon, A. B., & Sutton, R. I. (2000). Building an innovation factory. *Harvard Business Review, 78*(3), 157–166.

Hope, J. A. (1996). A better mousetrap, *American Heritage,* 90–97.

Hounshell, D. A. (1984). *From the American system to mass production.* Baltimore: Johns Hopkins University Press.

Hughes, T. P. (1989). *American genesis: A century of invention and technological enthusiasm, 1870–1890.* New York: Viking.

Israel, P. B. (1998). *Edison: A life of invention.* New York: John Wiley.

Kurtzberg, T. R., & Amabile, T. M. (2001). From Guilford to creative synergy: Opening the black box of team level creativity. *Creativity Research Journal,13,* 285–294.

Lave, J. (1988). *Cognition in practice: Mind, mathematics, and culture in everyday life.* Cambridge, New York: Cambridge University Press.

Levitt, B., & March, J. G. (1988). Organizational learning. *Annual Review in Sociology,14,* 319–340.

March, J. G. (1991). Exploration and Exploitation in Organizational Learning. *Organization Science, 2,* 71–87.

Millard, A. (1990). *Edison and the business of innovation.* Baltimore: Johns Hopkins University Press.

Neustadt, R. E., & May, E. R. (1986). *Thinking in time: The uses of history for decision makers.* New York: Free Press.

Reeves, L. M., & Weisberg, R. W. (1993). On the concrete nature of human thinking: Content and context in analogical transfer. *Educational Psychology, 13*(3), 245–258.

Reeves, L. M., & Weisberg, R. W. (1994). The role of content and abstract information in analogical transfer. *Psychological Bulletin 115*(3), 381–400.

Rosenberg, N. (1979). Technological interdependence in the American economy. *Technology and Culture, 20*(1), 25–50.

Schank, R., & Abelson, R. P. (1977). *Scripts, plans, goals, and understanding: An inquiry into human knowledge structures.* Hillsdale, NJ: Lawrence Erlbaum.

Schon, D. A. (1983). *The Reflective Practitioner.* New York: Basic Books.

Schon, D. A. (1993). Generative metaphor: A perspective on problem-setting in social policy. In A. Ortony (Ed.), *Metaphor and thought* (pp. 137–163). Cambridge: Cambridge University Press.

Schumpeter, J. A. (1934). *The theory of economic development.* Cambridge, MA: Harvard University Press.

Segaller, S. (1998). *Nerds 2.0.1: A brief history of the Internet.* New York: TV Books.

Simonton, D. K. (1995). Foresight and insight: A Darwinian answer. In R.J. Sternberg and J. Davidson (Eds.), *The nature of insight.* Cambridge: MIT Press.

Weick, K. (1979). *The social psychology of organizing reading.* MA: Addison-Wesley.

Weick, K. E. (1995). *Sensemaking in organizations.* Thousand Oaks, CA: Sage.

Wise-Quotes.com. http://www.wise-quotes.com/florence-luscomb (accessed July 26, 2007).

Words of Wisdom 4U. http://www.wow4u.com/thomas-edison/index.html (accessed July 26, 2007).

Yates, J. (1999). The structuring of early computer use in life insurance. *Journal of Design History, 12*(1), 5–24.

SECTION IV

Suggestions for Future Organizational Creativity Research

CHAPTER 15

Expanding the Scope and Impact of Organizational Creativity Research

Jing Zhou
Rice University

Christina E. Shalley
Georgia Institute of Technology

INTRODUCTION

Although creativity in the workplace is still an emerging research field, considerable progress has been made toward an understanding of what factors promote or restrict creativity in the workplace. Indeed, chapters in this volume represent a constellation of distinctive research contributions. This research ranges from identifying critical factors operating at the individual level of analysis (e.g., leadership, feedback, goals, and roles), to creativity in groups and teams, social networks, climate and culture, and to an organizational level analysis such as organizing structure and politics. Also, creativity research is linked to other research areas such as research on organizational change and innovation. Finally, practical and managerial implications of creativity research are explored. The chapters represent both the breadth and depth of research on creativity in the workplace, and they allow the readers to appreciate this body of work through both a historical and a contemporary lens.

In this concluding chapter, we will first provide an integration of the chapters in this volume and then offer suggestions on future research directions. Elsewhere (Shalley, Zhou, & Oldham, 2004; Zhou & Shalley,

2003) we provided detailed discussions on future research directions. Thus, in this concluding chapter, we will not repeat the research directions we already discussed previously. Instead, we will focus on discussing future research directions inspired by chapters included in this volume. It is our goal that future research will bring creativity research to an even more exciting level by broadening its scope and deepening its impact.

EXPANDING RESEARCH ON ANTECEDENTS OF CREATIVITY TO MULTILEVEL ANALYSIS

As is evident in this volume and in recent reviews of the organizational creativity literature (e.g., Shalley et al., 2004; Zhou & Shalley, 2003), research on organizational creativity has overwhelmingly focused on antecedents of creativity. Moreover, much of this research has been on the individual level of analysis.

Several researchers have called for more multilevel research on creativity (e.g., Anderson, De Dreu, & Nijstad, 2004; Shalley et al., 2004; Woodman, Sawyer, & Griffin, 1993; Zhou & Shalley, 2003). However, research of this type has been rare. One possibility for the lack of progress in this aspect of creativity research may be that it is inherently difficult to collect multilevel data. For example, to collect data for quantitative analysis that would allow the researchers to draw reliable statistical inferences, the researchers would have to make sure that sample sizes at multiple levels are large enough. This sample-size requirement could increase the cost of data collection and could create problems for finding appropriate data sites (e.g., a manufacturing plant that has 100 employees organized in three teams might not provide adequate sample sizes for a multilevel investigation). To make the matter more complex, although some researchers suggest that to ensure adequate statistical power one needs to have a sample size of 30 individuals per team and 30 teams, much still needs to be learned concerning precisely what the cutoffs are for sample sizes in a multilevel investigation (Hofmann, Griffin, & Gavin, 2000).

Another possibility may be that the creativity research field has not developed a unified typology that would provide theoretical guidance on how to conceptualize and design multilevel research on creativity. A typology elaborated by Rousseau (1985) could be a useful starting point in this regard. Rousseau (1985) described three different kinds of models in multilevel research in organizational science. The first type is called the composition model (e.g., Chan, 1998; Rousseau, 1985). In composition models, constructs at different levels of analysis are assumed to hold the same meaning or refer to similar phenomena at different levels. The composition models depict relationships among those constructs. When these constructs have the same functional relationships with other constructs in nomological networks at different levels of analysis, isomorphism is said to exist. In creativity research, one example is leadership at different levels of analysis. Tierney (chap. 4, this volume) points out that there are four levels of leadership in the workplace (i.e., individual, dyadic, team, and organizational levels), and extant research concerning effects of leadership on creativity has focused on leadership at lower levels (e.g., individual and team level) of analysis. She suggests that there may be functional relationships among leadership at lower levels and leadership at higher levels of the organization (e.g., leaders at the top level of the organization). Clearly, this could be an exciting topic for future research.

Another example is the relationship between the constructs of climate or culture for creativity at the team level and the organizational level of analysis. An interesting question would be: Is there a corresponding construct at the individual level of analysis? In addition, Michael West and colleagues have done extensive research on climate for creativity at the team level of analysis. Given that a corresponding construct has already been defined at the organizational level of analysis, it would be interesting to see whether isomorphism exists at the team and organizational levels of analysis. That is, future research could examine whether the same pattern of relationships among the team creativity climate-related constructs investigated by West and colleagues also exists at the organizational level of analysis. If a corresponding construct also can be defined at the individual level of analysis, it would be useful to investigate whether isomorphism exists at all three levels of analysis.

The second type of multilevel model is called the cross-level model. In a cross-level model, variables at different levels affect variables at different levels. The most straightforward example of a cross-level model on creativity would be that independent variable X_1 at individual level, and independent variable X_2 at the group level affect the dependent variable—creativity—at the individual level of analysis. Researchers could examine main effects of X_1 and X_2 on creativity. They could also investigate the interaction effects of X_1 and X_2 on creativity. The latter can be tested by examining the significance of the statistical interactions between X_1 and X_2 on the dependent variable—creativity.

While this example shows the most straightforward form of a cross-level model, there could be other forms of cross-level models. For example, Zhou (chap. 5, this volume) suggests the value added of cross-level research on feedback and creativity by asking how a "deviant" negative feedback provided by a coworker or a manager would affect an individual's creativity. A deviant feedback is one that is significantly different from a group mean level of feedback. Zhou provides a hypothetical scenario in which an individual received negative feedback from a coworker, and yet the group mean feedback was positive. This is a special case of cross-level models (Rousseau, 1985). Research is needed to identify various forms of cross-level models concerning antecedents of creativity in the workplace. Unfortunately, there have been few studies on creativity using cross-level models. Since individual and team behaviors including creativity in the workplace are inherently affected by factors at different levels (e.g., individual, team, and organizational levels), we call for more studies to be conducted using cross levels to investigate individual and team creativity.

According to Rousseau (1985), the third type of multilevel model is concerned with relationships among independent and dependent variables that are generalizable across different levels of analysis. Although the term "multilevel" frequently has been used in the literature rather loosely to represent different kinds of models that involve variables in two or more levels of analysis, strictly speaking, multilevel models refer to the situation in which the meaning of both constructs and the causal relationships among them at one level can be generalized to other levels. Previous researchers (Klein, Dansereau, & Hall, 1994; Rousseau, 1985) rely on the threat-rigidity theory formulated by Staw, Sandelands, and Dutton (1981) to illustrate a prototypical multilevel model in the field of organizational behavior. According to the threat-rigidity theory, individuals, groups, and organizations all experience negative events originated from the external environment, which are called threats. Individuals tend to respond to these threats with rigidity, narrowing information search and processing, and limiting production of novel responses, which often result in inappropriate and ineffective responses to the current threats. Staw and colleagues (1981) theorized that parallel and similar phenomena and relationships can be found at the group and organizational levels as well.

A truly comprehensive, precise, and testable multilevel theory has yet to be formulated in the creativity research arena. Nonetheless, chapters included in this volume suggest that as we move toward more in-depth understanding of creativity in the workplace, developing and testing multilevel theories of creativity could be a promising direction for future theorizing and research.

Taken as a whole, chapters in this volume suggest that two issues derived from the creativity literature may be the prime targets for multilevel theorizing and research. The first issue is concerned with how antecedents at different levels in the workplace jointly affect creativity. The antecedents of creativity that are identified and discussed in the chapters in this volume include leadership (Tierney), feedback (Zhou), goal setting (Shalley), diversity (Paulus), task structure (Paulus), climate and culture (West & Richter), social networks (Perry-Smith), and methods of organizing (Dougherty & Tolboom). In addition, previous reviews of the creativity literature (Shalley et al., 2004; Zhou & Shalley, 2003) identified additional antecedents of creativity: different supervisory behaviors, presence of coactors, presence of creative role models, presence of competitive others, autonomy, rewards, and spatial configurations as contextual factors from employees' work environment. Also, individual differences including creative personality, "Big-Five" personality factors, and cognitive styles have been related to individuals' motivation and ability to be creative. While the individual differences are clearly at the individual level of analysis, some of the contextual variables could be at the individual level and others could be defined both at the individual and higher levels of analysis. For instance, it is not clear from the literature what combination of personal factors or cognitive styles is best for teams to be creative. Moreover, the answer to this question may change based on the teams' engagement in different stages of the creative process. For example, having individuals or teams relatively high on openness to experience may be best for preliminary stages of the creative process. However, for more final stages of the creative process, having teams high on conscientiousness may be the necessary driver for successful closure of the project. Future research is needed to examine how contextual variables at the individual and higher levels of analysis, and individual differences variables at the individual level of analysis jointly affect creativity. Cross-level models appear to be most suitable in this line of research.

The second issue is concerned with whether the same predictor predicts creativity at different levels in the same way. As the chapters in this volume suggest, considerable progress has been made on an understanding of how contextual factors affect creativity at the individual level of analysis. In particular, leadership (Tierney), goal setting (Shalley), and feedback and expected evaluation (Zhou) are three of the most important contextual factors that have been found to influence individual creativity. Compared with research at the individual level, we know relatively less about whether, how, when, and why leadership, goal setting, and feedback affect creativity at the group or team level of analysis. We know even less about cross-level influences involving leadership, goal setting, and feedback on creativity. Research addressing these issues could use all three models for multilevel theorizing and research: composition models, cross-level models, and multilevel models.

A number of chapters in this volume suggest several starting points for researchers to address this second issue. For example, Gilson (chap. 13, this volume) argues that creativity is a homologous construct in the sense that its antecedents function in the same manner at different levels of analysis. She provided the example of the effects of goals, which have been found to affect creativity at both the individual level (Shalley, 1991, 1995) and the group level of analysis (Gilson & Shalley, 2004). Will the other antecedents that have been found to affect creativity at the individual level of analysis, such as leadership or feedback, also affect creativity at the group level of analysis in the same fashion?

As another example, Dougherty and Tolboom (chap. 10, this volume) theorize three deep structures for innovative organizing that would enable sustained product innovation: defining work as professional practice, differentiating work into distinct problems in value creation, and integrating work via enactable standards of practice. They then discuss how each of these three deep structures affects different aspects of the entire product development process, from relatively individual or microlevel aspects such as generating knowledge or gaining the freedom to act, to more macrolevel aspects such as community-bound collaboration and enacting standards that would provide clear innovation guidelines across communities. Their chapter raises interesting questions and possibilities for expanding creativity research to multilevel investigation by suggesting that methods of organizing, which are what they term deep structures, affect innovation or product development at individual, collective, and organizational levels of analysis. In addition, one wonders whether their notion of deep structures will only have beneficial effects on product innovation. That is, are the cross-level and multilevel relationships between methods of organizing and product innovation generalizable to other types of creativity and innovation?

As a third example, West and Richter (chap. 9, this volume) assert that organizational culture and climate influence creativity and innovation at the individual, group or team, and organizational levels of analysis. They identify two aspects of culture and climate that influence creativity, and two aspects of culture and climate that influence innovation at the individual level of analysis. The aspects that influence individual creativity are a climate that is safe, positive, and unpressured, and job characteristics. The aspects that influence individual innovation are job characteristics, high work demands, and extrinsic rewards. At the group level of analysis, West and Richter identify six climate factors for innovation, which include clarifying and ensuring commitment, participation in decision making, managing conflict and minority influence constructively, supporting innovation, developing intragroup safety and trust, and reflexivity.

In comparing the aforementioned individual-level and group-level climate factors, it is interesting to note that while both sets of factors include elements of psychological safety and social support, they differ in other elements. For example, at the individual level, extrinsic rewards are said to influence creative idea implementation, whereas at the team level no extrinsic rewards are mentioned and they are not expected to influence individual ideation.

Thus, it would appear that one possibility for expanding multilevel research on creativity and innovation is to further identify culture or climate factors at the individual, team, and organizational levels, and investigate their differential influences on creativity and innovation at these three levels of analysis. Another interesting aspect of multilevel research on creativity is that in addition to the typical three levels of analysis (i.e., individual, team, and organizational), two other levels, namely, dyadic level (see Tierney, chap. 4, this volume) and project level (see Amabile & Mueller; Drazin et al., chap. 11, this volume), have been mentioned. Research on these and other multilevel topics could benefit from the guidelines proposed by Klein, Dansereau, and Hall (1994), Klein and Kozlowski (2000), Morgeson and Hofmann (1999), and Rousseau (1985). For example, Morgeson and Hofmann argue that researchers interested in multilevel theory development should pay attention to the structure and function of constructs. Structures are the results of interaction among individuals in a collective entity (e.g., a team). Over time, structures can influence subsequent interactions. Functions address causal relationships among constructs.

EXPANDING THE SCOPE OF CREATIVITY RESEARCH

In addition to advocating multilevel analysis and introducing a typology for doing so, we also believe that researchers can substantially advance our understanding of creativity by untangling the complex influences of several factors (e.g., affect, reward) on creativity, by paying attention to the temporal dimension of creativity, and by engaging in more interdisciplinary research. In this section, we will discuss each of these potential research areas.

Affect

Although not the focus of an independent chapter, affect is mentioned in several chapters in this volume (e.g., Amabile & Mueller; Zhou). These chapters, as well as a small but rapidly growing body of work on relationships between affect and creativity, suggest that understanding the complex influences of affect on creativity is one of the most promising and exciting directions for future research on creativity in work organizations.

As a recent review of the creativity literature (Shalley et al., 2004) indicates, much of early research concerning effects of affect on creativity focused on the role of positive affect. In particular, in a series studies conducted in the behavioral laboratory, Isen and colleagues found that positive affect was related to better performance (e.g., uniqueness of research participants' responses) on unusual word association tasks (Isen, Johnson, Mertz, & Robinson, 1985) or creatively solving the functional fixedness problem demonstrated by Duncker's candle task (1945) (Isen, Daubman, & Nowicki, 1987). Word associations were rated as unique or unusual if, for example, they were produced by equal to or fewer than 2.5 percent of the participants. In those lab experiments, positive affect was usually induced by showing the research participants a short film clip for a few minutes or by giving them a small bag of candy.

Effects of positive affect on creativity continue to fascinate researchers. For example, Amabile and Mueller (chap. 2, this volume) describe a longitudinal field study published by Amabile, Barsade, Mueller, and Staw (2005), which showed that positive affect was an antecedent of creativity. Positive affect was measured by self-reported items (e.g., satisfaction with the team) tapping the pleasantness dimension of affect (see Russell, 1980).

On the other hand, previous research conducted in the behavioral laboratory found that negative affect could have a functional impact on creativity (e.g., Kaufmann & Vosburg, 1997). In a series of studies conducted in the workplace (George & Zhou, 2002, 2007; Zhou & George, 2001), systematically theorized and investigated conditions under which job dissatisfaction or negative affect may be beneficial for creativity. In the first of this series of studies, Zhou and George (2001) formulated a voice perspective of creativity that theorized conditions under which job dissatisfaction led to creativity. According to this perspective, under certain circumstances (e.g., continuance commitment and useful coworker feedback), *dis*satisfied employees may engage in creative activities as an expression of voice. Results supported their theoretical predictions.

In the second study, George and Zhou (2002), on the basis of the mood-as-input model in the affect literature (e.g., Martin & Stoner, 1996), hypothesized that under certain conditions, negative moods might foster creativity and positive moods might inhibit it. Mood was defined as a pervasive affective state that was experienced over short periods of time and that could be affected by contextual factors and fluctuate (George & Brief, 1992). According to the mood-as-input model, individuals' mood states provided them with information (e.g., Schwarz & Clore, 2003) and the significance and consequences of the information depended upon the context (Martin & Stoner, 1996). Adapting this model to creativity research, George and Zhou argued that employees' work environment or contexts provide them with cues concerning their ongoing creative activities. These cues are valuable to them because when they are engaged in creative activities at work, they often have little objective information and have to decide for themselves when they have tried hard enough to come up with a new and improved procedure, or put forth enough effort to come up with a new and better way of completing tasks. Consistent with their theoretical arguments, these researchers found that negative moods were positively related to creativity when perceived recognition and rewards for creativity and clarity of feelings (a meta-mood process) were high. They also found that under the same conditions, positive moods were *negatively* related to creativity.

In their most recent study, George and Zhou (2007) continued the quest to untangle the complex relations between mood states and creativity. They theorized and tested a dual-tuning perspective concerning interactive effects of positive mood, negative mood, and supportive contexts on creativity. According to the mood-as-information theoretical framework, moods can exert tuning effects on cognitive processes. Thus, both positive and negative moods may be functional for creativity in the workplace. By signaling a satisfactory state of affairs, positive moods lead to more use of integrative top-down strategies, simplifying heuristics, and schemas and scripts (e.g., Fiedler, 1988; Kaufmann, 2003; Schwarz, 2002; Schwarz & Clore, 2003). They lead to less systematic and effortful information processing. By signaling a problematic state of affairs, negative moods push individuals to address and correct problems. They encourage a bottom-up, detail-oriented, analytic approach to understanding the situation, more focused on understanding the data at hand and less focused on preexisting schemas, scripts, and simplifying heuristics (Kaufmann, 2003; Schwarz & Clore, 2003). As such, both positive and negative moods can benefit creativity. Negative moods alert employees to problems, cause them to focus on the current situation rather than on preexisting assumptions, and motivate them to exert high levels of effort to make improvements (George & Zhou, 2002; Kaufmann, 2003; Martin & Stoner, 1996; Schwarz, 2002). Positive moods allow employees to be playful with ideas, to be willing to take risks and explore novel ways of doing things, and facilitate divergent thinking. Notably, the joint effects of positive and negative moods only manifested themselves in a supportive context provided by supervisors (i.e., when the supervisors provided developmental feedback, demonstrated interactional justice, and were trustworthy). Indeed, results showed that positive mood, negative mood, and a supportive context interacted to affect creativity in such a way that when positive mood and a supportive context were both high, negative mood had the strongest positive relation with creativity.

While the before-reviewed studies investigated affect as an antecedent of creativity, in a study conducted by Madjar, Oldham, and Pratt (2002), affect was used as a mediator explaining relations between creativity-related support received by employees from sources inside or outside their work organizations and those employees' creative performance at work. No doubt, either as an antecedent that influences creativity perhaps under a host of contextual conditions, or as a mediating mechanism linking contextual factors to employee creativity, affect holds considerable promise in advancing our understanding of creativity in the workplace.

Reward

Whether rewards promote or inhibit creativity in the workplace is not a new question. As two extensive reviews of the organizational creativity literature (Shalley et al., 2004; Zhou & Shalley, 2003) concluded, research results have not yet provided clear answers to this important question. Little has changed since the publication of those two reviews, and there is still a lack of definitive answers concerning whether rewards facilitate or inhibit creativity in the workplace. For example, Amabile and colleagues (e.g., Amabile, Hennessey, & Grossman, 1986) found that contingent reward undermined creativity. In contrast, Eisenberger and colleagues (e.g., Eisenberger & Armeli, 1997) demonstrated that the promise of reward had a positive impact on creativity.

Most of the previous studies on the effects of rewards were conducted in the behavioral laboratory. This makes sense because it would be difficult and potentially unethical to use different incentive schemes for employees performing the same job in an organization. Therefore, we see real value in continuing to try to tease out the relationship between rewards and creativity in the laboratory. Once a clear pattern of results emerges in the laboratory, there would be more merit to the testing of different incentive schemes in an organizational field study.

Also, since the research on rewards, thus far, has been laboratory based this could be providing a different context than what you have in the workplace, affecting the reward–creativity relationship. In work organizations, employees go to work and make contributions to their organizations in exchange for being financially compensated. Thus, the role of norms and expectations may be a potential hidden moderator of some of these results.

In the only workplace study that we are aware of, looking at rewards and creativity, George and Zhou (2002) found an interaction effect in which negative moods were positively related to employee creativity when employees perceived that their creativity would be rewarded and recognized and when their clarity of feelings was high. They did not hypothesize nor did they find a main effect of reward on creativity.

This state of affairs (i.e., inconsistent and inconclusive results obtained in lab studies and lack of research in organizational settings) concerning what we know about effects of reward on creativity is not satisfactory. Hence, we believe more research in both the laboratory and the workplace is needed to illuminate the effects of reward on employees' creativity.

Temporal Dimension

Elsewhere (Zhou & Shalley, 2003), we suggested that creativity theorizing and research should take the temporal dimension of creativity more seriously by tracking how the creative process unfolds over time. The Amabile and colleagues' work diaries study described in Amabile and Mueller (chap. 2, this volume) serves as an excellent example of a longitudinal investigation of creativity. In addition, the sensemaking approach to studying creativity, which was developed by Drazin, Kazanjian, and Glynn (chap. 11, this volume), also requires that researchers use longitudinal and qualitative case studies. As Drazin and colleagues point out, as an alternative to the structural-functional approach to studying creativity, the sensemaking approach holds considerable promise in advancing our knowledge about creativity and the creative process.

Taking the temporal dimension seriously includes, but is not limited to, simply studying creativity longitudinally. Another alternative approach might be to develop a typology of how time and individuals' perceptions of time influence the creative idea production process, as well as the temporal rhythm of producing creative ideas. Several recent papers in the creativity literature are noteworthy in this regard. For example, Ford and Sullivan (2004) adapted Gersick's (1988) punctuated equilibrium model to theorizing the value of novel contributions in project teams. They maintain that at early stages of a project team's life cycle, novel contributions are particularly beneficial. However, after the team has reached the midpoint transition in its life cycle, novel ideas may not be that helpful and may even be disruptive. This is because, after the midpoint, the team members' attention is switched to execution, feasibility, and completion prior to a deadline.

As another example, Yuan and Zhou (forthcoming) adapted Campbell's (1960) variation and selective retention model to theorize that variation or idea generation, and selective retention or idea modification and selection are two main parts of the creative idea production process. These two parts determine the novelty and appropriateness of the final creative idea, respectively. More detail of the Yuan and Zhou study can be found in Zhou (chap. 5, this volume). What is relevant here is the idea that the novelty and appropriate dimensions of creativity may be addressed at different points in time in the creative idea production process. Thus, Campbell's notion of variation and selective retention could be another useful theoretical foundation that serves to guide research concerning time and creativity.

The third option involves examining the effectiveness of training and other interventions that are designed to enhance individual or teams' creativity skills and strategies. Although there is some evidence suggesting that creativity techniques can help individuals to improve their performance at creativity or ideation tasks (Amabile, 1996; Scott, Leritz, & Mumford, 2004), more systematic research is needed to demonstrate which training methods are most effective at helping individuals or teams master which aspects of ideation or which components of their creativity skills and strategies. In addition, previous research demonstrated that modeling facilitated observers' creativity (Shalley & Perry-Smith, 2001; Zhou, 2003), which presumably took place because the observers learned creativity skills and strategies by watching creative role models in action. Thus, research is also needed to address the question: To what extent can creativity skills and strategies be learned and improved upon, and how does this learning process unfold over time?

A related issue is that there is very little systematic evidence that creativity training programs work at changing employees' actual behavior in the workplace, and that any behavioral change sustains over a relatively long period of time. It would be useful to the field, and in particular for managers, if research was conducted to examine the various success rates of different creativity training programs. Also, research could determine whether some training programs are better at developing skills needed in the initial stages of ideation versus at later stages. Furthermore, are certain training techniques and programs more beneficial for individuals or teams to learn creativity skills and strategies? Future research could help to determine this, as well as assess the long-term impact of training and what training techniques are better at enabling individuals or teams to have successful transfer of skills learned in training to being creative in their job, day to day.

BRIDGING CREATIVITY RESEARCH
WITH OTHER FIELDS OF RESEARCH

As Hargadon's (chap. 14, this volume) interesting examples and Perry-Smith's (chap. 3, this volume) fascinating work on social networks suggest, creativity is a social process. Connecting with others, building networks, and interacting with those not in one's own field could allow one to make novel combinations of ideas and practices and hence promote creativity. Hargadon's notion of knowledge brokering is not only applicable to product design and business practices, it is equally valuable for researchers who are interested in researching and understanding creativity. In addition, Ford and Kuenzi (chap. 3, this volume) analyze several classic and foundational texts on management, and argue that much can be learned by considering and investigating creating and organizing simultaneously. They emphasize that while in its earlier stages of development the field of organizational creativity relied heavily on social psychological theory and methods, the field has grown and matured to the point of being able to offer much insight to other research domains in the broad field of management.

Interestingly enough, Woodman (chap. 12, this volume) discusses how research on organizational creativity and research on organizational change and development can inform each other. For example, Woodman argues that Van de Ven and Poole's (1995) typology of four process theories describing organizational change can inform theory development in the organizational creativity research area. He goes on to speculate how creativity researchers might be inspired by Van de Ven and Poole's typology, and formulate a typology of creativity motors such as stage advancement, social construction, dialectical tension, and biological imperative.

Woodman's insights provide an excellent example of the tremendous opportunities that could be created if creativity researchers were to bridge with other fields of scientific inquiry. For example, there is a plausible link between the research fields of organizational creativity and entrepreneurship. The creation, funding, development, and growth of new ventures inside or outside of an organization would seem to require a great deal of creativity. Also, one could argue that all entrepreneurs need some level of creativity, whether it is in identifying an opportunity, coming up with new ideas, being creative in how they seek venture capital funding, or pitching their ideas to potential investors. We believe that entrepreneurial research and creativity research have natural connections, and we think the two fields would benefit from a discussion of some shared research interests.

There is also an obvious link between research on creativity and innovation. While traditionally creativity research has been carried out by social psychologists and researchers in the field of micro-organizational behavior, and innovation research has been conducted by sociologists and researchers in the field of organizational theory and strategy, this division of labor seems to be more of a result of disciplinary traditions than what the objective reality requires. In reality, creativity and innovation are not so clearly separate from each other. Perhaps it is time to seriously consider how these two largely separate research streams can inform each other and benefit from each other. In order to do that, we need to do a better job of talking to each other across disciplines. Perhaps by the use of research forums, panels, and small conferences we can bring together researchers interested in various aspects of creativity and innovation to explore potential links, opportunities, and overlapping areas for our research.

In addition, there could be a link between research on creativity and research on strategy. If creativity is part of every organization's member's job, then there is no reason to exclude organizational decision makers and top management from creative endeavors. Indeed, West and Anderson (1996) investigated relationships between top management team composition and processes on innovation in the health care industry. More research along this line is needed, particularly seeing creativity not as a separate outcome of top management team processes, but as an integral part of top management teams' strategy formation and implementation.

Finally, there appears to be a link between research on organizational creativity and research on human resource management. Elsewhere (Zhou & Shalley, 2003), we discussed implications of creativity research for human resource management practices such as performance appraisal, reward and compensation programs, employee relations, recruitment and selection, and training. Although in that paper our emphasis was on how research might inform practice, there is reason to believe that research on creativity and research on human resource management can inform each other. For example, theory and research on training effectiveness could be used to investigate the effectiveness of various creativity training programs. Likewise, theory and research on effects of rewards on creativity could inform research on compensation programs.

EXPANDING THE CONTEXT OF CREATIVITY RESEARCH

A striking omission from this volume is work focused on studying creativity via a cross-cultural or international lens. As creativity research continues to grow in its breadth and depth, and as work organizations continue to become interconnected globally, it is necessary to expand the context of creativity research to the international arena.

Cheng (1994) identified two types of international research. In the first and traditional type, research is designed to test generalizability of extant research results. Typically, the results obtained in prior studies were based on theory developed in Western countries such as the United States and Europe. Subsequent research is then conducted to see whether the results obtained in prior studies would still hold in a new country or cultural context. Results of the subsequent research are expected to be invariant in different countries and cultures.

In the second type of international research, the goal is not so much on testing for generalizability or finding invariant results across different cultures and nations. Instead, unique and specific cultural and country characteristics are taken into consideration in the hope that the richness and uniqueness of the specific cultural or national context in which research is conducted would allow the researchers to discover the unknowns, rather than confirming what was already known in other contexts. Cheng (1994) argues that the second type of research represents new thinking in international research in that it provides a complementary approach to the traditional generalizability type of studies, and together, those two approaches would allow researchers to develop a set of universal knowledge that would not have been possible to discover had they relied on only the generalizability type of research.

A survey of the organizational creativity literature reveals that there have been few studies conducted in non-Western countries. Most research on antecedents of creativity in the workplace has been conducted in the United States or Europe. In the few studies that were conducted in non-Western countries, the first, traditional type of approach to international research seemed to be the starting point for research design. That is, these studies set out to test or validate theories developed in the West. For example, Madjar and colleagues (2002) conducted a study on relationships between work and nonwork support and employees' creativity in Bulgaria. On the basis of prior theory and research on social support, mood states, and creativity, they found that support from supervisors and coworkers, and support from friends and family members were positively related to employees' creativity in the workplace. These relationships were mediated by positive mood states. Although as a set these results were new, the authors argued that because some of their results were consistent with results found in prior studies, their results may be generalizable to different cultures.

Two other studies also appeared to start off using largely generalizability type of research designs, and yet their interesting findings were consistent with the second type of international research identified by Cheng (1994)—research that reveals unique phenomenon or relationships among variables in a specific cultural context. In particular, on the basis of prior theory and research on role identity and creativity that were mainly developed in the Western countries such as the United States, Farmer, Tierney, and Kung-McIntyre (2003) set out to investigate the impact of creative role identity on employees' creativity in Taiwan. They also explored antecedents of creative role identity. Interestingly, and consistent with the second, contextual approach identified by Cheng (1994), Farmer and colleagues hypothesized and found that perceived coworker creativity expectations were positively related to employees' creative role identity. Those researchers developed this hypothesis on the basis of the unique contexts in Taiwan, where individuals' social context and relationships with others play a role in defining the individuals' self construals.

In a study conducted in Korea, Shin and Zhou (2003) also were largely interested in testing whether theoretical arguments rooted in prior theory and research on transformational leadership, intrinsic motivation, and creativity that were developed in the West were applicable to an Eastern country, namely Korea. As such, a large part of the Shin and Zhou study design was the first, traditional type of international research identified by Cheng (1994). However, in anticipation of possible cultural effects,

Shin and Zhou did include a variable that was directly related to cultural contexts—the value of conservation. Interestingly, these researchers found that the positive relation between transformational leadership and creativity was even stronger for employees who scored high on the conservation measure.

More recently, Zhou (2006) formulated a model of team creativity that continues to move creativity research to the direction of the second type of international research. She identified the construct of paternalistic organizational control, which is defined as the degree to which an organization exerts influence on its work groups' personnel and task arrangements. She theorizes that in the East, more paternalistic organizational control would lead to greater group creativity. The construct of paternalistic organizational control and its theorized effects on group creativity were developed on the basis of analyzing the unique cultural and societal context of the East, where paternalistic leadership is often the preferred leadership style (Aycan, 2006; Farh & Cheng, 2000).

As the three empirical studies and one conceptual paper reviewed before suggest, there are exciting opportunities in investigating antecedents of workplace creativity in different cultures and countries, especially in non-Western countries. Since the extant creativity literature is overwhelmingly based on theory and research developed in the West, and because business organizations operate in an interconnected world, both types of research identified by Cheng (1994) would contribute to building universal knowledge on antecedents of creativity in the workplace.

In addition to research that exclusively focuses on either generalizability of extant constructs and theories developed in the West, or indigenous constructs, phenomena, and relationships among the constructs, research on creativity in the international context can benefit from a "third way" recently suggested by Brewer (2006). She suggests that it is possible to create a middle ground for international research by both acknowledging the profound influences of culture on cognition, emotion, motivation, and behaviors, and using fundamental principles as substrates for illustrating and understanding cultural differences and variations. Because cross-cultural theorizing and research on creativity in the workplace are still in their infancy, generalizability studies, indigenous studies, and the "third way" in which fundamental principles and cultural specificities are combined to inform and guide the research are all needed for the field to advance. All in all, we consider expanding creativity research to the international context as an important direction for future research.

CONSEQUENCES OF CREATIVITY

The tremendous interest in creativity is partly driven by intellectual curiosity and partly driven by the assumption that employee creativity is always beneficial to organizations' effectiveness and success. This assumption has seldom been put to direct scientific investigation. Nonetheless, several authors in this volume, as well as other researchers (e.g., Mumford, 2003), suggest that employee creativity may result in both positive and negative consequences.

Positive Consequences

Gilson (this volume) reviewed a wide range of correlates or consequences of creativity at the individual, group, and organizational levels. For example, she found some suggestive evidence that creativity resulted in or was associated with general performance, innovation, job satisfaction, and reduced strain at the individual level of analysis.

West (2002a, 2002b) suggests that the correlation between individual employees' and teams' potential to produce creative ideas and the actual performance of the organization as a whole may not be very strong. If so, it would be necessary to investigate the process through which creative ideas produced at lower levels of the organization (i.e., at the individual or the team level) are translated into the overall performance at the organizational level. Are the ideas fully and properly implemented? Are ideas that are selected for implementation not truly new and useful, as suggested by Paulus (this volume)? Is there some inherent calculation going on in organizations between the merit of highly creative ideas versus the risk of them failing, as compared to choosing ideas from a more moderate level of creativity that may have a safer rate of risk?

Negative Consequences

In addition to presenting evidence showing positive consequences of creativity, Gilson (chap. 13, this volume) also wonders about negative consequences of creativity. Compared with positive consequences, even less research attention has been devoted to negative consequences of creativity. However, this could be an exciting area for future research. Questions that can be addressed in future research include: Are creative ideas always good for the organization? Under what conditions are ideas produced valuable to the individual but detrimental to the organization? If ideas produced benefit the organization but ultimately are detrimental to the individual who produced the idea or to other individuals working in the organization, what happens to the ideas? Are they implemented or squashed?

CONCLUDING REMARKS

In conclusion, although organizational creativity is still a young and emerging field, considerable progress has been made to enhance our understanding of what factors positively or negatively influence employee creativity in the workplace. Chapters included in this volume provide only a sample of the knowledge accumulated over such a short period of time. More importantly, these chapters share common threads, which we believe will serve as inspiration to those who have been conducting research on organizational creativity and for those who are new to the field. We hope this volume sparks researchers to embark on an exciting journey aimed at gaining broader and more in-depth understanding of antecedents, processes, and consequences of employee creativity.

REFERENCES

Amabile, T. M. (1996). *Creativity in context: Update to the social psychology of creativity*. Boulder, CO: Westview.

Amabile, T. M., Barsade, S. G., Mueller, J. S., & Staw, B. M. (2005). Affect and creativity at work. *Administrative Science Quarterly, 50*, 367–403.

Amabile, T. M., Hennessey, B. A., & Grossman, B. S. (1986). Social influences on creativity: The effects of contracted-for reward. *Journal of Personality and Social Psychology, 50*, 14–23.

Anderson, N., De Dreu, C. K. W., & Nijstad, B. A. (2004). The routinization of innovation research: A constructively critical review of the state-of-the-science. *Journal of Organizational Behavior, 25*, 147–173.

Aycan, Z. (2006). Paternalism: Towards conceptual refinement and operationalization. In K. S. Yang, K. K. Huang, & U. Kim (Eds.), *Scientific advances in indigenous psychologies: Empirical, philosophical, and cultural contributions* (pp. 445–466). London: Cambridge University Press.

Brewer, M. B. (2006). Bringing culture to the table. In E. A. Mannix & M. A. Neale (Series Ed.) & Y. Chen (Ed.), *Research on managing groups and teams. National culture and groups* (Vol. 9, pp. 353–365).

Campbell, D. T. (1960). Blind variation and selective retention in creative thought as in other knowledge processes. *Psychological Review, 67*, 380–400.

Chan, D. (1998). Functional relations among constructs in the same content domain at different levels of analysis: A typology of composition models. *Journal of Applied Psychology, 83*, 234–246.

Cheng, J. L. C. (1994). On the concept of universal knowledge in organizational science: Implications for cross-national research. *Management Science, 40*, 162–168.

Duncker, K. (1945). On problem solving. *Psychological Monographs, 58*(5, Whole No. 270).

Eisenberger, R., & Armeli, S. (1997). Can salient reward increase creative performance without reducing intrinsic creative interest? *Journal of Personality and Social Psychology, 72*, 652–663.

Farh, J. L., & Cheng, B. S. (2000). A cultural analysis of paternalistic leadership in Chinese organizations. In J. T. Li, A. S. Tsui, & E. Weldon (Eds.), *Management and organizations in the Chinese context.* United Kingdom: Macmillan Press.

Farmer, S. M., Tierney, P., & Kung-McIntyre, K. (2003). Employee creativity in Taiwan: An application of role identity theory. *Academy of Management Journal, 46,* 618–630.

Fiedler, K. (1988). Emotional mood, cognitive style, and behavior regulation. In K. Fiedler and J. Forgas (Eds.), *Affect, cognition and social behavior* (pp. 101–119). Toronto: J. Hogrefe.

Ford, C., & Sullivan, D. M. (2004). A time for everything: How the timing of novel contributions influences project team outcomes, *Journal of Organizational Behavior, 25,* 279–292.

George, J. M., & Brief, A. P. (1992). Feeling good—Doing good: A conceptual analysis of the mood at work-organizational spontaneity relationship. *Psychological Bulletin, 112,* 310–329.

George, J. M., & Zhou, J. 2002. Understanding when bad moods foster creativity and good ones don't: The role of context and clarity of feelings. *Journal of Applied Psychology, 87,* 687–697.

George, J. M., & Zhou, J. (in press). Dual tuning in a supportive context: Joint contributions of positive mood, negative mood, and supervisory behaviors to employee creativity. *Academy of Management Journal.*

Gersick, C. J. G. (1988). Time and transition in work teams: Toward a new model of group development. *Academy of Management Journal, 31*(1), 9–41.

Gilson, L. L., & Shalley, C. E. (2004). A little creativity goes a long way: An examination of teams' engagement in creative processes. *Journal of Management, 30,* 453–470.

Hofmann, D. A., Griffin, M. A., & Gavin, M. B. (2000). The application of hierarchical linear modeling to organizational research. In K. J. Klein & S. W. J. Kozlowski (Eds.), *Multilevel theory, research, and methods in organizations: Foundations, extensions, and new directions* (pp. 467–511). San Francisco: Jossey-Bass.

Isen, A. M., Daubman, K. A., & Nowicki, G. P. (1987). Positive affect facilitates creative problem solving. *Journal of Personality and Social Psychology, 52,* 1122–1131.

Isen, A. M., Johnson, M. M. S., Mertz, E., & Robinson, G. F. (1985). The influence of positive affect on the unusualness of word associations. *Journal of Personality and Social Psychology, 48,* 1413–1426.

Kaufmann, G. (2003). The effect of mood on creativity in the innovation process. In L. V. Shavinina (Ed.), *The international handbook on innovation* (pp. 191–203). Oxford, UK: Elsevier Science.

Kaufmann, G., & Vosburg, S. K. (1997). "Paradoxical" mood effects on creative problem-solving. *Cognition and Emotion, 11,* 151–170.

Klein, K. J., Dansereau, F., & Hall, R. J. (1994). Levels issues in theory development, data collection, and analysis. *Academy of Management Review, 19,* 195–229.

Klein, K. J., & Kozlowski, S. W. J. (2000). From micro to meso: Critical steps in conceptualizing and conducting multilevel research. *Organizational Research Methods, 3,* 211–236.

Madjar, N., Oldham, G. R., & Pratt, M. G. (2002). There's no place like home? The contributions of work and nonwork creativity support to employees' creative performance. *Academy of Management Journal, 45,* 757–767.

Martin, L. L., & Stoner, P. (1996). Mood as input: What we think about how we feel determines how we think. In L. L. Martin and A. Tesser (Eds.), *Striving and feeling: Interactions among goals, affect, and self-regulation* (pp. 279–301). Mahwah, NJ: Erlbaum.

Morgeson, F. P., & Hofmann, D. A. (1999). The structure and function of collective constructs: Implications for multilevel research and theory development. *Academy of Management Review, 24,* 249–265.

Mumford, M. D. (2003). Where have we been, where are we going? Taking stock in creativity research. *Creativity Research Journal, 15,* 107–120.

Rousseau, D. (1985). Issues of level in organizational research: Multilevel and cross-level perspectives. In L. L. Cummings & B. M. Staw (Eds.), *Research in organizational behavior* (Vol. 7, pp. 1–37). Greenwich, CT: JAI Press.

Russell, J. A. (1980). A circumplex model of affect. *Journal of Personality and Social Psychology, 39,* 1161–1178.

Schwarz, N. (2002). Situated cognition and the wisdom of feelings: Cognitive tuning. In L. Feldman Barrett & P. Salovey (Eds.), *The wisdom in feelings* (pp. 144–166). New York: Guilford.

Schwarz, N., & Clore, G. L. (2003). Mood as information. *Psychological Inquiry, 14,* 296–303.

Scott, G., Leritz, L. E., & Mumford, M. D. (2004). The effectiveness of creativity training: A quantitative review. *Creativity Research Journal, 16,* 361–388.

Shalley, C. E. (1991). Effects of productivity goals, creativity goals, and personal discretion on individual creativity. *Journal of Applied Psychology, 76,* 179–185.

Shalley, C.E. (1995). Effects of coaction, expected evaluation, and goal setting on creativity and productivity. *Academy of Management Journal, 38,* 483–503.

Shalley, C. E., & Perry-Smith, J. E. (2001). Effects of social-psychological factors on creative performance: The role of informational and controlling expected evaluation and modeling experience. *Organizational Behavior and Human Decision Processes, 84,* 1–22.

Shalley, C. E., Zhou, J., & Oldham, G. R. (2004). The effects of personal and contextual characteristics on creativity: Where should we go from here? *Journal of Management, 30,* 933–958.

Shin, S., & Zhou, J. (2003). Transformational leadership, conservation, and creativity: Evidence from Korea. *Academy of Management Journal, 46,* 703–714.

Staw, B. M., Sandelands, L., & Dutton, J. (1981). Threat-rigidity effects in organizational behavior: A multi-level analysis. *Administrative Science Quarterly, 26,* 501–524.

Van de Ven, A. H., & Poole, M. S. (1995). Explaining development and change in organizations. *Academy of Management Review, 20,* 510–540.

West, M. A. (2002a). Sparkling fountains or stagnant ponds: An integrative model of creativity and innovation implementation in work groups. *Applied Psychology: An International Review, 51,* 355–387.

West, M. A. (2002b). Ideas are ten a penny: It's team implementation not idea generation that counts. *Applied Psychology: An International Review, 51,* 411–424.

West, M. A., & Anderson, N. (1996). Innovation in top management teams. *Journal of Applied Psychology, 81,* 680–693.

Woodman, R.W., Sawyer, J. E., & Griffin, R. W. (1993). Toward a theory of organizational creativity. *Academy of Management Review, 18,* 293–321.

Yuan, F., & Zhou, J. (forthcoming). Differential effects of expected external evaluation on different parts of the creative idea production process and on final product creativity. *Creativity Research Journal.*

Zhou, J. (2003). When the presence of creative coworkers is related to creativity: Role of supervisor close monitoring, developmental feedback, and creative personality. *Journal of Applied Psychology, 88,* 413–422.

Zhou, J. (2006). A model of paternalistic organizational control and group creativity. In E. A. Mannix & M. A. Neale (Series Ed.) & Y. Chen (Ed.), *National culture and groups. Research on managing groups and teams* (Vol. 9, pp. 75–94). Oxford: Elsevier Science.

Zhou, J., & George, J. M. (2001). When job dissatisfaction leads to creativity: Encouraging the expression of voice. *Academy of Management Journal, 44,* 682–696.

Zhou, J., & Shalley, C. E. (2003). Research on employee creativity: A critical review and directions for future research. In J. Martocchio (Ed.), *Research in Personnel and Human Resource Management, 22,* 165–217.

AUTHOR INDEX

A

Abbey, A., 159
Abelson, R.P., 333
Ackerman, P.L., 154
Adams, M., 238
Agrell, A., 222
Aguilar, F., 274
Alba, R.D., 197
Albert, R.S., 323
Albrecht, T.L., 205
Allen, N.J., 133, 165, 175
Allen, T.J., 149, 200, 202
Amabile, T.M., 5, 6, 9, 10, 12, 16,
    17, 20, 21, 22, 34, 37, 39, 42, 49,
    50, 51, 55, 56, 57, 66, 78, 87, 88,
    96, 97, 98, 102, 103, 104, 105,
    107, 108, 109, 110, 112, 113, 126,
    128, 129, 130, 135, 148, 149, 151,
    156, 160, 174, 175, 177, 189, 191,
    205, 222, 225, 226, 227, 228,
    229, 241, 243, 245, 263, 267, 268,
    275, 284, 290, 291, 294, 297,
    304, 306, 308, 323, 353, 354,
    356, 357, 358
Ancona, D.G., 181, 202
Anderson, C.A., 166
Anderson, N.R., 21, 37, 218, 219,
    222, 267, 313, 314, 318, 348, 360
Anderson, P., 276
Andrews, F.M., 19, 102, 160, 217,
    267
Andrews, S.B., 199
Anthony, W.P., 267

Appelbaum, E., 175
Archambault, S., 55
Argyris, C., 213
Armeli, S., 159, 356
Asch, S.E., 202
Ashby, W.R., 221
Ashe, D.K., 214
Astley, W.G., 265
Atchley, F.K., 19
Avolio, B.J., 21, 98, 106, 111, 113,
    178, 179, 317
Axtell, C.J., 308
Aycan, Z., 363

B

Bacon, G., 237, 240
Baden-Fuller, C., 268
Baer, M., 23, 98, 105, 305
Bailey, D.E., 175, 312
Baker, W.E., 326
Balkundi, P., 201
Bandura, A., 160, 197
Barabba, N., 221
Barki, H., 171
Barley, S., 247, 268, 274
Barney, J., 243
Baron, R.S., 176, 221
Barr, S.H., 309, 318
Barrett, K.M., 100
Barron, F., 4, 6, 7, 8, 9, 33, 284
Barron, R., 150
Barsade, S.G., 21, 55, 56, 189, 241,
    245, 354

SUBJECT INDEX